HISTORY

OF THE

UNITED STATES,

FROM THE

DISCOVERY OF THE AMERICAN CONTINENT.

BY GEORGE BANCROFT.

VOL. III.

FOURTEENTH EDITION.

BOSTON:
LITTLE, BROWN, AND COMPANY.
1856.

HISTORY

OF THE

COLONIZATION

OF THE

UNITED STATES.

BY GEORGE BANCROFT.

VOL. III.

FOURTEENTH EDITION.

BOSTON:

LITTLE, BROWN, AND COMPANY.

1856.

Entered according to Act of Congress, in the year 1840,
By George Bancroft,
In the Clerk's Office of the District Court of Massachusetts.

CONTENTS.

CHAPTER XIX.

THE ABSOLUTE POWER OF PARLIAMENT.

CHAPTER XX.

FRANCE AND THE VALLEY OF THE MISSISSIPPI.

CHAPTER XXI.

FRANCE CONTENDS FOR THE FISHERIES AND THE GREAT WEST.

CHAPTER XXII.

THE ABORIGINES EAST OF THE MISSISSIPPI.

CHAPTER XXIII.

THE COLONIES OF FRANCE AND ENGLAND ENCROACH MORE AND MORE ON THE RED MEN.

CHAPTER XXIV.

ENGLISH ENCROACHMENTS ON THE COLONIAL MONOPOLY OF SPAIN, PREPARE AMERICAN INDEPENDENCE.

COLONIAL HISTORY.

CHAPTER XIX.

THE ABSOLUTE POWER OF PARLIAMENT

THE Stuarts passed from the throne of England. Their family, distinguished by a blind resistance to popular opinion, was no less distinguished by misfortunes. During the period of their separate sovereignty over Scotland, but three of the race escaped a violent death. The first of them who aspired to the crown of Great Britain was by an English monarch doomed to death on the scaffold; her grandson was beheaded in the name of the English people. The next in the line, long a needy exile, is remembered chiefly for his vices; and, as if a domestic crime could alone avenge the national wrongs, James II. was reduced from royalty to beggary by the conspiracy of his own children. Yet the New World has monuments of the Stuarts; North America acquired its British colonies during their rule, and towns, rivers, headlands, and even states bear their names. The pacific disposition of James I. promoted the settlement of Virginia; a timely neglect fostered New England; the favoritism of Charles I. opened the way for religious liberty in Maryland; Rhode Island long cherished the charter which its importunity won from Charles II.; the honest friendship of James II. favored the grants which gave

CHAP. XIX. liberties to Pennsylvania, and extended them to Delaware; the crimes of the dynasty banished to our country men of learning, virtue, and fortitude. Thus did despotism render benefits to freedom. "The wisdom of God," as John Knox had predicted, "compelled the very malice of Satan, and such as were drowned in sin, to serve to his glory and the profit of his elect."

Four hundred and seventy-four years after the barons at Runnymede had extorted Magna Charta from their legitimate king, the aristocratic revolution of 1688 established for England and its dominions the sovereignty of Parliament and the supremacy of law. Its purpose was the security of property and existing franchises, and not the abolition of privilege, or the equalization of political power. The chiefs of the nobility who, in 1640, had led the people in its struggle for liberty, had, from the passionate enthusiasm of "a generous inexperience," been hurried, against their design, into measures which their interests opposed. Made circumspect by the past, the renewed contest did not disturb their prudence, nor triumph impair their moderation. Avoiding the collisions with established privileges that spring from the fanatical exaggeration of abstract principles, still placing the hope of security on the system of checks and the balance of opposing powers, they made haste to finish the work of establishing the government. The character of the new monarch of Great Britain could mould its policy, but not its constitution. True to his purposes, he yet wins no sympathy. In political sagacity, in force of will, far superior to the English statesmen who environed him; more tolerant than his ministers or his parliaments, the childless man seems like the unknown character in algebra which is introduced to form the equation, and dismissed when the problem is solved. In his person thin and feeble, with eyes of a hectic lustre, of a temperament inclining to the melancholic, in conduct cautious, of a self-relying humor, with abiding impressions respecting men, he sought no favor, and relied for success on his own inflexibility and the greatness and maturity of his designs. Too wise to be cajoled, too firm to be complaisant, no address could sway his resolve. In Holland, he had not scrupled to derive an increase of power from the crimes of rioters and assassins; in England, no filial respect diminished the energy of his ambition. His exterior was chilling; yet he had a passionate delight in horses and the chase. In conversation he was abrupt, speaking little and slowly, and with repulsive dryness; in the day of battle, he was all activity, and the highest energy of life, without kindling his passions, animated his frame. His trust in Providence was so connected with faith in general laws, that, in every action, he sought the principle which should range it on an absolute decree. Thus, unconscious to himself, he had sympathy with the people, who always have faith in Providence. "Do you dread death in my company?" he cried to the anxious sailors, when the ice on the coast of Holland had almost crushed the boat that was bearing him to the shore. Courage and pride pervaded the reserve of the prince who, spurning an alliance with a bastard daughter of Louis XIV., had made himself the centre of a gigantic opposition to France. For England, for the English people, for English liberties, he had no affection, indifferently employing the whigs, who found their pride in the revolution, and the tories, who had opposed his eleva-

CHAP. XIX. tion, and who yet were the fittest instruments "to carry the prerogative high." One great passion had absorbed his breast—the independence of his native country. The harsh encroachments of Louis XIV., which, in 1672, had made William of Orange a revolutionary stadtholder, now assisted to constitute him a revolutionary king, transforming the impassive champion of Dutch independence into the defender of the liberties of Europe.

The English statesmen who settled the principles of the revolution, careless of ideal excellence, took experience for their guide. It is true that Somers, the acknowledged leader of the whig party, of plebeian origin, and unsupported by inherited fortune, was ready, with the new king from a Calvinistic commonwealth, to admit corresponding maxims of government and religion. Yet, free from fanaticism, even to indifference, by nature, by his profession as a lawyer, and by the tastes which he had cultivated, averse to metaphysical abstractions, he labored to confirm English liberties, not to establish the rights of man; to make an inventory of the privileges of Englishmen, and imbody them in a public law, and not to introduce a new capitulation, or to establish a perfect republic. Freedom sought its title-deeds, not in the nature of man, but in the experience of the past, in records, charters, and prescription. The revolution of 1688 was made, not on a theory of absolute justice, but on the facts friendly to freedom which were claimed as the inheritance of the nation. The bill of rights was regarded as a distinct, written recapitulation of ancient, well-established national possessions; English liberties, questioned by the abdicated king, were now adapted to the spirit of the age, and, with some

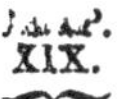

increase, were reasserted and confirmed as an inalienable property. The tide of English liberty was advancing; the rising wave rolled beyond the highest mark of that which was receding.

In the progress of civilization, the human mind had been steadily tending towards the principle of inquiry and freedom. This principle could not as yet conquer for itself a place in the laws; yet the only ground on which its admission could consistently be refused was abandoned. The Anglican church, which, under the guardianship of authority, had aspired to assert for England unity of faith, as the Catholic church had claimed to assert it for the whole human race, still retained the monopoly of political power; but a statute, narrow, indeed, in theory, and penuriously conceding a limited enfranchisement of mind as a privilege, tolerated dissenters, and opened a career to freedom of religious opinion. With unrelenting zeal, the "Protestant" revolution did, indeed, persecute the Roman Catholics as a defeated tyranny, oppressed them with civil disfranchisements, and left them without allies, exposed to the vindictive severities of legal despotism; but for Protestant liberty and philosophic freedom the victory was decisive.

The ancient monarchical system, which had connected the unity of truth with authority, had also asserted the necessity of order in the state, under the doctrine of the personal, divine right of the king to the sovereignty. This right was maintained by the Catholic church against every power but its own. Protestantism abolished the supremacy of the Roman see; and the monarchical reformers, Luther, Cranmer, Ridley, Latimer, the homilies of the Anglican church, recognized legitimacy without reserve, and, opposing

CHAP. XIX.

the Roman pretension to a power of dispensing from allegiance, taught passive obedience. The right of resistance—familiar to Calvin and Knox, to the early Puritans and the Presbyterians, not of itself a democratic doctrine, but rather the most cherished principle of feudal liberty, familiar to the nobles of every monarchy in Europe—was the next conquest in the progress of popular freedom: the idea of popular power would follow, but was not yet ripe. The revolution of 1688 dismissed the doctrine of passive obedience from the statute-book, to take its place, for the English world, among exploded superstitions. The old system of legitimacy, as it had existed in the monarchies of Christendom, was summoned to expire, and yielded, not as in Denmark, and afterwards in Prussia, to a military monarchy, nor yet to the supremacy of reason as expressed by the popular conviction, but to the transition theory of a social compact, to constitutional monarchy. The commons, by a vast majority, declared the executive power to be a conditional trust; and the hereditary assembly of patricians, struggling in vain for a compromise with legitimacy by the appointment of a regency friendly to the church, or by simply acknowledging the accession of the next unquestioned heir, at length, after earnest debates, submitted to confess an original contract between king and people. The election of William III. to be king for life was a triumph of the perseverance of the more popular party in the commons over the deep, inherited prejudices of the high aristocracy. In this lies the democratic tendency that won to the revolution the scattered remnant of "the good old" republican "cause;" this appropriated to the whigs the glory of the change, in which they exulted, and of which the tories regretted and excused the necessity. This also has commended to the friends of freedom the epoch in which the great European world beheld a successful insurrection against legitimacy and authority over mind.

By resolving that James II. had abdicated, the representatives of the English people assumed to sit in judgment on its kings. By declaring the throne vacant, they annihilated the principle of legitimacy. By disfranchising a dynasty for professing the Roman faith, they not only exerted the power of interpreting the original contract, but of introducing into it new conditions. By electing a king, they made themselves his constituents; and the parliament of England became the fountain of sovereignty for the English world.

The royal prerogative of a veto on English legislation soon fell into disuse. The dispensing power was expressly abrogated, or denied. The judiciary was rendered independent of the crown; so that enfranchisements were safe against executive interference, and state trials ceased to be collisions between bloodthirsty hatred and despair. For England, parliament was absolute.

The progress of civilization had gradually elevated the commercial classes, and given importance to towns. It now set up, as its landmark and evidence of advancement, the acknowledged influence and power of the men of business; of those who make the exchanges between the consumer and the producer, and those also who assist the exchanges by advances. The reverence for the landed aristocracy was deeply branded into the rural mind; in the parliament of Richard Cromwell, it had even been said that the country people were ready to become insurgents for

CHAP. XIX. their restoration. It was in cities and towns, among those engaged in commerce, in which the ancient patricians had no share, that the spirit of liberty became active, and was quickened by the cupidity which sought new benefits for trade through political influence. The day for shouting liberty and equality had not come; the cry was, "Liberty and property." The revolution was made by the property of the country, and wealth became a power in the state; and when, at elections, the country people were first invited to seek other representatives than the large landholders, it was not the leveller or the republican, but the merchant, or a candidate in the interest of the merchant, who taught the timid electors their first lessons in independence.

But the moneyed class gained influence in two other modes—the manner of granting supplies, and the credit system. The civil list was fixed for the whole reign; all other supplies were granted annually, and were subjects of special appropriation; so that the king, who had been elected by parliament, was subject to its enactments, and, dependent on its annual supplies, was also held responsible for the expenditure of the public treasure.

Moreover, as the expenses of wars soon exceeded the revenue of England, the government prepared to avail itself of the largest credit which, not the accumulations of wealth only, but the floating credits of commerce and the funding system, could supply. The price of such aid was political influence. That the government should, as its paramount policy, promote commerce, domestic manufactures, and a favorable balance of trade; that the classes benefited by this policy should sustain the government with their credit and their wealth, was the reciprocal relation and compromise, on which rested the fate of parties in England. The floating credits of commerce, aided by commercial accumulations, soon grew powerful enough to balance the landed interest: stock aristocracy competed with feudalism. So imposing was the spectacle of the introduction of the citizens and of commerce as the arbiter of alliances, the umpire of factions, the judge of war and peace, that it roused the attention of speculative men; that, at last, Bolingbroke, claiming to speak for the landed aristocracy, described his opponents, the whigs, as the party of the banks, the commercial corporations, and, "in general, the moneyed interest;" and the gentle Addison, espousing the cause of the burghers, declared nothing to be more reasonable than that "those who have engrossed the riches of the nation should have the management of its public treasure, and the direction of its fleets and armies." In a word, the old English aristocracy was compelled to respect the innovating element imbodied in the moneyed interest.

Still more revolutionary was the political theory developed by the revolution. The old idea of a Christian monarchy resting on the law of God was exploded, and political power sought its origin in compact. Absolute monarchy was denied to be a form of civil government. Nothing, it was held, can bind freemen to obey any government save their own agreement. Political power is a trust; and a breach of the trust dissolves the obligation to allegiance. The supreme power is the legislature, to whose guardianship it has been sacredly and unalterably delegated. By the fundamental law of property, no taxes may be levied on the people but by its own

Hallam, iv. 374.

CHAP. XIX. consent, or that of its authorized agents. These were the doctrines of the revolution, dangerous to European institutions, and dear to the colonies; menacing the Old World with convulsive struggles and reforms, and establishing for America the sanctity of its own legislative bodies. Throughout the English world, the right to representation could never again be separated from the power of taxation. The theory gave to vested rights in England a bulwark against the monarch; it encouraged the colonists to assert their privileges, as possessing a sanctity which tyranny only could disregard, and which could perish only by destroying allegiance itself.

But the revolution is still further marked as a consequence of public opinion, effected without bloodshed in favor of the strongest conviction. Far from being a result of force, it refused to confirm itself by force, and would not tolerate standing armies. It even compelled William III. to dismiss his Dutch guards. A free discussion of the national policy and its agents was more and more demanded and permitted. The English government, which used to punish censure of its measures or its ministers with merciless severity, began to lean on public conviction. The whigs could not consistently restrain debate; the tories, from their interests, as usually a minority, desired freedom to appeal to popular sympathy; and the adherents of the fallen dynasty loved to multiply complaints against impious usurpation. All were clamorous for liberty; and even Jacobites and patriots could, at last, frame a coalition. The nation had elected its dynasty from a commonwealth which had allowed a home to Spinoza, and had sheltered skepticism itself in Bayle; and it was no longer possible to set limits to the active spirit of inquiry. The philosophy of Locke, cherishing the variety that is always the first fruit of analysis and free research, was protected and admired, even though it seemed to endanger some dogmas of the Church, of which the denial was still, by the statutes, a crime. The English chancellor would have become openly the friend of Bayle, if the self-respect of the scholar had not refused his patronage. Men not only dissented from the unity of faith, but even denied the reality of faith; and philosophy, passing from the ideal world to the actual, claimed the right of observing, weighing, measuring, and doubting, at its will. The established censorship of the press, by its own limitation, drew near its end, and, after a short renewal, was suffered to expire, never again to be revived. England enjoyed the liberty of unlicensed printing. If prosecutions for libels still continued, if the cowardice of the courts hesitated to assert the freedom of the press, the torrent, destined to swell with advancing years, was already irresistible. Its force was increased by the unlimited freedom of parliamentary debate, the freedom of elections, and the right of petition, which belonged to every Englishman.

Here, and here only, lies the democratic character of the revolution. Its authors had carefully sought to reconcile the new with the old, had been unwilling to agitate the public mind, had avoided glaring reforms. "In the revolution of 1688, there was certainly no appeal to the people." In the contest between the nation and the throne, the aristocracy constituted itself the mediating lawgiver, and made privilege the bulwark of the commons against despotism. The free press carried political discussions every where. By slow degrees, a popular opinion would gather a con-

Hallam, iv. 381.

CHAP. XIX. sciousness of existence. By slow degrees, the common people would gain hardihood enough to present petitions; to convene for the consideration of public grievances. If the aristocracy refused to abdicate the control of parliament; if Lord Somers did not propose a reform of boroughs, such as the people of that day had not learned to desire; the liberty of unlicensed printing opened an avenue for diffusing political instruction, and was a pledge of the ultimate concession of every reform which increasing intelligence might obtain the moral force to demand.

Thus the revolution of 1688, narrow in its principles, imperfect in its details, frightfully intolerant towards Catholics, forms an era in the history of the liberty of England and of mankind. Henceforward, the title of the king to the crown was bound up with the title of the aristocracy to its privileges, and of the people to its liberties: it sprung from the nation, and not from a power superior to the nation; from law, and not from divine right; and its responsibility was therefore not to God alone, but to God and the nation. The revolution respected existing possessions, yet made conquests for freedom; preserved the ascendency of the aristocracy, yet increased the weight and the numbers of the middling class. It mitigated the evils which it did not absolutely abolish, increasing the securities of personal liberty, of opinion, of the press, and of the responsibility of the executive. England became the star of constitutional liberty, shining brilliantly as a beacon on the horizon of Europe. Her institutions won respect in the heart of despotic countries, compelling the eulogies of Montesquieu and the homage of Voltaire. Never in the history of man had so large a state been blessed with institutions so favorable to public happiness, to the arts of peace, to the development of the natural resources. Of old, Greece, in collision with the East, had spread the civilization of Hellas through Asia Minor and the regions that encircle the Levant; Rome, entering into relations with Greece, as the conqueror of her soil, became imbued with her civilization, and by its sword carried that civilization to the Danube and the Rhine, to Western Europe and to Britain. The destiny of Great Britain was still more grand: her commerce connected her with every quarter of the globe; she sought to make the world a tributary to her industry; and her colonies, her commercial stations, and her trade, were so many pledges that the whole race would participate in the benefit of her liberties and her culture.

To the English people, the supremacy of parliament was the source of hope: the colonies could not fail to perceive that, as the revolution of 1688 had been made for the rights of Englishmen, not for the rights of man, so, in its external policy, the dominant motive was the interest of England, and not the reciprocity of justice.

To the proprietaries of Carolina the respect of the 1689
revolution for vested rights secured their possessions. In the territory itself, south and west of Cape Fear, political parties had already become passionate, if they had not acquired consistency. Of "the pretended Churchmen" who were among the early emigrants, Archdale.
some were known as "ill livers," having the manners of the time of Charles II. The larger part of the settlers were dissenters, bringing with them the faith and the staid sobriety of the Calvinists of that age. At first, "the ill livers," averse to restraint, opposed

CHAP. XIX. the proprietaries, whose government the grave Presbyterians, as friends to order, sustained. When the
1689. obstinate perversity of the proprietaries drove the Presbyterians into opposition, those who were styled "the nobility," together with the High Church party, constituted a colonial oligarchy against the great mass of the people. The dissenters, who, from respect to an established government, had favored the proprietaries, now joined even with "ill livers" in behalf of colonial rights.

1690. The people had deposed Colleton. His successor was Seth Sothell, who to pretensions as a proprietary added the choice of the people. His administration is the triumph of the more popular party; and its enactments were made, with silent disregard of the nobility,
Statutes at large, ii. 38,39. by the exclusive consent of the commons. The "wise, moderate, and well-living" Thomas Smith, who had advised martial law, and those who had established it,
40—42. were disfranchised for two years. Methods of colonial
1691. defence were adopted, and were, in the following years,
64—68. improved by providing military stores, and establishing
1691. May 1. a revenue; and, in May, the Huguenots were fully
Statutes ii. 58—60. enfranchised, as though they had been freeborn citizens. The statute-book of South Carolina attests the moderation and liberality of the government, which derived its chief sanction from the people.

But tranquillity did not return. As the revolution of 1688 respected the rights of the proprietaries, the insurrectionary government soon came to an end. Factions multiplied in a colony which had as yet gained no moral unity. The legal sovereigns would not expend their private fortunes in reducing their insurgent liegemen; the colonial oligarchy, which they favored, was too feeble a minority to conduct the government; and the people were forbidden by law to take care of themselves. To this were added the evils of an uncertain boundary on the south, and of disordered finances. CHAP. XIX.

All the acts of the democratic legislature were rejected by the proprietaries; while, as a remedy for anarchy, Philip Ludwell, a moderate adherent of Berkeley, once collector of customs in Virginia, a man of a candid mind, a complainant in England against Effingham, and since 1689 governor of North Carolina, was sent to establish order and the supremacy of the proprietaries. But he had power to inquire into grievances, not to redress them. Disputes respecting quitrents and the tenure of lands continued; and, after floating for a year between the wishes of his employers and the necessities of the colonists, Ludwell gladly withdrew into Virginia. 1692. Hewatt Martin, i. 194. MS

A concession followed. In April, 1693, the proprietaries voted "That, as the people have declared they would rather be governed by the powers granted by the charter, without regard to the fundamental constitutions, it will be for their quiet, and for the protection of the well-disposed, to grant their request." So perished the legislation of Shaftesbury and Locke. It had been promulgated as immortal, and, having never gained life in the colony, was, within a quarter of a century, abandoned by the proprietaries themselves. Palatines, landgraves, and caciques, "the nobility" of the Carolina statute-book, were doomed to pass away. 1693

On the abrogation of the constitutions, Thomas Smith was by the proprietaries appointed governor. The system of biennial assemblies, which, with slight changes, still endures, was immediately instituted by

CHAP. XIX.
the people; but, as the political opinions of Smith were at variance with those of the majority, his per-
1693. sonal virtues could not conciliate for him confidence. Despairing of success, he proposed that one of the
1694 proprietaries should visit Carolina, with ample powers alike of inquiry and of redress.

The advice pleased; and the grandson of Shaftesbury, the pupil and antagonist of Locke, was elected dictator. He declined; and the choice fell upon John Archdale, an honest member of the society of Friends.

The disputes in South Carolina had grown out of the selfish zeal of a High Church oligarchy, sustained by the proprietaries, in opposition to the great body of the freemen. Now the peaceful Archdale, the mediator between the factions, was himself, as a dissenter, pledged to freedom of conscience. Yet his powers
1695. permitted him to infuse candor into his administration,
Aug. 17. rather than into the constitution of Carolina. Not rejecting the best men of "the party of high pretended Churchmen, that had lain latent from the beginning" of the colony, and conscious that "dissenters could kill wolves and bears, fell trees, and clear ground, as well as Churchmen;" acknowledging that emigrants should ever expect "an enlargement of their native rights in a wilderness country,"—he selected for the council two men of the moderate party to one High Churchman. Thus the balance of power was in harmony with colonial opinion. By remitting quitrents for three and for four years, by regulating the price of land and the form of conveyances, by giving the planter the option of paying quitrents in money or in the products of the country, he quieted the jarrings between the colonists and their feudal sovereigns. To cultivate

friendship with the Indians, he established a board to decide all contests between them and the white men. The natives round Cape Fear obtained protection against kidnappers, and requited this security by kindness towards mariners shipwrecked on their coast. The government was organized as it had been in Maryland, the proprietaries appointing the council, the people electing the house of assembly. The defence of the colony rested on the militia. With the Spaniards at St. Augustine friendly relations sprung up: a Quaker could respect the faith of a Papist. Four Indians, converts of the Spanish priests, captives to the Yammasees, and exposed to sale as slaves, were ransomed by Archdale, and sent to the governor of St. Augustine. "I shall manifest reciprocal kindness," was his reply, "and shall always observe a good correspondence with you;" and, when an English vessel was wrecked on Florida, the Spaniards retaliated the benevolence of Archdale.

The fame of Carolina, the American Canaan, that flowed with milk and honey, began to increase. The industrious Scotch, zealous alike for liberty and property, were soon to be attracted. Already New England men were allured to the region that now "stood circumstanced with the honor of a true English government, zealous for the increase of virtue, as well as outwa d trade and business." And the representatives of the freemen of the colony declared that Archdale, "by his wisdom, patience, and labor, had laid a firm foundation for a most glorious superstructure."

1696 June 26. Archdale, 21

Immediately after the return of the Quaker legislator, the Huguenots were once more and successfully enfranchised by the colonial legislature. Liberty of conscience was also conferred on all Christians, unhap-

1697 March 10.

CHAP. XIX. pily with the exception of Papists. This was the first act in Carolina disfranchising religious opinion.

Soon after Archdale reached England, the work of
1698. proprietary legislation was renewed. The new code asserted the favorite maxim of the reformers of that day, that "all power and dominion are most naturally founded in property." But this maxim, which, in England, was, in the progress of freedom, a conquest of commercial industry over the pride of birth, was, with the laws resting on it, rejected in Carolina. The
1702. Sept. 1. journals of the provincial assembly show that, after they had been read and debated, paragraph by para-
Statutes i. 42. graph, the question of ordering them to a second reading was carried in the negative. Carolina refused alike an hereditary nobility and the dominion of wealth.

The colonial oligarchy next looked for favor to an exclusive religion of state. Even the consent of non-
1699. conformists had been given to the public maintenance
Statutes ii. 135. of one minister of the Church of England; and ortho-
1703. doxy had, as in nearly every colony, been protected by
May 6. 1704. the menace of disfranchisement and prisons. In 1704,
Statutes ii. 196, 197. "the high pretended Churchmen," having, by the arts of Nathaniel Moore, obtained a majority of one in an
Archdale, 25. assembly representing a colony of which two thirds were dissenters, abruptly disfranchised them all, and,
Statutes ii. 232. after the English precedent, gave to the Church of England a monopoly of political power. The council, no longer composed on the principles of Archdale, joined in the eager assent of the governor. In the court of the proprietaries, Archdale opposed the bill; but Lord Granville, the palatine, an opponent to occasional conformity, scorned the gentle remonstrances of the Quaker. "You," said he, "are of one opinion;

I of another; and our lives may not be long enough CHAP. XIX.
to end the controversy. I am for this bill, and this is
the party that I will head and countenance." Dis- Oldmixon, i. 486.
senters having thus been excluded from the house of
commons, the Church of England was easily established 1704. Nov.
by law. At the same time, a body of lay commissioners was nominated by the oligarchy from its own number, to supersede the authority of the bishop. Thus the intolerant spirit which persecuted dissenters assumed "a haughty dominion over the clergy itself."

The dissenters, excluded from the colonial legislature, rejected with contumely by the proprietaries, Dalcho, 64—69.
appealed to the house of lords, where the spirit of
Somers prevailed. An address to the queen, in behalf 1706. March 12.
of the dissenters of Carolina, was adopted; the lords
of trade and plantations reported that the proprietaries May 24.
had forfeited their charter, and advised its recall by a
judicial process; the intolerant acts were, by royal June 10.
authority, declared null and void. In November of the
same year, they were repealed by the colonial assem- Statutes ii. 281, 282.
bly; but, while dissenters were tolerated, and could 282-295.
share political power, the Church of England was immediately established as the religion of the province.

This compromise continued till the revolution. Meantime, the authority of the proprietaries was tainted by the declaration of the queen, and the opinion of English lawyers. Strifes ensued perpetually respecting quitrents and finances; and, as the proprietaries provided no sufficient defence for the colony, their power, which had no guaranty even in their own interests, and still less in the policy of the English government, or the good will of the colonists, awaited only an opportunity to expire.

This period of turbulence and insurrection, of angry

CHAP. XIX. factions and popular excitements, was nevertheless a period of prosperity. The country rapidly increased in population and the value of its exports. The prolific rice-plant had, at a very early period, been introduced from Madagascar; in 1691, the legislature was already busy in rewarding the invention of new methods for cleansing it; its culture steadily increased; and the rice of Carolina was esteemed the best in the world. Hence the opulence of the colony; hence, also, its swarms of negro slaves. The profits of the rice-fields tempted the planter to enlarge his domains, and Africa furnished laborers.

The cereal grains were ill adapted to the sands near the sea, or the alluvial swamps. The woods were more inviting. Early in the eighteenth century, the Carolina Indian trader had penetrated a thousand miles into the interior The skins of bears, beaver, wildcats, deer, foxes, and raccoons, invited commerce. The oak was cleft into staves for the West Indies: the trunk of the pine was valued for masts, boards, and joists; its juices yielded turpentine; from the same tree, when dry, fire extracted tar.

But naval stores were still more the produce of North Carolina, where, as yet, slaves were very few, and the lonely planters, under their mild sky, mingled a leisurely industry with the use of the fowling-piece. While the world was set on fire by wars of unparalleled extent, the unpolished inhabitants of North Carolina multiplied and spread in the enjoyment of the highest personal liberty. Five miles below Edenton, just a hundred yards from the sound, beneath the shade of a large cedar, the stone that marks the grave of Henderson Walker keeps the record that "North Carolina, during his administration, enjoyed tranquillity." This is the history of four years in which the people, without molestation, enjoyed their wild independence. It was the liberty of freemen in the woods. "North Carolina," like ancient Rome, was famed "as the sanctuary of runaways;" seventy years after its origin, Spotswood describes it as "a country where there's scarce any form of government;" and it long continued to be said, with but slight exaggeration, that "in Carolina, every one did what was right in his own eyes, paying tribute neither to God nor to Cæsar."

CHAP. XIX.

Spotswood, MS.

Bland, MS.

In such a country, which was almost an utter stranger to any public worship, among a people made up of Presbyterians and Independents, of Lutherans and Quakers, of men who drew their politics, their faith, and their law from the light of nature,—where, according to the royalists, the majority "were Quakers, atheists, deists, and other evil-disposed persons,"—the pious zeal or the bigotry of the proprietaries, selecting Robert Daniel, the deputy-governor, as the fit instrument, resolved on establishing the Church of England. The legislature, chosen without reference to this end, after much opposition, acceded to the design; and further enacted that no one, who would not take the oath prescribed by law, should hold a place of trust in the colony. Then did North Carolina first gain experience of disfranchisements for opinions; then did it first hear of glebes, and a clergy; then were churches first ordered to be erected at the public cost. But a people does not bend in a generation: the laws could not be enforced; and, six years afterwards, the people still "labored under such a total absence of religion, that there was but one clergyman in the whole country." The Quakers, led by their faith, were foremost

Spotswood, MS.

1704

Spotswood, MS

CHAP. XIX. in opposition. They were "not only the principal fomenters of the distractions in Carolina," but the governor of the Old Dominion complained that they "made it their business to instil the like pernicious notions into the minds of his majesty's subjects in Virginia, and to justify the mad actions of the rabble by arguments destructive to all government."

1705. On a vacancy in the office of governor, anarchy prevailed. "The North had been usually governed by a Spotswood, MS. deputy, appointed by the governor of South Carolina," and Thomas Cary obtained a commission in the wonted form. The proprietaries disapproved the appointment, and gave leave to the little oligarchy of their own deputies to elect the chief magistrate. Their choice fell on William Glover; and the colony was forthwith rent with divisions. On the one side were Churchmen and royalists, the immediate friends of the proprietaries; on the other, "a rabble of profligate persons," that is, the Quakers and other dissenters, and that majority of the people which was unconsciously swayed by democratic instincts. Each party had its governor; 1706 to 1710 each elected its house of representatives. Neither could entirely prevail. The one wanted a legal sanction, the other popular favor; and, as "it had been the Spotswood, MS. common practice for them in North Carolina to resist and imprison their governors," till they came "to look upon that as lawful which had been so long tolerated," the party of the proprietaries was easily "trodden under foot." "The Quakers were a numerous people there, and, having been fatally trusted with a large share in the administration of that government," were resolved 1710 1711. "to maintain themselves therein." To restore order, Edward Hyde was despatched to govern the province; but he was to receive his commission as deputy from

CHAP. XIX. 1710, 1711

Tynte, the governor of the southern division; and, as Tynte had already fallen a victim to the climate, Hyde could show no evidence of his right, except private letters from the proprietaries; and "the respect due to his birth could avail nothing on that mutinous people." Affairs grew worse than ever; for the legislature which he convened, having been elected under forms which, in the eyes of his opponents, tainted the whole action with illegality, showed no desire to heal by prudence the distractions of the country, but, blinded by zeal for revenge, made passionate enactments, "of which they themselves had not power to enforce the execution," and which, in Virginia, even royalists condemned as unjustifiably severe. At once "the true spirit of Quakerism appeared" in an open disobedience to unjust laws: Cary and some of his friends took up arms; it was rumored that they were ready for an alliance with the Indians; and Spotswood, an experienced soldier, now governor of Virginia, was summoned by Hyde as an ally. The loyalty of the veteran was embarrassed. He could not esteem "a country safe which had in it such dangerous incendiaries." He believed that, unless "measures were taken to discourage the mutinous spirits, who had become so audacious as to take up arms, it would prove a dangerous example to the rest of her majesty's plantations." But "the difficulties of marching forces into a country so cut with rivers, were almost insuperable;" there were no troops but the militia; the counties bordering on Carolina were "stocked with Quakers," or, at least, with "the articles of those people;" and the governor of Virginia might almost as well have undertaken a military expedition against foxes and raccoons, or have attempted to enforce religious uniformity among the conies, as

CHAP. XIX. employ methods of invasion against a people whose dwellings were so sheltered by creeks, so hidden by forests, so protected by solitudes. The insurgent people "obstructed the course of justice, demanding the dissolution of the assembly, and the repeal of all laws they disliked." Spotswood could only send a party of marines from the guard-ships, as evidence of his disposition. No effusion of blood followed. Cary, and the leaders of his party, on the contrary, boldly appeared in Virginia, for the purpose, as they said, of appealing to England in defence of their actions; and Spotswood compelled them to take their passage in the men-of-war that were just returning. But North Carolina remained as before; its burgesses, obeying the popular judgment, "refused to make provision for
1711 to 1712. defending any part of their country," unless "they could introduce into the government the persons most obnoxious for the late rebellion;" and therefore the
1712. Feb. assembly was promptly dissolved. There was little hope of harmony between the proprietaries and the people of North Carolina.

But here, as elsewhere in America, this turbulence of freedom did not check the increase of population. Notwithstanding the contradictory accounts, the province, from its first permanent settlement by white men, has constantly been advancing, and has, I think, always exceeded South Carolina in numbers. The country
1710. between the Trent and the Neuse was occupied; and at the confluence of those rivers, where sands abound instead of glaciers, and a wide champaign instead of highlands and mountains, emigrants from Switzerland began the settlement of New Berne. Germans, also, fugitives from the devastated Palatinate, found a home in the same vicinity. In these early days, few negroes

were introduced into the colony. Its trade was chiefly engrossed by New England. The increasing expenses of the government amounted, in 1714, to nine hundred pounds. While the people were establishing a commonwealth, the surplus revenue to the proprietaries, by sales of land and the quitrents from their boundless domains, was but one hundred and sixty-nine pounds, or twenty guineas to each proprietary. Such was the profit from the ownership of a wilderness.

For Virginia, the revolution gave to her liberties the regularity of law; in other respects, the character of her people and the forms of her government were not changed. The first person who, in the reign of King William, entered the Ancient Dominion as lieutenant-governor, was the same Francis Nicholson who, in the days of King James, had been the deputy of Andros for the consolidated provinces of the north, and had been expelled from New York by the insurgent people; and his successor was Andros himself, fresh from im- 1692.
prisonment in Massachusetts. The earlier administration of the ardent but narrow-minded Nicholson was signalized by the establishment of the college of William and Mary, the first fruits of the revolution, in age second only to Harvard; at the instance of the learned and persevering commissary Blair, whose zeal for future generations was aided by subscriptions, by a gift of quitrents from the king, by an endowment from the royal domain, and by a tax of a penny a pound on tobacco exported to other plantations. To the care of Andros the historical inquirer owes the preservation of those few early papers of Virginia which have escaped official neglect, fires, time, and civil wars; but neither from them nor from their successors was there hope of an enlargement of civil freedom.

CHAP. XIX.

The powers of the governor were exorbitant; he was at once lieutenant-general and admiral, lord treasurer and chancellor, the chief judge in all courts president of the council, and bishop, or ordinary; so that the armed force, the revenue, the interpretation of law, the administration of justice, the church,—all were under his control or guardianship.

The checks on his power existed in his instructions, in the council, and in the general assembly. But the instructions were kept secret; and, besides, they rather confirmed his prerogatives. The members of the council owed their appointment to his recommendation, their continuance to his pleasure, and, moreover, looked to him for advancement to places of profit. The assembly was restrained by the prospect of a negative from the governor and from the crown, was compelled to solicit the concurrence of the council, was exposed to influence from royal patronage, was watched in its actions by a clerk whom the governor appointed, and was always sure of being dissolved if complaints began to grow loud or opposition too ardent. It had, moreover, lost the method of resistance best suited to the times, since, in addition to quitrents, a former legislature had already established a perpetual revenue.

Yet the people of Virginia still found methods of nourishing the spirit of independence. The permanent revenue was sure to be exhausted on the governor and his favorites; when additional supplies became necessary, the burgesses, as in Jamaica and in other colonies, claimed the right of nominating a treasurer of their own, subject to their orders, without further warrant
Hening, iii. 92, 197, 476, 495. from the governor. The statutes of Virginia show that the first assembly after the revolution set this
1691. example, which was often imitated. The denial of

this system by the crown increased the aversion to CHAP. XIX.
raising money; so that Virginia refused to contribute
its quota to the defence of the colonies against France, Present State, p 62.
and not only disregarded the special orders for assisting
Albany, but with entire unanimity, and even with
the assent of the council, justified its disobedience.
While other provinces were exhausted by taxation, in
eleven years, eighty-three pounds of tobacco for each Spotswood.
poll was the total sum levied by all the special acts of 1707
the assembly of Virginia. to 1718

The very existence of the forms of representation
led to comparison. Virginia was conscious of its importance to the mother country; and its inhabitants,
long aware that their liberties were less than those of
New England, were put "upon a nice inquiry into the Quarry
circumstances of the government." England also provoked a generous rivalry. "The assembly concluded
itself entitled to all the rights and privileges of an
English parliament;" and the records of the house
of commons were examined in search of precedents
favorable to legislative freedom.

The constitution of the Church in Virginia cherished colonial freedom; for the act of 1642, which established it, reserved the right of presentation to the parish. The license of the bishop of London, and the recommendation of the governor, availed, therefore, but little. Sometimes the parish rendered the establishment nugatory by its indolence of action; sometimes
the minister, if acceptable to the congregation, was Jones, 103.
received, but not presented. It was the general custom Present State.
to hire the minister from year to year. A legal opinion 1703.
was obtained from England, that the minister is an Barradale, MS.
incumbent for life, and cannot be displaced by his
parishioners; but the vestry kept themselves the

CHAP. XIX. parson's master by preventing his induction, so that he acquired no freehold in his living, and might be removed at pleasure. Nor was the character of the clergy who came over always suited to win affection or respect. The parishes, moreover, were of such length, that some lived fifty miles from the parish church; and the assembly would not increase the taxes by changing the bounds, even from fear of impending "paganism, atheism, or sectaries." "Schism" threatened "to creep into the Church," and to generate "faction in the civil government;" and when Virginia and the crown came to a first violent collision, the strife related to the rights of "the parsons."

Hawks, 88, 89.

Spotswood, MS.

But the greatest safeguard of liberty in Virginia was the individual freedom of mind, which formed, of necessity, the characteristic of independent landholders living apart on their plantations. In the age of commercial monopoly, Virginia had not one market town, not one place of trade. "As to outward appearance, it looked all like a wild desert;" and the mercantile world, founding its judgment on the absence of cities, regarded it as "one of the poorest, miserablest, and worst countries in all America." It did not seek to share actively in the profits of commerce; it had little of the precious metals, and still less of credit; it was satisfied with agriculture. Taxes were paid in tobacco; remittances to Europe were made in tobacco; the revenue of the clergy, and the magistrates, and the colony, was collected in the same currency; the colonial tradesman received his pay in straggling parcels of it; and ships from abroad were obliged to lie whole months in the rivers, before boats, visiting the several plantations on their banks, could pick up a cargo. In the season of a commercial revolution, the commercial element did not

CHAP. XIX.

enter into the character of the colony. Its inhabitants "daily grew more and more averse to cohabitation." All royalists and Churchmen as they were by ancestry, habit, and established law, they reasoned boldly in their seclusion, making their own good pleasure their rule of conduct. "Pernicious notions, fatal to the royal prerogative, were improving daily;" and, though Virginia protested against the charge of "republicanism," as an unfounded reproach, yet colonial opinion, the offspring of free inquiry, which seclusion awakened, the woods sheltered, and the self-will of slaveholders fortified, was more than a counterpoise to the prerogative of the British crown. In former ages, no colony had ever enjoyed a happier freedom. From the days of the insurrection of Bacon, for a period of three quarters of a century, Virginia possessed uninterrupted peace. On its own soil, the strife with the Indians was ended; the French hesitated to invade the western frontier, on which they lowered: if sometimes alarm was spread by privateers upon the coast, a naval foe was not attracted to a region which had neither town nor magazines, where there was nothing to destroy but a field of tobacco, nothing to plunder but the frugal stores of scattered plantations. The soil was stained by nothing but the sweat of the laborer. In such scenes of tranquil happiness, the political strifes were but the fitful ebullitions of a high spirit, which, in the wantonness of independence, loved to tease the governor; and, again, if the burgesses expressed loyalty, they were loyal only because loyalty was their humor. Hence the reports forwarded to England were often contradictory. "This government," wrote Spotswood, in 1711, "is in perfect peace and tranquillity, under a due obedience to the royal authority, and a gentlemanly

1703. Quarry

1709, 1710.

CHAP. XIX. conformity to the Church of England;" and the letter had hardly left the Chesapeake before he found himself thwarted by the impracticable burgesses, dissolving the assembly, and fearing to convene another till opinion should change. But Spotswood, the best in the line of Virginia governors, was soon restored to colonial favor. Like schoolboys of old at a barring out, the Virginians resisted their government, not as ready for independence, but as resolved on a holiday.

The English revolution was a "Protestant" revolution: of the Roman Catholic proprietary of Maryland it sequestered the authority, while it protected the fortunes.

During the absence of Lord Baltimore from his province, his powers had been delegated to nine deputies, over whom William Joseph presided. The spirit that swayed their counsels sprung from the doctrine of legitimacy, which the revolution had prostrated; and they fell with it. Distrusting the people, they provoked opposition by demanding of the assembly, as a qualification of its members, an oath of fidelity to the proprietary. On resistance to the illegal demand, the house was prorogued; and, even after the successful invasion of England became known, the deputies of Lord Baltimore hesitated to proclaim the new sovereigns.

1689. April. The delay gave birth to an armed association for asserting the right of King William; and the deputies were easily driven to a garrison on the south side of Patuxent River, about two miles above its mouth. Aug 1. There they capitulated, obtaining security for themselves, and yielding their assent to the exclusion of Papists from all provincial offices. A convention of the associates, "for the defence of the Protestant religion," assumed the government, and, in an address

to King William, denounced the influence of Jesuits, CHAP. XIX.
the prevalence of Popish idolatry, the connivance by
the government at murders of Protestants, and the
danger from plots with the French and Indians.

The privy council, after a debate on the address, advised the forfeiture of the charter by a process of law; but King William, heedless of the remonstrances of the proprietary, who could be convicted of no crime 1691.
but his creed, and impatient of judicial forms, by his June 1.
own power constituted Maryland a royal government. Chalmers's
The arbitrary act was sanctioned by a legal opinion Opinions, 29.
from Lord Holt. In 1692, Sir Lionel Copley arrived 1692.
with a royal commission, dissolved the convention, assumed the government, and convened an assembly. Its first act recognized William and Mary; its second established the Church of England as the religion of the state, to be supported by general taxation. Thus were the barons of Baltimore superseded for a generation. The ancient capital, inconvenient in its site, was, moreover, tenanted chiefly by Catholics, and surrounded by proprietary recollections: under Protestant auspices, the city sacred to the Virgin Mary was aban- 1694
doned, and Annapolis became the seat of government. The system of a religion of state, earnestly advanced by the boastful eagerness of Francis Nicholson, who 1694 to
passed from Virginia to the government of Maryland, 1698
and by the patient, the disinterested, but unhappily too exclusive earnestness of the commissary Thomas Bray, became the settled policy of the government. The first act, as it had contained a clause giving validity in 1692
the colony to the Great Charter of England, was not accepted by the crown. Again, in 1696, the inviolable claim of the colony to English rights and liberties was engrafted by the assembly on the act of establishment;

CHAP. XIX. and this also was disallowed. In 1700, the presence and personal virtues of Bray, who saw Christianity only in the English Church, obtained by unanimity a law commanding conformity in every "place of public worship." Once more the act was rejected in England from regard to the rights of Protestant dissenters;
1702. and when, at last, Episcopacy was established by the colonial legislature, and the right of appointment and induction secured to the governor, the English acts of toleration were at the same time put in force. Thus was a religion of state established in Maryland, as well as in Virginia. In the latter province, the right of presentation remained with the parish; in the former, with the governor. In Virginia, sectaries found no favor from the law; in Maryland, they were tolerated. Protestant dissent was, therefore, safe; for the difficulty of obtaining English missionaries, the remoteness of the ecclesiastical tribunals, the scandal arising from
Hawks, 100. the profligate lives and impunity in crime of many clergymen, the zeal of the numerous Quakers for intellectual freedom, and the powerful activity of a sort of "wandering pretenders from New England," deluding even "Churchmen by their extemporary prayers and preachments,"—all united as a barrier against persecution. The Roman Catholics alone were left without an ally, exposed to English bigotry and colonial injustice. They alone were disfranchised on the soil which, long before Locke pleaded for toleration or Penn for religious freedom, they had chosen, not as their own asylum only, but, with catholic liberality, as the asylum of every persecuted sect. In the land which Catholics had opened to Protestants, the Catholic inhabitant was
1704. the sole victim to Anglican intolerance. Mass might not be said publicly. No Catholic priest or bishop

might utter his faith in a voice of persuasion. No Catholic might teach the young. If the wayward child of a Papist would but become an apostate, the law wrested for him from his parents a share of their property. The disfranchisement of the proprietary related to his creed, not to his family. Such were the methods adopted "to prevent the growth of Popery." Who shall say that the faith of the cultivated individual is firmer than the faith of the common people? Who shall say that the many are fickle, that the chief is firm? To recover the inheritance of authority, Benedict, the son of the proprietary, renounced the Catholic Church for that of England; the persecution never crushed the faith of the humble colonists.

CHAP. XIX.

It was not till 1715 that the power of the proprietary was restored. In the mean time, the administration of Maryland resembled that of Virginia. Nicholson and Andros were governors in each. Like Virginia, Maryland had no considerable town, was disturbed but little by the Indians, and less by the French. Its staple was tobacco; yet hemp and flax were raised, and both, like tobacco, were sometimes used as currency. In Somerset and Dorchester, the manufacture 1706
of linen, and even of woollen cloth, was attempted. Industry so opposite to the system of mercantile monopoly needed an apology, and the assembly pleaded, in excuse of the weavers, that they were driven to their tasks "by absolute necessity." As Maryland lies in the latitude where, in the collision of negro labor and white labor, climate gives the white man a decided advantage, and as the large introduction of slaves drove free laborers to more northern regions, this province surpassed every other in the number of its white servants. The market was always supplied with them,

CHAP. XIX. the price varying from twelve to thirty pounds. By its position, also, Maryland was connected with the north; it is the most southern colony which, in 1695, consented to pay its quota towards the defence of New York, thus forming, from the Chesapeake to Maine, an imperfect confederacy. The union was increased by a public
1695. post. Eight times in the year, letters might be forwarded from the Potomac to Philadelphia. During the period of the royal government, the assembly still retained influence; for it firmly refused to establish a permanent revenue. Education was neglected; yet a legislative enactment promised a library and a free school to every parish—a proof of the zeal of the commissary and the good intentions of the assembly. The population of the colony increased, but not so rapidly as elsewhere. The usual estimates for this period are too low. In 1710, the number of bond and free must have exceeded thirty thousand; yet a bounty for every
1715. wolf's head continued to be offered, the roads to the capital were long marked by notches on trees, and water-mills still solicited legislative encouragement. Such was Maryland as a royal province. In 1715, the authority of the infant proprietary was vindicated in the person of his guardian.

More happy than Lord Baltimore, the proprietary of Pennsylvania recovered his authority without surrendering his principles. Accepting the resignation of the narrow and imperious but honest Blackwell, who, at the period of the revolution, acted as his deputy, the Quaker chief desired "to settle the government in a condition to please the generality," to "let them be the choosers."—"Friends,"—such was his message, —"I heartily wish you all well, and beseech God to guide you in the ways of righteousness and peace.

I have thought fit, upon my further stop in these parts, CHAP. XIX.
to throw all into your hands, that you may see the
confidence I have in you, and the desire I have to give
you all possible contentment." And, as the council Minutes, i. 274.
of his province was, at that time, elected directly by
the people, that body collectively was constituted his 1690. June 2.
deputy. Of its members, Thomas Lloyd, from North
Wales, an Oxford scholar, was universally beloved as a
bright example of the integrity of virtue. The path
of preferment had opened to him in England, but he
chose rather the internal peace that springs from
"mental felicity." This Quaker preacher, the oracle
of "the patriot rustics" on the Delaware, was now, by
free suffrage, constituted president of the council. But
the lower counties were jealous of the superior weight
of Pennsylvania; disputes respecting appointments to Nov. 21.
office grew up, the council divided; protests ensued; 1691
the members from the territories withdrew, and would April 1.
not be reconciled; so that, with the reluctant consent
of William Penn, who, though oppressed with persecutions and losses, never distrusted the people of his
province, and always endured hardships as though they
"were, in the end, every way for good," the lower
counties were constituted a separate government under
Markham. Thus did the commonwealth of Delaware
begin an independent existence. It was the act of its
own citizens.

Uncertainty rested on the institutions of the prov- 1691
inces; an apparent schism among the Quakers increased the gloom. Who denies that the heart of man is deceitful, and desperately wicked? Often, an apostate from a party, in the incipient stages of apostasy, is unconscious of his change; and the delusions of self-love nurse the belief that the perverse community from

CHAP. XIX.

1691, 1692.

which he separates leaves him alone to vindicate their principles in unaltered purity. So it was with George Keith. Amidst the applause of the malignant opponents of Quakers, the apostate, conciliating other Protestants by a more formal regard for the Bible, which the Quakers reverenced, and would not even seem to undervalue, asserted his own exclusive adhesion to the principles of Friends by pushing the doctrine of non-resistance to an absolute extreme. No true Quaker, he asserted, can act in public life, either as a lawgiver or as a magistrate. The inferences were plain. The liberties of the province, fruits of Quaker legislation, were subverted; and, if Quakers could not be magistrates in a Quaker community, King William must send Churchmen to govern them. Conforming his conduct to his opinion, Keith resisted the magistracy of Pennsylvania with defiance and contumely. The grand jury found him guilty of a breach of the laws; an indictment, trial, and conviction followed. The punishment awarded was a fine of five pounds; yet, as his offence was, in its nature, a contempt of court, the scrupulous Quakers, shunning the punishment of impertinence, lest it should seem the punishment of opinion, forgave the fine. Meantime, the envious world, vexed at the society which it could neither corrupt nor intimidate, set up the cry that the Quakers were turned persecutors. Not a word of explanation would be listened to. The expressions of indignation, which the bluntness of the Quaker magistrates had not restrained, were quoted as proofs of intolerance. But, in the great conflict of parties, the devices of an apostate to deceive have but an accidental and transient interest: the unchanged Quaker, disowned by those who had cherished and advanced him,

was soon left without a faction, and, tired of his posi- CHAP XIX.
tion, made a true exposition of the strife by accepting
an Episcopal benefice.

The disturbance by Keith, creating questions as to
the administration of justice, confirmed the disposition 1692
of the English government to subject Pennsylvania to Oct. 21.
a royal commission; and, in April, 1693, Benjamin 1693
Fletcher, assuming power as governor for William and April 26.
Mary, once more united Delaware to Pennsylvania.
If no open opposition was made, "yet some, who held
commissions from the proprietor, withdrew at the
publishing of their majesties' commission, and others Minutes, i. 360.
refused to act under that power."

When the house of representatives assembled, resist- May 15.
ance was developed. It was the object of Fletcher to
gain supplies; the wary legislators were intent on
maintaining their privileges. The laws founded on
the charter of Penn they declare to be "yet in
force; we desire the same may be confirmed to us as
our right and liberties."—"If the laws," answered
Fletcher, "made by virtue of Mr. Penn's charter, be of
force to you, and can be brought into competition with
the great seal which commands me hither, I have no
business here;" and he pleaded the royal prerogative
as inalienable. "The grant of King Charles," replied
Joseph Growdon, the speaker, "is itself under the
great seal. Is that charter in a lawful way at an end?"

To reconcile the difference, Fletcher proposed to
reënact the greater number of the former laws. "We May 24.
are but poor men," said John White, "and of inferior
degree, and represent the people. This is our difficulty; we durst not begin to pass one bill to be enacted
of our former laws, least by soe doing we declare the
rest void."

CHAP. XIX.

1693. May 25.

The royalists next started a technical objection: the old laws are invalid because they do not bear the great seal of the proprietary. "We know the laws to be our laws," it was answered; "and we are in the enjoyment of them; the sealing does not make the law, but the consent of governor, council, and assembly."

The same spirit pervaded the session; and the grant of a penny in the pound, which, it was promised, "should not be dipt in blood," was connected with a capitulation recognizing the full legislative rights of the representatives. And a public manifesto, signed by all the members from Pennsylvania, declared it to be "the right of the assembly that, before any bill for supplies be presented, aggrievances ought to be redressed."—"My door was never shut," said Fletcher on parting; "but it was avoided, as if it were treason for the speaker, or anie other representative, to be seen in my company during your sessions."

One permanent change in the constitution was the fruit of this administration: the house originated its bills, and retained this right ever after. Fletcher would gladly have changed the law for "yearlie delegates;" for "where," thought the royalist, "is the hurt, if a good assemblie should be continued from one year to another?" But the people saved their privilege by having elected an assembly of which Fletcher could "give no good character at Whitehall," and which he could have no wish to continue.

1694 The assembly of the next year was still more impracticable, having for its speaker David Lloyd, the keenest discoverer of grievances, and the most quiet and persevering of political scolds. "If you will not

May levy money to make war,"—such was the governor's

message,—"yet I hope you will not refuse to feed the hungrie, and clothe the naked." The assembly was willing to give alms to the sufferers round Albany; but it claimed the right of making specific appropriations, and collecting and disbursing the money by officers of its own appointment. The demand was rejected as an infringement on the royal prerogative; and, after a fortnight's altercation, the assembly was dissolved. Such was the success of a royal governor in Pennsylvania. CHAP XIX. 1694.

Meantime, the proprietary recovered his authority. Thrice, within two years after the revolution, had William Penn been arrested and brought before court, and thrice he had been openly set free. He prepared 1690
to embark once more for America; emigrants crowded round him; a convoy was granted; the fleet was almost ready to sail, when, on his return from the funeral of George Fox, messengers were sent to apprehend him. Having been thrice questioned, and thrice acquitted, he now went into retirement. Locke would have interceded for his pardon; but Penn refused clemency, waiting rather for justice. The delay completed the wreck of his fortunes; sorrow lowered over his family; the wife of his youth yielded to a mortal disease; his eldest son had no vigorous hold on life; even among Friends, some cavilled at his conduct; Jesuit, Papist, rogue, and traitor, were the gentlest calumnies of the world; yet Penn preserved his serenity, and, true to his principles, in a season of passionate and almost universal war, published a plea for eternal peace among the nations.

But, among the many in England whom Penn had benefited, gratitude was not extinct. On the restora- 1693
tion of the whigs to power, Rochester, who, under

CHAP. XIX. James II., had given up office, rather than profess Romanism, the less distinguished Ranelagh, and Henry, the brother of Algernon Sidney, of old the correspondent of the prince of Orange, as well as the warm friend of William Penn, interceded for the restoration of the proprietary of Pennsylvania. "He is my old acquaintance," answered William; "he may follow his business as freely as ever; I have nothing to say
1694. against him." Appearing before the king in council,
Aug. 20. his innocence was established; and, in August, 1694, the patent for his restoration passed the seals.

1695. March 26. The pressure of poverty delayed the return of the proprietary to the banks of the Delaware; and Markham was invested with the executive power. The
Sept. 9. members of the assembly, which he convened, anxious for political liberties, which the recent changes had threatened to efface, found a remedy within themselves, and, assuming the power of fundamental legislation, framed a democratic constitution. They would have "their privileges granted before they would give anie monie." Doubtful of the extent of his authority, Markham dissolved the assembly.

1696. Oct. The legislature of the next year persevered, and, by its own authority, subject only to the assent of the proprietary, established a purely democratic government. The governor was but chairman of the council The council, the assembly, each was chosen by the people. The time of election, the time of assembling, the period of office, were placed beyond the power of the executive. The judiciary depended on the legislature. The people constituted themselves the foun-
Proud, App. iv. tain of honor and of power. When the assembly
1697. next came together, Markham could say to them,
May 12. "You are met, not by virtue of any writ of mine,

WILLIAM PENN.

but of a law made by yourselves." The people ruled, CHAP. XIX.
and, after years of strife, all went happily. Nothing was wanting but concert with the proprietary.

Before the close of the century, William Penn was 1699. Nov. 30.
once more within his colony. The commonwealth, which had been as an infant, nestling under his wing, had ripened into self-reliance. Passing over all intermediate changes, the proprietary acknowledged the present validity of the old fundamental law. "Let's 1700. April.
make a constitution," said a member of the council, "that may be firm and lasting to us and ours;" and Penn invited them "to keep what's good in the charter and frame of government, to lay aside what is burdensome, and to add what may best suit the common good." And the old charter was surren- June 7.
dered, with the unanimous consent of the assembly and council.

Yet the framing of a new constitution was delayed by colonial jars. The counties of Delaware dreaded the loss of their independence by a union with the extending population of Pennsylvania. Besides, in the lower province, the authority of William Penn rested but on sufferance; in the larger state, it was sanctioned by a royal charter; and a passionate strife 1700
delayed the establishment of government. 1701

Meantime, the proprietary endeavored to remove the jealousy with which his provinces were regarded in England. The parliament ever insisted on the colonial monopoly, and the colony readily passed laws against piracy and illicit trade; but it could not assent to propitiate the English sovereigns by granting its quota for the defence of New York.

In regard to the improvement of the negroes, Penn attempted to legislate, not for the abolition of slavery,

CHAP. XIX. but for the sanctity of marriage among the slaves, and for their personal safety. The last object was effected; the first, which would have been the forerunner of freedom, was defeated.

Neither did philanthropy achieve permanent benefits for the Indian. Treaties of peace were renewed with the men of the wilderness from the Potomac to Oswego, and the trade with them was subjected to regulations; but they could not be won to the faith or the habits of civilized life.

These measures were adopted amidst the fruitless
1701. wranglings between the delegates from Delaware and
Aug. 21. those from Pennsylvania. At last, the news was received that the English parliament was about to render all their strifes and all their hopes nugatory by the general abrogation of every colonial charter. An as-
Aug. 22. sembly was summoned instantly; and, when it came together, the proprietary, eager to return to England to defend the common rights of himself and his province,
Sept. 15. urged the perfecting of their frame of government. "Since all men are mortal,"—such was his weighty message,—"think of some suitable expedient and provision for your safety, as well in your privileges as property, and you will find me ready to comply with whatever may render us happy by a nearer union of our interests. Review again your laws; propose new ones, that may better your circumstances; and what you do, do it quickly. Unanimity and despatch may contribute to the disappointment of those that too long have sought the ruin of OUR YOUNG COUNTRY."

The relations of Penn to his colony were twofold; he was their sovereign, and he was the owner of the unappropriated domain. The members of the assembly, impelled by an interest common to every one of

CHAP. XIX. 1701

their constituents, were disposed to encroach on his private rights. If some of their demands were resisted, he readily yielded every thing which could be claimed, even by inference, from his promises, or could be expected from his liberality; making his interests of less consideration than the satisfaction of his people; rather remitting than rigorously exacting his revenues.

Minutes, and Gordon, i. 896.

Of political privileges, he conceded all that was desired. The council, henceforward to be appointed by the proprietary, became a branch of the executive government; the assembly assumed to itself the right of originating every act of legislation, subject only to the assent of the governor. Elections to the assembly were annual; the time of its election and the time of its session were fixed; it was to sit upon its own adjournments. Sheriffs and coroners were nominated by the people; no questions of property could come before the governor and council; the judiciary was left to the discretion of the legislature. Religious liberty was established, and every public employment was open to every man professing faith in Jesus Christ. Happy Pennsylvania! While, in revolutionized England, the triennial parliaments were dependent for the time of their election, prorogation, and dissolution, on the will of the sovereign; while Papists were persecuted, and dissenters disfranchised; in Pennsylvania, human rights were respected. The fundamental law of William Penn, even his detractors concede, was in harmony with universal reason, and true to the ancient and just liberties of the people.

On returning to America, William Penn had designed to remain here for life, and to give a home to his family and his posterity in the New World. But his work was accomplished. Divesting himself and his suc-

CHAP. XIX. cessors of all power to injure, he had founded a democracy. By the necessity of the case, he remained its
1701. feudal sovereign; for it was only as such that he could have granted or could maintain the charter of colonial liberties. His resignation would have been a surrender of the colony to the crown. But time and the people would remove the inconsistency. And now, having given freedom and popular power to his provinces, no strifes remaining but strifes about property, happily for himself, happily for his people, happily for posterity, he departed from the "young countrie" of his affections, and exiled himself to the birthplace of his fathers.

For the separation of the territories, contingent
1702. provision had been made by the proprietary. In 1702, Pennsylvania convened its legislature apart, and the two colonies were never again united. The lower counties became at once almost an independent democracy; for, as the authority of the proprietary was one
1708. of sufferance merely, and was often brought into question, the executive power intrusted to the governor of Pennsylvania was too feeble to limit the power of the people. Delaware had its own legislature, its own tribunals, its own subordinate executive offices, and virtually enjoyed an absolute self-government.

1701 to 1710. The subsequent years in Pennsylvania exhibit constant collisions between the proprietary, as owner of the unappropriated public territory, and a people eager to enlarge their freeholds. The scoldings of David Lloyd may be consigned to oblivion; the integrity of the mildly aristocratic James Logan, to whose judicious care the proprietary estates were intrusted, has preserved its purity unsullied by the accusations or impeachments of the assembly. Strifes also existed on political questions. The end of government was declared to be the happiness of the people, and from this maxim the duties of the governor were derived. But the organization of the judiciary was the subject of longest controversy. That the tenure of the judicial office should be the will of the people, was claimed as "the people's right." The rustic legislators insisted on their right to institute the judiciary, fix the rules of court, define judicial power with precision, and by request displace judges for misbehavior. Neither would they, even in the highest courts, have English lawyers for judges. "Men skilled in the law," said they, "of good integrity, are very desirable; yet we incline to be content with the best men the colony affords." And the courts obtained no permanent organization till the accession of the house of Hanover. The civil constitution included feudalism and democracy; from this there could be no escape but through the sovereignty of the people. Twice, indeed, the province had almost become a royal one—once by act of parliament, and once by treaty. But, in England, a real regard for the sacrifices and the virtues of William Penn gained him friends among English statesmen; and the malice of the pestilent English office-seekers, of Quarry, and the men employed in enforcing the revenue laws, valuing a colony only by the harvest it offered of emoluments and jobs, and ever ready to appeal selfishly to the crown, the church, or English trade, was never able to overthrow his influence. His poverty, consequent on his disinterested labors, created a willingness to surrender his province to the crown; but he insisted on preserving the colonial liberties, and the crown hardly cared to buy a democracy. If the violent conflicts of the assembly, in their eagerness to engross all

CHAP. XIX.

1707. Minutes, ii. 324.

1706. Minutes, ii. 277

CHAP. XIX. authority, and gain control over the questions of property between the province and its proprietary, seemed sometimes to compel a surrender of his powers of government, yet the bare apprehension of such a result always brought the colonists to a gentler temper.

Thus did Penn perfect his government. An executive dependent for its support on the people; all subordinate executive officers elected by the people; the judiciary dependent for its existence on the people; all legislation originating exclusively with the people; no forts, no armed police, no militia; perfect freedom of opinion; no established church; no difference of rank; and a harbor opened for the reception of all mankind, of children of every language and every creed;—could it be that the invisible power of reason would be able to order and to restrain, to punish crime and to protect property? Would not confusion, discord, and rapid ruin successively follow such a government? Or was it a conceivable thing that, in a country without army, without militia, without forts, and with no sheriffs but those elected by the rabble, with their liberty shouts, wealth and population should increase, and the spectacle be given of the happiest and most prospered land?

In New Jersey, had the proprietary power been vested in the people, or reserved to one man, it would have survived; but it was divided among speculators in land, who, as a body, had gain, and not freedom, for their end.

Smith, 568, 211. In April, 1688, "the proprietors of East New Jersey had surrendered their pretended right of government," and the surrender had been accepted. In October of the same year, the council of the proprietaries, not of the people, of West New Jersey, voted to surrender to the secretary-general for the dominion of New England, "all records relating to government." Thus the whole province fell, with New York and New England, under the consolidated government of Andros. At the revolution, therefore, the sovereignty over New Jersey was merged in the crown; and the legal maxim, soon promulgated by the lords of trade, that the domains of the proprietaries might be bought and sold, but not their executive power, weakened their attempts at the restoration of their authority.

Will you know with how little government a community of husbandmen may be safe? For twelve years, the whole province was not in a settled condition. From June, 1689, to August, 1692, East New Jersey had no government whatever, being, in time of war, without military officers, as well as without magistrates; and afterwards commissions were issued by two sets of proprietors, of which each had its adherents· while a third party, swayed by disgust at the confusion, and also by disputes about land titles, rejected the proprietaries altogether. In the western moiety, Daniel
Coxe, as largest owner of the domain, claimed exclu- 1689.
sive proprietary powers; yet the people disallowed his claim, rejecting his deputy under the bad name of a Jacobite. In 1691, Coxe conveyed such authority as he had to the West Jersey Society; and in 1692, Andrew Hamilton was accepted in the colony as governor under their commission. Thus did West New Jersey continue, with a short interruption in 1698, till the
government was surrendered. But the law officers of 1694
the crown questioned even the temporary settlement, and the lords of trade claimed New Jersey as a royal
province, and they proposed a settlement of the ques- 1699
tion by "a trial in Westminster Hall on a feigned

CHAP. XIX. issue." The proprietaries, threatened with the ultimate interference of parliament, in respect to provinces "where," it was said, "no regular government had ever been established," resolved rather to resign their pretensions. In the first year of Queen Anne, the surrender took place before the privy council.

Journals of Commons, Feb. 5, 1701-2.

1702. April 17.

It is worthy of remark, that the domain, ceasing to be connected with proprietary powers, remained, under the rules of private right, safe to its possessors, and was never confiscated. After the revolution, even to the present time, their rights have been respected like other titles to estates. So true it is, that the separation of private property from political questions tends to its security.

The surrender of "the pretended" rights to government being completed, the two Jerseys were united in one province; and the government was conferred on Edward Hyde, Lord Cornbury, who, like Queen Anne, was the grandchild of Clarendon.

New Jersey never again obtained a charter: the royal commission and the royal instructions to Lord Cornbury constituted the form of its administration. To the governor appointed by the crown belonged the power of legislation, with consent of the royal council and the representatives of the people. A freehold, or property qualification, limited the elective franchise. The governor could convene, prorogue, or dissolve the assembly at his will, and the period of its duration depended on his pleasure. The laws were subject to an immediate veto from the governor, and a veto from the crown, to be exercised at any time. The governor, with the consent of his council, instituted courts of law, and appointed their officers. The people took no part in constituting the judiciary. Liberty of conscience was granted to all but Papists, but favor was invoked for the Church of England. At the same time, its prosperity was made impossible by investing the governor with the right of presentation to benefices. CHAP. XIX.

In suits at law, the governor and council formed a court of appeal: if the value in dispute exceeded two hundred pounds, the English privy council possessed ultimate jurisdiction. Two instructions mark, one a declining bigotry, the other an increasing interest. "Great inconvenience," says Queen Anne, "may arise by the liberty of printing in our province" of New Jersey; and therefore no printing press might be kept, "no book, pamphlet, or other matters whatsoever, be printed without a license." And, in conformity with English policy, especial countenance of the traffic "in merchantable negroes" was earnestly enjoined. Thus the courts, the press, the executive, became dependent on the crown, and the interests of free labor were sacrificed to the cupidity of the Royal African Company. 1702 April.

One method of influence remained to the people of New Jersey. The assembly must fix the amount of its grants to the governor. The queen did not venture to prescribe, or to invite parliament to prescribe, a salary,—still less, herself to concede it from colonial resources. Urgent that all appropriations should be made directly for the use of the crown, to be audited by her officers, she wished a fixed revenue to be settled; but the colonial deliberations were respected, and the wise assembly, which never established a permanent revenue, often embarrassed its votes of supplies by insisting on an auditor of its own.

The freemen of the colony were soon conscious of

CHAP. XIX. the diminution of their liberties. For absolute religious freedom, they obtained only toleration; for courts resting on enactments of their own representatives, they now had courts instituted by royal ordinances; and the sense of their loss quickened their love of freedom by an undefined sentiment of having suffered a wrong. By degrees they claimed to hold their former privileges by the nature of an inviolable compact. The surrender of their charter could change the authority of the proprietaries, but not impair their concessions of political liberties. Inured to self-reliance and self-government, no thought of independence sprung up among them; but the Quakers and Puritans of East and West New Jersey, cordially joining to vindicate their common liberties, never feared an encounter with a royal governor, and were ever alert to resist encroachments on their rights.

1702. Retaining its own legislature, New Jersey was, for a season, included in the same government with New York. The first governor of West New Jersey had been the peaceful Thomas Olive, who, as a magistrate, had quietly dispensed justice seated on a stump in his fields, and, as governor, had been content with twenty pounds a year. Did hopes dawn of a brighter day with a kinsman to the queen as governor of the united royal province? In the administration of Olive, there had been tranquillity and contentment,—the happiness of a blameless community under its own guardianship. Would more even justice be administered by one so nearly allied to the nobility and the throne of England?

In New York, the dread of Popery and despotism bewildered the hasty judgment of the less cultivated. There were differences in origin; the Dutch were not blended with the English; and if, of the latter, the stern dissenters opposed the Churchmen and those who had gathered round the royal governor, among the Dutch, also, the humbler class of people had not amalgamated with "the gentlemen of figure." From the first, feudal distinctions had existed among the emigrants from Holland. In assuming power, Leisler rested chiefly for his support upon the less educated classes of the Dutch, and English dissenters were not heartily his friends. The large Dutch landholders, many of the English merchants, the friends to the Anglican Church, the cabal that had grown up round the royal governors, were his wary and unrelenting opponents. But his greatest weakness was in himself. Too restless to obey, and too passionate to command, as a Presbyterian, Leisler was averse to the Church of England; as a man of middling fortunes, to the aristocracy; while, as a Dutchman and a Calvinist, he was an enthusiast for William of Orange. Destitute of equanimity, his failure was inevitable.

The Protestant insurgents had, immediately after the revolution in New England, taken possession of the fort in New York. A few companies of militia, from the first, sided with Leisler openly, and nearly five hundred men in arms soon joined him. Their declaration, published to the world, avows their purposes: "As soon as the bearer of orders from the June 3.
prince of Orange shall have let us see his power, then, without delay, we do intend to obey, not the orders only, but also the bearer thereof."

A committee of safety of ten assumed the task of 1689.
reorganizing the government, and Jacob Leisler re- June 8.
ceived their commission to command the fort of New York. Of this he gained possession without a struggle. An address to King William was forwarded, and a letter

CHAP. XIX. from Leisler was received by that prince, if not with favor, yet with respect, and without rebuke. Nicholson, July 25. the deputy-governor, had been heard to say, what was afterwards often repeated, that the people of New York were a conquered people, without claim to the rights of Englishmen; that the prince might lawfully govern them by his own will, and appoint what laws he pleased. The dread of this doctrine sunk deeply into the public mind, and afterwards attracted the notice of the assemblies of New York. At that period of Aug. 16. disorder, the committee of safety reassembled; and "Leisler, an insolent alien, assisted," say "the principal men" of New York, "by those who formerly were Chalmers, 610. thought unfit to be in the meanest offices," was constituted the temporary governor of the province.

The appointment was, in its form, open to censure Courtland, the mayor of the city, Bayard, and others of the council, after fruitless opposition, retired to Albany, where the magistrates, in convention, proclaimed their allegiance to William and Mary, and their resolution to disregard the authority of Leisler. When Milborne, the son-in-law of Leisler, first came to demand the fort, he was successfully resisted. In December, letters were received addressed to Nicholson, or, in his absence, to "such as, for the time being, take care for preserving the peace and administering the law" in New York. A commission to Nicholson accompanied them. The commission proved the royal favor to be with the tory party, the friends of the late government; but, as Nicholson was absent, Leisler esteemed his own authority to have received the royal sanction.

1690 Jan. 17. A warrant was soon issued for the apprehension of Bayard; and Albany, in the spring, terrified by the calamity of an Indian invasion, and troubled by the anger and the outrages of domestic factions, yielded to Milborne. CHAP XIX.

To protect the frontier, and invade and conquer Canada, was the ruling passion of the northern colonies; but the summer was lost in fruitless preparations, and closed in strife.

Meantime, a house of representatives had been convened, and, amidst distress and confusion, the govern ment constituted by the popular act.

In January of 1691, the Beaver arrived in New 1691
York harbor with Ingoldsby, who bore a commission as captain. Leisler offered him quarters in the city: "Possession of his majesty's fort is what I demand," Jan. 30
replied Ingoldsby, and issued a proclamation requiring submission. Thus the aristocratic party obtained as a leader one who held a commission from the new sovereign. Leisler, conforming to the original agreement Jan. 31
made with his fellow-insurgents, replied, that Ingoldsby had produced no order from the king, or from Sloughter, who, it was known, had received a commission as governor, and, promising him aid as a military officer, refused to surrender the fort. Feb. 1.
The troops, as they landed, were received with all courtesy and accommodation; yet passions ran high, and a shot even was fired at them. The outrage was severely reproved by Leisler, who, amidst proclamations and counter-proclamations, promised obedience to Sloughter on March 10.
his arrival.

On the evening on which the profligate, needy, and March 19.
narrow-minded adventurer, who held the royal commission, arrived in New York, Leisler sent messengers to receive his orders. The messengers were detained. Next morning, he asked, by letter, to whom he should 20.

CHAP. XIX. surrender the fort. The letter was unheeded; and Sloughter, giving no notice to Leisler, commanded Ingoldsby "to arrest Leisler, and the persons called his council."

1691. The prisoners, eight in number, were promptly arraigned before a special court constituted for the purpose by an ordinance, and having inveterate royalists as judges. Six of the inferior insurgents made their defence, were convicted of high treason, and were reprieved. Leisler and Milborne denied to the governor the power to institute a tribunal for judging his predecessor, and they appealed to the king. On their refusal to plead, they were condemned of high treason as mutes, and sentenced to death, — Joseph Dudley, of New England, now chief justice in New York, giving the opinion that Leisler had had no legal authority

May 7. whatever. "Certainly never greater villains lived," wrote Sloughter; but he "resolved to wait for the royal pleasure, if by any other means than hanging he could keep the country quiet."

Meantime the assembly, for which warrants had been

April 9. issued on the day of Leisler's arrest, came together. In its character it was thoroughly royalist, establishing a revenue, and placing it in the hands of the receiver-general, at the mercy of the governor's warrant. It passed several resolves against Leisler, especially declaring his conduct at the fort an act of rebellion; and Sloughter, in a time of excitement, assented to the

May 14. vote of the council, that Leisler and Milborne should be executed. "The house, according to their opinion

15. given, did approve of what his excellency and council had done."

Accordingly, on the next day, amidst a drenching rain, Leisler, parting from his wife Alice, and his numerous family, was, with his son-in-law, Milborne, led to the gallows. Both acknowledged the errors which they had committed "through ignorance and jealous fear, through rashness and passion, through misinformation and misconstruction;" in other respects, they asserted their innocence, which their blameless private lives confirmed. "Weep not for us, who are departing to our God,"—these were Leisler's words to his oppressed friends,—"but weep for yourselves, that remain behind in misery and vexation;" adding, as the handkerchief was bound round his face, "I hope these eyes shall see our Lord Jesus in heaven." Milborne exclaimed, "I die for the king and queen, and the Protestant religion, in which I was born and bred. Father, into thy hands I commend my spirit."

CHAP. XIX.

Saturday, May 16.

MS

The appeal to the king, which had not been permitted during their lives, was made by Leisler's son; and, though the committee of lords of trade reported that the forms of law had not been broken, the estates of "the deceased" were restored to their families. Dissatisfied with this imperfect redress, the friends of Leisler persevered till an act of parliament, strenuously but vainly opposed by Dudley, reversed the attainder.

1692. Jan. 7.

1695

Private Acts, 6 and 7 Wil. III. c. xxx. Hutchinson, ii. 84.

Thus fell Leisler and Milborne, victims to party spirit. The event struck deep into the public mind. Long afterwards, their friends, whom a royalist of that day described as "the meaner sort of the inhabitants," and who were distinguished always by their zeal for popular power, for toleration, for opposition to the doctrine of legitimacy, formed a powerful, and ultimately a successful, party. The rashness and incompetency of Leisler were forgotten in sympathy for the judicial

CHAP. XIX. murder by which he fell; and the principles which he upheld, though his opponents might rail at equality of
MS. suffrage, and demand for the man of wealth as many votes as he held estates, necessarily became the principles of the colony.

1691. There existed in the province no party which would sacrifice colonial freedom. Even the legislature, composed of the deadly enemies of Leisler, asserted the right to a representative government, and to English liberties, to be inherent in the people, and not a consequence of the royal favor. This act received the veto of King William. "No tax whatever shall be levied on his majestie's subjects in the province, or on their estates, on any pretence whatsoever, but by the act and consent of the representatives of the people in general assembly convened:"—"supreme legislative power belongs to the governor and council, and to the people by their representatives:"—such was the voice of the most royalist assembly that could ever be convened in New
1697. York. What though the enactment was annulled by the English sovereign? The spirit lived, and was openly displayed. It was soon said by a royal governor to the mixed races of legislators in the province, "There are none of you but what are big with the privileges of Englishmen and Magna Charta."

1692. In the administration of the covetous and passionate
Sept. Fletcher, a man of great mobility and feeble judgment, the people of New York were soon disciplined into more decided resistance. As to territory, the old hope of extending from Connecticut River to Delaware Bay revived; and, for the security of the central province, the command of the militia of New Jersey and Connecticut was, by a royal commission, conferred on Fletcher.

An address was also sent to the king, representing the great cost of defending the frontiers, and requesting that the neighboring colonies might be compelled to contribute to the protection of Albany. In the necessity of common defence lay the root of the parliamentary attempt at taxation; for it created the desire of a central will, and this desire looked sometimes to the English monarch as the fountain of sovereignty, sometimes to the idea of a confederacy of the colonies, and at last to the action of parliament. In this age, 1695.
it led only to instructions. All the colonies north of Carolina were directed to furnish quotas for the defence of New York or the attacks on Canada; but the instructions, though urgently renewed, were never enforced, and were by some colonies openly disregarded.

In its relations towards Canada, New York shared the strong passion for conquest which gradually extended to all the colonies. In its internal affairs, bordering on Puritan New England, it is the most northern colony that admitted by enactment the partial establishment of the Anglican Church. The time had passed when religious sects constituted the forms under which political questions were discussed. The Presbyterians had never had dominion in New York, but had originally introduced themselves under compacts with the Dutch government. The original settlers from Holland were Calvinists, yet with a church organization far less popular than the system of New England, and having many points of sympathy with the ecclesiastical polity of Episcopacy. During the ascendency of the Dutch, the established authority of their church had often been asserted in an exclusive spirit; when the colony became English, the conquest

CHAP. XIX. was made by men devoted to the English throne and the English Church, and the influence of Churchmen was at once predominant in the council. The idea of toleration was still imperfect in New Netherlands; equality among religious sects was unknown. It is not strange, therefore, that the efforts of Fletcher to privilege the English Church were partially successful. The house framed a bill, in which they established certain churches and ministers, reserving also the right of presentation to the vestry-men and church-wardens. The governor interpreted the act by limiting its meaning to the English service, and framed an amendment giving the right of presentation to the representative of the crown. The assembly asserted it for the people, rejecting the amendment. "Then I must tell you," retorted Fletcher, this "seems very unmannerly. There never was an amendment desired by the council board, but what was rejected. It is a sign of a stubborn ill temper. I have the power of collating or suspending any minister in my government by their majesties' letters patent; and, whilst I stay in this government, I will take care that neither heresy, schism, or rebellion, be preached among you, nor vice and profanity encouraged. You seem to take the whole power into your hands, and set up for every thing."

1695. April 12. The "stubborn temper" of the house was immovable; and, two years afterwards, that the act might not be construed too narrowly, it was declared that the vestry-men and church-wardens of the church established in New York might call a dissenting Protestant minister. Not a tenth part of the population of that day adhered to the Episcopal Church; the public spirit demanded toleration; and if, on the one hand, the English Church

CHAP. XIX.

succeeded in engrossing the provision made by the ministry acts, on the other, the dissenters were wakened to jealousy, lest the Episcopal party, deriving countenance from England, might nourish a lust for dominion.

The differences were tranquillized in the short administration of the kindlier earl of Bellamont, an Irish peer, with a sound heart and honorable sympathies for popular freedom. He arrived in New York after the peace of Ryswick, with a commission extending to the 1698
borders of Canada, including all the northern British April 2.
possessions, except Connecticut and Rhode Island. In New York, Lord Bellamont, who had served on the committee of parliament to inquire into the trials of Leisler and Milborne, was indifferent to the little oligarchy of the royal council, of which he reproved the vices and resisted the selfishness. The memory of the wrongs of Leisler was revived; and the assembly, by an appropriation of its own in favor of his family, confirmed the judgment of the English parliament.

The enforcement of the acts of trade, which had been violated by the connivance of men appointed to execute them; the suppression of piracy, which, as the turbulent offspring of long wars and of the false principles of the commercial systems of that age, infested every sea from America to China,—were the great purposes of Bellamont; yet for both he accomplished little. The acts of trade, despotic in their nature, contradicting the rights of humanity, were evaded every where; but in New York, a city, in part, of aliens, owing allegiance to England, without the bonds of common history, kindred, and tongue, they were disregarded without scruple. No voice of conscience declared their violation a moral offence; respect

CHAP. XIX. for them was but a calculation of chances. In the attempt to suppress piracy, the prospect of infinite booty to be recovered from pirates, or to be won from the enemies of England, had gained from the king and the admiralty a commission for William Kidd, and had deluded Bellamont into a partnership in a private expedition. Failing in his hopes of opulence, Kidd found his way as a pirate to the gallows. In the house of commons, the transaction provoked inquiry, and hardly escaped censure.

Documents in Journals of Commons, Dec. 4, 1699, and March 28, 1701.

On questions of finance, the popularity of Bellamont prevented collisions by an honest promise,—"I will pocket none of the public money myself, nor shall there be any embezzlement by others;"—and the necessity of the promise is the strongest commentary upon the character of his predecessors. The confiding house of representatives voted a revenue for six years, and placed it, as before, at the disposition of the governor. His death interrupted the short period of harmony in the colony; and, happily for New York, Lord Cornbury, his successor, had every vice of character necessary to discipline a colony into self-reliance and resistance.

Of the same family with the queen of England; brother-in-law to a king, whose service he had betrayed; the grandson of a prime minister; himself heir to an earldom,—Lord Cornbury, destitute of the virtues of the aristocracy, illustrated the worst form of its arrogance, joined to intellectual imbecility. Of the sagacity of the common mind, of its firmness, he knew nothing; of political power he had no conception, except as it emanates from the self-will of a superior; to him popular rights existed only as a condescension. Educated at Geneva, he yet loved Episcopacy, as a religion of state subordinate to executive power. And now, at about forty years of age, with self-will and the pride of rank for his counsellors, without fixed principles, without perception of political truth, he stood among the plebeians of New Jersey and the mixed people of New York as their governor.

The royalists anticipated his arrival with the incense 1702
of flattery; and the hospitality of the colony, which was not yet provoked to defiance, elected a house of assembly disposed to confide in the integrity of one who had been represented as a friend to Presbyterians. The expenses of his voyage were compensated by a grant of two thousand pounds, and an annual revenue for the public service provided for a period of seven years. In April, 1703, a further grant was made of fifteen hundred pounds to fortify the Narrows, "and for no other use whatever." But should Lord Cornbury regard the limitations of a provincial assembly? The money, by his warrant, disappeared from the treasury, while the Narrows were still defenceless; and the assembly, awakened to distrust, by addresses 1703
to the governor and the queen, solicit a treasurer of its June 19.
own appointment.

The general revenue had been fixed for a period of years; no new appropriations could be extorted; and, 1704
heedless of menaces or solicitation, the representatives of the people asserted "the rights of the house." Lord Cornbury expressed his whole character as a statesman in his answer: "I know of no right that you have as an assembly, but such as the queen is pleased to allow you."

The firmness of the assembly won its first victory; 1705
for the queen permitted specific appropriations of incidental grants of money, and the appointment by the

CHAP. XIX. general assembly of its own treasurer to take charge of extraordinary supplies.

In affairs relating to religion, Lord Cornbury was equally imperious, disputing generally the right of either minister or schoolmaster to exercise his vocation without his license. The question of the freedom of the pulpit no longer included the whole question of intellectual freedom; the victory for toleration had been won; and the spirit of political freedom found its organ in the provincial legislature. The captious reference to the standing instructions in favor of the English Church, sometimes encouraging arbitrary acts of power in its behalf, and always tending to bias every question in its favor, led only to acts of petty tyranny, useless to English interests, and benefiting the people by compelling their active vigilance. The power of the people redressed the griefs. If Francis Makemie, a Presbyterian, was indicted for preaching without a license from the governor; if the chief justice advised a special verdict,—the jury, composed, it is said, of Episcopalians, constituted themselves the judges of the law, and readily agreed on an acquittal. In like manner, at Jamaica, the church which the whole town had erected, was, by the connivance of Lord Cornbury, reserved exclusively for the Episcopalians—an injustice which was afterwards reversed in the colonial courts.

1708. Aug. 19. Twice had Lord Cornbury dissolved the assembly. The third which he convened proved how rapidly the political education of the people had advanced. Dutch, English, and New England men, were all of one spirit. The rights of the people, with regard to taxation, to courts of law, to officers of the crown, were asserted with an energy to which the governor could offer no resistance. Without presence of mind, subdued by the colonial legislature, and now appearing dispirited as he was indigent, he submitted to the ignominy of reproof, and thanked the assembly for the simplest act of justice. CHAP. XIX.

Shall we glance at his career in New Jersey? There are the same demands for money, and a still more wary refusal; representatives, elected by a majority of votes, 1704 excluded by the governor; assemblies convened, and angrily dissolved. At last, necessity compels a third assembly, and among its members are Samuel Jennings and Lewis Morris. The latter was of a liberal mind, yet having no fixed system; intrepid, but not exclusive. The former, elected speaker of the assembly, was a true Quaker, of a hasty yet benevolent temper, faithful in his affections, "stiff and impracticable in politics." These are they whom Lord Cornbury describes "as capable of any thing but good;" whom Quarry and other subservient counsellors accuse as "turbulent and disloyal," "encouraging the governments in America to throw off the royal prerogative, declaring openly that the royal instructions bind no further than they are warranted by law." The assembly, according to the usage of that day, wait on 1707 the governor with their remonstrance. The Quaker April 7. speaker reads it for them most audibly. It charges Lord Cornbury with accepting bribes; it deals sharply with "his new methods of government," his "encroachment" on the popular liberties by "assuming a negative voice to the freeholders' election of their representatives;" "they have neither heads, hearts, nor souls, that are not forward with their utmost power lawfully to redress the miseries of their country."—"Stop!" exclaimed Lord Cornbury, as the undaunted Quaker delivered the remonstrance; and Jennings meekly and

CHAP. XIX. distinctly repeated the charges, with greater emphasis than before. What could Lord Cornbury do? He attempted to retort, charging the Quakers with disloyalty and faction; and they answered, in the words of Nehemiah to Sanballat, "There is no such thing done as thou sayest, but thou feignest them out of thine own heart." And they left, for the instruction of future governors, this weighty truth:—"To engage the affections of the people, no artifice is needful, but to let them be unmolested in the enjoyment of what belongs to them of right."

Lord Cornbury had fulfilled his mission; more successful than any patriot, he had taught New York the necessity and the methods of incipient resistance.
1709. April. The assembly which met Lord Lovelace, his shortlived successor, began the contest that was never to cease but with independence. The crown demanded a permanent revenue, without appropriation; New York henceforward would raise only an annual revenue, and appropriate it specifically.

Such was the inheritance of controversies provided for Robert Hunter, the friend of Swift, an adventurer, who came to his government in quest of good cheer. "Here," he writes, "is the finest air to live upon in the universe: the soil bears all things, but not for me; for, according to the custom of the country, the sachems are the poorest of the people." "Sancho Panza," he avers, "was indeed but a type of me."

1710. Sept. 1. In less than five months after his arrival, he was disputing with an assembly. The house, to prevent misapplications of the public revenue, secured to their own treasurer a check on payments; the council negatived the restraint on the governor's prerogative; no compromise could be made, and a prorogation followed.

In the following spring, Hunter bade the assembly beware, "lest some insinuations, much repeated of late years, should gain credit at last, that, however their resentment has fallen upon the governor, it is the government they dislike;" and the house, remaining inflexible, was dissolved. CHAP. XIX. 1711.

The desire to conquer Canada prevailed, in the summer of 1711, to obtain a specific grant of bills of credit for £10,000; but no concession was made in regard to the ordinary expenses of the government.

The contest was again renewed. The council, claiming the right to make amendments to the money bills, asserted that the house, like itself, existed only "by the mere grace of the crown." The assembly, defying the opinion of the lords of trade, as concluding nothing, rose to the doctrine required by the emergency. The share of the council in legislation, they agree, comes "from the mere pleasure of the prince;" but for themselves they claim an "inherent right" to legislation, spinging "not from any commission or grant from the crown, but from the free choice and election of the people, who ought not, nor justly can, be divested of their property without their consent."

In 1712, the same spirit was manifested. Hunter 1712
cannot effectually obey the lords of trade. They instruct him as to what the legislature shall do, and the legislature is inflexible. "I am used like a dog," wrote the really well-disposed man; and, again, "I have spent three years in such torment and vexation, that nothing in life can ever make amends for it." Concession and philosophical indifference afterwards gave him calm; but the spirit roused in New York was never lulled.

New York would willingly, after the revolution, have

CHAP. XIX. extended her boundary over a part of Connecticut; but the people of the colony themselves vindicated its liberties and the integrity of its territory.

1689. May 9. Governor Treat having resumed his office, the assembly, which soon convened, obeying the declared opinion of the freemen, organized the government according to their charter.

May 26. On the joyful news of the accession of William and Mary, every fear vanished, every countenance brightened with joy. "Great was that day," said the loyal June 13. address of Connecticut to King William, "when the Lord, who sitteth upon the floods, did divide his and your adversaries like the waters of Jordan, and did begin to magnify you like Joshua, by the deliverance of the English dominions from Popery and slavery. Because the Lord loved Israel forever, therefore hath he made you king, to do justice and judgment." And, describing their acquiescence in the rule of Andros as "an involuntary submission to an arbitrary power," they announce that, by the consent of the major part Trumbull, i. 539. of the freemen, they have themselves resumed the government.

1690. In prosecuting its claim in London, Whiting, the agent of Connecticut, was aided by all the influence which the religious sympathy of the Presbyterians could enlist for New England. The English corporations had been restored; and Edward Ward gave his opinion, that a surrender, of which no legal record existed, did not invalidate a patent. Somers assented. "There is no ground of doubt," reiterated George Treby. And the sanctity attached to the democratic charter and government of Connecticut, is the most honorable proof of the respect which was cherished by the revolution of 1688 for every existing franchise.

CHAP. XIX.

Thus was the rule of the people restored. They elected their own governor, council, and assembly-men, all their magistrates, and all annually. Connecticut was the most perfect democracy which had ever been organized. It rested on free labor, and upheld equality: the people were the sources of all power.

The English crown would willingly have resumed, at least, the command of the militia, which, after having been, at one time, assigned to the governor of Massachusetts, by whom it was never challenged, was claimed as a part of the royal prerogative, and conferred 1692
on the governor of New York. The legislature resisted, and referred the question to the people, who resolved on a petition to the king, by the hands of Fitz John 1693 Sept.
Winthrop. To give the command of the militia, it was said, to the governor of another colony, is, in effect, to put our persons, interests, and liberties entirely into his power: by our charter, the governor and company themselves have a commission of command.

Meantime, Fletcher, refusing to await the decision 1693
in England, appeared in Hartford, and, after fruitless Oct. 26.
negotiation, ordered its militia under arms, that he might beat up for volunteers for the war.

Hartford was then a small, but delightful township, with its meeting-house and cluster of dwellings, built on land just above the rich meadows, which the lovely Connecticut annually overflows—a community of farmers, the unmixed progeny of Puritans. William Wadsworth, the senior captain of the town, walked in front of the assembled train-bands, "busy in exercising them." Fletcher advances, to assume command, ordering Bayard, of New York, to read his commission and the royal instructions.

It is the fortune of our America, that if, at any mo-

CHAP. XIX. ment, the happiness of a state depended on the will of one man, that man was true to his duty. At the order of Captain Wadsworth, the drums began to roll, beating some of the old marches that may have been handed down from the veterans of Gustavus or the volunteers of Naseby. The petulant Fletcher commanded silence. "I will not"—such had been his words to the governor of Connecticut—"I will not set my foot out of this colony, till I have seen his majesty's commission obeyed;" and Bayard, of New York, once more began to read. Once more the drums beat. "Silence!' exclaimed Fletcher. "Drum, drum, I say!" shouted Wadsworth, adding, as he turned to the governor of New York, "If I am interrupted again, I will make the sun shine through you in a moment." Fletcher was daunted; and, as the excited people came swarming into Hartford, in spite of his expressed determination, he fled from the scene to his government in New York.

1694. April 19. In England, the king, in council, decided, on the advice of Ward and Treves, that the ordinary power of the militia in Connecticut, and in Rhode Island, belonged to their respective governments; and Winthrop, returning from his agency to a joyful welcome, was soon elected governor of a colony of which he had asserted the freedom.

The decisions which established the rights of Connecticut included those of Rhode Island. The assaults of the royalists were always made upon the more powerful colony, in the assurance that the fate of both would be included in its overthrow. These two commonwealths were the portion of the British empire distinguished above all others by the largest liberty. Each presented the anomaly of a nearly absolute democracy under the shelter of a monarchy. But the results in the two were not strictly parallel. CHAP XIX.

Rhode Island had asserted entire freedom of mind; it had, therefore, apparently, less unity in its population, and less cohesion. In consequence, it was inferior in all that required joint action, but had, perhaps, a greater regard for personal liberty and independence. No bitter conflict with the crown had excited any deep hostilities; and the colony yielded, for a season, to quiet influence, what it might have refused to force or entreaty. It interpolated into the statute-book the exclusion of Papists from the established equality. Less liberal than Connecticut, it attached the franchise, not "to the inhabitant," but to the soil; and, as a wrong principle always leads to practical error, it fostered family pride, by a distant imitation of the English law of primogeniture.

In Connecticut, no other influence gave a bias, except that of the Puritan clergy, who were there, and there only, consociated by the legislature. And it was first the custom, and afterwards the order, that "the 1708
ministers of the gospel should preach a sermon on the day appointed by law for the choice of civil rulers, proper for the direction of the towns in the work before them." Trum bull i. 43?

But danger was not passed. The crown, reserving to itself the right of appeal, had still a method of interfering in the internal concerns of the little republics. Besides, their charters were never safe; absolute sovereignty being claimed in England, their freedom rested on forbearance. Both were included among the colonies in which the lords of trade advised a complete restoration of the prerogatives of the crown. Both 1701
were named in the bill which was introduced into par- April 21.

CHAP. XIX. liament for the abrogation of all American charters. The journals of the house of lords relate that Con-
1701. May 8. necticut was publicly heard against the bill, contending that its liberties were held by contract, in return for services that had been performed; that the taking away of so many charters would destroy all confidence in royal promises, and would afford a precedent dangerous to all the chartered corporations of England. Yet the bill was read a second time, and its principle, as applied to colonies, was advocated by the mercantile interest and by "great men" in England. The impending war with the French postponed the purpose till the accession of the house of Hanover.

But the object was not left out of mind. Lord Cornbury, who had in vain solicited money of Con-
1703. June. necticut, wrote home, that "this vast continent would never be useful to England, till all the proprietary and
Trumbull, i. 417. charter governments were brought under the crown." Quarry, also, reported to the lords of trade, that "the roguery and villany of Connecticut were enough to fill a volume;" and, appealing to the powerful sympathy in the English policy of that age, declared that, "if the government be continued longer in these men's hands, the honest trade of these parts will be ruined." And Dudley, a native New England man, now governor of Massachusetts, took the lead in the conspiracy against the liberties of New England, preparing a volume of complaints, and urging the appointment of a governor
1705. over Connecticut by the royal prerogative. These, and their associates, are the men who first filled the world with calumnies against that commonwealth. The lords of trade were too just to condemn the colony unheard, and it succeeded in its vindication; only an obsolete law against Quakers, which had never been

enforced, after furnishing an excuse for outcries against Puritan intolerance, was declared null and void by the queen in council. CHAP. XIX.

The insurrection in Boston, which had overthrown the dominion of Andros, had sprung spontaneously from the people. Among the magistrates, and especially among the ministers, some distrusted every popular movement, and sought to control a revolution, of which they feared the tendency. The insurgent people insisted on the restoration of the colonial charter; but Cotton Mather, claiming only English liberties, and not charter liberties, and selfishly jealous of popular power, was eager to thwart the design; and, against the opinion of the venerable Bradstreet, the charter magistrates, joining to themselves "the principal inhabitants" of Boston, became a self-constituted "council for the safety of the people." Thus was the popular will defeated. It had demanded its ancient liberties; and the men on whom it was compelled to rely, constituting themselves its guardians, "humbly" waited "for direction of the crown of England." Thus was lost the only opportunity for Massachusetts to vindicate its sequestered freedom. "Had they, at that time,"—it is the confession of Increase Mather,—"entered upon the full exercise of their charter government, as their undoubted right, wise men in England were of opinion they might have gone on without disturbance."

Calef's Post-script, ed. 1828 p. 310, and 205 Danforth to Increase Mather; Hutch. Hist. i. 339. Some Few Remarks, 1702, p. 45, 46. Cotton Mather's own words, p. 45, 46. 1689 April 20. Calef. Records, Hutch i. 340. Increase Mather's Account, p. 18.

When the convention of the people assembled, they, too, were jealous of their ancient privileges. Instead of recognizing the self-constituted council, they excluded the new associates, and declared the governor, deputy-governor, and assistants, chosen and sworn in 1686, according to charter rights, and the deputies sent by the freemen of the towns, to be the government

1689. May 9. Increase Mather's Account p. 18.

CHAP. XIX. now settled in the colony. The council resisted; and the question was referred to the people. Nearly four 1689. May 22. fifths of the towns instructed their representatives to reassume; but the pertinacity of a majority of the June 5. council permitted only a compromise. In June, the representatives, upon a new choice, assembled in Boston. Again they refuse to act, till the old charter officers shall assume their power as of right. The council accepted the condition, but still as subject to directions from England. Indeed, the time had gone by. Already an address to King William had contained the assurance that "they had not entered upon the full exercise of the charter government," and was soon Hutch. i. 347, 348. answered by the royal assent to the temporary organization which the council had adopted. But the popular party, jealous of the dispositions of Increase Mather, joined with him, in the agency for New England, Sir Henry Ashurst and two of their own adherents, the patriot Elisha Cook, and the honest but less able Thomas Oakes.

A revolution in opinion was impending. The reformation had rested truth on the Bible, as the Catholic church had rested it on tradition; and a slavish interpretation of the Bible had led to a blind idolatry of the book. But true religion has no alliance with bondage; and, as the spirit of the reformation, which was but a less perfect form of freedom of mind, was advancing, reason was summoned to interpret the records of the past, and to separate time-hallowed errors from truths of the deepest moment. The statute-book, in obedience to this adoration of the letter, had asserted the existence of witchcraft by establishing death as its penalty; sustaining both the superstition and its punishment by reference to the Jewish records.

CHAP. XIX. 1688.

New England, like Canaan, had been settled by fugitives. Like the Jews, they had fled to a wilderness; like the Jews, they looked to heaven for a light to lead them on; like the Jews, they had no supreme ruler but God; like the Jews, they had heathen for their foes; and they derived their legislation from the Jewish code. But, for the people of New England, the days of Moses and of Joshua were past; for them there was no longer a promised land—they were in possession. Reason now insisted on bringing the adopted laws to the proof, that it might hold fast only the good. Skepticism began to appear; not the giant skepticism which, in Europe, was beginning to overthrow the accumulated abuses of centuries, but a cautious doubt, which should eliminate the errors adhering to the glorious faith by which New England had been created. Belief in witchcraft had sprung alike from the letter of the Mosaic law and from the natural wonder excited by the mysteries of nature. Man feels that he is a dependent being. The reverence for universal laws is implanted in his nature too deeply to be removed. The infinite is every where; and every where man has acknowledged it, beholding in every power the result of an infinite attribute. The same truth superstition admits, yet disguises, when it fills the air with spectres, or startles ghosts among the tombs; or studies the stars to cast a horoscope; or gazes on the new moon with confiding credulity; or, yielding blindly to fear, beholds in the evil that is in the world, the present malignity of Satan. The belief in witchcraft had fastened itself on the elements of religious faith, and become deeply branded into the common mind. Do not despise the credulity. The people did not rally to the error; they accepted the superstition

CHAP. XIX. only because it had not yet been disengaged from religion.

1688. The same causes which had given energy to the religious principle had given weight to the ministers. In the settlement of New England, the temple, or, as it was called, the meeting-house, was the centre round which the people gathered. As the church had successfully assumed the exclusive possession of civil franchises, the ambition of the ministers had been both excited and gratified. They were not only the counsellors by an unwritten law; they also were the authors of state papers, often employed on embassies, and, at home, speakers at elections and in town-meetings. "New England," says Cotton Mather, "being a country whose interests are remarkably inwrapped in ecclesiastical circumstances, ministers ought to concern themselves in politics." But their political mission was accomplished. Under their guidance, God's people had entered into possession of the promised land, and had planted commonwealths free from the presence of royalty, of feudalism, and of prelacy. The power of the ministers over the magistrates, having now no effect but to narrow and restrain, reposed no longer on the energy of religion, but on a superstitious veneration. It is the beauty of truth that nothing can rest upon it but justice. The ministers, desirous of unjust influence, could build their hope of it only on error; and the struggle for greater freedom of mind—the struggle against superstition, and against the slavish interpretation of the Bible—was one with the struggle against their dominion in the state.

In the last year of the administration of Andros, who, as the servant of arbitrary power, had no motive to dispel superstition, the daughter of John Goodwin,

CHAP. XIX.

1688.

Cotton Mather passim.

a child of thirteen years, charged a laundress with having stolen linen from the family; Glover, the mother of the laundress, a friendless emigrant, almost ignorant of English, like a true woman, with a mother's heart, rebuked the false accusation. Immediately the girl, to secure revenge, became bewitched. The infection spread. Three others of the family, the youngest a boy of less than five years old, soon succeeded in equally arresting public attention. They would affect to be deaf, then dumb, then blind, or all three at once; they would bark like dogs, or purr like so many cats; but they ate well, and slept well. Cotton Mather went to prayer by the side of one of them, and, lo! the child lost her hearing till prayer was over. What was to be done? The four ministers of Boston, and the one of Charlestown, assembled in Goodwin's house, and spent a whole day of fasting in prayer. In consequence, the youngest child, the little one of four years old, was "delivered." But if the ministers could thus by prayer deliver a possessed child, then there must have been a witch; the honor of the ministers required a prosecution of the affair; and the magistrates, William Stoughton being one of the judges, and all holding commissions exclusively from the English king, and being irresponsible to the people of Massachusetts, with a "vigor" which the united ministers commended as "just," made "a discovery of the wicked instrument of the devil." The culprit was evidently a wild Irish woman, of a strange tongue. Goodwin, who made the complaint, "had no proof that could have done her any hurt;" but "the scandalous old hag," whom some thought "crazed in her intellectuals," was bewildered, and made strange answers, which were taken as confessions; sometimes, in excite

Cotton Mather's Mem. Prov.

John Goodwin's Account.

Cotton Mather

CHAP. XIX. ment, using her native dialect. One Hughes testified that, six years before, she had heard one Howen say she had seen Glover come down her chimney. It was plain the prisoner was a Roman Catholic, she had never learned the Lord's prayer in English; she could repeat the paternoster fluently enough, but not quite correctly: so the ministers and Goodwin's family had the satisfaction of getting her condemned as a witch, and executed. "Here," it was proclaimed, "was food for faith." So desperately wicked is the heart of man: the girl, who knew herself to be a deceiver, had no remorse; and to the ministers, in their self-righteousness, it never occurred that vanity and love of power had blinded their judgment.

Goodwin, 48, 49.

There were skeptics in Boston. The age, thought the ministers, "was a debauched one," given up "to Sadducism;" and, as the possessed damsel obtained no relief, Cotton Mather, eager to learn the marvels of the world of spirits, and "wishing to confute the Sadducism" of his times, invited her to his house; and the artful girl easily imposed upon his credulity. The devil would permit her to read in Quaker books, or the Common Prayer, or Popish books; but a prayer from Cotton Mather, or a chapter from the Bible, would throw her into convulsions. By a series of experiments, in reading aloud passages from the Bible in various languages, the minister satisfied himself, "by trials of their capacity," that devils are well skilled in languages, and understand Latin, and Greek, and even Hebrew; though he fell "upon one inferior Indian language which the dæmons did not seem so well to understand." Experiments were made, with unequal success, to see if devils can know the thoughts of others;

C. Mather's Memorable Providences, p. 34, ed. 1689

and the inference was that "all devils are not alike sagacious." The vanity of Cotton Mather was further gratified; for the bewitched girl would say that the demons could not enter his study, and that his own person was shielded by God against blows from the evil spirits. CHAP XIX. C. Mather, Mem Prov. p. 39. p. 27.

The revolution in New England seemed to open, once more, a career to the ambition of ministers. Yet great obstacles existed. The rapid progress of free inquiry was alarming. "There are multitudes of Sadducees in our day," sighed Cotton Mather. "A devil, in the apprehension of these mighty acute philosophers, is no more than a quality or a distemper."—"We shall come," he adds, "to have no Christ but a light within, and no heaven but a frame of mind."—"Men counted it wisdom to credit nothing but what they see and feel. They never saw any witches; therefore, there are none."—"How much," add the ministers of Boston and Charlestown, "how much this fond opinion has gotten ground, is awfully observable."—"Witchcraft," shouted Cotton Mather from the pulpit, "is the most nefandous high treason against the Majesty on high;" "a capital crime." "A witch is not to be endured in heaven or on earth." And, because men were skeptical on the subject, "God is pleased," said the ministers, "to suffer devils to do such things in the world, as shall stop the mouths of gainsayers, and extort a confession."* The Discourse of Cotton Mather was therefore printed, with a copious narrative of the recent case of witchcraft. The story was confirmed by Goodwin, and recommended by all the ministers of Boston and Charlestown as an answer to atheism, proving clearly that "there is both a God and a devil, and witchcraft;" and Cotton Mather, an- 1689 C. M.'s Discourse, p. 14. C. M.'s Discourse, p. 10.

CHAP. XIX. nouncing himself as an eye-witness, resolved hencefor-ward to regard "the denial of devils, or of witches," as a personal affront, the evidence "of ignorance, incivility, and dishonest impudence."

"I was myself an eye-witness," p. 40.

This book, thus prepared and recommended, and destined to have a wide circulation, was printed in 1689, and distributed through New England. Unhappily, it gained fresh power from England, where it was "published by Richard Baxter," who declared the evidence strong enough to convince all but "a very obdurate Sadducee."

This tale went abroad at a moment when the enthusiasm of the country was engrossed by the hopes that sprung from the accession of King William. The conquest of New France was the burning passion of New England, in harmony with its hatred of legitimacy and the old forms of Christianity. To subdue the French dominions—this was the joint object which was to foster a common feeling between England and the American colonies. This passion advanced even to action, but, at that time, was only fruitful of disasters.

Meantime, the agents of Massachusetts, appealing to the common enmity towards France, solicited a restoration of its charter. King William was a friend to

1689. March 14.

Calvinists, and, on the first interview with Increase Mather, conceded the recall of Sir Edmund Andros. The convention parliament voted that the taking away of the New England charters was a grievance; and the English Presbyterians, with singular affection, declared that "the king could not possibly do any thing more grateful to his dissenting subjects in England, than by restoring to New England its former privileges." The dissolution of the convention parliament, followed by one in which an influence friendly to the tories was perceptible, destroyed the hope of relief from the English legislature: to attempt a reversal of the judgment by a writ of error was hopeless. There was no avenue to success but through the favor of a monarch who loved authority. The people of New England "are like the Jews under Cyrus," said Wiswall, the agent for Plymouth colony: with a new monarch "on the throne of their oppressors, they hope in vain to rebuild their city and their sanctuary." CHAP XIX.

Yet William III. professed friendship for Massachusetts. The hope of colonial conquests over the French was excited; his subjects in New England, said Increase Mather, if they could but enjoy "their ancient rights and privileges," would make him "the emperor of America." In the family of Hampden, Massachusetts inherited a powerful intercessor. The countess of Sunderland, whom the Princess, afterwards Queen, Anne describes as "a hypocrite," "running from church to church after the famousest preachers, and keeping a clatter with her devotions," is remembered in America as a benefactress. The aged Lord Wharton, last surviving member of the Westminster assembly of divines, "a constant and cordial lover of all good men," never grew weary in his zeal. I take pleasure in recording that the tolerant archbishop of Canterbury, the rational Tillotson, charged the king "not to take away from the people of New England any of the privileges which Charles I. had granted them."—"The charter of New England," said the feebler Burnet, "was not an act of grace, but a contract between the king and the first patentees, who promised to enlarge the king's dominion at their own charges, provided they and their posterity might enjoy certain privileges." Yet Somers resisted the restoration of the charter of Massachusetts, 1689. July 4.

CHAP. XIX. pleading its imperfections. The charter sketched by Sir George Treby was rejected by the privy council for its liberality; and that which was finally conceded reserved such powers to the crown, that Cooke, the popular envoy, declined to accept it. Somers and King William were less liberal to Massachusetts than Clarendon and Charles II.

Correct Ebeling, i. 1015, by I. Mather's Account p. 9.

1691. Oct. 7.

The freemen of Massachusetts, under the old charter, had elected their governor annually; he was henceforward appointed by the king during the royal pleasure. The governor had been but first among the magistrates; he was now the representative of English royalty, and could convene, adjourn, or dissolve the general court. The freemen had, by popular vote, annually elected their magistrates, or judicial officers; the judges were now appointed, with consent of council, by the royal governor. The decisions in the courts of New England had been final; appeals to the privy council were now admitted. The freemen had exercised the full power of legislation within themselves by their deputies; the warrior king reserved a double veto —an immediate negative to the governor of the colony, while, at any time within three years, the king might cancel any act of colonial legislation. In one respect, the new charter was an advancement. Every form of Christianity, except, unhappily, the Roman Catholic, was enfranchised; and, in civil affairs, the freedom of the colony, no longer restricted to the members of the church, was extended so widely as to be, in a practical sense, nearly universal. The legislature continued to encourage by law the religion professed by the majority of the inhabitants, but it no longer decided controversies on opinions; and no synod was ever again convened. The charter government of Massachusetts, as established by the revolutionary monarch of England, differed from that of the royal provinces in nothing but the council. In the royal colonies, that body was appointed by the king; in Massachusetts, it was, in the first instance, appointed by the king, and, subject to a negative from the governor, was ever after elected, in joint ballot, by the members of the council and the representatives of the people. As the councillors were twenty-eight in number, they generally, by their own vote, succeeded in effecting their own reëlection; and, instead of being, as elsewhere, a greedy oligarchy, were famed for their unoffending respectability. For long years, they ventured on nothing that could displease royalty or the people. CHAP. XIX.

The territory of Massachusetts was by the charter vastly enlarged. On the south, it embraced Plymouth colony and the Elizabeth Islands; on the east, it included Maine and all beyond it to the Atlantic; on the north, it was described as swept by the St. Lawrence —the fatal gift of a wilderness, for the conquest and defence of which Massachusetts expended more treasure, and lost more of her sons, than all the English continental colonies beside.

From the Elizabeth Islands to the St. Lawrence, and eastward to the Atlantic, Massachusetts now included the whole vast region, except New Hampshire. That colony became henceforward a royal province. Its inhabitants had assembled in convention to institute gov- 1689.
ernment for themselves; at their second session, they 1690.
resolved to unite, and did actually unite, with Massachusetts; and both colonies desired that the union might be permanent. But England, if it annexed to Massachusetts the burden of the unconquered desert east and north of the Piscataqua, held itself bound by

CHAP. XIX. no previous compact to concede to New Hampshire any charter whatever. The right to the soil, which Samuel Allen, of London, had purchased of Mason, was recognized as valid; and Allen himself received the royal commission to govern a people whose territory, including the farms they had redeemed from the wilderness, he claimed as his own. His son-in-law Usher, of Boston, formerly an adherent of Andros, and a great speculator in lands, was appointed, under him, lieutenant-governor. Such was the English revolution of 1688. It valued the uncertain claims of an English merchant more than the liberties of a province. Indeed, that revolution loved, not liberty, but privilege, and respected popular liberty only where it had the sanction of a vested right.

1692. Aug. 13. In 1692, the new government for New Hampshire was organized by Usher. The civil history of that colony, for a quarter of a century, is a series of lawsuits about land. Complaints against Usher were met by counter complaints, till New Hampshire was placed, with Massachusetts, under the government of Bella-
1699. mont, and a judiciary, composed of men attached to the colony, was instituted. Then, and for years afterwards, followed scenes of confusion;—trials in the colonial courts, resulting always in verdicts against the pretended proprietary; appeals to the English monarch in council; papers withheld; records of the court under Cranfield destroyed; orders from the lords of trade and the crown disregarded by a succession of inflexible juries; a compromise proposed, and rendered of no avail by the death of one of the parties; an Indian deed manufactured to protect the cultivators of the soil; till, at last, the heirs of the proprietary abandoned
1715. their claim in despair. The yeomanry of New Hamp-

shire gained quiet possession of the land which their labor had redeemed and rendered valuable. The waste domain reverted to the crown. A proprietary, sustained by the crown, claimed the people of New Hampshire as his tenants; and they made themselves freeholders. CHAP. XIX.

For Massachusetts, the nomination of its first officers under the charter was committed to Increase Mather. As governor he proposed Sir William Phipps, a native of New England, who honestly loved his country,—of a dull intellect, headstrong, and with a reason so feeble that, in politics, he knew nothing of general principles, in religion, was the victim to superstition. Accustomed, from boyhood, to the axe and the oar, he had gained distinction only by his wealth, the fruits of his enterprise with the diving-bell in raising treasures from a Spanish wreck. His partners in this enterprise gained him the honor of knighthood; his present favor was due to the honest bigotry and ignorance which left him open to the influence of the ministers. Intercession had been made by Cotton Mather for the advancement of William Stoughton, a man of cold affections, proud, self-willed, and covetous of distinction. He had acted under James II. as deputy-president—a fit tool for such a king, joining in all "the miscarriages of the late government." The people had rejected him, in their election of judges, giving him not a vote. Yielding to the request of his son, Increase Mather assigned to Stoughton the office of deputy-governor. "The twenty-eight assistants, who are the governor's council, every man of them," wrote the agent, "is a friend to the interests of the churches."—"The time for favor is come," exulted Cotton Mather; "yea, the set time is come. Instead of my being made a sacrifice to 1691

Increase Mather's Account, p. 20

CHAP. XIX. wicked rulers, my father-in-law, with several related to me, and several brethren of my own church, are among the council. The governor of the province is not my enemy, but one whom I baptized, and one of my own flock, and one of my dearest friends." And, uttering a midnight cry, he wrestled with God to awaken the churches to some remarkable thing. A religious excitement was resolved on. "I obtained of the Lord that he would use me," says the infatuated man, "to be a herald of his kingdom now approaching;" and, in the gloom of winter, among a people desponding at the loss of their old liberties, and their ill success against Quebec, the wildest imaginations might prevail.

C. Mather's Diary.

Midnight Cry. 1692.

It must be remarked that, in modern times, the cry of witchcraft had been raised by the priesthood rarely, I think never, except when free inquiry was advancing. Many a commission was empowered to punish alike heresy and witchcraft. The bold inquirer was sometimes burned as a wizard, and sometimes as an insurgent against the established faith. In France, where there were most heretics, there were most condemnations for witchcraft. Rebellion, it was said, is as the sin of witchcraft; and Cotton Mather, in his Discourse, did but repeat the old tale: "Rebellion is the Achan, the trouble of us all."

C. M.'s Discourse, p. 13.

In Salem village, now Danvers, there had been, between Samuel Parris, the minister, and a part of his people, a strife so bitter, that it had even attracted the attention of the general court. The delusion of witchcraft would give opportunities of terrible vengeance. In the family of Samuel Parris, his daughter, a child of nine years, and his niece, a girl of less than twelve, began to have strange caprices. "He that will read

1692. Feb.

Cotton Mather's Book of Memorable Providences, may read part of what these children suffered:" and Tituba, an Indian female servant, who had practised some wild incantations, being betrayed by her husband, was scourged by Parris, her master, into confessing herself a witch. The ministers of the neighborhood held, at the afflicted house, a day of fasting and prayer; and the little children became the most conspicuous personages in Salem. Of a sudden, the opportunity of fame, of which the love is not the exclusive infirmity of noble minds, was placed within the reach of persons of the coarsest mould; and the ambition of notoriety recruited the little company of the possessed. There existed no motive to hang Tituba: she was saved as a living witness to the reality of witchcraft; and Sarah Good, a poor woman, of a melancholic temperament, was the first person selected for accusation. Cotton Mather, who had placed witches "among the poor, and vile, and ragged beggars upon earth," and had staked his own reputation for veracity on the reality of witchcraft, prayed "for a good issue." As the affair proceeded, and the accounts of the witnesses appeared as if taken from his own writings, his boundless vanity gloried in "the assault of the evil angels upon the country, as a particular defiance unto himself." Yet the delusion, but for Parris, would have languished. Of his own niece, the girl of eleven years of age, he demanded the names of the devil's instruments who bewitched the band of "the afflicted;" and then became at once informer and witness. In those days, there was no prosecuting officer, and Parris was at hand to question his Indian servants and others, himself prompting their answers, and acting as recorder to the magistrates. The recollection of the old contro-

CHAP. XIX.

Hale, 24.

1692.

March 11.

C. M.'s Discourse, p. 31, 32.

CHAP. XIX. versy in the parish could not be forgotten ; and Parris, moved by personal malice, as well as by blind zeal,
1692. "stifled the accusations of some,"—such is the testimony of the people of his own village,—and, at the same time "vigilantly promoting the accusation of others," was "the beginner and procurer of the sore afflic-
March 21. tions to Salem village and the country." Martha Cory, who, on her examination in the meeting-house before a throng, with a firm spirit, alone, against them all, denied the presence of witchcraft, was committed to
March 24. prison. Rebecca Nurse, likewise, a woman of purest life, an object of the special hatred of Parris, resisted the company of accusers, and was committed. And Parris, filling his prayers with the theme, made the
April 3. pulpit ring with it. "Have not I chosen you twelve," —such was his text,—"and one of you is a devil?" At this, Sarah Cloyce, sister to Rebecca Nurse, rose up and left the meeting-house; and she, too, was cried out upon, and sent to prison.

The subject grew interesting; and, to examine Sarah Cloyce and Elizabeth Procter, the deputy-governor,
April 11 and five other magistrates, went to Salem. It was a great day; several ministers were present. Parris officiated; and, by his own record, it is plain that he himself elicited every accusation. His first witness, John, the Indian servant, husband to Tituba, was rebuked by Sarah Cloyce, as a grievous liar. Abigail Williams, the niece to Parris, was also at hand with her tales: the prisoner had been at the witches' sacrament. Struck with horror, Sarah Cloyce asked for water, and sank down "in a dying fainting fit."—"Her spirit," shouted the band of the afflicted, "is gone to prison to her sister Nurse." Against Elizabeth Procter, the niece of Parris told stories yet more foolish than false. the

prisoner had invited her to sign the devil's book. CHAP. XIX.
"Dear child," exclaimed the accused in her agony, "it
is not so. There is another judgment, dear child;" 1692.
and her accusers, turning towards her husband, declared that he, too, was a wizard. All three were
committed. Examinations and commitments multi- April 18.
plied. Giles Cory, a stubborn old man of more than four- April 14.
score years, could not escape the malice of his minister
and his angry neighbors, with whom he had quarrelled.
Edward Bishop, a farmer, cured the Indian servant of
a fit by flogging him; he declared, moreover, his belief
that he could, in like manner, cure the whole company
of the afflicted; and, for his skepticism, found himself April 22.
and his wife in prison. Mary Easty, of Topsfield, another sister to Rebecca Nurse,—a woman of singular
gentleness and force of character, deeply religious, yet
uninfected by superstition,—was torn from her children, and sent to jail. Parris had had a rival in George April 22.
Burroughs, who, having formerly preached in Salem
village, had had friends there desirous of his settlement. He, too, a skeptic in witchcraft, was accused May 8.
and committed. Thus far, there had been no success
in obtaining confessions, though earnestly solicited.
It had been hinted, also, that confessing was the avenue to safety. At last, Deliverance Hobbs owned May 11.
every thing that was asked of her, and was left un-
harmed. The gallows was to be set up, not for those
who professed themselves witches, but for those who
rebuked the delusion.

Simon Bradstreet, the governor of the people's
choice, deemed the evidence insufficient ground of
guilt. On Saturday, the 14th of May, the new char- 1692 May 14.
ter and the royal governor arrived in Boston. On the
next Monday, the charter was published, and the 16.

CHAP. XIX. 1692. parishioner of Cotton Mather, with the royal council, was installed in office. The triumph of Cotton Mather was perfect. Immediately a court of oyer and terminer was instituted by ordinance, and Stoughton appointed by the governor and council its chief judge: by the 2d of June, the court was in session at Salem, making its first experiment on Bridget Bishop, a poor and friendless old woman. The fact of the witchcraft was assumed as "notorious:" to fix it on the prisoner, Samuel Parris, who had examined her before her commitment, was the principal witness to her power of inflicting torture; he had seen it exercised. Deliverance Hobbs had been whipped with iron rods by her spectre; neighbors, who had quarrelled with her, were willing to lay their little ills to her charge; the poor creature had a preternatural excrescence in her flesh; "she gave a look towards the great and spacious meeting-house of Salem,"—it is Cotton Mather who records this,—"and immediately a dæmon, invisibly entering the house, tore down a part of it." She was a witch by the rules and precedents of Keeble and Sir Matthew Hale, of Perkins and Bernard, of Baxter and Cotton Mather; and, on the 10th of June, protesting her innocence, she was hanged. Of the magistrates at that time, not one held office by the suffrage of the people: the tribunal, essentially despotic in its origin, as in its character, had no sanction but an extraordinary and an illegal commission; and Stoughton, the chief judge, a partisan of Andros, had been rejected by the people of Massachusetts. The responsibility of the tragedy, far from attaching to the people of the colony, rests with the very few, hardly five or six, in whose hands the transition state of the government left, for a season, unlimited influence. Into

Cotton Mather, Wonders.

Hale, 37.

the interior of the colony the delusion did not spread at all. CHAP XIX.

The house of representatives, which assembled in June, was busy with its griefs at the abridgment of the old colonial liberties. Increase Mather, the agent, was heard in his own defence; and, at last, Bond, the speaker, in the name of the house, tardily and languidly thanked him for his faithful and unwearied exertions. No recompense was voted. "I seek not yours, but you," said Increase Mather; "I am willing to wait for recompense in another world;" and the general court, after prolonging the validity of the old laws, adjourned to October. 1692. June 8 to July 2. June 9. June 24. Some Few Remarks, 1702, p. 20. July 2.

But Phipps and his council had not looked to the general court for directions; they turned to the ministers of Boston and Charlestown; and from them, by the hand of Cotton Mather, they receive gratitude for their sedulous endeavors to defeat the abominable witchcrafts; prayer that the discovery may be perfected; a caution against haste and spectral evidence; a hint to affront the devil, and give him the lie, by condemning none on his testimony alone; while the direful advice is added—"We recommend the speedy and vigorous prosecution of such as have rendered themselves obnoxious." The obedient court, at its next session, condemned five women, all of blameless lives, all declaring their innocence. Four were convicted easily enough; Rebecca Nurse was, at first, acquitted. "The honored court was pleased to object against the verdict;" and, as she had said of the confessing witnesses, "they used to come among us," meaning that they had been prisoners together, Stoughton interpreted the words as of a witch festival. The jury withdrew, and could as yet not agree; but, as the June 30.

CHAP. XIX. prisoner, who was hard of hearing, and full of grief, made no explanation, they no longer refused to find her guilty. Hardly was the verdict rendered, before the foreman made a statement of the ground of her condemnation, and she sent her declaration to the court in reply. The governor, who himself was not unmerciful, saw cause to grant a reprieve; but Parris had preached against Rebecca Nurse, and prayed against her; had induced "the afflicted" to witness against her; had caused her sisters to be imprisoned for their honorable sympathy. She must perish, or the delusion was unveiled; and the governor recalled the reprieve. On the next communion day, she was taken in chains to the meeting-house, to be formally excommunicated by Noyes, her minister; and was hanged with the rest. "You are a witch; you know you are," said Noyes to Sarah Good, urging a confession. "You are a liar," replied the poor woman; "and, if you take my life, God will give you blood to drink."

1692. July 4.

Mass. Hist. Coll. xxiii 175

July 19.

Confessions rose in importance. "Some, not afflicted before confession, were so presently after it." The jails were filled; for fresh accusations were needed to confirm the confessions. "Some, by these their accusations of others,"—I quote the cautious apologist Hale,—"hoped to gain time, and get favor from the rulers." "Some of the inferior sort of people did ill offices, by promising favor thereby, more than they had ground to engage. Some, under these temptations, regarded not as they should what became of others, so that they could thereby serve their own turns. Some have since acknowledged so much." If the confessions were contradictory; if witnesses uttered apparent falsehoods, "the devil," the judges would say, "takes away their memory, and imposes on their brain." And who now

Hale, p. 89.

Hale, p. 89.

Brattle, in Mass Hist. Coll. v. 65.

would dare to be skeptical? who would disbelieve confessors? Besides, there were other evidences. A callous spot was the mark of the devil: did age or amazement refuse to shed tears; were threats after a quarrel followed by the death of cattle or other harm; did an error occur in repeating the Lord's prayer; were deeds of great physical strength performed,—these all were signs of witchcraft. In some instances, the phenomena of somnambulism would appear to have been exhibited; and "the afflicted, out of their fits, knew nothing of what they did or said in them." 1692. Hale, 56

Aug. 3. Again, on a new session, six are arraigned, and all are convicted. John Willard had, as an officer, been employed to arrest the suspected witches. Perceiving the hypocrisy, he declined the service. The afflicted immediately denounced him, and he was seized, convicted, and hanged.

At the trial of George Burroughs, the bewitched persons pretended to be dumb. "Who hinders these witnesses," said Stoughton, "from giving their testimonies?"—"I suppose the devil," answered Burroughs. "How comes the devil," retorted the chief judge, "so loath to have any testimony borne against you?" and the question was effective. Besides, he had given proofs of great, if not preternatural muscular strength. Cotton Mather calls the evidence "enough:" the jury gave a verdict of guilty.

July 23. John Procter, who foresaw his doom, and knew from whom the danger came, sent an earnest petition, not to the governor and council, but to Cotton Mather and the ministers. Among the witnesses against him were some who had made no confessions till after torture. "They have already undone us in our estates, and that will not serve their turns without our innocent

CHAP. XIX. blood;" and he begs for a trial in Boston, or, at least, for a change of magistrates. His entreaties were vain,
1692. as also his prayers, after condemnation, for a respite.
Calef, 225, 226. Among the witnesses against Martha Carrier, the mother saw her own children. Her two sons refused to perjure themselves till they had been tied neck and heels so long that the blood was ready to gush from them. The confession of her daughter, a child of seven years old, is still preserved.

The aged Jacobs was condemned, in part, by the evidence of Margaret Jacobs, his granddaughter. "Through the magistrates' threatenings and my own vile heart,"—thus she wrote to her father,—"I have confessed things contrary to my conscience and knowledge. But, oh! the terrors of a wounded conscience who can bear?" And she confessed the whole truth before the magistrates. The magistrates refused their belief, and, confining her for trial, proceeded to hang her grandfather.

Aug. 19. These five were condemned on the third, and hanged on the nineteenth of August; pregnancy reprieved Elizabeth Procter. To hang a minister as a witch was a novelty; but Burroughs denied absolutely that there was, or could be, such a thing as witchcraft, in the current sense. This opinion wounded the self-love of the judges, for it made them the accusers and judicial murderers of the innocent. On the ladder, Burroughs cleared his innocence by an earnest speech, repeating the Lord's prayer composedly and exactly, and with a fervency that astonished. Tears flowed to the eyes of many; it seemed as if the spectators would rise up to hinder the execution. Cotton Mather, on horseback among the crowd, addressed the people, cavilling at the ordination of Burroughs, as though he had been no true minister; insisting on his guilt, and hinting that the devil could sometimes assume the appearance of an angel of light: and the hanging proceeded. CHAP XIX. 1692.

Meantime, the confessions of the witches began to be directed against the Anabaptists. Mary Osgood was dipped by the devil. The court still had work to do. On the ninth, six women were condemned; and more convictions followed. Giles Cory, the octogenarian, seeing that all were convicted, refused to plead, and was condemned to be pressed to death. The horrid sentence, a barbarous usage of English law, never again followed in the colonies, was executed forthwith.

On the twenty-second of September, eight persons were led to the gallows. Of these, Samuel Wardwell had confessed, and was safe; but, from shame and penitence, he retracted his confession, and, speaking the truth boldly, he was hanged, not for witchcraft, but for denying witchcraft. Martha Cory was, before execution, visited in prison by Parris, the two deacons, and another member of his church. The church record tells that, self-sustained, she "imperiously" rebuked her destroyers, and "they pronounced the dreadful sentence of excommunication against her." In the calmness with which Mary Easty exposed the falsehood of those who had selected from her family so many victims, she joined the noblest fortitude with sweetness of temper, dignity, and resignation. But the chief judge was positive that all had been done rightly, and "was very impatient in hearing any thing that looked another way."—"There hang eight firebrands of hell," said Noyes, the minister of Salem, pointing to the bodies swinging on the gallows. Brattle, 74.

Already twenty persons had been put to death for

CHAP. XIX. 1692

witchcraft; fifty-five had been tortured or terrified into penitent confessions. With accusations, confessions increased; with confessions, new accusations. Even "the generation of the children of God" were in danger of "falling under that condemnation." The jails were full. It was also observed, that no one of the condemned confessing witchcraft had been hanged. No one that confessed, and retracted a confession, had escaped either hanging or imprisonment for trial. No one of the condemned, who asserted innocence, even if one of the witnesses confessed perjury, or the foreman of the jury acknowledged the error of the verdict, escaped the gallows. Favoritism was shown in listening to accusations, which were turned aside from friends or partisans. If a man began a career as a witch-hunter, and, becoming convinced of the imposture, declined the service, he was accused and hanged. Persons accused, who had escaped from the jurisdiction in Massachusetts, were not demanded, as would have been done in case of acknowledged crime; so that the magistrates acted as if witch-law did not extend beyond their jurisdiction. Witnesses convicted of perjury were cautioned, and permitted still to swear away the lives of others. It was certain, people had been tempted to become accusers by promise of favor. Yet the zeal of Stoughton was unabated, and the arbitrary court adjourned to the first Tuesday in November. "Between this and then," wrote Brattle, "will be the great assembly, and this matter will be a peculiar subject of agitation. Our hopes," he adds, "are here." The representatives of the people must stay the evil, or "New England is undone and undone."

Far different was the reasoning of Cotton Mather. He was met "continually with all sorts of objections and objectors against the work doing at Salem." The obstinate Sadducees, "the witch advocates," who esteemed the executions to be judicial murders, gained such influence as to embarrass the governor. But Cotton Mather, still eager "to lift up a standard against the infernal enemy," undertook the defence of his friends; and he sent to Salem for an account strong enough "to knock down" "one that believed nothing reasonable," promising "to box it about among his neighbors till it come he knows not where at last." Before the opening of the adjourned session of the general court, the indefatigable man had prepared his narrative of "the Wonders of the Invisible World," in the design of promoting "a pious thankfulness to God for justice being so far executed among us." For this book he received the approbation of the president of Harvard College, the praises of the governor, and the gratitude of Stoughton.

CHAP XIX. 1692. Sept 20. Oct. 12. I. Mather's Cases of Conscience.

On the second Wednesday in October, 1692, about a fortnight after the last hanging of eight at Salem, the representatives of the people assembled; and the people of Andover, their minister joining with them, appeared with their remonstrance against the doings of the witch tribunals. "We know not," say they, "who can think himself safe, if the accusations of children, and others under a diabolical influence, shall be received against persons of good fame." Of the discussions that ensued no record is preserved; we know only the issue. The general court did not place itself in direct opposition to the advocates of the trials: as to legislation, it adopted what King William rejected, —the English law, word for word as it stood in the English statute-book; but they abrogated the special court, establishing a tribunal by public law. Phipps

1692. Oct 18.

CHAP. XIX. 1692. had, instantly on his arrival, employed his illegal court in hanging; the representatives of the people delayed the first assembling of the legal colonial court till January of the following year. Thus an interval of more than three months from the last executions gave the public mind security and freedom; and, though Phipps still conferred the place of chief judge on Stoughton, yet jurors, representing the public mind, acted independ-
1693. Jan. ently. When the court met at Salem, six women of Andover, at once renouncing their confessions, treated the witchcraft but as something so called, the bewil-
Abbot's Andover, 164 dered but as "seemingly afflicted." A memorial of like tenor came from the inhabitants of Andover.

Of the presentments the grand jury dismissed more than half, and, if it found bills against twenty-six, the trials did but show the feebleness of the testimony on which others had been condemned. The same testimony was produced, and there, at Salem, with Stoughton on the bench, verdicts of acquittal followed: "Error expired amidst its worshippers." Three had, for special reasons, been convicted: one was a wife, whose testimony had sent her husband to the gallows, and whose confession was now used against herself. All were at once reprieved, and soon set free.

Feb. Still reluctant to yield, the party of superstition were resolved on one conviction. The victim selected was Sarah Daston, a woman of eighty years old, who for twenty years had enjoyed the undisputed reputation of a witch: if ever there were a witch in the world, she, it was said, was one. In the presence of a throng, the trial went forward at Charlestown: there was more evidence against her than against any at Salem; but the common mind was disinthralled, and asserted itself, through the jury, by a verdict of acquittal.

To cover his confusion, Cotton Mather got up a case of witchcraft in his own parish. Miracles, he avers, were wrought in Boston. Believe his statements, and you must believe that his prayers healed diseases. But he was not bloodthirsty; he wished his vanity protected, not his parishioners hanged; and his bewitched neophyte, profiting by his cautions, was afflicted by veiled spectres. The imposture was promptly exposed to ridicule by "a malignant, calumnious, and reproachful man," "a coal from hell," the unlettered but rational and intelligent Robert Calef. Was Cotton Mather honestly credulous? Ever ready to dupe himself, he limited his credulity only by the probable credulity of others. He changes, or omits to repeat, his statements, without acknowledging error, and with a clear intention of conveying false impressions. He is an example how far selfishness, under the form of vanity and ambition, can blind the higher faculties, stupefy the judgment, and dupe consciousness itself. His self-righteousness was complete, till he was resisted. As the recall of Phipps—a consequence of impetuous imbecility—left the government for some years in the hands of Stoughton, the press was re strained: when, at last, the narrative of Calef appeared, Cotton Mather endeavored to shield himself by calling his adversaries the adversaries of religion; and, though hardly seven or eight of the ministers, and no magistrate of popular appointment, had a share in the guilt, he endeavored, but ineffectually, to denounce the book as "a libel upon the whole government and ministry of the land." Denying the jurisdiction of popular opinion, he claims the subject as "too dark and deep for ordinary comprehension," and appeals for a decision to the day of judgment. But the sentence was not de-

CHAP. XIX.

Bentley.

layed. The inexorable indignation of the people of Salem village drove Parris from the place; Noyes regained favor only by a full confession, asking forgiveness always, and consecrating the remainder of his life to deeds of mercy. Sewall, one of the judges, by the frankness and sincerity of his undisguised confession, recovered public esteem. Stoughton and Cotton Mather never repented. The former lived proud, unsatisfied, and unbeloved; the latter attempted to persuade others and himself that he had not been specially active in the tragedy. But the public mind would not be deceived. His diary proves that he did not wholly escape the rising impeachment from the monitor within; and Cotton Mather, who had sought the foundation of faith in tales of wonders, himself "had temptations to atheism, and to the abandonment of all religion as a mere delusion."

The common mind of Massachusetts was more wise. It never wavered in its faith; more ready to receive every tale from the invisible world, than to gaze on the universe without acknowledging an Infinite Intelligence. But, employing a gentle skepticism, eliminating error, rejecting superstition as tending to cowardice and submission, cherishing religion as the source of courage and the fountain of freedom, the common mind in New England refused henceforward to separate belief and reason. To the west of Massachusetts, and to Connecticut, to which the influence of Cotton Mather and its consequences did not extend, we must look for the unmixed development of the essential character of New England; yet there, also, faith and "common sense" were reconciled. In the vicinity of Boston, the skepticism of free inquiry conducted some minds to healthy judgments; others asserted God to be the true being,

Brattle.

the devil to be but a nonentity, and disobedience to God to be the only possible compact with Satan; others, still clinging to the letter of the Bible, yet showed the insufficiency of all evidence for the conviction of a witch; others denied witchcraft, as beyond comprehension, involving a contradiction, and not sustained by the evidence of experience. The invisible world began to be less considered; men trusted more to observation and analysis; and this philosophy, derived from the senses, was analogous to their civil condition. The people in the charter governments could hope from England for no concession of larger liberties. Instead, therefore, of looking for the reign of absolute right, they were led to reverence the forms of their privileges as exempt from change. We hear no more of the theocracy where God was alone supreme lawgiver and king; no more of the expected triumph of freedom and justice anticipated "in the second coming of Christ:" liberty, in Massachusetts, was defended by asserting the sanctity of compact.

Maule.

Hale.

But the political morality of England did not recognize the sanctity of the compacts with colonies. "The regulation of charters was looked on as part of the public economy," and Massachusetts was included in the bill for their abrogation.

The colony, moreover, had the grief of receiving as its governor, under a commission that included New Hampshire, its own apostate son, Joseph Dudley, the great supporter of Andros, "the wolf," whom the patriots of Boston had "seized by the ears," whom the people had insisted on having "in the jail," and who, for twenty weeks, had been kept in prison, or, as he himself termed it, had been "buried alive." He obtained the place by the request of Cotton Mather, who

CHAP. XIX. at that time continued, though erroneously, to be regarded in England as representing the general wish of the ministers.

1702. On meeting his first assembly, Dudley gave "instances of his remembering the old quarrel, and the people, on their parts, resolved never to forget it." "All his ingenuity could not stem the current of their prejudice against him." A stated salary was demanded for the governor. "As to settling a salary for the governor," replied the house, "it is altogether new to us; nor can we think it agreeable to our present constitution; but we shall be ready to do what may be proper for his support." Here began the controversy which nothing but independence could solve. In vain did Dudley endeavor to win from the legislature concessions to the royal prerogative; and he, and, for a season, his son also, became the active opponents of the chartered liberties of New England, endeavoring to effect their overthrow and the establishment of a general government as in the days of Andros. "This country would never be worth living in, for lawyers and gentlemen, till the charter is taken away."

Quarry.

The character of Dudley was that of profound selfishness. He possessed prudence and the inferior virtues, and was as good a governor as one could be who loved neither freedom nor his native land. His grave is among strangers; his memory has perished from among those whose interests he flattered, and is preserved only in the country of his birth. He who loved himself more than freedom or his country, is left without one to palliate his selfishness.

The contest with France having engrossed the attention of England and of New England, Massachusetts, at this time, suffered no further diminution of her liberties, except through the general action of parliament, which had made itself supreme by electing monarchs and a dynasty for the British dominions. Its absolute power was, in general terms, unquestioned in England even by American agents, and was by itself interpreted to extend over all the colonies, with no limitation but its own pleasure; it was "absolute and unaccountable." Dummer.

England, at "the abdication" of its throne by the Stuarts, was, as it were, still free from debt; and a direct tax on America, for the benefit of the English treasury, was, I think, at that time, not dreamed of. That the respective colonies should contribute to the common defence against the French and Indians, was desired in America, was earnestly enjoined from England; but the demand for quotas was directed to the colonies themselves, and was refused or granted by the colonial assemblies, as their own policy prompted. The want of concert, and the refusal of contributions, readily suggested the interference of parliament. I find the suggestion to have been actually made, in 1705, by a royalist in the colonies, in a memorial to the lords of trade; but the proposition seems to have remained unnoticed by the ministry: our colonial records exhibit no alarm. The institution of a general 1710
post-office was valued as a convenience, not dreaded as a tax. If the declaratory acts, by which every one of the colonies asserted their right to the privileges of Magna Charta, to the feudal liberty of freedom from taxation except with their own consent, were always disallowed by the crown, it was done silently, and the strife on the power of parliament to tax the colonies was certainly adjourned. The colonial legislatures had their own budgets; and financial questions arose—

CHAP. XIX. Shall the grants be generally for the use of the crown, or carefully limited for specific purposes? Shall the moneys levied be confided to an officer of royal appointment, or to a treasurer responsible to the legislature? Shall the revenue be granted permanently, or from year to year? Shall the salaries of the royal judges and the royal governor be fixed, or depend annually on the popular contentment? These were questions consistent with the relations between metropolis and colony; but the supreme power of parliament to tax at its discretion, was not yet maintained in England—was always denied in America.

The colonial press, in spite of royal instructions, was generally as free in America as in any part of the world. In matters of religion, intellectual freedom was viewed, in the colonies as in England, as a Protestant question; and the outcry against "Popery and slavery" generated equally bitter hostility towards the Roman Catholic church. England, moreover, cherished a steady purpose of disseminating Episcopacy; yet the political effect of this endeavor was inconsiderable. Similarity in religious institutions would, it is true, nurse a sympathy with England; but in South Carolina, in Maryland, laymen aspired to dominion over the church. American Episcopacy, without an American bishop, was a solecism; and an American bishop was feared as an emblem of independence. Besides, if the advowson of the churches was reserved to the governor, the people took no interest in them; and religion can be propagated only by consent. If, on the contrary, the advowson remained with the parish, the church became popular, and inclined to independence. If, as in Virginia, the relations between priest and people were not accurately defined; if, among the missionaries, some, of feeble minds and uncertain morals, prodigious zealots from covetousness, sought, by appeals to England, to clutch at a monopoly of ecclesiastical gains; if legal questions arose,—the institution became the theme of dispute, and an instrument for educating the people into strife with their English superiors. The crown ncorporated and favored the Society for Propagating the Gospel in Foreign Parts.

The security of personal freedom was not formally denied to America. Massachusetts, in an enactment, 1692
claimed the full benefit of the writ of habeas corpus: "the privilege had not yet been granted to the plantations," was the reply even of Lord Somers; it was not become a vested right; and the act was disallowed. When, afterwards, the privilege was affirmed by Queen Anne, the burgesses of Virginia, in their gratitude, did but esteem it "an assertion to her subjects of their just rights and properties." England conceded the security of personal freedom as a boon; America claimed it as a birthright.

In the contests respecting the judiciary, the crown gained the advantage. New England had not permitted appeals to the king in council; the permission of appeal was insisted upon in all the colonies. Thus, in the settlement of American disputes, the ultimate tribunal was in England; and the English crown gained the appointment of the judges in nearly every colony. Where the people selected them, as in Connecticut and Rhode Island, they were chosen annually, and the public preference, free from fickleness, gave stability to the office; where the appointment rested with the royal governor, the popular instinct desired for the judges an independent tenure.

To "make most of the money centre in England,"

CHAP. XIX. the lords of trade proposed a regulation of the colonial currency, by reducing all the coin of America to one standard. The proclamation of Queen Anne was not designed to preserve among the colonies the English basis: on the contrary, it confirmed to all the colonies a depreciated currency, but endeavored to make the depreciation uniform and safe against change. In a word, England sought to establish for itself a fixed standard of gold and silver; for the colonies, a fixed standard of depreciation. As the necessities of the colonies had led them of themselves to depreciate their currency, the first object of England was gained, and it therefore monopolized all gold and silver. Even the shillings of early coinage in Massachusetts were nearly all gathered up, and remitted; but the equality of depreciation could never be maintained against the rival cupidity of the competitors in bills of credit.

The enforcement of the mercantile system, in its intensest form, is also a characteristic of the policy of the aristocratic revolution of England. By the corn-laws, English agriculture became an associate in the system of artificial legislation. "The value of lands" began to be urged as a motive for oppressing the colo-
1696. May. nies. The affairs of the plantations were, in 1696, intrusted permanently to the commissioners who formed the board of trade; and all questions on colonial liberty and affairs were decided from the point of view of English commerce.

12 Car II. c. xviii. 15 Car. II. c. vii. 22 and 23 Car. II. c. xxvi. 25 Car. II. c. vii 7 and 8 W. III. c. xxii. All former acts giving a monopoly of the colonial trade to England were renewed, and, to effect their rigid execution, the paramount authority of parliament was strictly asserted. Colonial commerce could be conducted only in ships built, owned, and commanded by the people of England or of the colonies. All gov-

ernors, in the charter colonies, as well as the royal provinces, were compelled to take oath to do their utmost that every clause in these acts be punctually observed. Officers of the revenue in America were invested with all the powers conferred by act of parliament on those in England. The intercolonial trade had been burdened with taxation, and the payment of the tax was interpreted as giving to the goods the right of being exported any where: this liberty was denied. The immense American domain was reserved exclusively for English subjects, or for those who obtained from the privy council a permission to purchase. The proprietary charters were modified—it is the first act of parliament of that nature—by conferring on the crown a negative on the choice of the governors in the charter colonies; and the paramount legislative authority of parliament was asserted by declaring illegal, null, and void, every colonial act or usage, present or future, which might be in any wise repugnant "to this present act, or to any other law hereafter to be made in the kingdom, so far as such law shall relate to the plantations." Such was the spirit of English legislation for its colonies, at the great moment when England asserted its aristocratic liberties.

CHAP. XIX.

Compare 8 and 9 W. III. c. XX. § 69.

§ 16.

As yet the owners of land were not sufficiently pledged to the colonial system. Wool was the great staple of England, and its growers and manufacturers envied the colonies the possession of a flock of sheep, a spindle, or a loom. The preamble to an act of parliament avows the motive for a restraining law, in the conviction that colonial industry would "inevitably sink the value of lands" in England. The public mind of the mother country could esteem the present interest of its landholders paramount to natural justice.

10 and 11 W. III. c. X.

CHAP. XIX.

§ 19. The clause, which I am about to cite, is a memorial of a delusion which once pervaded all Western Europe, and which has already so passed away, that men grow incredulous of its former existence:—"After the first day of December, 1699, no wool, or manufacture made or mixed with wool, being the produce or manufacture of any of the English plantations in America, shall be loaden in any ship or vessel, upon any pretence whatsoever,—nor loaden upon any horse, cart, or other carriage,—to be carried out of the English plantations to any other of the said plantations, or to any other place whatsoever." Thus the fabrics of Connecticut might not seek a market in Massachusetts, or be carried to Albany to traffic with the Indians. An English mariner might not purchase in Boston woollens of a greater value than forty shillings. The mercantile system of England, in its relations with foreign states, sought a convenient tariff; in the colonies, it prohibited industry.

11 and 12 W. III. c. xiii. § 9.

And the intolerable injustice was not perceived. The interests of the landed proprietors with the monopolies of commerce and manufactures, jointly fostered by artificial legislation, corrupted the public judgment, so that there was no secret compunction. Even the bounty on naval stores was not intended as a compensation, but grew out of the efforts of Sweden to infringe the mercantile system of England, and was accompanied by a proviso which extended the jurisdiction of parliament to every grove north of the Delaware. Every pitch-pine tree, not in an enclosure, was henceforward sacred to the purposes of the English navy; and, in the undivided domain, no tree fit for a mast might be cut without the queen's license. Thus the bounty of the English parliament was blended with monopoly, while the colonists were constantly invited

3 and 4 Anne, c. x.

9 Anne, xvii

to cease the manufacture of wool, and produce naval stores. CHAP. XIX.

In Virginia, the poverty of the people compelled them to attempt coarse manufactures, or to go unclad; yet Nicholson, the royal governor, calmly advised that parliament should forbid the Virginians to make their own clothing. Spotswood repeats the complaint— Beverley, 92. "The people, more of necessity than of inclination, attempt to clothe themselves with their own manufactures;" adding that "it is certainly necessary to divert their application to some commodity less prejudicial to the trade of Great Britain." The charter colonies are 1701. reproached by the lords of trade, "with promoting and Journals of Commons, 448, 479. propagating woollen and other manufactures proper to England." The English need not fear to conquer Canada;—such was the reasoning of an American agent;—for, in Canada, "where the cold is extreme, Dummer's Letter 6. and snow lies so long on the ground, sheep will never thrive so as to make the woollen manufactures possible, which is the only thing that can make a plantation unprofitable to the crown." The policy was continued by every administration. "Should our sovereign authority of legislative and commercial control be denied," said the elder Pitt, seventy years afterwards, "I would not suffer even a nail for a horseshoe to be manufactured in America;" and, at the beginning of the eighteenth century, the lords of trade and plantations, to effect their purposes of monopoly, proposed that every charter should, by the legislative power of the kingdom, be reassumed to the crown.

The charters were royal grants, and a parliament which had disfranchised a dynasty disdained to consider their violation a just ground for resistance. It placed its own power alike above the authority by which

CHAP. XIX. they had been conceded, and above the colonies which possessed them. From legislating on commerce and industry, it proceeded to legislate on government; and, if it omitted to startle the colonies by the avowal, it plainly held the maxim as indisputable, that it might legislate for them in all cases whatsoever.

These relations, placing the property, the personal freedom, the industry, the chartered liberties of the colonies, in the good will, and under "the absolute power," of the English legislature, could not but lead to independence; and the English were the first to perceive the tendency.

The insurrection in New England, in 1689, excited alarm, as an indication of a daring spirit. In 1701, the lords of trade, in a public document, declared "the independency the colonies thirst after is now notorious."—"Commonwealth notions improve daily," wrote Quarry, in 1703; "and, if it be not checked in time, the rights and privileges of English subjects will be thought too narrow." In 1705, it was said in print, "The colonists will, in process of time, cast off their allegiance to England, and set up a government of their own;" and by degrees it came to be said, "by people of all conditions and qualities, that their increasing numbers and wealth, joined to their great distance from Britain, would give them an opportunity, in the course of some years, to throw off their dependence on the nation, and declare themselves a free state, if not curbed in time, by being made entirely subject to the crown." "Some great men professed their belief of the feasibleness of it, and the probability of its some time or other actually coming to pass."

Dummer, p. 32, 33.

CHAPTER XX.

FRANCE AND THE VALLEY OF THE MISSISSIPPI.

If our country, in the inherent opposition between its principles and the English system, was as ripe for governing itself in 1689 as in 1776, the colonists disclaimed, and truly, a present passion for independence. A deep instinct gave assurance that the time was not yet come. They were not merely colonists of England, but they were riveted into an immense colonial system, which every commercial country in Europe had assisted to frame, and which bound in its strong bonds every other quarter of the globe. The question of independence would be not a private strife with England, but a revolution in the commerce and in the policy of the world,—in the present fortunes, and, still more, in the prospects of humanity itself. As yet, there was no union among the settlements that fringed the Atlantic; and but one nation in Europe would, at that day, have tolerated—not one would have fostered—an insurrection. Spain, Spanish Belgium, Holland, and Austria, were then the allies of England against France, which, by centralizing its power, and by well-considered plans of territorial aggrandizement, excited the dread of a universal monarchy. When Austria, with Belgium, shall abandon its hereditary warfare against France. when Spain and Holland, favored by the armed neutrality of Portugal, Sweden, Denmark, Prussia, and

CHAP. XX. Russia, shall be ready to join with France in repressing the commercial ambition of England;—then, and not till then, American independence becomes possible. Those changes, extraordinary and improbable as they might have seemed, were to spring from the false principles of the mercantile system, which made France and England enemies. Our borders were become the scenes of jealous collision; our soil was the destined battle-ground on which the grand conflict of the rivals for commercial privilege was to begin. The struggles for maritime and colonial dominion, which transformed the unsuccessful competitors for supremacy into the defenders of the freedom of the seas, having, in their progress, taught our fathers union, secured to our country the opportunity of independence.

The mercantile system placed the benefit of commerce, not in a reciprocity of exchanges, but in a favorable balance of trade. Its whole wisdom was, to sell as much as possible—to buy as little as possible. Pushed to its extreme, the policy would destroy all commerce: it might further the selfish aims of an individual nation; the commerce of the world could flourish only in spite of it. In its mitigated form, it was a necessary source of European wars; for each nation, in its traffic, sought to levy tribute in favor of its industry, and the adjustment of tariffs and commercial privileges was the constant subject of negotiations among states. The jealousy of one country envied the wealth of a rival as its own loss.

Territorial aggrandizement was also desired and feared, in reference to its influence on European commerce; and, as France, in its ambitious progress, encroached upon the German empire and the Spanish Netherlands, the mercantile interests of England led directly to an alliance with Austria as the head of the empire, and with Spain as the sovereign of Belgium.

Thus the commercial interest was, in European politics, become paramount; it framed alliances, regulated wars, dictated treaties, and established barriers against conquest.

The discovery of America, and of the ocean-path to India, had created maritime commerce, and the great European colonial system had united the world. Now, for the first time in the history of man, the oceans vindicated their rights as natural highways; now, for the first time, great maritime powers struggled for dominion on the high seas. The world entered on a new epoch.

Ancient navigation kept near the coast, or was but a passage from isle to isle; commerce now selected, of choice, the boundless deep.

The three ancient continents were divided by no wide seas, and their intercourse was chiefly by land. Their voyages were, like ours on Lake Erie, a continuance of internal trade; the vastness of their transactions was measured, not by tonnage, but by counting caravans and camels. But now, for the wilderness commerce substituted the sea; for camels, merchantmen; for caravans, fleets and convoys.

The ancients were restricted in the objects of commerce; for how could rice be brought across continents from the Ganges, or sugar from Bengal? But now commerce gathered every production from the East and the West; tea, sugar, and coffee, from the plantations of China and Hindostan; masts from American forests; furs from Hudson's Bay; men from Africa.

With the expansion of commerce, the forms of business were changing. Of old, no dealers in credit existed between the merchant and the producer. The Greeks and Romans were hard-money men; their language has no word for bank notes or currency; with them there was no stock market, no brokers' board, no negotiable scrip of kingdom or commonwealth. Public expenses were borne by direct taxes, or by loans from rich citizens, soon to be cancelled, and never funded. The expansion of commerce gave birth to immense masses of floating credits; larger sums than the whole revenue of an ancient state were transferred from continent to continent by bills of exchange; and, when the mercantile system grew strong enough to originate wars, it also gained power to subject national credit to the floating credits of commerce.

Every commercial state of the earlier world had been but a town with its territory; the Phœnician, Greek, and Italian republics, each was a city government, retaining its municipal character with the enlargement of its jurisdiction and the diffusion of its colonies. The great European maritime powers were vast monarchies, grasping at continents for their plantations. In the tropical isles of America and the East, they made their gardens for the fruits of the torrid zone; the Cordilleras and the Andes supplied their mints with bullion; the most inviting points on the coasts of Africa and Asia were selected as commercial stations; and the temperate regions of America were to be filled with agriculturists, whose swarming increase—such was the universal metropolitan aspiration—should lead to the infinite consumption of European goods.

That the mercantile system should be applied by each nation to its own colonies, was universally tolerated by the political morality of that day. Thus each metropolis was at war with the present interests and natural rights of its colonies; and, as the European colonial system was established on every continent; as the single colonies were, each by itself, too feeble for resistance; colonial oppression was destined to endure as long, at least, as the union of the oppressors. But the commercial jealousies of Europe extended, from the first, to European colonies; and the home relations of the states of the Old World to each other were finally surpassed in importance by the transatlantic conflicts with which they were identified. The mercantile system, being founded in error and injustice, was doomed not only itself to expire, but, by overthrowing the mighty fabric of the colonial system, to emancipate commerce, and open a boundless career to human hope. CHAP. XX.

That colonial system all Western Europe had contributed to build. Even before the discovery of Amer- 1419.
ica, Portugal had reached Madeira and the Azores, the 1448.
Cape Verd Islands and Congo; within six years after 1449. 1484.
the discovery of Hayti, the intrepid Vasco de Gama, following where no European, where none but Africans from Carthage, had preceded, turned the Cape of Good Hope, and arrived at Mozambique; and, passing the Arabian peninsula, landed at Calicut, and made an establishment at Cochin.

Within a few short years, the brilliant temerity of Portugal achieved establishments on Western and Eastern Africa, in Arabia and Persia, in Hindostan and the Eastern isles, and in Brazil. The intense application of the system of monopoly, combined with the despotism of the sovereign and the priesthood, precipitated the decay of Portuguese commerce in advance of the decay of the mercantile system; and the Moors,

CHAP. XX. the Persians, Holland, and Spain, dismantled Portugal of her possessions at so early a period, that she was never involved, as a leading party, in the early wars of North America.

Far different were the relations of Spain with our colonial history. The world had been divided by Pope Alexander VI. between Portugal and Spain: to the former the East had been allotted; and, therefore, Spain never reached the Asïatic world except by travelling west, and, obedient to the Roman see, never claimed possession of any territory in Asia beyond the Philippine Isles. But in America there grew up a Spanish world safe against conquest, from its boundless extent, yet doubly momentous to our fathers, from its vicinity and its commercial system. Occupying Florida on our south, Spain was easily involved in controversy with England on the subject of reciprocal territorial encroachments; and, carefully excluding foreigners from all participation in her colonial trade, she could not but arouse the cupidity of English commerce, bent on extending itself, if necessary, by force. Yet the colonial maxims, in conformity with which Spain had spread its hierarchy, its missions, its garrisons, and its inquisition, over islands and half a continent, were recognized by England; and both powers were, by their legislation, pledged to the system of colonial monopoly.

Holland had emerged into existence as the advocate and example of maritime freedom, and had, moreover, been ejected from the continent of North America. Yet, as a land power, it needed the alliance of England as a barrier against France; and the aristocratic republic, now itself possessing precious spice islands in the Indian Seas, cherished also the maxim of monopoly

But the two powers, of which the ambition was most actively interested in the colonial system, were France and England, both stern advocates of colonial monopoly, and both jealous competitors for new acquisitions.

Chateaubriand.

The political condition of France rendered her commercial advancement possible. "Louis XIV., on coming of age, entering parliament with a whip in his hand, is the emblem of absolute monarchy." The feudal system, that great antagonist to free industry, was subdued; the struggle between monarchy and the aristocracy of blood was over; and the people of France,—aided by Louis XIV., who detested aristocracy, and left as a legacy to his posterity his advice to a continuance of that hatred,—emerged into existence, one day to assert its power. While absolute monarchy was the period of transition from hereditary privilege to equality; while the memory of republican virtues was kept alive by the poetry of Corneille, and the vices of courts were rebuked in the fictions of Fenelon,—the policy of France gave dignity to the class of citizens. In the magistracy, as in the church, they could reach high employments; the meanest burgher could have audience of the king; and the members of the royal council were, almost without exception, selected from the ignoble. Colbert and Louvois were not of the high nobility. Thus the great middling class was constantly increasing in importance; and the energies of France, if not employed in arms for aggrandizement, began to be husbanded for commerce and the arts.

Even before the days of Colbert, the colonial rivalry with England had begun. When Queen Elizabeth gave a charter to a first not very successful English

CHAP. XX. East India company, France, under Richelieu, strug
gled also, though vainly, to share the great commerce
with Asia. The same year in which England took
possession of Barbadoes, Frenchmen occupied the half
of St. Christopher's. Did England add half St. Christopher's, Nevis, and, at last, Jamaica,—France gained
Martinique and Guadaloupe, with smaller islets, founded a colony at Cayenne, and, by the aid of bucaniers,
took possession of the west of Hayti. England, by its
devices of tariffs and prohibitions, and by the royal
assent to the act of navigation, sought to call into ac-
1664 tion every power of production, hardly a year before
to 1667. Colbert hoped, in like manner, by artificial legislation,
to foster the manufactures and finances of France, and
to insure to that kingdom spacious seaports, canals,
colonies, and a navy. The English East India company had but just revived, under Charles II., when
1664 France also gave privileges to an East India commercial corporation; and, if the folly of that corporation in
planting on the Island of Madagascar, where there was
nothing to sell or to buy, effected its decline, still the
1675. banner of the Bourbons reached Malabar and Coro-
mandel. The fourth African company, with the
1674. Stuarts for stockholders, and the slave trade for its
1679. object, soon found a rival in the Senegal company;
and, just at the time when the French king was most
1685. zealous for the conversion of the Huguenots, he established a Guinea company to trade from Sierra Leone
to the Cape of Good Hope. France was, through
Colbert and Seignelay, become a great naval power,
and had given her colonial system an extent even
vaster than that of the British. So eager was she in
her rivalry on the ocean, so menacing was the compe-

tition of her workshops in every article of ingenious manufacture, that the spirit of monopoly set its brand upon language, and men's consciences became so far debauched as to call England and France natural enemies.

Memory fostered the national antipathy; France had not forgotten English invasions of her soil, English victories over her sons.

France adhered to the old religion, and the revocation of the edict of Nantz made it a Catholic empire; England succeeded in a Protestant revolution, which made political power a monopoly of the Anglican Church, disfranchised all Catholics, and even subjected them, in Ireland, to a legal despotism.

In England, freedom of mind made its way through a series of aristocratic and plebeian sects, each of which found its support in the Bible; and the progress was so gradual, and under such variety of forms, both among the people and among philosophers, that the civil institutions were not endangered, even when freedom degenerated into skepticism or infidelity. In France, freedom of mind was introduced by philosophy, and, making its way, at one bound, to the absolute skepticism of pure reason, rejected every prejudice, and menaced the institutions of church and of state with an overthrow.

In England, philosophy existed as an empirical science; men measured and weighed the outward world, and constructed the prevailing systems of morals and metaphysics on observation and the senses. In France, the philosophic mind, under the guidance of Descartes, of Fenelon, of Leibnitz,—who belongs to the French world,—of Malebranche, assumed a character alike spiritual and universal.

CHAP. XX. Still more opposite were the governments. In France, feudal monarchy had been quelled by a military monarchy; in England, it had yielded to a parliamentary monarchy, in which government rested on property. France sustained the principle of legitimacy; England had selected its own sovereign, and to dispute his claims involved not only a question of national law, but of English independence.

To these causes of animosity, springing from the rivalry in manufactures and in commercial stations, from contrasts in religion, philosophy, opinion, and government, there was added a struggle for territory in North America. Not only in the West Indies, in the East Indies, in Africa, were France and England neighbors,—over far the largest part of our country Louis XIV. claimed to be the sovereign; and the prelude to the overthrow of the European colonial system, which was sure to be also the overthrow of the mercantile system, was destined to be the mighty struggle for the central regions of our republic.

The first permanent efforts of French enterprise, in colonizing America, preceded any permanent English settlement north of the Potomac. Years before the Pilgrims anchored within Cape Cod, the Roman church had been planted, by missionaries from France, in the
1615, 1616. eastern moiety of Maine; and Le Caron, an unambitious Franciscan, the companion of Champlain, had penetrated the land of the Mohawks, had passed to the north into the hunting-grounds of the Wyandots, and, bound by his vows to the life of a beggar, had, on foot, or paddling a bark canoe, gone onward and still onward, taking alms of the savages, till he reached the rivers of Lake Huron.

Sagard, Hist. du Canada.

1623, 1625 While Quebec contained scarce fifty inhabitants,

priests of the Franciscan order—Le Caron, Viel, Sa- CHAP. XX.
gard—had labored for years as missionaries in Upper Canada, or made their way to the neutral Huron tribe 1626.
that dwelt on the waters of the Niagara.

After the Canada company had been suppressed, 1622.
and their immunities had, for five years, been enjoyed by the Calvinists William and Emeric Caen, the hundred associates,—Richelieu, Champlain, Razilly, and 1627
opulent merchants, being of the number,—by a charter from Louis XIII., obtained a grant of New France, and, after the restoration of Quebec by its English 1632
conquerors, entered upon the government of their province. Its limits embraced specifically the whole basin of the St. Lawrence, and of such other rivers in New France as flowed directly into the sea; they included, moreover, Florida, or the country south of Virginia, esteemed a French province in virtue of the unsuccessful efforts of Coligny. Champlain, Voyages de.

Religious zeal, not less than commercial ambition, had influenced France to recover Canada; and Champlain, its governor, whose imperishable name will rival 1632, 1635
with posterity the fame of Smith and of Hudson, ever disinterested and compassionate, full of honor and probity, of ardent devotion and burning zeal, esteemed "the salvation of a soul worth more than the conquest of an empire." The commercial monopoly of a privileged company could not foster a colony; the climate of the country round Quebec, "where summer hurries through the sky," did not invite to agriculture; no persecutions of Catholics swelled the stream of emigration; and, at first, there was little, except religious enthusiasm, to give vitality to the province. Touched by the simplicity of the order of St. Francis, Champlain had selected its priests of the contemplative class for his

CHAP. XX. companions; "for they were free from ambition." But the aspiring honor of the Gallican church was interested; a prouder sympathy was awakened among the
1632. devotees at court; and, the Franciscans having, as a mendicant order, been excluded from the rocks and deserts of the New World, the office of converting the
Le Jeune, Brieve Relation 1632. heathen of Canada, and thus enlarging the borders of French dominion, was intrusted solely to the Jesuits.

The establishment of "the Society of Jesus" by Loyola had been contemporary with the reformation, of which it was designed to arrest the progress; and
1539, 1540. its complete organization belongs to the period when the first full edition of Calvin's Institutes saw the light. Its members were, by its rules, never to become prelates, and could gain power and distinction only by influence over mind. Their vows were, poverty, chastity, absolute obedience, and a constant readiness to go on missions against heresy or heathenism. Their cloisters became the best schools in the world. Emancipated, in a great degree, from the forms of piety, separated from domestic ties, constituting a community essentially intellectual as well as essentially plebeian, bound together by the most perfect organization, and having for their end a control over opinion among the scholars and courts of Europe and throughout the habitable globe, the order of the Jesuits held, as its ruling maxims, the widest diffusion of its influence, and the closest internal unity. Immediately on its institution, their missionaries, kindling with a heroism that defied every danger and endured every toil, made their way to the ends of the earth; they raised the emblem of man's salvation on the Moluccas, in Japan, in India, in Thibet, in Cochin China, and in China; they pene-

trated Ethiopia, and reached the Abyssinians; they planted missions among the Caffres: in California, on the banks of the Marañhon, in the plains of Paraguay, they invited the wildest of barbarians to the civilization of Christianity.

1632 The genius of Champlain, whose comprehensive mind planned enduring establishments for French commerce, and a career of discovery that should carry the lilies of the Bourbons to the extremity of North America, could devise no method of building up the dominion of France in Canada but by an alliance with the Hurons, or of confirming that alliance but by the establishment of missions. Such a policy was congenial to a church which cherishes every member of the human race, without regard to lineage or skin. It was, moreover, favored by the conditions of the charter itself, which recognized the neophyte among the savages as an enfranchised citizen of France.

Thus it was neither commercial enterprise nor royal ambition, which carried the power of France into the heart of our continent: the motive was religion. Religious enthusiasm colonized New England; and religious enthusiasm founded Montreal, made a conquest of the wilderness on the upper lakes, and explored the Mississippi. Puritanism gave New England its worship, and its schools; the Roman church created for Canada its altars, its hospitals, and its seminaries. The influence of Calvin can be traced in every New England village; in Canada, the monuments of feudalism and the Catholic church stand side by side; and the names of Montmorenci and Bourbon, of Levi and Condé, are mingled with memorials of St. Athanasius and Augustin, of St. Francis of Assisi, and Ignatius Loyola.

CHAP. XX.

1633, 1636.

Relation de ce qui s'est passé en la Nouvelle France, en l'année 1633.

Within three years after the second occupation of Canada, the number of Jesuit priests in the province reached fifteen; and every tradition bears testimony to their worth. They had the faults of ascetic superstition; but the horrors of a Canadian life in the wilderness were resisted by an invincible passive courage, and a deep internal tranquillity. Away from the amenities of life, away from the opportunities of vain-glory, they became dead to the world, and possessed their souls in unalterable peace. The few who lived to grow old, though bowed by the toils of a long mission, still kindled with the fervor of apostolic zeal. The history of their labors is connected with the origin of every celebrated town in the annals of French America: not a cape was turned, nor a river entered, but a Jesuit led the way.

Relation, &c 1634, 1635, &c.

Behold, then, the Jesuits Brebeuf and Daniel, soon to be followed by the gentler Lallemand, and many others of their order, bowing meekly in obedience to
1634 their vows, and joining a party of barefoot Hurons, who were returning from Quebec to their country. The journey, by way of the Ottawa and the rivers that interlock with it, was one of more than three hundred leagues, through a region horrible with forests. All day long, the missionaries must wade, or handle the oar. At night, there is no food for them but a scanty measure of Indian corn mixed with water; their couch is the earth or the rocks. At five-and-thirty waterfalls, the canoe is to be carried on the shoulders for leagues through thickest woods, or over roughest regions; fifty times, it was dragged by hand through shallows and rapids, over sharpest stones; and thus, swimming, wading, paddling, or bearing the canoe across the portages, with garments torn, with feet

mangled, yet with the breviary safely hung round the neck, and vows, as they advanced, to meet death twenty times over, if it were possible, for the honor of St. Joseph, the consecrated envoys made their way, by rivers, lakes, and forests, from Quebec to the heart of the Huron wilderness. There, to the north-west of Lake Toronto, near the shore of Lake Iroquois, which is but a bay of Lake Huron, they raised the first hum- 1634 Sept. ble house of the Society of Jesus among the Hurons— the cradle, it was said, of his church who dwelt at Bethlehem in a cottage. The little chapel, built by Creuxius, 163 aid of the axe, and consecrated to St. Joseph, where, in the gaze of thronging crowds, vespers and matins began to be chanted, and the sacred bread was consecrated by solemn mass, amazed the hereditary guardians of the council-fires of the Huron tribes. Beautiful testimony to the equality of the human race! the sacred wafer, emblem of the divinity in man, all that the church offered to the princes and nobles of the European world, was shared with the humblest of the savage neophytes. The hunter, as he returned from his wide roamings, was taught to hope for eternal rest; the braves, as they came from war, were warned of the wrath which kindles against sinners a never-dying fire, fiercer far than the fires of the Mohawks; the idlers of the Indian villages were told the exciting tale of the Savior's death for their redemption. Two new Christian villages, St. Louis and St. Ignatius, bloomed among the Huron forests. The dormant sentiment of pious veneration was awakened in many breasts, and there came to be even earnest and ascetic devotees uttering prayers and vows in the Huron tongue,— while tawny skeptics inquired, if there were indeed, in the centre of the earth, eternal flames for the unbelieving.

CHAP. XX.

The missionaries themselves possessed the weaknesses and the virtues of their order. For fifteen years enduring the infinite labors and perils of the Huron mission, and exhibiting, as it was said, "an absolute pattern of every religious virtue," Jean de Brebeuf, respecting even the nod of his distant superiors, bowed his mind and his judgment to obedience. Besides the assiduous fatigues of his office, each day, and sometimes twice in the day, he applied to himself the lash; beneath a bristling hair-shirt he wore an iron girdle, armed on all sides with projecting points; his fasts were frequent;
Creuxius, 553. almost always his pious vigils continued deep into the night. In vain did Asmodeus assume for him the forms of earthly beauty; his eye rested benignantly on visions of divine things. Once, imparadised in a trance, he beheld the Mother of Him whose cross he bore, surrounded by a crowd of virgins, in the beatitudes of
1640. heaven. Once, as he himself has recorded, while engaged in penance, he saw Christ unfold his arms to embrace him with the utmost love, promising oblivion of his sins. Once, late at night, while praying in the silence, he had a vision of an infinite number of crosses, and, with mighty heart, he strove, again and again, to grasp them all. Often he saw the shapes of foul fiends, now appearing as madmen, now as raging beasts; and often he beheld the image of Death, a bloodless form, by the side of the stake, struggling with bonds, and, at last, falling, as a harmless spectre,
1638. at his feet. Having vowed to seek out suffering for the greater glory of God, he renewed that vow every day, at the moment of tasting the sacred wafer; and,
Ragueneau, Relation, &c. 1648, p. 63, 64. as his cupidity for martyrdom grew into a passion, he exclaimed, "What shall I render to thee, Jesus, my Lord, for all thy benefits? I will accept thy cup, and

invoke thy name;" and, in sight of the Eternal Father and the Holy Spirit, of the most holy Mother of Christ and St. Joseph, before angels, apostles, and martyrs, before St. Ignatius and Francis Xavier, he made a vow never to decline the opportunity of martyrdom, and never to receive the death-blow but with joy. CHAP. XX.

The life of a missionary on Lake Huron was simple and uniform. The earliest hours, from four to eight, were absorbed in private prayer; the day was given to schools, visits, instruction in the catechism, and a service for proselytes. Sometimes, after the manner of St. Francis Xavier, Brebeuf would walk through the village and its environs, ringing a little bell, and inviting the Huron braves and counsellors to a conference. There, under the shady forest, the most solemn mysteries of the Catholic faith were subjected to discussion. It was by such means that the sentiment of piety was unfolded in the breast of the great warrior Ahasistari. Nature had planted in his mind the seeds of religious faith: "Before you came to this country," he would say, "when I have incurred the greatest perils, and have alone escaped, I have said to myself, 'Some powerful spirit has the guardianship of my days;'" and he professed his belief in Jesus, as the good genius and protector, whom he had before unconsciously adored. After trials of his sincerity, he was baptized; and, enlisting a troop of converts, savages like himself, "Let us strive," he exclaimed, "to make the whole world embrace the faith in Jesus."

As missionary stations multiplied, the central spot 1639.
was called St. Mary's, upon the banks of the Matchedash, the pleasant watercourse which joins Lake
Toronto to Huron. There, at the humble house dedi-
cated to the Virgin, in one year, three thousand guests Creuxius, 493.

CHAP. XX. from the cabins of the red man received a frugal welcome.

The news from this Huron Christendom awakened in France the strongest sympathy; religious communities, in Paris and in the provinces, joined in prayers for its advancement; the king sent magnificently embroidered garments as presents to the neophytes; the queen, the princesses of the blood, the clergy of France, even Italy listened with interest to the novel tale; and the pope himself expressed his favor. To confirm the missions, the first measure was the establishment of a college in New France; and the parents of the marquis de Gamache, pleased with his pious importunity, assented to his entering the order of the Jesuits, and added from their ample fortunes the means of endowing a seminary for education at Quebec. Its
1635. foundation was laid, under happy auspices, in 1635, just before Champlain passed from among the living, two years before the emigration of John Harvard, and one year before the general court of Massachusetts had made provision for a college.

The fires of charity were at the same time kindled. The duchess d'Aiguillon, aided by her uncle, the Cardinal Richelieu, endowed a public hospital, dedicated to the Son of God, whose blood was shed in mercy for all mankind. Its doors were open, not only to the sufferers among the emigrants, but to the maimed, the sick, and the blind of any of the numerous tribes between the Kennebec and Lake Superior; it received misfortune without asking its lineage. From the hospital nuns of Dieppe three were selected, the youngest but twenty-two, the eldest but twenty-nine, to brave the famine and the rigors of Canada in their patient missions of benevolence.

The same religious enthusiasm, inspiring Madame CHAP. XX.
de la Peltier, a young and opulent widow of Alençon,
with the aid of a nun from Dieppe and two others from 1639
Tours, established the Ursuline convent for the education of girls. As the youthful heroines stepped on Aug. 1.
shore at Quebec, they stooped to kiss the earth which Relation 1639.
they adopted as their country, and were ready, in case of need, to tinge with their blood. The governor, with the little garrison, received them at the water's edge; Hurons and Algonquins, joining in the shouts, filled the air with yells of joy; and the motley group escorted the new comers to the church, where, amidst a general thanksgiving, the Te Deum was chanted. Is it wonderful that the natives were touched by a benevolence which their poverty and squalid misery could not appall? Their education was also attempted; and the venerable ash-tree still lives, beneath which Mary of the Incarnation, so famed for chastened piety, genius, and good judgment, toiled, though in vain, for the culture of Huron children.

Meantime, a colony of the Hurons had been estab- 1637.
lished in the vicinity of Quebec; and the name of Silleri is the monument to the philanthropy of its projector. Here savages were to be trained to the faith and the manners of civilization.

Of Montreal, selected to be a nearer rendezvous for
converted Indians, possession was taken, in 1640, by a 1640
solemn mass, celebrated beneath a tent. In the following February, in France, at the cathedral of Our Lady 1641
of Paris, a general supplication was made that the Queen of Angels would take the Island of Montreal under her protection. In August of the same year, in the presence of the French gathered from all parts of Canada, and of the native warriors summoned from the wil-

CHAP. XX. derness, the festival of the assumption was solemnized on the island itself. Henceforward, the hearth of the sacred fires of the Wyandots was consecrated to the Virgin. "There the Mohawk and the feebler Algonquin," Relation 1640, 1641, p 211. said Le Jeune, "shall make their home; the wolf shall dwell with the lamb, and a little child shall guide them."

Yet the occupation of Montreal did not immediately 1641 to 1644. produce nearer relations with the Huron missionaries, who, for a period of three years, received no supplies whatever,—so that their clothes fell in pieces; they had no wine for the chalice but the juices of the wild grape, and scarce bread enough for consecration. Yet the efforts of the Jesuits were not limited even to the 1634 to 1647. Huron race. Within thirteen years, this remote wilderness was visited by forty-two missionaries, members of the Society of Jesus, besides eighteen others, who, if not initiated, were yet chosen men, ready to shed their blood for their faith. Twice or thrice a year, they all assembled at St. Mary's; for the rest of the time, they were scattered through the infidel tribes.

I would willingly trace their progress, as they gradually surveyed the coast of our republic, from the waters of the "Unghiara," or, as we write it, the Niagara, to the head of Lake Superior; but their narratives do but incidentally blend description with their details of conversions. Yet the map which was prepared by the order, at Paris, in 1660, proves that, in this earliest period, they had traced the highway of waters from Lake Erie to Lake Superior, and had gained a glimpse, at least, of Lake Michigan.

1638, 1639. Within six years after the recovery of Canada, the plan was formed of establishing missions, not only Relation 1638, 1639. p. 23, 24. among the Algonquins in the north, but south of Lake Huron, in Michigan, and at Green Bay; thus to gain access to the immense regions of the west and the north-west, to the great multitude from all nations, whom no one can number; but the Jesuits were too feeble, and too few, to attempt the spiritual conquest of so many countries: they pray for recruits; they invoke the blessing of the Divine Majesty on their thoughts and enterprises. CHAP. XX. Relation 1640, p. 211.

At the various missions, Indians from the remotest points appeared. In 1638, there came to the Huron mission a chief of the Huron tribe that dwelt on the head waters of the Ohio; and we find constant mention of Algonquins from the west, especially from Green Bay. Relation 1645-6, p. 86.

In the autumn of 1640, Charles Raymbault and Claude Pijart reached the Huron missions, destined for service among the Algonquins of the north and the west. By continual warfare with the Mohawks, the French had been excluded from the navigation of Lake Ontario, and had never even launched a canoe on Lake Erie. Their avenue to the west was by way of the Ottáwa and French River; so that the whole coast of Ohio and Southern Michigan remained unknown, except as seen by missionaries from their stations in Canada. In 1640, Brebeuf had been sent to the villages of the neutral nation which occupied the territory on the Niagara. Of these some villages were extended, on the southern shore of Lake Erie, beyond Buffalo; but it is not certain that Brebeuf visited them, or that he was at any time on the soil of our republic. His mission perfected the knowledge of the great watercourse of the valley of the St. Lawrence. "Could we but gain the mastery," it was said, "of the shore of Ontario on the side nearest the abode of the Iroquois, we could ascend by the St. Lawrence, with- Relation 1641, p. 12.

CHAP. XX. out danger, and pass free beyond Niagara, with a great saving of time and pains." Thus did Jesuits see Relation 1641. p. 50. the necessity of possessing a post in Western New York, seven years after the restoration of Quebec. At this time, no Englishman had reached the basin of the St. Lawrence. The country on the sea was held by the Dutch; that part of New York which is watered by streams that flow to the St. Lawrence, was first visited exclusively by the French.

But the fixed hostility and the power of the Five Nations left no hope of success in gaining safe intercourse by the St. Lawrence. To preserve the avenue to the west by the Ottáwa, Pijart and Charles Raymbault, in 1640, on their pilgrimage to the Huron country, attempted the conversion of the roving tribes that
1641. May 8. were masters of the highways; and, in the following
Relation 1642 p. 152. year, they roamed as missionaries with the Algonquins of Lake Nipissing.

Ibid. p. 153. Towards the close of summer, these wandering tribes prepared to celebrate "their festival of the dead,"—to gather up the bones of their deceased friends, and give them jointly an honorable sepulchre. To this ceremony all the confederate nations were
1641. Sept. invited; and, as they approach the shore, on a deep bay in Lake Iroquois, their canoes advance in regular array, and the representatives of nations leap on shore, uttering exclamations and cries of joy, which the rocks echo. The long cabin for the dead had been prepared; their bones are nicely disposed in coffins of bark, and wrapped in such furs as the wealth of Europe would have coveted; the mourning-song of the war-chiefs had been chanted, all night long, to the responsive wails of the women. The farewell to the dead, the dances, the councils, the presents,—all were

finished. But, before the assembly dispersed, the Jesuits, by their presents and their festivals, had won new affection, and an invitation was given to visit the nation of Chippewas at Sault Ste. Marie. CHAP. XX.

For the leader of this first invasion of the soil of our republic in the west, Charles Raymbault was selected; and, as Hurons were his attendants, Isaac Jogues was given him as a companion.

It was on the seventeenth day of September, 1641, that the birch-bark canoe, freighted with the first envoys from Christendom, left the Bay of Penetangushene for the Falls of St. Mary. Passing to the north, they floated over a wonted track till beyond the French River; then they passed onward over the beautifully clear waters and between the thickly clustering archipelagoes of Lake Huron, beyond the Manitoulins and other isles along the shore, to the straits that form the outlet of Lake Superior. There, at the falls, after a navigation of seventeen days, they found an assembly of two thousand souls. They made inquiries respecting many nations, who had never known Europeans, and had never heard of the one God. Among other nations, they heard of the Nadowessies, the famed Sioux, who dwelt eighteen days' journey farther to the west, beyond the Great Lake, then still without a name—warlike tribes, with fixed abodes, cultivators of maize and tobacco, of an unknown race and language. Thus did the religious zeal of the French bear the cross to the banks of the St. Mary and the confines of Lake Superior, and look wistfully towards the homes of the Sioux in the valley of the Mississippi, five years before the New England Eliot had addressed the tribe of Indians that dwelt within six miles of Boston harbor. 1641 Oct 4.

CHAP. XX. The chieftains of the Chippewas invited the Jesuits to dwell among them, and hopes were inspired of a permanent mission. A council was held. "We will embrace you," said they, "as brothers; we will derive profit from your words."

After finishing this excursion, Raymbault designed to rejoin the Algonquins of Nipissing, but the climate forbade; and late in the season, he returned to the har-
Relation 1642, p. 167. bor of the Huron missions, wasting away with consump-
1642–3, p. 271. tion. In midsummer of the next year, he descended
to Quebec. After languishing till October, the self-
1642. Oct. 22. denying man, who had glowed with the hope of bearing the gospel across the continent, through all the American Barbary, even to the ocean that divides America from China, ceased to live; and the body of this first apostle of Christianity to the tribes of Michigan was buried in "the particular sepulchre,"
Relation 1642, 1643, p. 27. which the justice of that age had "erected expressly to honor the memory of the illustrious" Champlain.

Thus the climate made one martyr;—the companion of Raymbault was destined to encounter a far more dreaded foe. The war parties of the Five Nations, hereditary enemies of the Hurons, and the deadly opponents of the French, controlled the passes between Upper Canada and Quebec; and each missionary on his pilgrimage was in danger of captivity. Such was
1642. the fate of Isaac Jogues, who, having been one of the first to carry the cross into Michigan, was now the first to bear it through the villages of the Mohawks. From the Falls of St. Mary he had repaired to the
June 13. Huron missions, and thence, with the escort of Ahasistari and other Huron braves, he descended by the
Aug. 1. Ottáwa and St. Lawrence to Quebec. On his return with a larger fleet of canoes, a band of Mohawks,

whose war parties, fearlessly strolling through the illimitable forest, were ever ready to burst suddenly upon their foes, lay in wait for the pilgrims, as they ascended the St. Lawrence. "There can be but three canoes of them," said Ahasistari, as, at day-break, he examined their trail on the shore: "there is nothing to fear," added this bravest of the braves. Unhappy confidence! The Mohawks, from their ambush, attacked the canoes, as they neared the land: the thin bark is perforated; Hurons, and Frenchmen, alike make for the shore, to find security in the thick forests. Jogues might have escaped also; but there were with him converts, who had not yet been baptized,—and when did a Jesuit missionary seek to save his own life, at what he believed the risk of a soul? Ahasistari had gained a hiding-place: observing Jogues to be a captive, he returned to him, saying, "My brother, I made oath to thee that I would share thy fortune, whether death or life; here am I to keep my vow."

CHAP. XX. 1642. Creuxius, 338–358. Aug.

The horrible inflictions of savage cruelty ensued, and were continued all the way from the St. Lawrence to the Mohawk. There they arrived the evening before the festival of the assumption of the Virgin; and, as he ran the gantlet, Jogues comforted himself with a vision of the glory of the queen of heaven. In a second and a third village, the same sufferings were encountered; for days and nights, he was abandoned to hunger and every torment which petulant youth could devise. But yet there was consolation: an ear of Indian corn on the stalk was thrown to the good father; and see! to the broad blade there clung little drops of dew or of water, enough to baptize two captive neophytes.

Relation &c. 1642, 1643, 1644.

Creuxius, 346

CHAP. XX. Three Hurons were condemned to the flames. The brave Ahasistari, having received absolution, met his end with the enthusiasm of a convert and the pride of the most gallant war-chief of his tribe.

Sad was the fate of the captive novice, René Goupil. He had been seen to make the sign of the
1642. cross on an infant's brow. "He will destroy the vil-
Sept. 19. lage by his charms," said his master; and, summoned while reciting, alternately with Jogues, the rosary of the Virgin, a blow with the tomahawk laid him lifeless.

Father Jogues had expected the same fate; but his life was spared, and his liberty enlarged. On a hill apart, he carved a long cross on a tree, and there, in the solitude, meditated the imitation of Christ, and soothed his griefs by reflecting that he alone, in that vast region, adored the true God of earth and heaven. Roaming through the stately forests of the Mohawk valley, he wrote the name of Jesus on the bark of trees, graved the cross, and entered into possession of these countries in the name of God,—often lifting up his voice in a solitary chant. Thus did France bring its banner and its faith to the confines of Albany. The missionary himself was humanely ransomed from captivity by the Dutch, and, sailing for France, soon
ogues' Letter from Albany. returned to Canada.

Similar was the fate of Father Bressani. Taken
1644. prisoner while on his way to the Hurons; beaten,
May. mangled, mutilated; driven barefoot over rough paths, through briers and thickets; scourged by a whole village; burned, tortured, wounded, and scarred,—he was eye-witness to the fate of one of his companions, who was boiled and eaten. Yet some mysterious awe
Creuxius, 395 to 403. protected his life, and he, too, was, at last, humanely rescued by the Dutch.

CHAP. XX. 1645.

Meantime, to make good the possession of the country, a treaty of peace is sought by the French with the Five Nations, and at Three Rivers a great meeting is held. There are the French officers in their magnificence; there the five Iroquois deputies, couched upon mats, bearing strings of wampum. It was agreed to smooth the forest-path, to calm the river, to hide the tomahawk. "Let the clouds be dispersed," said the Iroquois; "let the sun shine on all the land between us." The Algonquins joined in the peace. "Here is a skin of a moose," said Negabamat, chief of the Montagnez; "make moccasins for the Mohawk deputies, lest they wound their feet on their way home."—"We have thrown the hatchet," said the Mohawks, "so high into the air, and beyond the skies, that no arm on earth can reach to bring it down. The French shall sleep on our softest blankets, by the warm fire, that shall be kept blazing all the night long. The shades of our braves that have fallen in war, have gone so deep into the earth that they never can be heard calling for revenge."—"I place a stone on their graves," said Pieskaret, "that no one may move their bones."

With greater sincerity, the Abenakis of Maine, touched by the charities of Silleri, had solicited missionaries. Conversion to Catholic Christianity would establish their warlike tribes as a wakeful barrier against New England; and, in August, 1646, Father Gabriel Dreuillettes, first of Europeans, made the long and painful journey from the St. Lawrence to the sources of the Kennebec, and, descending that stream to its mouth, in a bark canoe continued his roamings on the open sea along the coast. The cross was already planted there,—raised by the disciples of St.

1646. Aug. 29.

Relation 1647, p. 176 to 193.

CHAP. XX. Francis of Assisi over their humble lodge near the mouth of the Penobscot. After a short welcome, the earnest apostle returned to the wilderness; and, a few miles above the mouth of the Kennebec, the Indians, in large numbers, gathered about him, building a rude chapel. In the winter, he was their companion in their long excursions in quest of game. Who can tell all the hazards that were encountered? The sharp rocks in the channel of the river were full of perils for the frail canoe; winter turned the solitudes into a wilderness of snow; the rover, Christian or pagan, must carry about with him his house, his furniture, and his food. But the Jesuit succeeded in winning the affections of the savages; and, after a pilgrimage of ten
1647. June 15. months, an escort of thirty conducted him to Quebec, full of health and joy.

Thus, in September, 1646, within fourteen years from the restoration of Quebec, France, advancing rapidly towards a widely extended dominion in North America, had its outposts on the Kennebec, and on the shores of Lake Huron, and had approached the settlements round Albany. The missionaries, exalted by zeal, enjoyed a fearless tranquillity, and were pledged to obedience unto death.

The whole strength of the colony lay in the missions. The government was weakened by the royal
1646. jealousy; the population hardly increased; there was no military force; and the trading company, deriving no income but from peltries and Indian traffic, had no motive to make large expenditures for protecting the settlements or promoting colonization. Thus the missionaries were left, almost alone, to contend against the thousands of braves that roamed over Acadia and the vast basin of the St. Lawrence. But what could

sixty or seventy devotees accomplish amongst the CHAP XX.
countless wild tribes from Nova Scotia to Lake Superior? They were at war as well with nature as
with savage inhumanity, and had to endure perils and
sufferings under every form. The frail bark of the
Franciscan Viel had been dashed in pieces, and the 1623.
missionary drowned, as he was shooting a rapid, on
his way from the Hurons. Father Anne de Noué, in
the depth of winter, leaves Quebec for the mouth of
the Sorel, to shrive the garrison; and, losing his way
among pathless snows, perishes by the frosts of Canada. No faithful Jesuit would allow an infant to die
unbaptized; and the Indian father, interpreting the
sprinkling as a device to kill his child, avenged his
affections by the death of the missionary. Still
greater was the danger which sprung from the hostility of the tribes towards the French, or towards the
nations by whom their envoys were received.

A treaty of peace had, indeed, been ratified, and, 1645 1646
for one winter, Algonquins, Wyandots, and Iroquois,
joined in the chase. The wilderness seemed hushed
into tranquillity. Negotiations also continued. In
May, 1646, Father Jogues, commissioned as an en- 1646.
voy, was hospitably received by the Mohawks, and Relation 1647.
gained an opportunity of offering the friendship of
France to the Onondagas. On his return, his favora- June 27.
ble report raised a desire of establishing a permanent
mission among the Five Nations; and he himself, the
only one who knew their dialect, was selected as its
founder. "*Ibo, et non redibo*"—I shall go, but shall Oct.
never return—were his words of farewell. Immediately on arriving at the Mohawk castles, he was received as a prisoner, and, against the voice of the
other nations, was condemned by the grand council Oct. 18.

CHAP. XX. of the Mohawks as an enchanter, who had blighted their harvest. Timid by nature, yet tranquil from zeal, he approached the cabin where the death-festival was kept, and, as he entered, received the death-blow. His head was hung upon the palisades of the village, his body thrown into the Mohawk River.

This was the signal for war. The Iroquois renewed their invasions of the Huron country. In vain
1648. did the French seek to engage New England as an ally in the contest. The Huron nation was doomed; the ancient clans of the Wyandots were to be exterminated or scattered; and the missionaries on the Matchedash shared the dangers of the tribes with whom they dwelt.

Relation 1648, 8—17. Each sedentary mission was a special point of attraction to the invader, and each, therefore, was liable to the horrors of an Indian massacre. Such was the fate of the village of St. Joseph. On the morning of July 4, 1648, when the braves were absent on the chase, and none but women, children, and old men, remained at home, Father Anthony Daniel hears the cry of danger and confusion. He flies to the scene to behold his converts, in the apathy of terror, falling victims to the fury of Mohawks. No age, however tender, excites mercy; no feebleness of sex wins compassion. A group of women and children fly to him to escape the tomahawk,—as if his lips, uttering messages of love, could pronounce a spell that would curb the madness of destruction. Those who had formerly scoffed his mission, implore the benefit of baptism. He bids them ask forgiveness of God, and, dipping his handkerchief in water, baptizes the crowd of suppliants by aspersion. Just then, the palisades are forced. Should he fly? He first ran to the wigwams to baptize the sick; he next pronounced a general absolution on all who sought it, and then prepared to resign his life as a sacrifice to his vows. The wigwams are set on fire; the Mohawks approach the chapel, and the consecrated envoy serenely advances to meet them. Astonishment seized the barbarians. At length, drawing near, they discharge at him a flight of arrows. All gashed and rent by wounds, he still continued to speak with surprising energy,—now inspiring fear of the divine anger, and again, in gentle tones, yet of more piercing power than the whoops of the savages, breathing the affectionate messages of mercy and grace. Such were his actions till he received a death-blow from a halbert. The victim to the heroism of charity died, the name of Jesus on his lips: the wilderness gave him a grave; the Huron nation were his mourners. By his religious associates it was believed that he appeared twice after his death, youthfully radiant in the sweetest form of celestial glory; that, as the reward for his torments, a crowd of souls, redeemed from purgatory, were his honoring escort into heaven. 1648.

Not a year elapsed, when, in the dead of a Canadian winter, a party of a thousand Iroquois fell, before dawn, upon the little village of St. Ignatius. It was sufficiently fortified, but only four hundred persons were present, and there were no sentinels. The palisades were set on fire, and an indiscriminate massacre of the sleeping inhabitants followed. 1649. March 16.

The village of St. Louis was alarmed, and its women and children fly to the woods, while eighty warriors prepare a defence. A breach is made in the palisades; the enemy enter; and the group of Indian cabins becomes a slaughter-house. In this village

CHAP. XX. resided Jean de Brebeuf, and the younger and gentler, yet not less patient, Gabriel Lallemand. The character of Brebeuf was firm beyond every trial;—his virtue had been nursed in the familiar sight of death. Disciplined by twenty years' service in the wilderness work, he wept bitterly for the sufferings of his converts, but for himself he exulted in the prospect of martyrdom. Both the missionaries might have escaped; but here, too, there were converts not yet baptized; besides, the dying might, in the hour of agony, desire the ordinances; and both, therefore, remain. They exhort the combatants to fear God: they bend over the dying to give them baptism, and claim their spirits as redeemed.

Success was with the Mohawks: the Jesuit priests are now their prisoners, to endure all the tortures which the ruthless fury of a raging multitude could invent. Brebeuf was set apart on a scaffold, and, in the midst of every outrage, rebuked his persecutors, and encouraged his Huron converts. They cut his lower lip and his nose; applied burning torches to his body; burned his gums, and thrust hot iron down his throat. Deprived of his voice, his assured countenance and confiding eye still bore witness to his firmness.

The delicate Lallemand was stripped naked, and enveloped from head to foot with bark full of rosin. Brought into the presence of Brebeuf, he exclaimed, "We are made a spectacle unto the world, and to angels, and to men." The pine bark was set on fire, and, when it was in a blaze, boiling water was poured on the heads of both the missionaries. The voice of Lallemand was choked by the thick smoke; but, the fire having snapped his bonds, he lifted his hands to heaven, imploring the aid of Him who is an aid to the weak. What need of many words? Brebeuf was scalped while yet alive, and died after a torture of three hours; the sufferings of Lallemand were prolonged for seventeen hours. The lives of both had been a continual heroism; their deaths were the astonishment of their executioners.

It may be asked, if these massacres quenched enthusiasm. I answer, that the Jesuits never receded one foot; but as, in a brave army, new troops press forward to fill the places of the fallen, there were never wanting heroism and enterprise in behalf of the cross and French dominion.

It was intended to collect the scattered remnants of the Hurons in the Grand Manitoulin Isle, which was chosen to be the centre of the western missions. "We shall be nearer," wrote Rageneau, cheeringly, "to the Algonquins of the west;" and, as the way to Quebec, even by the Ottawa and the St. Lawrence, was no longer safe, it was thought that, through the remote wilderness, some safe avenue might yet be opened. But the Hurons, destined to be scattered through the widest regions, hovered, for a season, round the isles that were nearest the graves of their ancestors; and the mission on the Grand Manitoulin was abandoned.

1649.

Relation 1648-9, p. 92.

Ibid. 93.

But the great point of desire was the conversion of the Five Nations themselves. Undismayed by barbarism, or the martyrdom of their brethren, the missionaries were still eager to gain admission; but the Mohawks, and the other tribes, having now, through commerce with the Dutch, learned the use of fire-arms, seemed resolved on asserting their power in every direction,—not only over the barbarians of the north, the west, and the south-west, but over the

CHAP. XX. French themselves. They bade defiance to forts and entrenchments; their war parties triumphed at Three
1651. Rivers, were too powerful for the palisades of Silleri, and proudly passed by the walls of Quebec. The Ottáwas were driven from their old abodes to the forests in the Bay of Saginaw. No frightful solitude in the wilderness, no impenetrable recess in the frozen north, was safe against the passions of the Five Nations. Their chiefs, animated not by cruelty only, but by pride, were resolved that no nook should escape their invasions; that no nation should rule but themselves; and, as their warriors strolled by Three Rivers and Quebec, they killed the governor of the one settlement,
1653. and carried off a priest from the other.

At length, satisfied with the display of their power, they themselves desired rest. Besides, of the scattered Hurons, many had sought refuge among their oppressors, and, according to an Indian custom, had been incorporated with the tribes of the Five Nations. Of these, some retained affection for the French. When
1654. peace was concluded, and Father Le Moyne appeared as envoy among the Onondagas to ratify the treaty, he found there a multitude of Hurons, who, like the Jews at Babylon, retained their faith in a land of strangers. The hope was renewed of winning the whole west and north to Christendom.

The villages bordering on the settlements of the Dutch, were indifferent to the peace; the western tribes, who could more easily traffic with the French,
1654. adhered to it firmly. At last, the Mohawks also grew weary of the strife; and Le Moyne, selecting the banks of their river for his abode, resolved to persevere, in the vain hope of infusing into their savage nature the gentler spirit of civilization.

The Onondagas were more sincere; and when Chaumonot, an Italian priest, long a missionary among the Hurons, left Quebec for their territory, he was accompanied by Claude Dablon, a missionary, who had recently arrived from France. They were hospitably welcomed at Onondaga, the principal village of the tribe. A general convention was held, by their desire; and, before the multitudinous assembly of the chiefs and the whole people, gathered under the open sky, among the primeval forests, the presents were delivered; and the Italian Jesuit, with much gesture, after the Italian manner, discoursed so eloquently to the crowd, that it seemed to Dablon as if the word of God had been preached to all the nations of that land. On the next day, the chiefs and others crowded round the Jesuits, with their songs of welcome. "Happy land!" they sang; "happy land! in which the French are to dwell;" and the chief led the chorus, "Glad tidings! glad tidings! it is well that we have spoken together; it is well that we have a heavenly message." At once, a chapel sprung into existence, and, by the zeal of the natives, was finished in a day. "For marbles and precious metals," writes Dablon, "we employed only bark; but the path to heaven is as open through a roof of bark as through arched ceilings of silver and gold." The savages showed themselves susceptible of the excitements of religious ecstasy; and there, in the heart of New York, the solemn services of the Roman church were chanted as securely as in any part of Christendom. The charter of the hundred associates included the basin of every tributary of the St. Lawrence. The Onondagas dwelt exclusively on the Oswego and its tributary waters: their land was, therefore, a part of

CHAP. XX. 1655. Journal de Dablon Nov. 5. Nov 15. 16. 18.

CHAP. XX. the empire of France. The cross and the lily, emblems of France and Christianity, were now known in the basin of the Oswego.

The success of the mission encouraged Dablon to invite a French colony into the land of the Onondagas; and, though the attempt excited the jealousy of the Mohawks, whose war chiefs, in their hunt after Huron fugitives, still roamed even to the Isle of Orleans, a
1656. May 7. company of fifty Frenchmen embarked for Onondaga. Diffuse harangues, dances, songs, and feastings, were
July 11. their welcome from the Indians. In a general convo-
July 24. cation of the tribe, the question of adopting Christianity as its religion was debated; and sanguine hope already included the land of the Onondagas as a part of Christendom. The chapel, too small for the throng of worshippers that assembled to the sound of its little bell, was enlarged. The Cayugas also desired a missionary, and they received the fearless René Mesnard. In their village, a chapel was erected, with mats for the tapestry; and there the pictures of the Savior and of
Mesnard, in Relation 1656-7, p. 158. the Virgin mother were unfolded to the admiring children of the wilderness. The Oneidas also listened to
1657. the missionary; and, early in 1657, Chaumonot reached
Relation 1656-7, c. xvii. the more fertile and more densely peopled land of the Senecas. The influence of France was planted in the beautiful valleys of Western New York. The Jesuit priests published their faith from the Mohawk to the Genesee, Onondaga remaining the central station.

But the savage nature of the tribes was unchanged. At this very time, a ruthless war of extermination was waged against the nation of Erie, and in the north of
Jean de Quens, 115. Ohio. The crowded hamlet became a scene of carnage. Prisoners, too, were brought home to the villages,

and delivered to the flames;—and what could the Jesuits expect of nations who could burn even children with refinements of tortures? "Our lives," said Mesnard, "are not safe." In Quebec, and in France, men trembled for the missionaries. They pressed upon the steps of their countrymen, who had been boiled and roasted; they made their home among cannibals; hunger, thirst, nakedness, were to be encountered; nature itself offered trials; and the first colony of the French, making its home near the Lake of Onondaga, and encountering the forest with the axe, suffered from fever before they could prepare their tenements. Border collisions also continued The Oneidas murdered three Frenchmen, and the French retaliated by seizing Iroquois. At last, when a conspiracy was framed in the tribe of the Onondagas, the French, having vainly solicited reënforcements, abandoned their chapel, their cabins, and their hearths, and the valley of the Oswego. The Mohawks compelled Le Moyne to return; and the French and the Five Nations were once more at war. Such was the issue of the most successful attempt at French colonization in New York. The Dutch of New Amsterdam were to give way to the English; and the union of the English colonies was a guaranty that France could never regain the mastery.

CHAP. XX. 1657. 1658. March 19. 1658, 1659.

Meantime, the Jesuits reached our country in the far west. In August, 1654, two young fur traders, smitten with the love of adventure, joined a band of the Ottawas, or other Algonquins, and, in their little gondolas of bark, ventured on a voyage of five hundred leagues. After two years, they reappeared, accompanied by a fleet of fifty canoes, urged forward by five hundred arms. The natives ascend the cliff of St. Louis, wel-

1654. Aug. 6. Relation 1655, 6, c. xiv. xv. xvi.

CHAP. XX. comed by a salute from the ordnance of the castle They describe the vast lakes of the west, and the numerous tribes that hover round them; they speak of the Knisteneaux, whose homes stretched away to the Northern Sea; of the powerful Sioux, who dwelt beyond Lake Superior; and they demand commerce with the French, and missionaries for the boundless west.

1656. The request was eagerly granted; and Gabriel Dreuillettes, the same who carried the cross through the forests of Maine, and Leonard Gareau, of old a missionary among the Hurons, were selected as the first religious envoys to a land of sacrifices, shadows, and deaths. The canoes are launched; the tawny mariners embark; the oars flash, and sounds of joy and triumph mingle with the last adieus. But, just below Montreal, a band of Mohawks, enemies to the
Aug. 30. Ottawas, awaited the convoy; in the affray, Gareau was mortally wounded, and the fleet dispersed.

The remote nations, by the necessity of the case, still sought alliance with the French. The Mohawks, and their confederates, receiving European arms from Albany, exterminated the Eries, and approached the Miamis and the Illinois. The western Indians desired commerce with the French, that they might gain means to resist the Iroquois; and, as furs were abun-
Relation 1659, 1660. dant there, the traders pressed forward to Green Bay.
1659. Two of them dared to pass the winter of 1659 on the banks of Lake Superior. Enriched with knowledge of the western world, in the summer of 1660, they came down to Quebec, with an escort of sixty canoes, rowed by three hundred Algonquins, and laden with peltry.

If the Five Nations can penetrate these remote re-

gions, to satiate their passion for blood; if mercantile CHAP. XX.
enterprise can bring furs from the plains of the Sioux;—
why cannot the cross be borne to their cabins, and the 1660.
name of the king of France be pronounced in their
councils? The zeal of Francis de Laval, the bishop
of Quebec, kindled with a desire himself to enter on
the mission; but the lot fell to René Mesnard. He
was charged to visit Green Bay and Lake Superior,
and, on a convenient inlet, to establish a residence as
the common place of assembly for the surrounding nations. His departure was immediate, and with few
preparations; for he trusted—such are his words—"in
the Providence which feeds the little birds of the des- Letter of Mesnard.
ert, and clothes the wild flowers of the forests." Ev-
ery personal motive seemed to retain him at Quebec;
but "powerful instincts" impelled him to the enterprise. Obedient to his vows, the aged man entered Aug.
on the path that was red with the blood of his predecessors, and made haste to scatter the seeds of truth
through the wilderness, even though the sower cast
his seed in weeping. "In three or four months," he
wrote to a friend, "you may add me to the memento
of deaths." In October, he reached the bay which he Oct. 15.
called St. Theresa, and which may have been the Bay
of Keweena, on the south shore of Lake Superior.
After a residence of eight months, he yielded to the
invitation of Hurons who had taken refuge in the Isle 1661.
of St. Michael; and, bidding farewell to his neophytes
and the French, and to those whom he never more
should meet on earth, he departed, with one attendant,
for the Bay of Che-goi-me-gon. The accounts would
indicate that he took the route by way of Keweena
Lake and Portage. There, while his attendant was
employed in the labor of transporting the canoe, Mes- Aug. 20.

CHAP. XX. nard was lost in the forest, and was never again seen. Long afterwards, his cassock and his breviary were kept as amulets among the Sioux.

1660. Meantime, the colony of New France was too feeble to defend itself against the dangerous fickleness and increasing confidence of the Iroquois: the very harvest could not be gathered in safety; the convents were insecure; many prepared to return to France; in moments of gloom, it seemed as if all must be abandoned.
1661. True, religious zeal was still active. Le Moyne once more appeared among the Five Nations, and was received with affection at Onondaga. The deputies of the Senecas, the Cayugas, and the Onondagas, assem-
Aug. 12. bled to the sound of the bell that had belonged to the chapel of the Jesuits; and the resolve of the council was, peace. But he could influence only the upper nations. The Mohawks would not be appeased;
1662. Montreal was not safe—one ecclesiastic was killed near its gates; a new organization of the colony was needed, or it would come to an end.

1663. Feb. 14. The company of the hundred associates resolved, therefore, to resign the colony to the king; and immediately, under the auspices of Colbert, it was conceded to the new company of the West Indies.

A powerful appeal was made, in favor of Canada, to the king; the company of Jesuits publicly invited him to assume its defence, and become their champion against the Iroquois. After various efforts at fit appointments, the year 1665 saw the colony of New France protected by a royal regiment, with the aged but indefatigable Tracy as viceroy; with Courcelles, a veteran soldier, as governor; and with Talon, a man of business and of integrity, as intendant and representative of the king in civil affairs. Every omen was favorable, save the conquest of New Netherlands by the English. That conquest eventually made the Five Nations a dependence on the English world; and if, for twenty-five years, England and France sued for their friendship, with uncertain success, yet, afterwards, in the grand division between parties throughout the world, the Bourbons found in them implacable opponents. How wonderful are the decrees of Providence! The Europeans, in their struggle against legitimacy and for freedom, having come all the way into the wilderness, pursued the contest even there, making of the Iroquois allies, and of their hunting-fields battle-grounds.

CHAP. XX.

With better hopes,—undismayed by the sad fate of Gareau and Mesnard,—indifferent to hunger, nakedness, and cold, to the wreck of the ships of bark, and to fatigues and weariness, by night and by day,—in August, 1665, Father Claude Alloüez embarked on a mission, by way of the Ottawa, to the far west. Early in September, he reached the rapids, through which the waters of the upper lakes rush to the Huron, and admired the beautiful river, with its woody isles and inviting bays. On the second of that month, he entered the lake which the savages reverenced as a divinity, and of which the entrance presents a spectacle of magnificence rarely excelled in the rugged scenery of the north. He passed the lofty ridge of naked sand, which stretches along the shore its stupendous piles of drifting barrenness; he sailed by the cliffs of pictured sandstone, which, for twelve miles, rise three hundred feet in height, fretted by the violence of the chafing waves into arches and bastions, caverns and towering walls, heaps of prostrate ruins, and erect columns crowned with fantastic entabla-

1665 Aug. 8.

Schoolcraft

CHAP. XX. tures. Landing on the south shore, he said mass,—thus consecrating the forests, which he claimed for a Alloüez, Journal, 37. Christian king.

Sailing beyond the Bay of St. Theresa, and having vainly sought for a mass of pure copper, of which he 1665. Oct. 1. had heard rumors, on the first day of October he arrived at the great village of the Chippewas, in the Bay of Che-goi-me-gon. It was at a moment when the young warriors were bent on a strife with the warlike Sioux. A grand council of ten or twelve Relation 1666, 7, c. iv. neighboring nations was held to wrest the hatchet from the hands of the rash braves; and Alloüez was admitted to an audience before the vast assembly. In the name of Louis XIV. and his viceroy, he commanded peace, and offered commerce and an alliance against the Iroquois: the soldiers of France would smooth the path between the Chippewas and Quebec; would brush the pirate canoes from the rivers; would leave to the Five Nations no choice but between tranquillity and destruction. On the shore of the bay, 1665 to 1667. to which the abundant fisheries attracted crowds, a chapel soon rose, and the mission of the Holy Spirit was founded. There admiring throngs, who had never seen a European, came to gaze on the white man, and on the pictures which he displayed of the realms of hell and of the last judgment; there a choir of Chippewas were taught to chant the pater and the ave. During his long sojourn, he lighted the torch of faith for more than twenty different nations. The dwellers round the Sault, a band of "the Outehibouec," as the Jesuits called the Chippewas, pitched their tents near his cabin for a month, and received his instructions. The scattered Hurons and Ottawas, that roamed the deserts north of Lake Superior, appealed to his compassion, and, before his return, obtained his presence in their morasses. From the unexplored recesses of Lake Michigan came the Potawatomies; and these worshippers of the sun invited him to their homes. The Sacs and Foxes travelled on foot from their country, which abounded in deer, and beaver, and buffalo. The Illinois, also,—a hospitable race, unaccustomed to canoes, having no weapon but the bow and arrow,—came to rehearse their sorrows. Their ancient glory and their numbers had been diminished by the Sioux, on the one side, and the Iroquois, armed with muskets, on the other. Curiosity was roused by their tale of the noble river on which they dwelt, and which flowed towards the south. "They had no forests, but, instead of them, vast prairies, where herds of deer and buffalo, and other animals, grazed on the tall grasses." They explained, also, the wonders of their peace-pipe, and declared it their custom to welcome the friendly stranger with shouts of joy. "Their country," said Alloüez, "is the best field for the gospel. Had I had leisure, I would have gone to their dwellings, to see with my own eyes all the good that was told me of them."

CHAP. XX.

Relation 1666, 7, 105, 6.

Ibid. 106-108

Ibid. 110.

Then, too, at the very extremity of the lake, the missionary met the wild, impassive warriors of the Sioux, who dwelt to the west of Lake Superior, in a land of prairies, with wild rice for food, and skins of beasts, instead of bark, for roofs to their cabins, on the banks of the Great River, of which Alloüez reported the name to be "Messipi."

Ibid. 111

After residing for nearly two years chiefly on the southern margin of Lake Superior, and connecting his name imperishably with the progress of discovery in the west, Alloüez returned to Quebec to urge the

1667 Aug.

CHAP. XX. establishment of permanent missions, to be accompanied by little colonies of French emigrants;—and such Relation 1666, 7. 129. was his own fervor, such the earnestness with which he was seconded, that, in two days, with another priest, Louis Nicolas, for his companion, he was on his way, returning to the mission at Chegoimegon.

1668. The prevalence of peace favored the progress of French dominion; the company of the West Indies, resigning its monopoly of the fur trade, gave an impulse to Canadian enterprise; a recruit of missionaries had arrived from France; and Claude Dablon and James Marquette repaired to the Chippewas at the Sault, to establish the mission of St. Mary. It is the oldest settlement begun by Europeans within the present limits of the commonwealth of Michigan.

For the succeeding years, the illustrious triumvirate, Alloüez, Dablon, and Marquette, were employed in confirming the influence of France in the vast regions that extend from Green Bay to the head of Lake Superior,—mingling happiness with suffering, and winning enduring glory by their fearless perseverance. For to what inclemencies, from nature and from man, was each missionary among the barbarians exposed! He defies the severity of climate, wading through water or through snows, without the comfort of fire; having no bread but pounded maize, and often no food but the unwholesome moss from the rocks; laboring incessantly; exposed to live, as it were, without nourishment, to sleep without a resting-place, to travel far, and always incurring perils,—to carry his life in his hand, or rather daily, and oftener than every day, to hold it up as a target, expecting captivity, death from the tomahawk, tortures, fire. And yet the simplicity and the freedom of life in the wilderness had

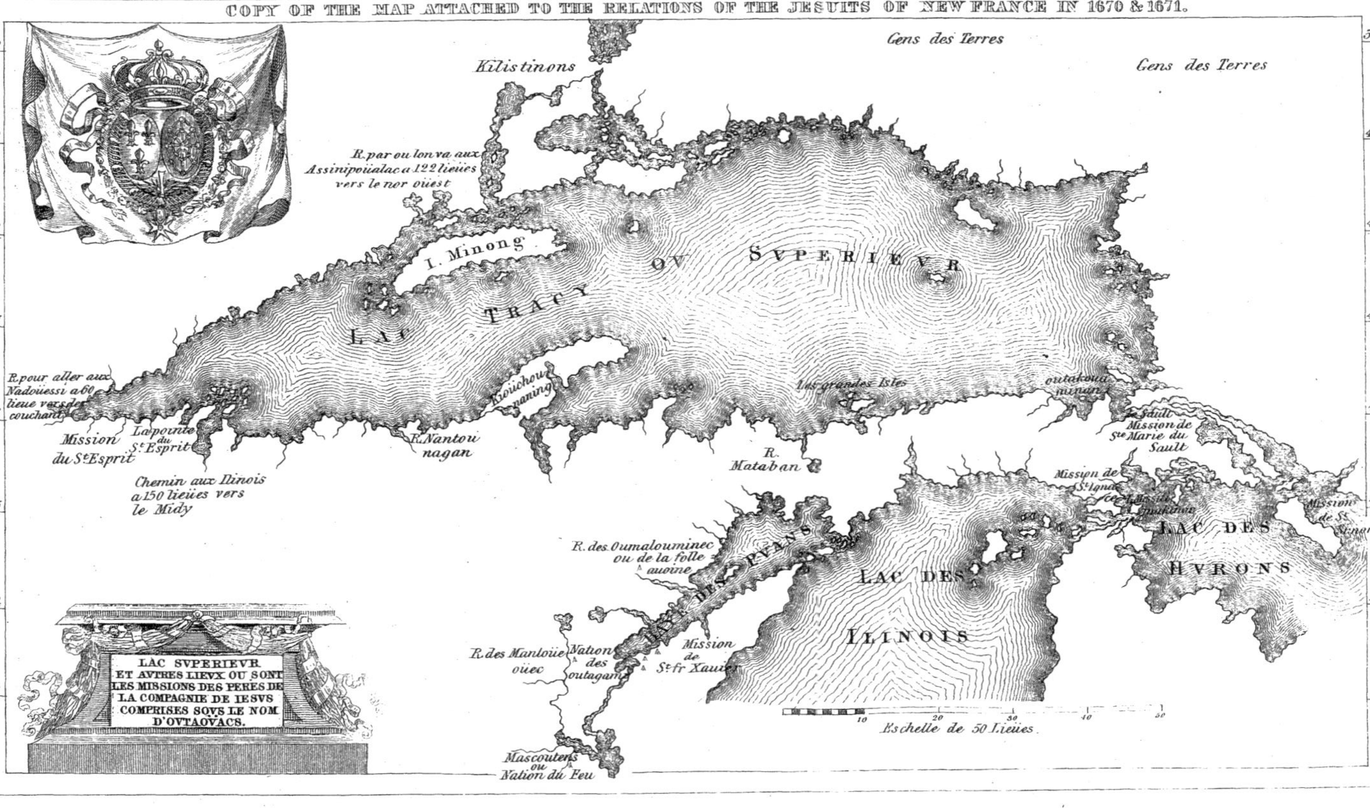
COPY OF THE MAP ATTACHED TO THE RELATIONS OF THE JESUITS OF NEW FRANCE IN 1670 & 1671.
Gens des Terres
Gens des Terres
Kilistinons
R. par ou lon va aux Assinipoüalac a 122 lieües vers le nor oüest
I. Minong
LAC TRACY OV SVPERIEVR
R. pour aller aux Nadoüessi a 60 lieue vers le couchant
Mission du St. Esprit
La pointe du St. Esprit
Chemin aux Ilinois a 150 lieües vers le Midy
R. Nantou nagan
Kioüchou aning
Les grandes Isles
outakoua minan
R. Mataban
Le Sault
Mission de Ste Marie du Sault
Mission de St. Ignace
Mission de St. Simon
LAC DES HVRONS
LAC DES ILINOIS
BAYE DES PVANS
R. des Oumalouminec ou de la folle auoine
R. des Manloüe oüec
Nation des outagami
Mission de St. fr Xauier
Mascoutens ou Nation du Feu
Eschelle de 50 Lieües
LAC SVPERIEVR ET AVTRES LIEVX OU SONT LES MISSIONS DES PERES DE LA COMPAGNIE DE IESVS COMPRISES SOVS LE NOM D'OVTAOVACS.

their charms. The heart of the missionary would swell CHAP. XX.
with delight, as, under a serene sky, and with a mild
temperature, and breathing a pure air, he moved over Relation 1659, 60.
waters as transparent as the most limpid fountain. Charlevoix, iii.
Every encampment offered his attendants the pleasures of the chase. Like a patriarch, he dwelt beneath a tent; and of the land through which he walked, he was its master, in the length of it and in the breadth of it, profiting by its productions, without the embarrassment of ownership. How often was the pillow of stones like that where Jacob felt the presence of God! How often did the ancient oak, of which the centuries were untold, seem like the tree of Mamre, beneath which Abraham broke bread with angels! Each day gave the pilgrim a new site for his dwelling, which the industry of a few moments would erect, and for which nature provided a floor of green inlaid with flowers. On every side clustered beauties, which art had not spoiled, and could not imitate.

The purpose of discovering the Mississippi, of which 1669
the tales of the natives had published the magnificence, Relation 1669, 70, p. 11.
sprung from Marquette himself. He had resolved on Ibid. 53.
attempting it, in the autumn of 1669; and, when delay intervened, from the necessity of employing him- Sept. 13.
self at Che-goi-me-gon, which Alloüez had exchanged for a new mission at Green Bay, he selected a young 1669,
Illinois as a companion, by whose instructions he be- 1670
came familiar with the dialect of that tribe.

Continued commerce with the French gave protec- 1670.
tion to the Algonquins of the west, and confirmed their attachment. A political interest grew up, and extended to Colbert and the ministry of Louis XIV. It became the fixed purpose of Talon, the intendant of the colony, to spread the power of France to the

CHAP. XX. utmost borders of Canada. To this end, Nicolas Perrot appeared as his agent in the west, to propose a congress of the nations at St. Mary's. The invitation reached the tribes of Lake Superior, and was carried even to the wandering hordes of the remotest north. Nor did the messenger neglect the south: obtaining, at Green Bay, an escort of Potawatomies, he, the first of Europeans, repaired on the same mission of friendship to the Miamis at Chicago.

1671. May. The day appointed for the unwonted spectacle of the congress of nations arrived; and, with Alloüez as his interpreter, St. Lusson, fresh from an excursion to Southern Canada,—that is, the borders of the Kennebec, where English habitations were already sown broadcast along the coast,—appeared at the Falls of St. Mary as the delegate of Talon. There are assembled the envoys of the wild republicans of the wilderness, and brilliantly-clad officers from the veteran armies of France. It was formally announced to the natives, gathered, as they were, from the head-springs of the St. Lawrence, the Mississippi, and the Red River, that they were placed under the protection of the French king. A cross of cedar was raised; and, amidst the groves of maple and pine, of elm and hemlock, that are strangely intermingled on the beautiful banks of the St. Mary, where the bounding river lashes its waters into snowy whiteness, as they hurry past the dark evergreen of the tufted islands in the channel,—the whole company of the French, bowing before the emblem of man's redemption, chanted to its glory a hymn of the seventh century:—

"Vexilla Regis prodeunt;
Fulget crucis mysterium."

The banners of heaven's King advance;
The mystery of the cross shines forth.

By the side of the cross a cedar column was planted, and marked with the lilies of the Bourbons. Thus were the authority and the faith of France uplifted, in the presence of the ancient races of America, in the heart of our continent. Yet this daring ambition of the servants of a military monarch was doomed to leave no abiding monument,—this echo of the middle age to die away.

In the same year, Marquette gathered the wandering remains of one branch of the Huron nation round a chapel at Point St. Ignace, on the continent north of the peninsula of Michigan. The climate was repulsive; but fish abounded, at all seasons, in the strait; and the establishment was long maintained as the key to the west, and the convenient rendezvous of the remote Algonquins. Here, also, Marquette once more gained a place among the founders of Michigan. 1671.

The countries south of the village founded by Marquette were explored by Alloüez and Dablon, who bore the cross through Eastern Wisconsin and the north of Illinois, visiting the Mascoutins and the Kickapoos on the Milwauke, and the Miamis at the head of Lake Michigan. The young men of the latter tribe were intent on an excursion against the Sioux, and they prayed to the missionaries to give them the victory. After finishing the circuit, Alloüez, fearless of danger, extended his rambles to the cabins of the Foxes on the river which bears their name. 1672.

The long-expected discovery of the Mississippi was at hand, to be accomplished by Joliet, of Quebec, of whom there is no record, but of this one excursion, that gives him immortality, and by Marquette, who, after years of pious assiduity to the poor wrecks of Hurons, whom he planted, near abundant fisheries, on 1673

CHAP. XX. the cold extremity of Michigan, entered, with equal humility, upon a career which exposed his life to perpetual danger, and, by its results, affected the destiny of nations.

The enterprise projected by Marquette had been favored by Talon, the intendant of New France, who, on the point of quitting Canada, wished to signalize the last period of his stay by ascertaining if the French, descending the great river of the central west, could bear the banner of France to the Pacific, or plant it, side by side with that of Spain, on the Gulf of Mexico.

Marquette, in Thevenot, and in Hennepin, Eng. ed. 1696.

A branch of the Potawatomies, familiar with Marquette as a missionary, heard with wonder the daring proposal. "Those distant nations," said they, "never spare the strangers; their mutual wars fill their borders with bands of warriors; the Great River abounds in monsters, which devour both men and canoes; the excessive heats occasion death."—"I shall gladly lay down my life for the salvation of souls," replied the good father; and the docile nation joined him in prayer.

1673. June 9.

At the last village on Fox River ever visited by the French,—where Kickapoos, Mascoutins, and Miamis dwelt together on a beautiful hill in the centre of prairies and magnificent groves, that extended as far as the eye could reach, and where Alloüez had already raised the cross, which the savages had ornamented with brilliant skins and crimson belts, a thank-offering to the Great Manitou,—the ancients assembled in council to receive the pilgrims. "My companion," said Marquette, "is an envoy of France to discover new countries; and I am ambassador from God to enlighten them with the gospel;" and, offering presents, he begged two guides

MARQUETTE.

Designed and etched for Bancroft's History of the U. States.

for the morrow. The wild men answered courteously, and gave in return a mat, to serve as a couch during the long voyage. CHAP XX. 1673.

Behold, then, in 1673, on the tenth day of June, the meek, single-hearted, unpretending, illustrious Marquette, with Joliet for his associate, five Frenchmen as his companions, and two Algonquins as guides, lifting their two canoes on their backs, and walking across the narrow portage that divides the Fox River from the Wisconsin. They reach the water-shed;—uttering a special prayer to the immaculate Virgin, they leave the streams that, flowing onwards, could have borne their greetings to the castle of Quebec;—already they stand by the Wisconsin. "The guides returned," says the gentle Marquette, "leaving us alone, in this unknown land, in the hands of Providence." France and Christianity stood in the valley of the Mississippi. Embarking on the broad Wisconsin, the discoverers, as they sailed west, went solitarily down the stream, between alternate prairies and hillsides, beholding neither man nor the wonted beasts of the forest: no sound broke the appalling silence, but the ripple of their canoe, and the lowing of the buffalo. In seven days, "they entered happily the Great River, with a joy that could not be expressed;" and the two birch-bark canoes, raising their happy sails under new skies and to unknown breezes, floated down the calm magnificence of the ocean stream, over the broad, clear sand-bars, the resort of innumerable waterfowl,—gliding past islets that swelled from the bosom of the stream, with their tufts of massive thickets, and between the wide plains of Illinois and Iowa, all garlanded with majestic forests, or checkered by island groves and the open vastness of the prairie.

CHAP XX. 1673 June 25. About sixty leagues below the mouth of the Wisconsin, the western bank of the Mississippi bore on its sands the trail of men; a little footpath was discerned leading into a beautiful prairie; and, leaving the canoes, Joliet and Marquette resolved alone to brave a meeting with the savages. After walking six miles, they beheld a village on the banks of a river, and two others on a slope, at a distance of a mile and a half from the first. The river was the Mou-in-gou-e-na, or Moingona, of which we have corrupted the name into Des Moines. Marquette and Joliet were the first white men who trod the soil of Iowa. Commending themselves to God, they uttered a loud cry. The Indians hear; four old men advance slowly to meet them, bearing the peace-pipe brilliant with many colored plumes. "We are Illinois," said they,—that is, when translated, "We are men;" and they offered the calumet. An aged chief received them at his cabin with upraised hands, exclaiming, "How beautiful is the sun, Frenchman, when thou comest to visit us! Our whole village awaits thee; thou shalt enter in peace into all our dwellings." And the pilgrims were followed by the devouring gaze of an astonished crowd.

Marquette's Map. Compare Charlevoix, iii. 397.

At the great council, Marquette published to them the one true God, their Creator. He spoke, also, of the great captain of the French, the governor of Canada, who had chastised the Five Nations and commanded peace; and he questioned them respecting the Mississippi and the tribes that possessed its banks. For the messengers, who announced the subjection of the Iroquois, a magnificent festival was prepared of hominy, and fish, and the choicest viands from the prairies.

After six days' delay, and invitations to new visits, the chieftain of the tribe, with hundreds of warriors, attended the strangers to their canoes; and, selecting a peace-pipe embellished with the head and neck of brilliant birds, and all feathered over with plumage of various hues, they hung round Marquette the mysterious arbiter of peace and war, the sacred calumet, a safeguard among the nations — CHAP. XX. 1673

The little group proceeded onwards. "I did not fear death," says Marquette; "I should have esteemed it the greatest happiness to have died for the glory of God." They passed the perpendicular rocks, which wore the appearance of monsters; they heard at a distance the noise of the waters of the Missouri, known to them by its Algonquin name of Pekitanoni; and, when they came to the most beautiful confluence of rivers in the world,—where the swifter Missouri rushes like a conqueror into the calmer Mississippi, dragging it, as it were, hastily to the sea,—the good Marquette resolved in his heart, anticipating Lewis and Clarke, one day to ascend the mighty river to its source; to cross the ridge that divides the oceans, and, descending a westerly flowing stream, to publish the gospel to all the people of this New World. — 1673. July

In a little less than forty leagues, the canoes floated past the Ohio, which was then, and long afterwards, called the Wabash. Its banks were tenanted by numerous villages of the peaceful Shawnees, who quailed under the incursions of the Iroquois.

The thick canes begin to appear so close and strong, that the buffalo could not break through them; the insects become intolerable; as a shelter against the suns of July, the sails are folded into an awning. The prairies vanish; and forests of whitewood, admirable

CHAP. XX. 1673. for their vastness and height, crowd even to the skirts of the pebbly shore. It is also observed that, in the land of the Chickasas, the Indians have guns.

Near the latitude of 33 degrees, on the western bank of the Mississippi, stood the village of Mitchigamea, in a region that had not been visited by Europeans since the days of De Soto. "Now," thought Marquette, "we must, indeed, ask the aid of the Virgin." Armed with bows and arrows, with clubs, axes, and bucklers, amidst continual whoops, the natives, bent on war, embark in vast canoes made out of the trunks of hollow trees; but, at the sight of the mysterious peace-pipe held aloft, God touched the hearts of the old men, who checked the impetuosity of the young, and, throwing their bows and quivers into the canoes, as a token of peace, they prepared a hospitable welcome.

The next day, a long, wooden canoe, containing ten men, escorted the discoverers, for eight or ten leagues, to the village of Akansea, the limit of their voyage. They had left the region of the Algonquins, and, in the midst of the Sioux and Chickasas, could speak only by an interpreter. A half league above Akansea, they were met by two boats, in one of which stood the commander, holding in his hand the peace-pipe, and singing as he drew near. After offering the pipe, he gave bread of maize. The wealth of his tribe consisted in buffalo skins; their weapons were axes of steel,—a proof of commerce with Europeans.

Thus had our travellers descended below the entrance of the Arkansas, to the genial climes that have almost no winter but rains, beyond the bound of the Huron and Algonquin languages, to the vicinity of the Gulf of Mexico, and to tribes of Indians that had obtained European arms by traffic with Spaniards or with Virginia

So, having spoken of God, and the mysteries of the Catholic faith; having become certain that the Father of Rivers went not to the ocean east of Florida, nor yet to the Gulf of California, Marquette and Joliet left Akansea, and ascended the Mississippi. CHAP XX. 1673 July 17.

At the 38th degree of latitude, they entered the River Illinois, and discovered a country without its paragon for the fertility of its beautiful prairies, covered with buffaloes and stags,—for the loveliness of its rivulets, and the prodigal abundance of wild duck and swans, and of a species of parrots and wild turkeys. The tribe of Illinois, that tenanted its banks, entreated Marquette to come and reside among them. One of their chiefs, with their young men, conducted the party, by way of Chicago, to Lake Michigan; and, before the end of September, all were safe in Green Bay.

Joliet returned to Quebec to announce the discovery, of which the fame, through Talon, quickened the ambition of Colbert; the unaspiring Marquette remained to preach the gospel to the Miamis, who dwelt in the north of Illinois, round Chicago. Two years afterwards, sailing from Chicago to Mackinaw, he entered a little river in Michigan. Erecting an altar, he said mass after the rites of the Catholic church; then, begging the men who conducted his canoe to leave him alone for a half hour, 1675 May 18. Charlevoix, iii 313, 14.

> "in the darkling wood,
> Amidst the cool and silence, he knelt down,
> And offered to the Mightiest solemn thanks
> And supplication."

At the end of the half-hour, they went to seek him, and he was no more. The good missionary, discoverer of a world, had fallen asleep on the margin of the stream that bears his name. Near its mouth, the ca-

CHAP. XX. noemen dug his grave in the sand. Ever after, the forest rangers, if in danger on Lake Michigan, would invoke his name. The people of the west will build his monument.

At the death of Marquette, there dwelt at the outlet of Lake Ontario, Robert Cavalier de la Salle. Of a good family, he had renounced his inheritance by entering the seminary of the Jesuits. After profiting by the discipline of their schools, and obtaining their praise for purity and diligence, he had taken his discharge from the fraternity; and, with no companions but poverty and a boundless spirit of enterprise, about the year 1667, when the attention of all France was directed towards Canada, the young adventurer embarked for fame and fortune in New France. Established, at first, as a fur-trader, at La Chine, and encouraged by Talon and Courcelles, he explored
1669. Lake Ontario, and ascended to Lake Erie; and, when the French governor, some years after occupying the banks of the Sorel, began to fortify the outlet of Lake
1675. Ontario, La Salle, repairing to France, and aided by Frontenac, obtained the rank of nobility, and the grant of Fort Frontenac, now the village of Kingston, on condition of maintaining the fortress. The grant was, in fact, a concession of a large domain and the exclusive traffic with the Five Nations.

1675 to 1677. In the portion of the wilderness of which the young man was proprietary, cultivated fields proved the fertility of the soil; his herd of cattle multiplied; groups of Iroquois built their cabins in the environs; a few French settled under his shelter; Franciscans, now tolerated in Canada, renewed their missions under his auspices;—the noble forests invited the construction of log cabins, and vessels with decks; and no canoemen in Canada could shoot a rapid with such address as the pupils of La Salle. Fortune was within his grasp. But Joliet, as he descended from the upper lakes, had passed by the bastions of Fort Frontenac—had spread the news of the brilliant career of discoveries opened in the west. In the solitudes of Upper Canada, the secluded adventurer had inflamed his imagination by reading the voyages of Columbus, and the history of the rambles of De Soto; and the Iroquois had, moreover, described the course of the Ohio. Thus the young enthusiast framed plans of colonization in the south-west, and of commerce between Europe and the Mississippi. Once more he repaired to France; and from the policy of Colbert, who instinctively listened to the vast schemes which his heroic sagacity had planned, and the special favor of Seignelay, Colbert's son, he obtained, with the monopoly of the traffic in buffalo skins, a commission for perfecting the discovery of the Great River. With Tonti, an Italian veteran, as his lieutenant, and a recruit of mechanics and mariners; with anchors, and sails, and cordage for rigging a ship, and stores of merchandise for traffic with the natives; with swelling hopes, and a boundless ambition, La Salle, in the autumn of 1678, returned to Fort Frontenac. Before winter, "a wooden canoe" of ten tons, the first that ever sailed into Niagara River, bore a part of his company to the vicinity of the falls; at Niagara, a trading-house was established; in the mouth of the Cayuga Creek, the work of shipbuilding began; Tonti and the Franciscan Hennepin, venturing among the Senecas, established relations of amity,—while La Salle himself, skilled in the Indian dialects, was now urging forward the ship-builders, now gathering furs at his magazine, now gazing at the

CHAP. XX.

Hennepin, Nouveau Voyage, 2.

1678

CHAP. XX. 1679. mighty cataract,—fittest emblem of eternity,—now sending forward a detachment into the country of the Illinois to prepare the way for his reception.

Under the auspices of La Salle, Europeans first pitched a tent at Niagara; it was he who, in 1679, amidst the salvo from his little artillery, and the chanting of the Te Deum, and the astonished gaze of the Senecas, first launched a wooden vessel, a bark of sixty tons, on the upper Niagara River, and, in the Griffin, freighted with the colony of fur-traders for the valley of the Mississippi, on the seventh day of August, un-
Aug. 7. furled a sail to the breezes of Lake Erie. Indifferent to the malignity of those who envied his genius, or were injured by his special privileges, La Salle, first of mariners, sailed over Lake Erie and between the verdant isles of the majestic Detroit; debated planting
Aug. 17. a colony on its banks; gave a name to Lake St. Clair, from the day on which he traversed its shallow waters; and, after escaping from storms on Lake Huron, and
Aug. 27. planting a trading-house at Mackinaw, he cast anchor in Green Bay. Here having despatched his brig to Niagara River, with the richest cargo of furs, he himself, with his company in scattered groups, repaired in bark canoes to the head of Lake Michigan; and at the mouth of the St. Joseph's, in that peninsula where Alloüez had already gathered a village of Miamis, awaiting the return of the Griffin, he constructed the trading-house, with palisades, known as the Fort of the Miamis. It marks his careful forethought, that he sounded the mouth of the St. Joseph's, and raised buoys to mark the channel. But of his vessel, on which his fortunes so much depended, no tidings came. Weary
Dec. 3. of delay, he resolved to penetrate Illinois; and, leaving ten men to guard the Fort of the Miamis, La Salle

himself, with Hennepin and two other Franciscans, CHAP XX.
with Tonti and about thirty followers, ascended the
St. Joseph's, and, by a short portage over bogs and 1679
swamps made dangerous by a snow-storm, entered the Kankakee. Descending its narrow stream, before the end of December, the little company had reached the site of an Indian village on the Illinois, probably not far from Ottawa, in La Salle county. The tribe was absent, passing the winter in the chase.

On the banks of Lake Peoria, Indians appeared;— 1680. Jan. 4.
they were Illinois; and, desirous to obtain axes and fire-arms, they offered the calumet, and agreed to an alliance: if the Iroquois should renew their invasions, they would claim the French as allies. They heard with joy that colonies were to be established in their territory; they described the course of the Mississippi, and they were willing to guide the strangers to its mouth. The spirit and prudence of La Salle, who was the life of the enterprise, won the friendship of the natives. But clouds lowered over his path: the Griffin, it seemed certain, was wrecked, thus delaying his discoveries, as well as impairing his fortunes; his men began to despond: alone, of himself, he toiled to revive their courage;—there could be no safety but in union: "None," he added, "shall stay after the spring, unless from choice." But fear and discontent pervaded the company; and when La Salle planned and began to build a fort on the banks of the Illinois, four days' journey, it is said, below Lake Peoria, thwarted by destiny, and almost despairing, he named the fort Crevecœur.

Yet here the immense power of his will appeared. Dependent on himself, fifteen hundred miles from

CHAP. XX. 1680. the nearest French settlement, impoverished, pursued by enemies at Quebec, and in the wilderness surrounded by uncertain nations, he inspired his men with resolution to saw trees into plank and prepare a bark; he despatched Louis Hennepin to explore the Upper Mississippi; he questioned the Illinois and their southern captives on the course of the Mississippi; he formed conjectures respecting the Tennessee River; and then, as new recruits were needed, and sails and cordage for the bark, in the month of March, with a musket and a pouch of powder and shot, with a blanket for his protection, and skins of which to make moccasins, he, with three companions, set off on foot for Fort Frontenac, to trudge through thickets and forests, to wade through marshes and melting snows, having for his pathway the ridge of highlands which divide the basin of the Ohio from that of the lakes,—without drink, except water from the brooks,—without food, except supplies from the gun. Of his thoughts, on that long journey, no record exists.

Hennepin, 173 and 184. New Discovery, i. 111. Charlevoix, i. 461, copies the error of the publisher of Tonti.

1680 Mar.

During the absence of La Salle, Louis Hennepin, bearing the calumet, and accompanied by Du Gay and Michael d'Accault, as oarsmen, followed the Illinois to its junction with the Mississippi; and, invoking the guidance of St. Anthony of Padua, ascended the mighty stream far beyond the mouth of the Wisconsin—as he falsely held forth, far enough to discover its source. The great falls in the river, which he describes with reasonable accuracy, were named from the chosen patron of the expedition. On a tree near the cataract, the Franciscan engraved the cross, and the arms of France; and, after a summer's rambles, diversified by

a short captivity among the Sioux, he and his compan CHAP. XX.
ions returned, by way of the Wisconsin and Fox Riv
ers, to the French mission at Green Bay. 1680

In Illinois, Tonti was less fortunate. The quick perception of La Salle had selected, as the fit centre
of his colony, Rock Fort, near a village of the Illinois Joutel, 337-340.
—a cliff rising two hundred feet above the river that Schoolcraft, 320.
flows at its base, in the centre of a lovely country of verdant prairies, bordered by distant slopes, richly tufted with oak, and black walnut, and the noblest trees of the American forest. This rock Tonti was to fortify; and, during the attempt, men at Crevecœur deserted. Besides, the enemies of La Salle had instigated the Iroquois to hostility, and, in September, a large party of them, descending the river, threatened ruin to his enterprise. After a parley, Tonti and the few men that remained with him, excepting the aged Franciscan Gabriel de la Ribourde, fled to Lake Michigan, where they found shelter with the Potawatomies. On the authority of a legend made up in Paris from the adventures of Tonti,—a legend full of geographical contradictions, of confused dates, and manifest fiction,—some have placed this attack of the Iroquois on the Illinois in 1681. The narrative of Hennepin, the whole of which was printed in 1682, proves conclusively that it happened in 1680, as Frontenac, the governor of Canada, related at the time.

When, therefore, La Salle returned to Illinois, with large supplies of men and stores for rigging a brigan-
tine, he found the post in Illinois deserted. Hence 1681
came the delay of another year, which was occupied in visiting Green Bay, and conducting traffic there; in finding Tonti and his men, and perfecting a capacious barge. At last, in the early part of 1682, La Salle

CHAP. XX. 1682. and his company descended the Mississippi to the sea. His sagacious eye discerned the magnificent resources of the country. As he floated down its flood; as he framed a cabin on the first Chickasa bluff; as he raised the cross by the Arkansas; as he planted the arms of France near the Gulf of Mexico;—he anticipated the future affluence of emigrants, and heard in the distance the footsteps of the advancing multitude that were coming to take possession of the valley. Le Clerq, c. xxiii. Meantime, he claimed the territory for France, and gave it the name of Louisiana. The year of the descent has been unnecessarily made a question; its accomplishment was known in Paris before the end of 1682.

This was the period of the proudest successes and largest ambition of Louis XIV. La Salle will return, it was said, to give to the court an ample account of the terrestrial paradise of America;—there the king will at once call into being a flourishing empire. And,
1683. May 12. Nov. La Hontan. in fact, La Salle, remaining in the west till his exclusive privilege had expired, returned to Quebec to embark for France.

Colbert, whose genius had awakened a national spirit in behalf of French industry, and who yet had rested his system of commerce and manufactures on no firmer basis than that of monopoly, was no more; but Seignelay, his son, the minister for maritime affairs, listened confidingly to the expected messenger from the land which was regarded with pride as "the delight of the New World."

1684 July 24. In the early months of 1684, the preparations for colonizing Louisiana were perfected, and in July the fleet left Rochelle. Four vessels were destined for the Mississippi, bearing two hundred and eighty per-

sons, to take possession of the valley. Of these, one CHAP. XX.
hundred were soldiers—an ill omen, for successful colonists always defend themselves: about thirty were 1684
volunteers, two of whom—young Cavalier, and the rash, passionate Moranget—were nephews to La Salle: of ecclesiastics, there were three Franciscans, and three of St. Sulpice, one of them being brother to La Salle: there were, moreover, mechanics of various skill; and the presence of young women proved the design of permanent colonization. But the mechanics were poor workmen, ill versed in their art; the soldiers, though they had for their commander Joutel, a man of courage and truth, and afterwards the historian of the grand enterprise, were themselves spiritless vagabonds, without discipline and without experience; the volunteers were restless with indefinite expectations; and, worst of all, the naval commander, Beaujeu, was deficient in judgment, incapable of sympathy with the magnanimous heroism of La Salle, envious, self-willed, and foolishly proud.

Disasters lowered on the voyage at its commencement: a mast breaks; they return: the voyage begins anew amidst variances between La Salle and the naval commander. In every instance on the record, the judgment of La Salle was right.

At St. Domingo, La Salle, delayed and cruelly thwarted by Beaujeu, saw already the shadow of his
coming misfortunes. On leaving the island, they were Nov 25.
more at variance than ever. They double Cape Anto- Dec. 12.
nio; they discover land on the continent; aware of the 28.
easterly direction of the Gulf Stream, they sail slowly
in the opposite course. On the tenth day of January, 1685
1685, they must have been near the mouth of the Mis- Jan. 10.
sissippi; but La Salle thought not, and the fleet sailed

CHAP. XX.

1685

by. Presently, he perceived his error, and desired to return; but Beaujeu refused; and thus they sailed to the west, and still to the west, till they reached the Bay of Matagorda. Weary of differences with Beaujeu,—believing the streams that had their outlet in the bay might be either branches from the Mississippi, or lead to its vicinity, La Salle resolved to disembark. While he was busy in providing for the safety of his men, his store-ship, on entering the harbor, was wrecked by the careless pilot. Others gazed listlessly; La Salle, calming the terrible energy of his grief at the sudden ruin of his boundless hopes, borrowed boats from the fleet to save, at least, some present supplies. But with night came a gale of wind, and the vessel was dashed utterly in pieces. The stores, provided with the munificence that marked the plans of Louis XIV., lay scattered on the sea; little could be saved. To aggravate despair, the savages came down to pilfer, and murdered two of the volunteers.

Terror pervaded the group of colonists: the evils of the wreck and the gale were charged to La Salle,—as if he ought to have deepened the channel and controlled the winds; men deserted, and returned in the fleet. La Salle, who, by the powerful activity of his will, controlled the feeble and irritable persons that surrounded him, and even censured their inefficiency, their treachery, and their disobedience, with angry vehemence, was yet, in his struggle against adversity, magnanimously tranquil. The fleet sets sail, and there remain on the beach of Matagorda a desponding company of about two hundred and thirty, huddled together in a fort constructed of the fragments of their shipwrecked vessel, having no reliance but in the constancy and elastic genius of La Salle.

Joutel 92

CHAP. XX. 1685

Ascending the small stream at the west of the bay, in the vain hope of finding the Mississippi, La Salle selected a site on the open ground for the establishment of a fortified post. The spot, which he named St. Louis, was a gentle slope, which showed, towards the west and south-west, the boundless expansion of the beautiful landscape, verdant with luxuriant grasses, and dotted with groves of forest-trees, south and east was the Bay of Matagorda, skirted with prairies. The waters abounded with fish, and invited crowds of wild fowl· the fields were alive with deer, and bisons, and wild turkeys, and the dangerous rattlesnake, bright inhabitant of the meadows. There, under the suns of June, with timber felled in an inland grove, and dragged for a league over the prairie grass, the colonists prepared to build a shelter, La Salle being the architect, and himself marking the beams, and tenons, and mortises. With parts of the wreck, brought up in canoes, a second house was framed, and of each the roof was covered with buffalo skins.

This is the settlement which made Texas a part of Louisiana. In its sad condition, it had yet saved from the wreck a good supply of arms, and bars of iron for the forge. Even now, this colony possessed, from the bounty of Louis XIV., more than was contributed by all the English monarchs together for the twelve English colonies on the Atlantic. Its number still exceeded that of the colony of Smith in Virginia, or of those who embarked in the Mayflower. France took possession of Texas; her arms were carved on its stately forest-trees; and by no treaty, or public document, except the general cessions of Louisiana, did she ever after relinquish the right to the province as colonized under her banners, and made still more surely a part of her territory, because the colony found there its grave

CHAP. XX. Excursions into the vicinity of the Fort St. Louis had discovered nothing but the luxuriant productiveness of
1685. Dec. the country. La Salle proposed to seek the Mississippi in canoes; and, after an absence of about four
1686 months, and the loss of twelve or thirteen men, he re-
Mar. turned in rags, having failed to find "the fatal river," and yet renewing hope by his presence. In April, he plunged into the wilderness, with twenty companions, lured towards New Mexico by the brilliant fictions of the rich mines of Sainte Barbe, the El Dorado of Northern Mexico. There, among the Cenis, he succeeded in obtaining five horses, and supplies of maize and beans: he found no mines, but a country unsurpassed for beauty of climate and exuberant fertility.

On his return, he heard of the wreck of the little bark which had remained with the colony: he heard it unmoved. Heaven and man seemed his enemies; and, with the giant energy of an indomitable will, having lost his hopes of fortune, his hopes of fame,—with his colony diminished to about forty, among whom discontent had given birth to plans of crime,—with no Europeans nearer than the River Panuco, no French nearer than Illinois,—he resolved to travel on foot to his countrymen at the north, and return from Canada to renew his colony in Texas.

1687. Leaving twenty men at Fort St. Louis, in January,
Jan. 12. 1687, La Salle, with sixteen men, departed for Canada. Lading their baggage on the wild horses from the Cenis, which found their pasture every where in the prairies; in shoes made of green buffalo hides; for want of other paths, following the track of the buffalo, and using skins as the only shelter against rain; winning favor with the savages by the confiding courage of their leader;—they ascended the streams towards

LA SALLE

the first ridge of highlands, walking through beautiful plains and groves, among deer and buffaloes,—now fording the clear rivulets, now building a bridge by felling a giant tree across a stream,—till they had passed the basin of the Colorado, and, in the upland country, had reached a branch of Trinity River. In the little company of wanderers, there were two men, Duhaut and L'Archevêque, who had embarked their capital in the enterprise. Of these, Duhaut had long shown a spirit of mutiny: the base malignity of disappointed avarice, maddened by suffering, and impatient of control, awakened the fiercest passions of ungovernable hatred. Inviting Moranget to take charge of the fruits of a buffalo hunt, they quarrelled with him, and murdered him. Wondering at the delay of his nephew's return, La Salle, on the twentieth of March, went to seek him. At the brink of the river, he observed eagles hovering as if over carrion; and he fired an alarm gun. Warned by the sound, Duhaut and L'Archevêque crossed the river; the former skulked in the prairie grass; of the latter, La Salle asked, "Where is my nephew?" At the moment of the answer, Duhaut fired; and, without uttering a word, La Salle fell dead "You are down now, grand bashaw! you are down now!" shouted one of the conspirators, as they despoiled his remains, which were left on the prairie, naked and without burial, to be devoured by wild beasts. Such was the end of this daring adventurer. For force of will, and vast conceptions; for various knowledge, and quick adaptation of his genius to untried circumstances; for a sublime magnanimity, that resigned itself to the will of Heaven, and yet triumphed over affliction by energy of purpose and unfaltering hope,—he had no superior among his countrymen. He had

CHAP. XX.

1687

Joutel, 120, 137, 148

March 17.

CHAP. XX. 1687. won the affection of the governor of Canada, the esteem of Colbert, the confidence of Seignelay, the favor of Louis XIV. After beginning the colonization of Upper Canada, he perfected the discovery of the Mississippi from the Falls of St. Anthony to its mouth; and he will be remembered through all time as the father of colonization in the great central valley of the west.

But avarice and passion were not calmed by the blood of La Salle. Duhaut and another of the conspirators, grasping at an unequal share in the spoils, were themselves murdered, while their reckless associates joined a band of savages. Joutel, with the brother and surviving nephew of La Salle, and others, in all but seven, obtained a guide for the Arkansas; and—fording rivulets, crossing ravines, by rafts or boats of buffalo hides making a ferry over rivers, not meeting the cheering custom of the calumet till they reached the country above the Red River, leaving an esteemed companion in a wilderness grave, on which the piety of an Indian matron heaped offerings of maize—at last, as the survivors came upon a branch of the Mississippi,
July 24. they beheld on an island a large cross. Never did Christian gaze on that emblem with heartier joy. Near it stood a log hut, tenanted by two Frenchmen. Tonti had descended the river, and, full of grief at not finding La Salle, had established a post near the Arkansas.

CHAPTER XXI

FRANCE CONTENDS FOR THE FISHERIES AND THE GREAT WEST

CHAP XXI.

SUCH were the events which gave to the French not only New France and Acadia, Hudson's Bay and Newfoundland, but a claim to a moiety of Maine, of Vermont, and to more than a moiety of New York, to the whole valley of the Mississippi, and to Texas even, as far as the Rio Bravo del Norte. Throughout that wide region, it sought to introduce its authority, under the severest forms of the colonial system. That system was enforced, with equal eagerness, by England upon the sea-coast. Could France, and England, and Spain, have amicably divided the American continent; could they have been partners, and not rivals, in oppression; I know not whence hope could have beamed upon the colonies.

But the aristocratic revolution of England was the signal for a war with France, growing out of "a root of enmity," which Marlborough described as "irreconcilable to the government and the religion" of Great Britain. Louis XIV. took up arms in defence of legitimacy; and England had the glorious office of asserting the right of a nation to reform its government. But, though the progress of the revolutionary principle was the root of the enmity, France could not, at once, obtain the alliance of every European power which was

CHAP. XXI. unfriendly to change. She had encroached on every neighbor; and fear, and a sense of wrong, made all of them her enemies. From regard to the integrity of its territory, the German empire, with Austria, joined with England; and, as the Spanish Netherlands, which constituted the barrier of Holland and Germany against France, and the path of England into the heart of the continent, could be saved from conquest by France only through the interposition of England and Holland, an alliance followed between the Protestant revolutionary republic and monarchy, on the one side, and the bigoted defender of the Roman Catholic church and legitimacy, on the other. Hence, also, in the first war of King William, the frontiers of Carolina, bordering on the possessions of Spain, were safe against invasion: Spain and England were allies.

Thus the war of 1689, in Europe, roused Louis XIV. in behalf of legitimacy, and, at the same time, rallied against him, not England only, but every power which dreaded his lawless ambition. William III. was not only the defender of the nationality of England, but of the territorial freedom of Europe.

In the colonies, the strife was, on behalf of their respective mother countries, for the fisheries, and for territory at the north and west. The idea of weakening an adversary, by encouraging its colonies to assert independence, did not, at that time, exist; the universal maxim of European statesmen assumed the fact, that colonies have a master. In the contests that followed, the religious faith, and the roving enterprise of the French Canadians, secured to Louis XIV. their active support. The English colonists, on the contrary, sided heartily with England: the English revolution was to them the pledge for freedom of mind, as

marked by Protestantism; for national freedom, as il- CHAP XXI.
lustrated in the exile of a tyrant, and in the election of
a constitutional king. Thus the strife in America was 1689
between England and France for the possession of colonial monopolies; and, in that strife, England rallied her forces under the standard of advancing freedom.

If the issue had depended on the condition of the colonies, it could hardly have seemed doubtful. The French census for the North American continent, in 1688, showed but eleven thousand two hundred and forty-nine persons—scarcely a tenth part of the English population on its frontiers; about a twentieth part of English North America.

West of Montreal, the principal French posts, and 1688
those but inconsiderable ones, were at Frontenac, at Mackinaw, and on the Illinois. At Niagara, there was a wavering purpose of maintaining a post, but no permanent occupation. So weak were the garrisons, that English traders, with an escort of Indians, had ventured even to Mackinaw, and, by means of the Senecas, obtained a large share of the commerce of the lakes. French diplomacy had attempted to pervade 1687
the west, and concert an alliance with all the tribes from Lake Ontario to the Mississippi. The traders were summoned even from the plains of the Sioux; and Tonti and the Illinois were, by way of the Ohio and the Alleghany, to precipitate themselves on the Senecas, while the French should come from Montreal, and the Ottáwas and other Algonquins, under Durantaye, the vigilant commander at Mackinaw, should descend from Michigan. But the power of the Illinois was broken; the Hurons and Ottáwas were almost ready to become the allies of the Senecas. The savages still held the keys of the great west; no inter- 1688

CHAP. XXI. 1688. course existed but by means of the forest rangers, who penetrated the barren heaths round Hudson's Bay, the morasses of the north-west, the homes of the Sioux and Miamis, the recesses of every forest where there was an Indian with skins to sell. "God alone could have saved Canada this year," wrote Denonville, in 1688. But for the missions at the west, Illinois would have been abandoned, the fort at Mackinaw lost, and a general rising of the natives would have completed the ruin of New France.

1689 Personal enterprise took the direction of the fur trade: Port Nelson, in Hudson's Bay, and Fort Albany, were originally possessed by the French. The attention of the court of France was directed to the fisheries; and Acadia had been represented by De Meules as the most important settlement of France. To protect it, the Jesuits Vincent and James Bigot collected a village of Abenakis on the Penobscot; and a flourishing town now marks the spot where the baron de St. Castin, a veteran officer of the regiment of Carignan, established a trading fort. Would France, it was said, strengthen its post on the Penobscot, occupy the islands that command the Gulf of St. Lawrence, and send supplies to Newfoundland, she would be sole mistress of the fisheries for cod. Hence the strife with Massachusetts, in which the popular mind was so deeply interested, that, to this day, the figure of a cod-fish is suspended in the hall of its representatives.

Thus France, bounding its territory next New England by the Kennebec, claimed the whole eastern coast, Nova Scotia, Cape Breton, Newfoundland, Labrador, and Hudson's Bay; and, to assert and defend this boundless region, Acadia and its dependencies counted but nine hundred French inhabitants. The missiona-

-ies, swaying the mind of the Abenakis, were the sole source of hope. CHAP. XXI.

On the declaration of war by France against England, Count Frontenac, once more governor of Canada, was charged to recover Hudson's Bay; to protect Acadia; and, by a descent from Canada, to assist a fleet from France in making conquest of New York. Of that province De Callieres was, in advance, appointed governor; the English Catholics were to be permitted to remain,—other inhabitants, to be sent into Pennsylvania or New England. But, on reaching the Gulf of St. Lawrence, Frontenac learned the capture of Montreal. 1689. June 25. Sept. 25.

On the twenty-fifth of August, the Iroquois, fifteen hundred in number, reached the Isle of Montreal, at La Chine, at break of day, and, finding all asleep, set fire to the houses, and engaged in one general massacre. In less than an hour, two hundred people met death under forms too horrible for description. Approaching the town of Montreal, they made an equal number of prisoners, and, after a severe skirmish, became masters of the fort, and of the whole island, of which they retained unmolested possession till the middle of October. In the moment of consternation, Denonville had ordered Fort Frontenac, on Lake Ontario, to be evacuated and razed. From Three Rivers to Mackinaw, there remained not one French town, and hardly even a post. 1689. Aug. 25.

In Hudson's Bay, a band of brothers—De Sainte Helene and D'Iberville—sustained the honor of French arms. They were Canadians, sons of Charles Lemoine, an early emigrant from Normandy, whose numerous offspring gave also to American history the name of Bienville. Passing across the ridge that di- 1689. White's Recopilacion, ii. 645.

CHAP. XXI. 1689. vides the rivers of Hudson's Bay from those of the St. Lawrence, amidst marvellous adventures, by hardy resolution and daring presence of mind, they had, in 1686, conquered the English posts from Fort Rupert to Albany River, leaving the English no trading house in the bay, except that of which, in 1685, they had dispossessed the French at Port Nelson. That post remained to the English; but the sons of Lemoine intercepted the forces which were sent to pro-
1689. claim William of Orange monarch over jagged cliffs, and deep ravines never warmed by a sunbeam,—over the glaciers and mountains, the rivers and trading-houses in Hudson's Bay. Exulting in their success, they returned to Quebec.

1689. June 27. In the east, blood was first shed at Cocheco, where, thirteen years before, an unsuspecting party of three hundred and fifty Indians had been taken prisoners, and shipped for Boston, to be sold into foreign slavery. The memory of the treachery was indelible; and the Indian emissaries of Castin easily excited the tribe of Penacook to revenge. On the evening of the twenty-seventh of June, two squaws repaired to the house of Richard Waldron, and the octogenarian magistrate bade them lodge on the floor At night, they rise, unbar the gates, and summon their companions, who at once enter every apartment. "What now? what now?" shouted the brave old man; and, seizing his sword, he defended himself till he fell stunned by a blow from a hatchet. They then placed him in a chair on a table in his own hall: "Judge Indians again!"—thus they mocked him; and, making cruel sport of their debts to him as a trader, they drew gashes across his breast, and each one cried, "Thus I cross out my account!" At last, the mutilated man reeled from faintness, and died in the midst of tortures. The Indians, burning his house, and others that stood near it, having killed three-and-twenty, returned to the wilderness with twenty-nine captives. CHAP XXI.

August comes. The women and children, at the Penobscot village of Canibas, have confessed their sins to the Jesuit Thury, that so they may uplift purer hands, while their fathers and brothers proceed against the heretics;—in the little chapel, the missionary and his neophytes have established a perpetual rosary during the expedition, and even the hours of repast do not interrupt the edifying exercise. A hundred warriors, purified also by confession, in a fleet of bark canoes, steal out of the Penobscot, and paddle towards Pemaquid. Thomas Gyles and his sons are at work, in the sunny noontide, making hay: a volley whistles by them;—a short encounter ends in their defeat. "I ask no favor," says the wounded father, "but leave to pray with my children." Pale with the loss of blood, he commends his children to God, then bids them farewell for this world, yet in the hope of seeing them in a better. The Indians, restless at delay, use the hatchet, and, for burial, heap boughs over his body. After a defence of two days, the stockade at Pemaquid capitulates; and the warriors return to Penobscot to exult over their prisoners. Other inroads were made by the Penobscot and St. John Indians, so that the settlements east of Falmouth were deserted. 1689 Gyles, in Drake, 77, &c.

In September, commissioners from New England held a conference with the Mohawks at Albany, soliciting an alliance. "We have burned Montreal," said they; "we are allies of the English; we will keep the chain unbroken." But they refused to invade the Abenakis.

CHAP. XXI. Had Frontenac never left New France, Montreal would probably have been safe. He now used every effort to win the Five Nations to neutrality or to friendship. To recover esteem in their eyes; to secure to Durantaye, the commander at Mackinaw, the means of treating with the Hurons and the Ottáwas; it was resolved by Frontenac to make a triple descent into the English provinces.

1690. Jan. From Montreal, a party of one hundred and ten, composed of French, and of the Christian Iroquois,—having De Mantet and Sainte Helene as leaders, and D'Iberville, the hero of Hudson's Bay, as a volunteer,—for two-and-twenty days, waded through snows and morasses, through forests and across rivers, to Schenectady. The village had given itself calmly to slumber: through open and unguarded gates the invaders Feb. 8. entered silently, and having, just before midnight, reached its heart, the war-whoop was raised, (dreadful sound to the mothers of that place and their children!) and the dwellings set on fire. Of the inhabitants, some, half clad, fled through the snows to Albany; sixty were massacred, of whom seventeen were children, and ten were Africans. For such ends had the hardships of a winter's expedition, frost, famine, and frequent deaths, been encountered: such was war.

The party from Three Rivers, led by Hertel, and consisting of but fifty-two persons, of whom three March 27. were his sons, and two his nephews, surprised the settlement at Salmon Falls, on the Piscataqua, and, after a bloody engagement, burned houses, barns, and cattle in the stalls, and took fifty-four prisoners, chiefly women and children. The prisoners were laden by the victors with spoils from their own homes. Robert Rogers, rejecting his burden, was bound by the Indians to a tree, and dry leaves kindled about him, yet in such heaps as would burn but slowly. Mary Furguson, a girl of fifteen, burst into tears from fatigue, and was scalped forthwith. Mehetabel Goodwin would linger apart in the snow to lull her infant to sleep, lest its cries should provoke the savages: angry at the delay, her master struck the child against a tree, and hung it among the branches. The infant of Mary Plaisted was thrown into the river, that, eased of her burden, she might walk faster. CHAP XXI. 1690

Returning from this expedition, Hertel met the war party, under Portneuf, from Quebec, and, with them and a reënforcement from Castin, made a successful attack on the fort and settlement in Casco Bay. May.

Meantime, danger taught the colonies the necessity of union, and, on the first day of May, 1690, New York beheld the momentous example of an American "congress." The idea originated with the government of Massachusetts, established by the people in the period that intervened between the overthrow of Andros and the arrival of the second charter; and the place of meeting was New York, where, likewise, the government had sprung directly from the action of the people. Thus, without exciting suspicion, were the forms of independence and union prepared. The invitations were given by letters from the general court of Massachusetts, and extended to all the colonies as far, at least, as Maryland. Massachusetts, the parent of so many states, is certainly the parent of the American Union. At that congress, it was resolved to attempt the conquest of Canada by marching an army, by way of Lake Champlain, against Montreal, while Massachusetts should, with a fleet, attack Que-

CHAP. XXI. 1690. bec. Thus did Massachusetts, Connecticut, and New York, having, at that time, each a government constituted by itself, in the spirit of independence, not only provide for order and tranquillity at home, but, unaided by England, of themselves plan the invasion of Acadia and Canada.

Acadia was soon conquered: before the end of May, Sir William Phipps, failing to bring seasonable supplies to Falmouth, sailed to Port Royal, which readily surrendered. New England was mistress of the coast to the eastern extremity of Nova Scotia, though the native hordes of that wilderness still retained their affection for the French.

While the people of New England and New York were concerting the grand enterprise of the reduction of Canada, the French had, by their successes, inspired the savages with respect, and renewed their intercourse with the west. But, in August, Montreal became alarmed. An Indian announces that an army of Iroquois and English was busy in constructing canoes on Lake George; and immediately Frontenac himself placed the hatchet in the hands of his allies, and, with the tomahawk in his own grasp, old as he was, chanted the war-song, and danced the war-dance On the twenty-ninth of August, it was said that an army had reached Lake Champlain; but, on the second of September, the spies could observe no trail. The projected attack by land was defeated by divisions,—Leisler charging Winthrop of Connecticut with treachery, and the forces from Connecticut blaming Milborne, the commissary of New York, for the insufficiency of the supplies.

Oc. 1C But, just as Frontenac, in the full pride of security, was preparing to return to Quebec, he heard that an

1690.

Abenaki, hurrying through the woods in twelve days from Piscataqua, had announced the approach of a hostile fleet from Boston. The little colony of Massachusetts had sent forth a fleet of thirty-four sail, under the command of the incompetent Phipps, manned by two thousand of its citizens, who, as they now, without pilots, sounded their way up the St. Lawrence, anxious for the result of the expedition against Montreal, watched wistfully the course of the winds, and hoped in the efficacy of the prayers that went up, evening and morning, from every hearth in New England.

Walley Cotton Mather Hutchinson. Hawkins. Le Clercq Charlevoix

Had the excursion from Albany by land succeeded,—had pilots, or fair winds, or decision in the commander, conducted the fleet more rapidly but by three days,—the castle of St. Louis would have been surprised and taken. But, in the night of the fourteenth of October, Frontenac reached Quebec. The inhabitants of the vicinity were assembled; and the fortifications of the city had already been put in a tenable condition, when, on the sixteenth, at daybreak, the fleet from Boston came in sight, and soon cast anchor near Beauport, in the stream. It was too late. The herald from the ship of the admiral, demanding a surrender of the place, was dismissed with scoffs. What availed the courage of the citizen soldiers who effected a landing at Beauport? Before them was a fortified town defended by a garrison far more numerous than the assailants, and protected by marshes and a river fordable only at low tide. The diversion against Montreal had utterly failed: the New England men reëmbark, and sail for Boston. In Quebec there were great rejoicings. For the church in the lower town, the yearly festival of Our Lady of Victory was established; and

Oct. 8/18.

Oct. 11/21.

Hawkins, 140 and 228

CHAP. XXI. in France a medal commemorated the successes of Louis XIV. in the New World. The New England ships, on their return, were scattered by storms: of one, bearing sixty men, wrecked on Anticosti, five of the few who did not perish from the winter, boldest of navigators, landed in Boston in the following May, after a voyage of forty-four days in a skiff. Sir William Phipps reached home in November. The treas-
1690 Dec. 10. ury was empty. "Considering the present poverty of the country, and, through scarcity of money, the want of an adequate measure of commerce," issues of bills of credit were authorized, in notes from five shillings to five pounds, to "be in value equal to money, and accepted in all public payments." But, as confidence wavered, the bills of the colony, which continued to be issued, were made, in all payments, a legal tender, and, instead of bearing interest, were received at the treasury at five per cent. advance.

1691 to 1696. Repulsed from Canada, the exhausted colonies attempted little more than the defence of their frontiers. Their borders were full of terror and sorrow, of captivity and death; but no designs of conquest were
1691. formed. If Schuyler made an irruption into the French settlements on the Sorel, it was only to gain successes in a skirmish, and to effect a safe retreat.
Nov. 26. A French ship anchoring in Port Royal, the red cross that floated over the town made way for the banner of France; and Acadia was once more a dependence on
1692. Canada. In January, 1692, a party of French and Indians, coming in snow-shoes from the east, burst upon the town of York, offering its inhabitants no choice but captivity or death. The fort which was rebuilt at Pemaquid was, at least, an assertion of English supremacy over the neighboring region. In Eng-

land, the conquest of Canada was resolved on; but the fleet designed for the expedition, after a repulse at Martinique, sailed for Boston, freighted with the yellow fever, which destroyed two thirds of the mariners and soldiers on board. For a season, hostilities in Maine were suspended by a treaty of peace with the Abenakis; but, in less than a year, solely through the influence of the Jesuits, they were again in the field, led by Villieu, the French commander on the Penobscot; and the village at Oyster River, in New Hampshire, was the victim of their fury. Ninety-four persons were killed and carried away. The young wife of Thomas Drew was taken to the tribe at Norridgewock: there, in midwinter, in the open air, during a storm of snow, she gave birth to her first-born, doomed by the savages to instant death. In Canada, the chiefs of the Micmacs presented to Frontenac the scalps of English killed on the Piscataqua. Nor did the thought occur that such inroads were atrocious. The Jesuit historian of France relates, with pride, that they had their origin in the counsels and influence of the missionaries Thury and Bigot; and, extolling the hardihood and the success of the foray, he passes a eulogy on the daring of Taxus, the bravest of the Abenakis. Such is self-love; it has but one root, with a thousand branches. The despot believed his authority from God, and his own personality to constitute the state; the mistresses of kings were, without scruple, made by patent the mothers of hereditary legislators; the English monopolist had no self-reproach for prohibiting the industry of the colonists; Louis XIV., James II., and his successors, Queen Anne, Bolingbroke, and Lady Masham, thought it no harm to derive money from the slave-trade; and, in the pages of Charlevoix, the una-

1693.

Aug. 11.

1694 July 18.

CHAP. XXI. vailing cruelties of midnight incendiaries, the murder and scalping of the inhabitants of peaceful villages, and the captivity of helpless women and children, are diffusely narrated as actions that were brave and beautiful.

1697. March 15. Once, indeed, a mother achieved a startling revenge. Seven days after her confinement, the Indian prowlers raised their shouts near the house of Hannah Dustin, of Haverhill: her husband rode home from the field; but too late to provide for her rescue. He must fly, if he would save even one of his seven children, who had hurried before him into the forest. But, from the cowering flock, how could a father make a choice? With gun in his hand, he now repels the assault, now cheers on the innocent group of little ones, as they rustle through the dried leaves and bushes, till all reach a shelter. The Indians burned his home, and dashed his infant against a tree; and, after days of weary marches, Hannah Dustin and her nurse, with a boy from Worcester, find themselves on an island in the Merrimac, just above Concord, in a wigwam occupied by two Indian families. The mother planned escape. "Where would you strike," said the boy, Samuel Leonardson, to his master, "to kill instantly?" and the Indian told him where, and how to scalp. At night, while the household slumbers, the captives, two women and a boy, each with a tomahawk, strike vigorously, and fleetly, and with wise division of labor,—and, of the twelve sleepers, ten lie dead; of one squaw the wound was not mortal; one child was spared from design. The love of glory next asserted its power; and the gun and tomahawk of the murderer of her infant, and a bag heaped full with scalps, were choicely kept as the trophies of the heroine.—The streams are the guides which God has set for the stranger in the wilderness:

in a bark canoe, the three descended the Merrimac to the English settlements, astonishing their friends by their escape, and filling the land with wonder at their successful daring.

Such scenes had no influence on the question of boundaries between Canada and New England. In the late summer of 1696, the fort of Pemaquid was taken by D'Iberville and Castin. Thus the frontier of French dominion was extended into the heart of Maine; and Acadia was yet, for a season, secured to the countrymen of De Monts and Champlain.

In the west, after the hope of conquering Canada was abandoned, Frontenac had little strife but with the Five Nations, whom he alternately, by missions and treaties, endeavored to win, and, by invasions, to terrify into an alliance. In February, 1692, three hundred French, with Indian confederates, were sent over the snows against the hunting parties of the Senecas in Upper Canada, near the Niagara. In the fol- 1693 Jan. and Feb.
lowing year, a larger party invaded the country of the Mohawks, bent on their extermination. The first castle, and the second also, fell easily,—for the war-chiefs were absent; at the third, a party of forty, who were dancing a war-dance, gave battle,—and victory cost the invaders thirty men. The governor of Montreal had ordered no quarter to be given, unless to women and children; but the savage confederates insisted on showing mercy; and the French historian censures their humanity "as inexcusable;" for Schuyler, of Albany, collecting two hundred men, and pursuing the party as it retired, succeeded in liberating many of the captives.

Nor did the Five Nations continue their control 1695
over western commerce. After many vacillations, the

CHAP. XXI. 1696 prudence of the memorable La Motte Cadillac, who had been appointed governor at Mackinaw, confirmed the friendship of the neighboring tribes; and a party of Ottawas, Potawatomies, and Chippewas, surprised and routed a band of Iroquois, returning with piles of beaver and scalps as trophies.

1696. At this time, a messenger from Montreal brought tidings of extensive preparations for ravaging the whole country of the Five Nations; but the Indians of the west would not rally under the banner of Onondio; and the French of Canada, aided only by their immediate allies, made their last invasion of Western New York. Frontenac, then seventy-four years of age, himself conducted the army: from Fort Frontenac they
July 28. passed over to Oswego, and occupied both sides of that river; at night, they reached the falls three leagues above its mouth, and, by the light of bark torches, they dragged the canoes and boats above the portage. As they advanced, they found the savage defiance, in two bundles of reeds, suspended on a tree —a sign that fourteen hundred and thirty-four warriors (such was the number of reeds) defied them. As
Aug. they approached the great village of the Onondagas, that nation set fire to it, and, by night, the invaders beheld the glare of the burning wigwams. Early in
Aug. 3. August, the army encamped near the Salt Springs, while a party was sent to ravage the country of the Oneidas, with orders to cut up their corn, burn their villages, put to death all who should offer resistance,
Aug. 8. and take six chiefs as hostages. Meantime, an aged Onondaga captive, who had refused to fly, was abandoned to the fury of the allies of the French; and never did the marvellous fortitude of an Indian brave display more fully its character of passive grandeur.

All the tortures that more than four hundred savages could inflict on the decrepit old man, extorted from him not one word of weakness: he scoffed always at his tormentors as the slaves of those whom he despised. On receiving mortal wounds, his last words were, "You should have taken more time to learn how to meet death manfully! I die contented; for I have no cause for self-reproach." Such scenes were enacted at Salina.

After these successes against the Onondagas and Oneidas, it was proposed to go against the Cayugas, but Frontenac refused, as if uncertain of the result: "It was time for him to repose;" and the army returned to Montreal. He had humbled, but not subdued, the Five Nations, and left them to suffer from a famine, yet to recover their lands and their spirit,—having pushed hostilities so far that no negotiations for peace could easily succeed.

The last year of the war was one of especial alarm, 1697
as rumor divulged the purpose of the French king to send out a powerful fleet to devastate the coast of New England, and to conquer New York. But nothing came of it; and the peace of Ryswick occasioned, at least, a suspension of hostilities, though not till the English exchequer had been recruited by means of a great change in the internal and the financial policy of England. The people of Massachusetts, in their wants, authorized an emission of bills on the faith of the state; England accepted from individuals a loan of one and a half million pounds sterling, paying for it eight per cent. per annum, and constituting the subscribers to the loan an incorporated bank of circulation. 1694
The measure extorted a reluctant assent from the financial wants of the government; but, in its char-

CHAP. XXI. acter, it was in harmony with the principles of the aristocratic revolution of England. "It will make money plentiful," said one of its projectors, "will raise the price of land, and draw gold and silver into the hands of the common people." In the constitutional monarchy of England, the Bank of England, a privileged body, became the mediator between the government and the moneyed interest.

1697. Sept. The peace of Ryswick was itself a victory of the spirit of reform; for Louis XIV., with James II. at his court, recognized the revolutionary sovereign of England; and the encroachments of France on the German empire were restrained. In America, France retained all Hudson's Bay, and all the places of which she was in possession at the beginning of the war; in other words, with the exception of the eastern moiety of Newfoundland, France retained the whole coast and adjacent islands, from Maine to beyond Labrador and Hudson's Bay, besides Canada and the valley of the Mississippi. But the boundary lines were reserved as subjects for wrangling among commissioners.

1698. On the east, England claimed to the St. Croix, and France to the Kennebec; and, had peace continued, the St. George would have been adopted as a compromise.

The boundary between New France and New York was still more difficult to be adjusted. Delius, the envoy from New York, included in that province all the country of the Five Nations, and declared openly at Montreal, that the countries at the west, even Mackinaw, belonged to England. This extravagant ambition was treated with derision: the French, moreover, themselves laid claim to the lands of the Five Nations. In the negotiations for the restoration of prisoners, Bellamont sought to obtain an acknowledgment that the Iroquois were subject to England; but the count de Frontenac referred the matter to the commissioners to be appointed under the treaty of Ryswick. "That the Five Nations were always considered subjects of England," said Bellamont, "can be manifested to all the world;" but De Callieres, sending ambassadors directly to Onondaga to regulate the exchange of prisoners, avoided an immediate decision. The Iroquois were proud of their independence; France asserted its right to dominion; England claimed to be in possession. Religious sympathies inclined the nations to the French, but commercial advantages brought them always into connection with the English. As the influence of the Jesuits gave to France its only power over the Five Nations, the legislature of New York, in 1700, made a law for hanging every Popish priest that should come voluntarily into the province. "The law ought forever to continue in force," is the commentary of an historian wholly unconscious of the true nature of his remark.

CHAP. XXI.

Smith, 157

1697

Smith 160.

After many collisions and acts of hostility between the Iroquois and the allies of the French, especially the Ottawas; after many ineffectual attempts, on the part of Lord Bellamont, to constitute himself the arbiter of peace, and thus to obtain an acknowledged ascendency; the four upper nations, in the summer of 1700, sent envoys to Montreal "to weep for the French who had died in the war." After rapid negotiations, peace was ratified between the Iroquois, on the one side, and France and her Indian allies, on the other. The Rat, chief of the Hurons from Mackinaw, said, "I lay down the axe at my father's feet;" and the deputies of the four tribes of Ottawas echoed his words. The

1700

July 18.

CHAP. XXI. envoy of the Abenakis said, "I have no hatchet but that of my father, and, since my father has buried it, now I have none;" the Christian Iroquois, allies of France, assented. A written treaty was made, to which each nation placed for itself a symbol;—the Senecas and Onondagas drew a spider; the Cayugas a calumet; the Oneidas a forked stick; the Mohawks a bear; the Hurons a beaver; the Abenakis a deer; and the Ottawas a hare. It was declared, also, that war should cease between the French allies and the Sioux; that peace should reach beyond the Mississippi. As to limits in Western New York, Callieres, becoming governor-general, still proposed to the French minister to assert French jurisdiction over the land of the Iroquois, or, at least, to establish its neutrality.

1701. The question remained undecided, and, through the Five Nations, England shared in the Indian trade of the west; but France kept the mastery of the great lakes, and De Callieres resolved on founding an establishment at Detroit. The Five Nations, by their dep-
March 2. uties, remonstrated, but in vain; and, in the month of June, 1701, De la Motte Cadillac, with a Jesuit mis-
Charlevoix, ii. 284. sionary and one hundred Frenchmen, was sent to take possession of Detroit. This is the oldest permanent settlement in Michigan. That commonwealth began to be colonized before even Georgia; it is the oldest, therefore, of all the inland states, except, perhaps, Illinois. The country on the Detroit River and Lake St. Clair was esteemed the loveliest in Canada; Nature had lavished on it all her charms—slopes and prairies, plains and noble forests, fountains and rivers; the lands, though of different degrees of fertility, were all productive; the isles seemed as if scattered by art to delight the eye; the lake and the river abounded in

fish; the water was pure as crystal; the air serene; the genial climate, temperate and giving health, charmed the emigrant from Lower Canada. Two numerous Indian villages gathered near the fort; here were, at last, the wigwams of the Hurons, who, from their old country, had fled first to the Falls of St. Mary, and then to Mackinaw; and above, on the right, in Upper Canada, rose a settlement of the Ottawas, their inseparable companions.

The military occupation of Illinois seems to have continued, without interruption, from the time when 1681 La Salle returned from Fort Frontenac. Joutel found a garrison at Fort St. Louis in 1687; in 1689, La Hontan bears testimony that it still continued; in 1696, a public document proves its existence, and the wish of Louis XIV. to preserve it in good condition; and when, in 1700, Tonti again descended the Missis- 1700 sippi, he was attended by twenty Canadian residents in Illinois.

The oldest permanent European settlement in the valley of the Mississippi, is the village of the Immaculate Conception of the Holy Virgin, or Kaskaskia, the seat of a Jesuit mission, which gradually became a central point of French colonization. We know that Father Gravier was its founder, but it is not easy to fix the date of its origin. Marquette had been followed by Alloüez, who, in 1684, may have been at Rock Fort, but who was chiefly a missionary to the Miamis, among whom he died. Gravier followed Alloüez, but in what year is unknown. Sebastian Rasles, after a short residence among the Abenakis, received orders to visit the west; and, from his own narrative, it is plain that, after passing a winter at Mackinaw, he, in the spring of 1693, repaired to Illinois, where he re-

Marest, in Lett. Ed. iv. 208.

Rasles, in Lett. Ed. T. iv.

CHAP. XXI. mained two years before exchanging its prairies for the borders of the Kennebec. He was sent, perhaps, as a companion to Gravier, who is famed as having been the first to ascertain the principles of the Illinois language, and to reduce them to rules, and as having, in the midst of perpetual perils and opposition from sorcerers, succeeded in beginning the establishment which was destined to endure.

When the founder of Kaskaskia was recalled to Mackinaw, he was relieved by two missionaries—by Pinet, who became the founder of Cahokia, preaching with such success, that his chapel could not contain the multitude that thronged to him; and Binnetau, who left his mission among the Abenakis to die on the upland plains of the Mississippi. Having followed the tribe to which he was attached, in their July ramble over their widest hunting-grounds,— now stifled amongst the tall grasses, now panting with thirst on the dry prairies,—all day tortured with heat, all night exposed on the ground to chilling dews,—he was seized with a mortal fever, and left his bones on the wilderness range of the buffaloes.

Before his death, and before Tonti left Illinois, Gabriel Marest, the Jesuit,—who, after chanting an ave to the cross among the icebergs of Hudson's Bay, had been taken by the English, and, on his liberation at the peace, had returned, by way of France, to America,—joined the mission at Kaskaskia, and, for a season, after the death of Binnetau and Pinet, had the sole charge of it. Very early in the eighteenth century, he was joined by Mermet. It was Mermet who assisted the commandant Jucherau, from Canada, in collecting a village of Indians and Canadians, and thus founding the first French post on the Ohio, or, as the lower part of that river was then called, the Wabash. But a contagious disease invaded the mixed population; the Indians, with extravagant ceremonies, sacrificed forty dogs to appease their manitou; and, when they began to apprehend that the manitou of the French was more powerful than their own, the medicine men would walk round the fort in circles, crying out, "We are dead: gently, manitou of the French, strike gently; do not kill us all. Good manitou, master of life and death, leave death within thy coffer; give life." Thus they prayed; but the dreadful mortality broke up the settlement.

CHAP. XXI.

Marest, iv. 206.

About the same time, Gravier returned to Illinois to plant a mission near Rock Fort, which had been abandoned by Tonti. Here he was unsuccessful, falling a victim to the assaults of the natives; but, on the banks of the Mississippi, the settlements slowly increased. The more hardy services of the mission fell to the lot of Marest. "Our life," he writes, "is passed in roaming through thick woods, in clambering over hills, in paddling the canoe across lakes and rivers, to catch a poor savage who flies from us, and whom we can tame neither by teachings nor by caresses."

Lett. Ed. iv 197.

In 1711, on Good Friday, Marest started for the Peorias, who desired a new mission. In two days he reached Cahokia. "I departed," he writes again, "having nothing about me but my crucifix and my breviary, being accompanied by only three savages, who might abandon me from levity, or from fear of enemies might fly. The horror of these vast, uninhabited forest regions, where in twelve days not a soul was met, almost took away all courage. Here was a journey where there was no village, no bridge, no ferry, no boat, no house, no beaten path, and over boundless

CHAP. XXI. prairies, intersected by rivulets and rivers,—through forests and thickets filled with briers and thorns,—through marshes, where we plunged sometimes to the girdle. At night, repose was sought on the grass, or on leaves, exposed to wind and rain,—happy if by the side of some rivulet, of which a draught might quench thirst. A meal was prepared from such game as was killed on the way, or by roasting ears of corn."

Lett. Ed. iv 220.

The gentle virtues and fervid eloquence of Mermet made him the soul of the mission at Kaskaskia. At early dawn, his pupils came to church, dressed neatly and modestly, each in a large deer-skin, or in a robe stitched together from several skins. After receiving lessons, they chanted canticles; mass was then said in presence of all the Christians in the place, the French and the converts,—the women on one side, the men on the other. From prayer and instruction, the missionaries proceeded to visit the sick and administer medicine; and their skill as physicians did more than all the rest to win confidence. In the afternoon, the catechism was taught, in presence of the young and the old, where every one, without distinction of rank or age, answered the questions of the missionary. At evening, all would assemble at the chapel for instruction, for prayer, and to chant the hymns of the church On Sundays and festivals, even after vespers, a homily was pronounced; at the close of the day, parties would meet in the cabins to recite the chaplet, in alternate choirs, and sing psalms into the night. Their psalms were often homilies, with the words set to familiar tunes. Saturday and Sunday were the days appointed for confession and communion, and every convert confessed once in a fortnight. The success of the mission was such, that marriages of the French emi-

Marest, iv 208.

grants were sometimes solemnized with the daughters of the Illinois according to the rites of the Catholic church. The occupation of the territory was a cantonment of Europeans among the native proprietors of the forests and prairies. CHAP XXI.

Jesuits and fur-traders were the founders of Illinois; Louis XIV. and privileged companies were the patrons of Southern Louisiana; but the honor of beginning the work of colonization in the south-west of our republic belongs to the illustrious Canadian, Lemoine D'Iberville. Present, as a volunteer, in the midnight attack upon Schenectady, where he was chiefly remembered for an act of clemency; at Port Nelson, calm amidst the crash of icebergs in which his vessels had become involved, and, though exceedingly moved by the loss of his young brother in a skirmish with the English, yet, with marvellous firmness, preserving his countenance without a sign of disquiet,—putting his whole trust in God, and, with tranquil daring, making a conquest of the fort which controls the vast Indian commerce of the wide regions of Nelson River; the captor of Pemaquid; the successful invader of the English possessions on Newfoundland; and again, in 1697, in spite of icebergs and a shipwreck, victorious in naval contests on the gloomy waters of Hudson's Bay, and recognized as the most skilful naval officer in the service of France;—he, the idol of his Canadian countrymen, ever buoyant and brave, after the peace of Ryswick, sought and obtained a commission for establishing direct maritime intercourse between France and the Mississippi. Lett. Ed. iv 14.

1698. On the seventeenth day of October, 1698, two frigates, and two smaller vessels, with a company of marines, and about two hundred settlers, including a few

CHAP. XXI. women and children,—most of the men being disbanded Canadian soldiers,—embarked for the Mississippi,
1698. which, as yet, had never been entered from the sea. Happier than La Salle, the leader of the enterprise won confidence and affection every where: the gov-
Dec ernor of St. Domingo gave him a welcome, and bore a willing testimony to his genius and his good judgment. A larger ship of war from that station joined
1699 the expedition, which, in January, 1699, caught a
Jan. 27. glimpse of the continent, and anchored before the Island St. Rose. On the opposite shore, the fort of Pensacola had just been established by three hundred Spaniards from Vera Cruz. This prior occupation is the reason why, afterwards, Pensacola remained a part of Florida, and the dividing line between that province and Louisiana was drawn between the bays of Pensacola and Mobile. Obedient to his orders, and to the maxims of the mercantile system, the governor of Pensacola would allow no foreign vessel to enter the harbor. Sailing to the west, D'Iberville cast anchor south-south-east of the eastern point of Mobile, and
Feb. 2. landed on Massacre, or, as it was rather called, Dauphine Island. The water between Ship and Horn Islands being found too shallow, the larger ship from the station of St. Domingo returned, and the frigates anchored near the groups of the Chandeleur, while D'Iberville with his people erected huts on Ship Island, and made the discovery of the River Pascagoula and the tribes of Biloxi. The next day, a party of Bayagoulas, from the Mississippi, passed by: they were warriors returning from an inroad into the land of the Indians of Mobile.

Feb. 27. In two barges, D'Iberville and his brother Bienville, with a Franciscan, who had been a companion to La

Salle, and with forty-eight men, set forth to seek the Mississippi. Floating trees, and the turbid aspect of the waters, guided to its mouth. On the second day in March, they entered the mighty river, and ascended to the village of the Bayagoulas—a tribe which then dwelt on its western bank, just below the River Iberville, worshipping, it was said, an opossum for their manitou, and preserving in their temple an undying fire. There they found a letter from Tonti to La Salle, written in 1684, and safely preserved by the wondering natives. The Oumas also were visited; and the party probably saw the great bend at the mouth of the Red River. A parish and a bayou, that bear the name of Iberville, mark the route of his return, through the lakes which he named Maurepas and Pontchartrain, to the bay which he called St. Louis. At the head of the Bay of Biloxi, on a sandy shore, under a burning sun, he erected the fort which, with its four bastions and twelve cannon, was to be the sign of French jurisdiction over the territory from near the Rio del Norte to the confines of Pensacola. While D'Iberville himself sailed for France, his two brothers, Sauvolle and Bienville, were left in command of the station, round which the few colonists were planted. Thus began the commonwealth of Mississippi. Prosperity was impossible; hope could not extend beyond a compromise with the Spaniards on its flank, and the Indian tribes around,—with the sands, which it was vain to till, and the burning sun, that may have made the emigrants sigh for the cool breezes of Hudson's Bay. Yet there were gleams of light: the white men from Carolina, allies of the Chickasas, invaded the neighboring tribes of Indians, making it easy for the French to establish alliances. Missionaries, also, had

CHAP. XXI.

1699

May

May 9

CHAP. XXI. already conciliated the good will of remoter nations; and from the Taensas and the Yazoos, Davion—whose name belonged of old to the rock now called Fort Adams—and Montigny floated down the Mississippi to visit their countrymen. Already a line of communication existed between Quebec and the Gulf of Mexico. The boundless southern region—made a part of the French empire by lilies carved on forest trees, or crosses erected on bluffs, and occupied by French missionaries and forest rangers—was annexed to the command of the governor of Biloxi.

During the absence of D'Iberville, it became apparent that England was jealous of his enterprise. Already Hennepin had been taken into the pay of
1698. William III., and had published his new work, in which, to bar the French claim of discovery, he had, with impudent falsehood, claimed to have himself first descended the Mississippi, and had interpolated into his former narrative a journal of his pretended voyage down the river. This had been published in London at the very moment when the fort at Biloxi
1699. was in progress; and, at once, an exploring expedition, under the auspices of Coxe, a proprietor of New Jersey, sought also for the mouths of the Mississippi. When Bienville, who passed the summer in exploring the forks below the site of New Orleans, descended
Sept. 16. the river, he met an English ship of sixteen guns, commanded by Barr,—one of two vessels which had been sent to sound the passes of the majestic stream. Giving heed to the assertion of Bienville of French supremacy, as proved by French establishments, the English captain turned back; and the bend in the river which was the scene of the interview was named and is still called, English Turn.

Thus failed the vast project of Coxe to possess what he styled the English province of Carolana. But Hennepin—who, had he but loved truth, would have gained a noble reputation, and who now is remembered, not merely as a light-hearted, ambitious, daring discoverer, but also as a boastful liar—had had an audience of William III.; a memorial from Coxe was also presented to King William in council, and the members were unanimous in the opinion, that the settling of the banks of the Mississippi should be encouraged. "I will leap over twenty stumbling-blocks, rather than not effect it," said William of Orange; and he often assured the proprietor of his willingness to send over, at his own cost, several hundred Huguenot and Vaudois refugees. But England was never destined to acquire more than a nominal possession of the Mississippi; nor could Spain do more than protest against what it regarded as a dismemberment of the government of Mexico. France obtained, under Providence, the guardianship of Louisiana, not, as it proved, for its own benefit, but rather as the trustee for the infant nation by which it was one day to be inherited. Coxe's Carolana. 1700

It was at this time that Bienville received the memorial of French Protestants to be allowed, under French sovereignty, and in the enjoyment of freedom of conscience, to plant the banks of the Mississippi. "The king," answered Pontchartrain at Paris, "has not driven Protestants from France to make a republic of them in America;" and D'Iberville returned from Europe with projects far unlike the peaceful pursuits of agriculture. First came the occupation of the Mississippi, by a fortress built on its bank, on a point elevated above the marshes, not far from the sea, soon to be abandoned. In February, Tonti came down from 1699 Dec. 7. 1700 Jan. 17.

CHAP XXI. 1700. the Illinois; and, under his guidance, the brothers D'Iberville and Bienville ascended the Great River, and made peace between the Oumas and the Bayagoulas. Among the Natchez, the Great Sun, followed by a large retinue of his people, welcomed the illustrious strangers. His country seemed best suited to a settlement; a bluff, now known as Natchez, was selected for a town, and, in honor of the countess of Pontchartrain, was called Rosalie.

While D'Iberville descended to his ships, soon to embark for France, his brother, in March, explored Western Louisiana, and, crossing the Red River, approached New Mexico. No tidings of exhaustless wealth were gleaned from the natives; no mines of unparalleled productiveness were discovered among the troublesome morasses; and St. Denys, with a motley group of Canadians and Indians, was sent to ramble for six months in the far west, that he might certainly find the land of gold. In April, Le Sueur led a company, in quest of mineral stores, to mountains in our northwestern territory. Passing beyond the Wisconsin, beyond the Chippewa, beyond the St. Croix, he sailed north till he reached the mouth of the St. Peter's, and did not pause till, entering that river, he came to the confluence of the Blue Earth. There, in a fort among Iowas, he passed the winter, that he might take possession of a copper mine, and, on the return of spring, fill his boats with heaps of ore.

La Harpe MS. Long's Second Ex. i. 316. Martin. Charlevoix.

1701. May 30. Le Sueur had not yet returned to Biloxi, when news came from the impatient ministry of impoverished France, that certainly there were gold mines on the Missouri. But bilious fevers sent death among the dreamers about veins of precious metals and rocks of emerald. July 22. Sauvolle was an early victim, leaving the chief command to the youthful Bienville; and great havock was made among the colonists, who were dependent on the Indians for baskets of corn, and were saved from famine by the chase and the net and line. The Choctas and the Mobile Indians desired an alliance against the Chickasas, and the French were too weak to act, except as mediators. In December, D'Iberville, arriving with reënforcements, found but one hundred and fifty alive. CHAP. XXI.

Early in 1702, the chief fortress of the French was 1702
transferred from Biloxi to the western bank of the Mobile River, the first settlement of Europeans in Alabama; and, during the same season, though Dauphine Island was very flat, and covered with sands which sustained no grasses, and hardly nourished a grove of pines, its excellent harbor was occupied as a convenient station for ships. Such was Louisiana in the days of its founder. Attacked by the yellow fever, D'Iberville escaped with his life, but his health was broken; and, though he gained strength to render service to France in 1706, the effort was followed by a
severe illness, which terminated in his death at the 1706 July 9
Havana. In him the colonies and the French navy lost a hero worthy of their regret. But Louisiana, at White's Recopilacion, ii. 654.
his departure, was little more than a wilderness claimed 1702.
in behalf of the French king; in its whole borders, there were scarcely thirty families. The colonists were unwise in their objects, searching for pearls, for the wool of the buffalo, for productive mines. Their scanty number was scattered on discoveries, or among the Indians in quest of furs. There was no quiet agricultural industry. Of the lands that were occupied, the coast of Biloxi is as sandy as the deserts of Lybia; the soil on Dauphine Island is meagre: on the delta

CHAP. XXI. of the Mississippi, where a fort had been built, Bienville and his few soldiers were insulated and unhappy,

1702 at the mercy of the rise of waters in the river; and the buzz and sting of mosquitoes, the hissing of the snakes, the croakings of the frogs, the cries of alligators, seemed to claim that the country should still, for a generation, be the inheritance of reptiles,—while, at the fort of Mobile, the sighing of the pines, and the hopeless character of the barrens, warned the emigrants to seek homes farther within the land.

But, at least, the Spaniards at Pensacola were no longer hostile; Spain, as well as France, had fallen under the sovereignty of the Bourbons; and, after ineffectual treaties for a partition of the Spanish monarchy, all Europe was kindling into wars, to preserve the balance of power, or to refute the doctrine of legitimacy. This is the period when Spain became intimately involved in our destinies; and she long remained, like France, the enemy to our fathers as subjects of England—the friend to their independence.

The liberties of the provinces, of the military corporations, of the cities, of Spain, had gradually become merged in despotism. The position of the peninsula, separated from Europe by a chain of mountains, and intersected by high ridges, had not favored the spirit of liberal inquiry; and the inquisition had so manacled the national intelligence, that the country of Cervantes and Calderon had relapsed into inactivity. The contest against the Arabs had been a struggle of Catholic Christianity against Moslem theism, and, as it had been continued for seven centuries with inexorable consistency, had given to Spanish character the aspect of exclusiveness, which was heightened by the tranquil pride consequent on success. France had amalga-

mated provinces; Spain had to deal with nations: CHAP. XXI.
France had triumphed over sovereignties, and Spain over religions.

But Spain was not only deficient in active intelligence, and in toleration; she also had lost men. From Ferdinand the Catholic to Philip III., she had expelled three millions of Jews and Moors; her inferior nobility emigrated to America: in 1702, her census enumerated less than seven million souls. The nation that once would have invaded England, had no navy; and, having the mines of Mexico and South America, it needed subscriptions for its defence. Foreigners, by means of loans and mortgages, gained more than seven eighths of the wealth from America, and furnished more than nine tenths of the merchandise shipped for the colonies. Spanish commerce had expired; Spanish manufactures had declined; even agriculture had fallen a victim to mortmains and privilege. Inactivity was followed by poverty; and the dynasty itself became extinct. 1701 Oct. 30.

If the doctrine of legitimacy were to be recognized as of divine origin, and therefore paramount to treaties, the king of France could claim for his own family the inheritance of Spain. That claim had been sanctioned by the testament of the last Spanish king, and was desired by the Spanish people, of whom the anger had been roused by the attempts at partition. To the crown of Spain belonged the Low Countries, the Milanese, and the Two Sicilies, besides its world in the Indies; and the union of so many states in the family of the Bourbons might rouse Spain from its atrophy, but seemed to threaten the freedom of Europe, and to secure to France co onial supremacy. William III. resolved on war. Ever true to his ruling passion for the liberty

CHAP. XXI. of Holland against France; persevering in it in opposition to his ministry and parliament; in the last year of
1702. his life, suffering from a mortal disease,—with swollen feet, voice extinguished; too infirm to receive visits; alone, separate from the world, at the castle of St. Loo;
Schlosser, i. 40, 41. he still rallied new alliances, governed the policy of Europe, and, as to territory, shaped the destinies of
1701. Sept. 18. America. In the midst of negotiations, James II. died at St. Germain; and Louis roused the nationality of England by recognizing the son of the royal exile as the legitimate king of Great Britain. Thus the war for the balance of power, for colonial territory, and for commercial advantages, became also a war of opinion, in which England vindicated the independence of national power.

1702. Louis XIV. was an old man, and the men of energy in his cabinet and his army were gone. There was no Colbert, to put order into the finances; no Louvois, by his savage resoluteness, to inspire terror: Luxemburgh was dead, and the wise Catinat no more a favorite. Long wars had enfeebled agriculture, and had exhausted the population; and the excess of royal vanity insured defeat; for the monarch expected victory to obey his orders, and genius to start into action from his choice. Two years passed without reverses; but the
1704 battle of Blenheim, fatal to the military reputation of France, revealed the exhaustion of the kingdom. The armies of Louis XIV. were opposed by troops collected from England, the Empire, Holland, Savoy, Portugal, Denmark, Prussia, and Lorraine, led on by Eugene and Marlborough, who, completing the triumvirate with the grand pensionary Heinsius, combined in their service money, numbers, forethought, and military genius.

In North America, the central colonies of our republic scarce knew the existence of war, except as they were invited to aid in defending the borders, or were sometimes alarmed at a privateer hovering off their coast. The Five Nations, at peace with both France and England, protected New York by a mutual compact of neutrality. South Carolina, bordering on Spanish Florida; New England, which had so often conquered Acadia, and coveted the fisheries; were alone involved in the direct evils of war. CHAP. XXI. 1702

South Carolina began colonial hostilities. Its governor, James Moore, by the desire of the commons, placed himself at the head of an expedition for the reduction of St. Augustine. The town was easily ravaged; but the garrison retreated to the castle, and the besiegers waited the arrival of heavy artillery. To obtain it, a sloop was sent to Jamaica; but an emissary had already announced the danger to Bienville, at Mobile, who conveyed the intelligence to the Spanish viceroy; and, when two Spanish vessels of war appeared near the mouth of the harbor, Moore abandoned his ships and stores, and retreated by land. The colony, burdened with debt, pleaded the precedent "of great and rich countries," and, confident that "funds of credit have fully answered the ends of money, and given the people a quick circulation of their trade and cash," issued bills of credit to the amount of six thousand pounds. To Carolina, the first fruits of war were debt and paper money. 1702 Sept. S. C. Statutes ii. 189, 195. Marston, in Hawks MSS. i. 180 Martin, i. 158. Statutes at large, i. 210. Ramsay, i. 129

This ill success diminished the terror of the Indians. The Spaniards had long occupied the country on the Bay of Appalache; had gathered the natives into towns, built for them churches, and instructed them by missions of Franciscan priests. The traders of

CHAP. XXI. Carolina beheld with alarm the continuous line of
communication from St. Augustine to the incipient settlements in Louisiana; and, in the last weeks of 1705,
Marston, in Hawks' MSS. i. 29. Carroll's Coll. ii. 574 and 352. Charlevoix, iii. 473. Roberts' Florida, 14, 15. Mills, 223. Hewatt. Ramsay. a company of fifty volunteers, under the command
of Moore, and assisted by a thousand savage allies,
roamed through the woods by the trading path across
the Ocmulgee, descended through the regions which
none but De Soto had invaded, and came upon the Indian towns near the port of St. Mark's. There seems
no reason to doubt that the inhabitants spoke a dialect
of the language of the Muskhogees. They had already
learned the use of horses and of beeves, which multiplied without care in their groves. At sunrise, on the
Dec. 14. fourteenth of December, the bold adventurers reached
the strong place of Ayavalla. Beaten back from the
assault with loss, they succeeded in setting fire to the
church, which adjoined the fort. A "barefoot friar," the
only white man, came forward to beg mercy; more than
a hundred women and children, and more than fifty
warriors, were taken and kept as prisoners for the slave
15. market. On the next morning, the Spanish commander
on the bay, with twenty-three soldiers and four hundred Indians, gave battle, and was defeated; but the
Spanish fort was too strong to be carried by storm.
17. The tawny chief of Ivitachma "compounded for peace
with the plate of his church and ten horses laden with
provisions." Five other towns submitted without conditions. Most of their people abandoned their homes,
and were received as free emigrants into the jurisdiction of Carolina. Thus was St. Augustine insulated
by the victory over its allies. The Creeks, that dwelt
between Appalache and Mobile, being friends to Carolina, interrupted the communication with the French.
The English flag having been carried triumphantly

through the wilderness to the Gulf of Mexico, the savages were overawed; and Great Britain established a new claim to the central forests that were soon to be named Georgia. CHAP XXI.

In the next year, a French squadron from the Havana attempted revenge by an invasion of Charleston; but the brave William Rhett and the governor, Sir Nathaniel Johnson, inspired courage, and prepared defence. The Huguenots, also, panted for action. One of the French ships was taken; and, wherever a landing was effected, the enemy was attacked with such energy that, of eight hundred, three hundred were killed or taken prisoners. The colonists fought like brave men contending for their families and homes. Unaided by the proprietaries, South Carolina gloriously defended her territory, and, with very little loss, repelled the invaders. The result of the war at the south was evidently an extension of the English boundary far into the territory that Spain had esteemed as a portion of Florida. 1706

At the north, the province of Massachusetts alone was desolated: for her, the history of the war is but a catalogue of misery. The marquis de Vaudreuil, now governor of Canada, made haste to conciliate the Iroquois. A treaty of neutrality with the Senecas was commemorated by two strings of wampum: to prevent the rupture of this happy agreement, he resolved to send no war parties against the English on the side of New York.

The English were less successful in their plans of neutrality with the Abenakis. A congress of chiefs, from the Merrimac to the Penobscot, met Governor Dudley at Casco: "The sun," said they, "is not more distant from the earth, than our thoughts from war;" 1703 June 20. Penhallow

CHAP. XXI. 1703. and, giving the belt of wampum, they added new stones to the two piles which had been raised as memorials of friendship. Yet, within six weeks, the whole country from Casco to Wells was in a conflagration. On Aug. 10. one and the same day, the several parties of the Indians, with the French, burst upon every house or garrison in that region, sparing, says the faithful chronicler, "neither the milk-white brows of the ancient, nor the mournful cries of tender infants." Cruelty became an art, and honor was awarded to the most skilful contriver of tortures. The prowling Indian seemed near every farm-house; many an individual was suddenly snatched away into captivity. If armed men, rousing for the attack, penetrated to the fastnesses of their roving enemy, they found nothing but solitudes.

1704. Death hung on the frontier. The farmers, that had built their dwellings on the bank just above the beautiful meadows of Deerfield, had surrounded with pickets an enclosure of twenty acres—the village citadel. There were separate dwelling-houses, also fortified by a circle of sticks of timber set upright in the ground. Their occupants knew, through the Mohawks, that danger was at hand. All that winter, there was not a night but the sentinel was abroad; not a mother lulled her infant to rest, but knew that, before morning, the tomahawk might crush its feeble skull. The snow lay four feet deep, when the clear, invigorating air of mid-Feb. winter cheered the war party of about two hundred French and one hundred and forty-two Indians, who, with the aid of snow-shoes, and led by Hertel de Rouville, had walked on the crust all the way from Canada. On the last night in February, a pine forest near Deerfield gave them shelter till after midnight. When, at the approach of morning, the unfaithful sentinels retired, the war party entered within the palisades, which drifts of snow had made useless; and the war-whoop of the savages bade each family prepare for captivity or death. The village was set on fire, and all but the church and one dwelling-house were consumed. Of the inhabitants, but few escaped: forty-seven were killed; one hundred and twelve, including the minister and his family, were made captives. One hour after sunrise, the party began its return to Canada. But who would know the horrors of that winter march through the wilderness? Two men starved to death. Did a young child weep from fatigue, or a feeble woman totter from anguish under the burden of her own offspring, the tomahawk stilled complaint, or the helpless infant was cast out upon the snow. Eunice Williams, the wife of the minister, had not forgotten her Bible; and, when they rested by the way-side, or, at night, made their couch of branches of evergreen strown on the snow, the savages allowed her to read it. Having but recently recovered from confinement, her strength soon failed. To her husband, who reminded her of the "house not made with hands, eternal in the heavens," "she justified God in what had happened." The mother's heart rose to her lips, as she commended her five captive children, under God, to their father's care; and then one blow from a tomahawk ended her sorrows. "She rests in peace," said her husband, "and joy unspeakable and full of glory." In Canada, no entreaties, no offers of ransom, could rescue his youngest daughter, then a girl of but seven years old. Adopted into the village of the praying Indians near Montreal, she became a proselyte to the Catholic faith, and the wife of a Cahnewaga chief; and when, after long years, she visited her friends at Deerfield, she appeared in an Indian dress:

CHAP XXI. 1704.

Mar. 1.

CHAP. XXI. and, after a short sojourn, in spite of a day of fast of a whole village, which assembled to pray for her deliverance, she returned to the fires of her own wigwam, and to the love of her own Mohawk children.

There is no tale to tell of battles like those of Blenheim or of Ramillies, but only one sad narrative of rural dangers and sorrows. In the following years, the

1705 to 1707. Indians stealthily approached towns in the heart of Massachusetts, as well as along the coast, and on the southern and western frontiers. Children, as they gamboled on the beach; reapers, as they gathered the harvest; mowers, as they rested from using the scythe; mothers, as they busied themselves about the household,—were victims to an enemy who disappeared the moment a blow was struck, and who was ever present where a garrison or a family ceased its vigilance.

1708. In 1708, at a war-council at Montreal, a grand expedition was resolved on by the French Indians against New England, to be led by French officers, and assisted by a hundred picked Canadians. The party of the French Mohawks and the Hurons failed; but the French under Des Chaillons and Hertel de Rouville, the destroyer of Deerfield, willing to continue murdering helpless women and children, when a part, at least, of the savages were weary of it, with Algonquin Indians as allies, ascended the St. Francis, and, passing by the White Mountains,—having travelled near one hundred and fifty leagues through almost impracticable paths,—made their rendezvous at Winnipiseogee. There they failed to meet the expected aid from the Abenakis, and in consequence were too feeble for an attack on Portsmouth; they therefore descended the Merrimac to the town of Haverhill, resolving to sack a remote village, rather than return without striking a blow.

Mirick's Haverhill, 117, 133. Whittier. Hutchinson. Charlevoix. MS.

Haverhill was, at that time, a cluster of thirty cottages and log-cabins, embosomed in the primeval forests, near the tranquil Merrimac. In the centre of the settlement stood a new meeting-house, the pride of the village. On the few acres of open land, the ripening Indian corn rose over the charred stumps of trees, and on the north and west bordered on the illimitable, unbroken wilderness, which stretched far away to the White Mountains, and beyond them, and, by its very depth, seemed a bulwark against invasion. On the night of the twenty-ninth of August, the evening prayers had been said in each family, and the whole village fearlessly resigned itself to sleep. That night, the band of invaders slept quietly in the near forest. At daybreak, they assumed the order of battle; Rouville addressed the soldiers, who, after their orisons, marched against the fort, raised the shrill yell, and dispersed themselves through the village to their work of blood. The rifle rang; the cry of the dying rose. Benjamin Rolfe, the minister, was beaten to death; one Indian sunk a hatchet deep into the brain of his wife, while another caught his infant child from its dying mother, and dashed its head against a stone. Thomas Hartshorne and his two sons, attempting a rally, were shot; a third son was tomahawked. John Johnston was shot by the side of his wife: she fled into the garden, bearing an infant; was caught and murdered; but, as she fell, she concealed her child, which was found, after the massacre, clinging to her breast. Simon Wainwright was killed at the first fire. Mary, his wife, fearlessly unbarred the door; with cheerful mien, bade the savages enter; procured for them what they wished; and, when they demanded money, she retired as if to "bring it," and, gathering up all her children save one, succeeded in escaping.

CHAP. XXI. 1708

Aug 29.

Mirick.

CHAP. XXI.

All the attacks were made simultaneously. The English began to gather; the intrepid Davis sounded an alarm; and, as the destroyers retired, Samuel Ayer, ever to be remembered in village annals, with but a thirteenth part of their number, hung on their rear,—himself a victim, yet rescuing several from captivity.

The day was advanced when the battle ended. The rude epitaph on the moss-grown stone tells where the interment was made in haste: Rolfe, his wife, and child, fill one grave: in the burial-ground of the village, an ancient mound marks the resting-place of the little multitude of victims.

Such were the sorrows of that generation. At daybreak, the villagers seemed secure: a little later in the morning, while the dew was hardly dry on the willows by the river side, the smoke rose from smouldering ruins, and the sward was red with the blood of their pastor and brave men, of women and mangled babes. Nor did this savage warfare pass unreproved. "I hold it my duty towards God and my neighbor"—such was the message of the brave Peter Schuyler to the marquis de Vaudreuil—"to prevent, if possible, these barbarous and heathen cruelties. My heart swells with indignation, when I think that a war between Christian princes, bound to the exactest laws of honor and generosity, which their noble ancestors have illustrated by brilliant examples, is degenerating into a savage and boundless butchery. These are not the methods for terminating the war. Would that all the world thought with me on this subject."

Charlevoix, 239.

But enough of these heart-rending tales. Such fruitless cruelties inspired our fathers with a deep hatred of the French missionaries; they compelled the employment of a large part of the inhabitants as soldiers; so that there was one year, during this war, when even a fifth part of all who were capable of bearing arms were in active service. They gave birth, also, to a willingness to exterminate the natives. The Indians vanished when their homes were invaded; they could not be reduced by usual methods of warfare: hence a bounty was offered for every Indian scalp; to regular forces under pay, the grant was ten pounds,— to volunteers in actual service, twice that sum; but if men would, of themselves, without pay, make up parties, and patrol the forests in search of Indians, as of old the woods were scoured for wild beasts, the chase was invigorated by the promised "encouragement of fifty pounds per scalp."

Meantime, the English had repeatedly made efforts to gain the French fortress on Newfoundland, and New England had desired the reduction of Acadia, as essential to the security of its trade and fishery. In 1704, a fleet from Boston harbor had defied Port Royal; and, three years afterwards, under the influence of Dudley, Massachusetts attempted its conquest. The failure of that costly expedition, which was thwarted by the activity of Castin, created discontent in the colony, by increasing its paper money and its debts. But England was resolved on colonial acquistions; in 1709, a fleet and an army were to be sent from Europe: from Massachusetts and Rhode Island, twelve hundred men were to aid in the conquest of Quebec; from the central provinces, fifteen hundred were to assail Montreal; and, in one season, Acadia, Canada, and Newfoundland, were to be reduced under British sovereignty. The colonies kindled at the prospect: to defray the expenses of preparation, Connecticut, and New York, and New Jersey,

CHAP. XXI. then first issued bills of credit; stores were collected; the troops levied from the hardy agriculturists. But no English fleet arrived; and the energies that had been roused were wasted in inactive expectation.

1710. At last, in 1710, the final successful expedition against Acadia took place. At the instance of Nicholson, who had been in England for that purpose, and under his command, six English vessels, joined by thirty of New Sept. 18–29. England, and four New England regiments, sailed in September from Boston. In six days, the fleet anchored before the fortress of Port Royal. The garrison of Subercase, the French governor, was weak and disheartened, and could not be rallied; murmurs and desertions Oct. 1–12. multiplied: the terms of capitulation were easily concerted; the tattered garrison, one hundred and fifty-six Oct. 5–16. in number, marched out with the honors of war, to beg food as alms. Famine would have soon compelled Charlevoix, ii 343, 346. a surrender at discretion. In honor of the queen, the place was called Annapolis. The French were unwilling to abandon the hope of recovering possession. Vaudreuil, having appointed Castin his lieutenant for Acadia, in the winter of 1710, sent messengers over the snows to the missionaries, to preserve the zeal and patriotism of the Indian allies and the inhabitants; but, from that day to this, the English flag has been safe at Annapolis.

1710. Flushed with victory, Nicholson repaired to England to urge the conquest of Canada. The tories, who were in power, desired peace, and colonial successes might conciliate the mercantile interest in its favor by the prospect of commercial advantages. The legislature of New York had unanimously appealed to the queen on the dangerous progress of French dominion at the west. "It is well known," said their address, "that the French can go by water from Quebec to Montreal. From thence they can do the like, through rivers and lakes, at the back of all your majesty's plantations on this continent as far as Carolina; and in this large tract of country live several nations of Indians who are vastly numerous. Among those they constantly send emissaries and priests, with toys and trifles, to insinuate themselves into their favor. Afterwards they send traders, then soldiers, and at last build forts among them; and the garrisons are encouraged to intermarry, cohabit, and incorporate among them; and it may easily be concluded that, upon a peace, many of the disbanded soldiers will be sent thither for that purpose." At the same time, five sachems from the Iroquois had sailed with Schuyler for England. In London, amidst the gaze of crowds, dressed in English small-clothes of black, with scarlet ingrain cloth mantles, edged with gold, for their blankets, they were conducted in state in coaches to an audience with Queen Anne; and, giving her belts of wampum, they avowed their readiness to take up the hatchet and aid in the reduction of Canada. 1710.

At that time, the secretary of state was St. John, afterwards raised to the peerage as Viscount Bolingbroke, whom a keen observer described as "the greatest young man" of his day. He possessed wit, quickness of apprehension, good learning, and excellent taste. Though fond of pleasure, he was prompt, and capable of close and long-continued application. Winning friends by his good temper and admirable conver sation, he was the best orator in the house of commons; and the whole parliament, turned by his eloquence, would do nothing without him. But St. John had no faith, and therefore he could keep no faith. He could 1711

CHAP. XXI. 1711. be true in his attachment to a woman or a friend, bu not to a principle, or a people. "The rabble," he would say, "is a monstrous beast, that has passions to be moved, but no reason to be appealed to;.....plain sense will influence half a score of men, at most, while mystery will lead millions by the nose;" and, having no reliance in the power of the common mind to discern the right, or in the power of truth to resist opposition and guide through perils, he could give no fixedness to his administration, and no security to his fame. Pushing intellectual freedom even to libertinism, it was he who was author of the tax on newspapers. Indifferent, not to the forms of religion only, but to religion itself, he was the unscrupulous champion of the High Church, and supported the worst acts of its most intolerant policy. As he grew older, he wrote on patriotism and liberty, and became himself, from the dupe of the Pretender, the suitor for power through the king's mistress. Thus, though capable of great ideas, and catching glimpses of universal truth, his horizon was shut in by the selfishness of his ambition. Writing brilliant treatises on philosophy, he fretted at the bit which curbed his passions; and, from the unsettled character of his mind, though rapid in appropriating a scheme, he could neither inspire confidence, nor enjoy internal calm, nor arrange an enterprise with method. Capable of energy and present activity, he had no soundness of judgment, nor power of combination. Such was the statesman who planned the conquest of Canada. "As that whole design," wrote St. John, in June, 1711, "was formed by me, and the management of it singly carried on by me, I have a sort of paternal concern for the success of it." (Bo Cor. i 161)

CHAP. XXI. 1711.

The fleet, consisting of fifteen ships-of-war and forty transports, was placed under the command of Sir Hovenden Walker; the seven veteran regiments from Marlborough's army, with a battalion of marines, were intrusted to Mrs. Masham's second brother, whom the queen had pensioned and made a brigadier-general,—whom his bottle companions called honest Jack Hill,—whom, when a tall, ragged boy, the duchess of Marlborough had, from charity, put to school,—and whom the duke, refusing him a colonelcy, had properly described as good for nothing. In the preparations, the public treasury was defrauded for the benefit of favorites. "Improve to-day, instead of depending on to-morrow;"—such was the secretary's admonition to his admiral. "The queen is very uneasy at the unaccountable loss of time in your stay at Portsmouth." Yet the fleet did sail at last; and when St. John heard of its safe arrival at Boston, he wrote exultingly to the duke of Orrery, "I believe you may depend on our being masters, at this time, of all North America."

Harley's Brief Account. Bol. Cor. i. 154.

Bol. Cor. i. 208.

From June twenty-fifth to the thirtieth day of July, the fleet lay at Boston, taking in supplies and the colonial forces. At the same time, an army of men from Connecticut, New Jersey, and New York, Palatine emigrants, and about six hundred Iroquois, assembling at Albany, prepared to burst upon Montreal; while at the west, in Wisconsin, the English had, through the Iroquois, obtained allies in the Foxes, ever wishing to expel the French from Michigan.

Charlevoix, ii. 351–361

The news of the intended expedition was seasonably received in Quebec; and the measures of defence began by a renewal of friendship with the Indians. To deputies from the Onondagas and Senecas, the governor spoke of the fidelity with which the French

CHAP. XXI. had kept their treaty; and he reminded them of their promise to remain quiet upon their mats.

1711 A great war festival was next held, at which were present all the savages domiciliated near the French settlements, and all the delegates of their allies who had come down to Montreal. In the presence of seven or eight hundred warriors, the war-song was sung, and the hatchet uplifted. The savages of the remote west were wavering, till twenty Hurons from Detroit took up the hatchet, and swayed all the rest by their example. The influence of the Jesuits had never been so manifest: by their power over the natives, an alliance extending to the Chippewas constituted the defence of Montreal.

Descending to Quebec, Vaudreuil found Abenaki volunteers assembling for his protection. Measures for resistance had been adopted with hearty earnestness; the fortifications were strengthened; Beauport was garrisoned; and the people were resolute and confiding—even women were ready to labor for the common defence.

Men watched impatiently the approach of the fleet. Aug. 25. Towards the last of August, it was said that peasants at Matanes had descried ninety or ninety-six vessels with the English flag. Yet September came, and still from the heights of Cape Diamond no eye caught one sail of the expected enemy.

The English squadron, leaving Boston on the thirtieth of July, after loitering near the Bay of Gaspe, Aug. 14–20. at last began to ascend the St. Lawrence, while Sir Hovenden Walker puzzled himself with contriving how he should secure his vessels during the winter at Quebec. Fearing "the ice in the river, freezing to the bottom, would bilge them, as much as if they were

Hoven den Walker's Journal 121

to be squeezed between rocks," he could think of no way but to disencumber them, "and secure them on the dry ground, in frames and cradles, till the thaw." 171
While ascending the river, which was "a hundred fathom deep,"—and which yet was, in winter, to freeze to the bottom,—on the evening of the twenty-second of August, a thick fog came on, with an easterly breeze. The pilots, with one accord, advised that the fleet should lie to, with the heads of the vessels to the southward: this was done, and, even so, the vessels were carried towards the northern shore. Just as Walker was going to bed, the captain of his ship came down to say that land could be seen; and, without going on deck, the admiral wantonly ordered the ships to head to the north. There was on the quarter-deck a man of sense,—Goddard, a captain in the land service: he rushed to the cabin in great haste, and importuned the admiral at least to come on deck; but the self-willed man laughed at his fears, and refused. A second time Goddard returned. "For the Lord's sake, come on deck," cried he, "or we shall certainly be lost; I see breakers all around us!"—"Putting on my gown and slippers," writes Walker, "and coming upon deck, I found what he told me to be true." Even then the blind admiral shouted, "I see no land to the leeward!" but the moon, breaking through the mists, gave him the lie. The fleet was close upon the north shore, among the Egg Islands. Now the admiral believed the pilots, and made sail immediately for the middle of the river; but morning showed that eight ships had been wrecked, and eight hundred and eighty-four men drowned. A council of war voted unanimously that it was impossible to proceed. "Had we arrived safe at Quebec," wrote the admiral, "ten or twelve

CHAP. XXI. thousand men must have been left to perish of cold and hunger: by the loss of a part, Providence saved all 1712. the rest!" and he expected public honors for his successful retreat, which to him seemed as glorious as a victory. Walker, 28.

Such was the issue of hostilities in the north-east. The failure of the attack on Quebec left Nicholson no option but to retreat, and Montreal also was unmo-
1712. lested. Detroit, though not till the next year, almost fell before the valor of a party of the Ottagamies, or Foxes—a nation passionate and untamable, springing up into new life from every defeat, and, though reduced in the number of their warriors, yet present every where by their ferocious enterprise and savage daring. Resolving to burn Detroit, they pitched their lodgings near the fort, which Du Buisson, with but twenty Frenchmen, defended. Aware of their intention, he summoned his Indian allies from the chase; and, about the middle of May, Ottawas, and Hurons, and Potawatomies, with one branch of the Sacs, Illinois, Menomonies, and even Osages and Missouris, each nation with its own ensign, came to his relief. So wide was the influence of the missionaries in the west. "Father," said they, "behold! thy children compass thee round. We will, if need be, gladly die for our father—only take care of our wives and our children, and spread a little grass over our bodies to protect them against the flies." The warriors of the Fox nation, far from destroying Detroit, were themselves besieged, and, at last, compelled to surrender at discretion. Those who bore arms were ruthlessly murdered; the rest distributed as slaves among the confederates, to be saved or massacred, at the will of their masters.

Charlevoix, ii. 365–372. Cass. Lanman's Michigan.

Thus was Detroit, though claimed by the English, preserved to the French. Its loss would have been the ruin of New France, of which it was the centre. Cherished as the loveliest spot in Canada, its possession secured the intercourse with the upper Indians and the great highway to the Mississippi.

In the mean time, the preliminaries of a treaty had been signed between France and England; and the war, which had grown out of European changes and convulsions, was suspended by negotiations that were soon followed by the uncertain peace of Utrecht.

In 1706, the victories of Ramillies and of Turin were equally fatal; and France, driven from its outposts, was compelled to struggle for the defence of its 1708
own soil. The aged monarch, humbled in arms, reduced in power, chagrined as a king by the visible decline of the prosperity of his kingdom, dejected at the loss of foreign provinces, was now wounded in his affections. His children, his grandchildren, all but one feeble infant, were swept away: he remained alone. 1709
Bowing to the stroke of Providence, he desired peace, April 29.
even on humiliating terms. "I have always," said he, "submitted to the divine will. I make a sacrifice of what I cherished most—I forget my glory." And he assented to the dethronement of his grandson. The proud confederates demanded more—that he should himself assist in reducing the Spanish monarchy. This arrogant demand was rejected; but, on the defeat at Malplaquet, he offered to abandon Alsace, and to pay a million of livres a month towards the charge of expelling his grandson from the Spanish throne. The allies demanded that he himself should do it. "If I must have war," he answered, "it shall not be with my children;" and he immediately began to enlist on

CHAP. XXI. his side the sympathies of the dispassionate. From the banks of the Danube, the Tagus, and the Po, his armies had been driven back into the confines of his own kingdom. France could not threaten England with a king, or Holland with conquest, or the emperor with a dispute for power in the empire. The party of peace grew every day. Besides, the archduke Charles, whom the allies had proposed as king of Spain, was, by the death of Joseph, become emperor. If the sovereign over the Austrian dominions, and head of the empire, should also possess the undivided Spanish monarchy, the days of Charles V. would return, and the balance of power be as far removed as ever.

The debility of France became its safety, and the success of the archduke was the prevailing motive for neglecting his claims. Moreover, success in arms had, in 1710, under the auspices of the victorious duke de Vendome, and with the applause of the Spanish nation, conducted Philip V. to Madrid. His expulsion was become impossible. Public opinion demanded the peace; and in England, where public opinion could reach the government, the tories came into power as the party of peace. Marlborough, who gave utterance to the sentiment that the enmity between England and France was irreconcilable, was dismissed; and humanity was pleased at the dismissal.

1713. April 11. The treaty of peace concluded at Utrecht was momentous in its character and consequences. It closed the series of universal wars for the balance of power, and, establishing the territorial relations of the states adjoining France on a basis which endures even now, left no opportunity for future wars, except for commerce or opinion.

The Netherlands were the barrier against French

encroachment. As Spain was now, of necessity, thrown into the current of French policy, and doomed to be stationary, or to receive an impulse from France, the Netherlands were severed from Spain, and assigned to Austria, as the second land power on the continent.

The house of Savoy was raised to the rank of royalty, and Sicily at first, afterwards, instead of Sicily, the Island of Sardinia, was added to its sceptre.

The kingdom of Naples, at first wholly severed from Spain, and divided between the houses of Savoy and Austria, soon became united, and was constituted a secundogeniture of Spain. These subsequent changes were subordinate, and not inconsistent with the policy of the peace of Utrecht, and were therefore, at a later day, effected without a general conflagration of Europe.

For the house of Brandenburg, as for that of Savoy, a monarchy was established. We shall presently see its intimate relation with the fortunes of our country.

Thus, in regard to territorial arrangements, the policy of William III. was triumphant. The balance of power, as far as France and England were interested on the continent, was arranged in a manner that might have permitted between the two neighbors a perpetual peace.

The war between England and France had been not only a contest for the balance of power on the continent, but a conflict of opinions; and this, also, was amicably settled. France assented to the emancipation of England from the maxims of legitimacy, and not only recognized the reigning queen, but also the succession to the crown, as vested in the house of Hanover by act of parliament. For Spain it compromised the question, asserting the divine right of the

CHAP. XXI. family of the Bourbons, but agreeing that the two crowns should never be united. On the other hand, 1713 England took no interest in any question of freedom agitated on the continent, and never in a single instance asserted, or was suspected of asserting, any increase of popular power. Its faithful allies, the Catalonians, had maintained their liberties inherited from the middle age: the abolition of these liberties was their punishment from the Bourbons for having joined the opposition to legitimacy; and, in the treaty of peace, England mocked them by a clause which promised them "the privileges of Castile,"—that is, the loss of all their own liberties. The government of England was in the hands of an aristocracy; and the absolute monarchy of the continent, sure of the conservative influence of its foreign policy, had no dread of Great Britain as the supporter in arms of revolutionary principles. As no eye glanced across the Atlantic to watch the principles which were springing into powerful activity on the borders of the wilderness, it seemed as if European revolutions and European wars for opinion were forever at an end.

And yet the treaty of peace at Utrecht scattered the seeds of war broadcast throughout the globe. The world had entered on the period of mercantile privilege. Instead of establishing equal justice, England sought commercial advantages; and, as the mercantile system was identified with the colonial system of the great maritime powers of Europe, the political interest which could alone kindle universal war, was to be sought in the colonies. Hitherto the colonies were but subordinate to European politics: henceforward, the question of trade on our borders, the question of territory on our frontier, involved an interest which could excite the world to arms. For about two centuries, the wars of religion had prevailed;—the wars for commercial advantages were now prepared. The interests of commerce, under the narrow point of view of privilege and of profit, regulated diplomacy, swayed legislation, and marshaled revolutions.

First, then, by the peace of Utrecht, Spain lost all her European provinces, and retained all her colonies. The mother country, being thus left with a population of but six or seven millions, had no strength proportionate to the vast extent of her colonial possessions. She held them not by physical force, but by the power of established interests, usages, and religion, and in some measure on sufferance, at the will of the maritime powers which aspired to the dominion of the seas. Great Britain, moreover, remained in possession of Gibraltar, her strongest fortress, the key to the Mediterranean. By insisting on the cession of the Spanish Netherlands to Austria, England lost its only hold on Spain; and by taking Gibraltar, it made Spain its implacable enemy.

Again: by the peace of Utrecht, Belgium was compelled to forego the advantages with which she had been endowed by the God of nature; to gratify commercial jealousy, Antwerp was denied the use of the deep waters that flowed by her walls; and afterwards the Austrian efforts at trade with the East Indies were suffocated in their infancy. This policy was an open violation of international justice,—a fraud upon humanity,—a restriction, by covenant, of national industry and prosperity. It was a pledge that Belgium would look beyond treaties, and grow familiar with natural rights; and it was possible that, even in the line of Austrian monarchs, a wise ruler might one day be penetrated with indignation at the outrage.

CHAP XXI.

With regard to France, one condition of the treaty was still worse. Jealous of the growth of the French navy, England extorted the covenant, that the port of Dunkirk should be not merely abandoned, but filled up. A treaty of peace contained a stipulation for the ruin of a harbor!

On the opening of the contest with France, William III., though bearing the standard of freedom, was false to the principle of the liberty of the seas,—prohibiting all commerce with France,—and to the protest of Holland gave no other reply than that it was his will, and that he had power to make it good. To the tory ministry of Queen Anne belongs the honor of having inserted in the treaties of peace a principle, which, but for England, would, in that generation, have wanted a vindicator. But truth, once elicited, never dies. As it descends through time, it may be transmitted from state to state, from monarch to commonwealth; but its light is never extinguished, and never permitted to fall to the ground. A great truth, if no existing nation would assume its guardianship, has power—such is God's providence—to call a nation into being, and live by the life it imparts. What Holland asserted, England kept alive, and Prussia received, till it was safe against any possible combination. The idea which Grotius promulgated, Bolingbroke fostered, till the great Frederic could become its champion, and all the continent of Europe invoke America to secure its triumph. "Free ships"—such was international law, as interpreted by England at Utrecht—"Free ships shall also give a freedom to goods." The name of contraband was narrowly defined, and the right of blockade severely limited. Sailors, in those days, needed no special protections; for it was covenanted

1689. Aug. 22. Heeren, i 349.

1713.

Treaty with France, § 17.

Treaty of Commerce with Spain, § 21-25.

that, with the exception of soldiers in the actual service of the enemy, the flag shall protect the persons that sail under it. CHAP. XXI. 1713.

Further: England, guarding with the utmost strictness the monopoly of her own colonial trade, encroached by treaty on the colonial monopoly of Spain. There shall be trade, it was said, between Great Britain and Spain, and their respective plantations and provinces, "where hitherto trade and commerce have been accustomed;" so that a prescriptive right might spring from the continued successes of British smugglers. Besides, as England gained the assiento, it was agreed that the agents of the assientists might enter all the ports of Spanish America; might send their factors into inland places; might, for their own supplies, establish warehouses, safe against search until after proof of fraudulent importations; might send yearly a ship of five hundred tons, laden with merchandise, to be entered free of all duties in the Indies, and to be sold at the annual fair; might send the returns of this traffic, whether bars of silver, ingots of gold, or the produce of the country, directly to Europe in English vessels. The hope was further expressed, that, from Europe and the North American colonies, direct supplies might be furnished to the assientists in small vessels,—that is, in vessels most likely to engage in smuggling. Here, also, lay the seeds of war: the great colonial monopolists were divided against each other; and England sought to engross, if possible, every advantage. Many were the consequences to our fathers from these encroachments: they opened trade between our colonies and the Spanish islands; they stimulated England to aggressions which led to a war; they incensed Spain, so that she could wish to see the

Assiento, § 8, 9, 11, 15.

§ 34

CHAP. XXI. great colonial system impaired, if by that means she could revenge herself on England.

1713. But the assiento itself was, for English America, the most weighty result of the negotiations at Utrecht. It was demanded by St. John, in 1711; and Louis XIV. promised his good offices to procure this advantage for the English. "Her Britannic majesty did offer and undertake,"—such are the words of that treaty,—"by persons whom she shall appoint, to bring into the West Indies of America belonging to his Catholic majesty, in the space of thirty years, one hundred and forty-four thousand negroes, at the rate of four thousand eight hundred in each of the said thirty years,"—paying, on four thousand of them, a duty of thirty-three and a third dollars a head. The assientists might introduce as many more as they pleased, at the less rate of duty of sixteen and two thirds dollars a head—only, no scandal was to be offered to the Roman Catholic religion! Exactest care was taken to secure a monopoly. No Frenchman, nor Spaniard, nor any other persons, might introduce one negro slave into Spanish America. For the Spanish world in the Gulf of Mexico, on the Atlantic, and along the Pacific, as well as for the English colonies, her Britannic majesty, by persons of her appointment, was the exclusive slave trader. England extorted the privilege of filling the New World with negroes. As great profits were anticipated from the trade, Philip V. of Spain took one quarter of the common stock, agreeing to pay for it by a stock-note; Queen Anne reserved to herself another quarter; and the remaining moiety was to be divided among her subjects. Thus did the sovereigns of England and Spain become the largest slave merchants in the world. Lady Masham promised herself a share of

Cooke's Bolingbroke, i. 175.

Assiento, § 7.

§ 18.

CHAP. XXI.

the profits; but Harley, who had good sense, and was most free from avarice, advised the assignment of her majesty's portion of the stock to the South Sea company.

Controlling the trade in slaves, who cost nothing but trinkets, and toys, and refuse arms, England gained, by the sale of the children of Africa into bondage in America, the capital which built up and confirmed a British empire in Hindostan. The political effects of this traffic were equally perceptible in the West Indies. The mercantile system, of which the whole colonial system was the essential branch, culminated in the slave trade, and in the commercial policy adopted with regard to the chief produce of slave labor. The statesmen who befriended the system of colonial monopoly, showed their highest favor to the sugar colonies. We shall hereafter see England, not satisfied with monopolizing the traffic in negroes, seek also to engross every sugar plantation in the world.

Finally, England, by the peace of Utrecht, obtained from France large concessions of territory in America. The assembly of New York had addressed the queen against French settlements in the west; William Penn advised to establish the St. Lawrence as the boundary on the north, and to include in our colonies the valley of the Mississippi. It "will make a glorious country" —such were his prophetic words. Spotswood of Virginia, again and again, directed the attention of the English ministry to the progress of the French in the west. In St. John the colony of Louisiana excited "apprehensions of the future undertakings of the French in North America." The colonization of Louisiana had been proposed to Queen Anne; yet, at the peace, that immense region remained to France. But

Bol. Cor. ii. 272.

CHAP. XXI.

England obtained supremacy in the fisheries; the entire possession of the Bay of Hudson and its borders, of Newfoundland, and of all Nova Scotia or Acadia, according to its ancient boundaries. It was agreed, also, that "France should never molest the Five Nations subject to the dominion of Great Britain." But how far did Louisiana extend? It included, according to French ideas, the whole basin of the Mississippi. Did the treaty of Utrecht assent to such an extension of French territory? And what were the ancient limits of Acadia? Did it include all that is now New Brunswick? or had France still a large territory on the Atlantic between Acadia and Maine? And what were the bounds of the territory of the Five Nations, which the treaty appeared to recognize as a part of the English dominions? These were questions which were never to be adjusted amicably.

CHAPTER XXII.

THE ABORIGINES EAST OF THE MISSISSIPPI.

On the surrender of Acadia to England, the lakes, the rivulets, the granite ledges, of Cape Breton,—of which the irregular outline is guarded by reefs of rocks, and notched and almost rent asunder by the constant action of the sea,—were immediately occupied as a province of France; and, in 1714, fugitives from Newfoundland and Acadia built their huts along its coasts wherever safe inlets invited fishermen to spread their flakes, and the soil, to plant fields and gardens. In a few years, the fortifications of Louisburg began to rise—the key to the St. Lawrence, the bulwark of the French fisheries, and of French commerce in North America. From Cape Breton, the dominion of Louis XIV. extended up the St. Lawrence to Lake Superior, and from that lake, through the whole course of the Mississippi, to the Gulf of Mexico and the Bay of Mobile. Just beyond that bay began the posts of the Spaniards, which continued round the shores of Florida to the fortress of St. Augustine. The English colonies skirted the Atlantic, extending from Florida to the eastern verge of Nova Scotia. Thus, if on the east the strait of Canso divided France and England, if on the south a narrow range of forests intervened between England and Spain, every where else the colonies of the rival nations were separated from each

CHAP XXII.

Pichon, 3

1720.

CHAP. XXII. other by tribes of the natives. The Europeans had established a wide circle of plantations, or, at least, of posts; they had encompassed the aborigines that dwelt east of the Mississippi; and, however eager might now be the passion of the intruders for carving their emblems on trees, and designating their lines of anticipated empire on maps, their respective settlements were kept asunder by an unexplored wilderness, of which savages were the occupants. The great strife of France and England for American territory could not, therefore, but involve the ancient possessors of the continent in a series of conflicts, which have, at last, banished the Indian tribes from the earlier limits of our republic. The picture of the unequal contest inspires a compassion that is honorable to humanity. The weak demand sympathy. If a melancholy interest attaches to the fall of a hero, who is overpowered by superior force, shall we not drop a tear at the fate of nations, whose defeat foreboded the exile, if it did not indeed shadow forth the decline and ultimate extinction, of a race?

A. Humboldt, Nouv. Esp. i. 380.

The earliest books on America contained tales as wild as fancy could invent or credulity repeat. The land was peopled with pygmies and with giants; the tropical forests were said to conceal tribes of negroes and tenants of the hyperborean regions were white, like the polar bear or the ermine. Jaques Cartier had heard of a nation that did not eat; and the pedant Lafitau believed, if not in a race of headless men, at least, that there was a nation of men with the head not rising above the shoulders.

Lafitau 68, 69

Yet the first aspect of the original inhabitants of the United States was uniform. Between the Indians of Florida and Canada, the difference was scarcely per-

Charlevoix i. 29

ceptible. Their manners and institutions, as well as their organization, had a common physiognomy; and, before their languages began to be known, there was no safe method of grouping the nations into families. But when the vast variety of dialects came to be compared, there were found east of the Mississippi not more than eight radically distinct languages, of which five still constitute the speech of powerful communities, and three are known only as memorials of tribes that have almost disappeared from the earth.

CHAP. XXII.

Albert Gallatin's Synopsis.

I. The primitive language which was the most widely diffused, and the most fertile in dialects, received from the French the name of ALGONQUIN. It was the mother tongue of those who greeted the colonists of Raleigh at Roanoke, of those who welcomed the Pilgrims to Plymouth. It was heard from the Bay of Gaspe to the valley of the Des Moines; from Cape Fear, and, it may be, from the Savannah, to the land of the Esquimaux; from the Cumberland River of Kentucky to the southern bank of the Missinipi. It was spoken, though not exclusively, in a territory that extended through sixty degrees of longitude, and more than twenty degrees of latitude.

The Micmacs, who occupied the east of the continent, south of the little tribe that dwelt round the Bay of Gaspe, holding possession of Nova Scotia and the adjacent isles, and probably never much exceeding three thousand in number, were known to our fathers only as the active allies of the French. They often invaded, but never inhabited, New England.

Mass. Hist. Coll. x. 115

The Etchemins, or Canoemen, dwelt not only on the St. John's River, the Ouygondy of the natives, but on the St. Croix, which Champlain always called from their name, and extended as far west, at least, as Mount Desert.

Champlain i. 74.

CHAP. XXII.

Champlain. Relation, &c. Next to these came the Abenakis, of whom one tribe has left its name to the Penobscot, and another to the Androscoggin; while a third, under the auspices of Jesuits, had its chapel and its fixed abode in the fertile fields of Norridgewock.

The clans that disappeared from their ancient hunting-grounds did not always become extinct; they often migrated to the north and west. Relation 1646 Of the Sokokis, who appear to have dwelt near Saco, and to have had an alliance with the Mohawks, many, at an early day,
1646. abandoned the region where they first became known to European voyagers, and placed themselves under the shelter of the French in Canada. The example of emigration was often followed; the savage shunned the vicinity of the civilized: among the tribes of Texas, Duponceau. there are warriors who are said to trace their lineage to Algonquins on the Atlantic; and descendants from the New England Indians now roam over western prairies.

The forests beyond the Saco, with New Hampshire, and even as far as Salem, constituted the sachemship of Pennacook, or Pawtucket, and often afforded a refuge to the remnants of feebler nations around them. The tribe of the Massachusetts, even before the colonization of the country, had almost disappeared from the shores of the bay that bears its name; and the villages of the interior resembled insulated and nearly independent bands, that had lost themselves in the wilderness.

Of the Pokanokets, who dwelt round Mount Hope, and were sovereigns over Nantucket, Martha's Vineyard, and a part of Cape Cod; of the Narragansetts, who dwelt between the bay that bears their name and the present limits of Connecticut, holding dominion over Rhode Island and its vicinity, as well as a part of Long Island,—the most civilized of the northern nations; of the Pequods, the branch of the Mohegans that occupied the eastern part of Connecticut, and ruled a part of Long Island,—earliest victims to the Europeans,—I have already related the overthrow. The country between the banks of the Connecticut and the Hudson was possessed by independent villages of the Mohegans, kindred with the Manhattans, whose few "smokes" once rose amidst the forests on New York Island.

CHAP XXII

Gookin c. ii.

The Lenni Lenape, in their two divisions of the Minsi and the Delawares, occupied New Jersey, the valley of the Delaware far up towards the sources of that river, and the entire basin of the Schuylkill. Like the benevolent William Penn, the Delawares were pledged to a system of peace; but, while Penn forbore retaliation freely, the passiveness of the Delawares was to them the degrading confession of their defeat and submission to the Five Nations. Their conquerors had stripped them of their rights as warriors, and compelled them to endure taunts as women.

Heckewelder.

Beyond the Delaware, on the Eastern Shore, dwelt the Nanticokes, who disappeared without glory, or melted imperceptibly into other tribes; and the names of Accomac and Pamlico are the chief memorials of tribes that made dialects of the Algonquin the mother tongue of the natives along the sea-coast as far south, at least, as Cape Hatteras. It is probable, also, that the Corees, or Coramines, who dwelt to the southward of the Neuse River, spoke a kindred language—thus establishing Cape Fear as the southern limit of the Algonquin speech.

Lawson, 171

In Virginia, the same language was heard through-

CHAP. XXII. out the whole dominion of Powhatán, which had the tribes of the Eastern Shore as its dependencies, and included all the villages west of the Chesapeake, from the most southern tributaries of James River to the Patuxent. The power of the little empire was entirely broken in the days of Opechancanough; and after the insurrection of Bacon, the confederacy disappears from history.

The Shawnees connect the south-eastern Algonquins with the west. The basin of the Cumberland River is marked by the earliest French geographers as the home of this restless nation of wanderers. A Kirche-val, 53. part of them afterwards had their "cabins" and their "springs" in the neighborhood of Winchester. Their principal band removed from their hunting-fields in Law-son, 171. Kentucky to the head waters of one of the great rivers of South Carolina; and, at a later day, an encampment of four hundred and fifty of them, who had been Adair, 410. straggling in the woods for four years, was found not far north of the head waters of the Mobile River, on their way to the country of the Muskhogees. It was Logan, MSS. about the year 1698, that three or four score of their families, with the consent of the government of Pennsylvania, removed from Carolina, and planted themselves on the Susquehannah. Sad were the fruits of that hospitality. Others followed; and when, in 1732, the number of Indian fighting men in Pennsylvania was estimated to be seven hundred, one half of them were Shawnee emigrants. So desolate was the wilderness, that a vagabond tribe could wander undisturbed from Cumberland River to the Alabama, from the head waters of the Santee to the Susquehannah.

The Miamis were more stable, and their own traditions preserve the memory of their ancient limits.

CHAP XXII.

"My forefather," said the Miami orator Little Turtle, at Greenville, "kindled the first fire at Detroit; from thence he extended his lines to the head waters of Scioto; from thence to its mouth; from thence down the Ohio to the mouth of the Wabash; and from thence to Chicago, on Lake Michigan. These are the boundaries within which the prints of my ancestor's houses are every where to be seen." And the early French narratives confirm his words. The forests beyond Detroit were at first found unoccupied, or, it may be, roamed over by bands too feeble to attract a trader or win a missionary; the Ottáwas, Algonquin fugitives from the basin of the magnificent river whose name commemorates them, fled to the Bay of Saginaw, and took possession of the whole north of the peninsula as of a derelict country; yet the Miamis occupied its southern moiety, and their principal mission was founded by Alloüez on the banks of the St. Joseph, within the present state of Michigan.

American State Papers, iv. 570, 571

The Illinois were kindred to the Miamis, and their country lay between the Wabash, the Ohio, and the Mississippi. Marquette found a village of them on the Des Moines, but its occupants soon withdrew to the east of the Mississippi; and Kaskaskia, Cahokia, Peoria, still preserve the names of the principal bands, of which the original strength has been greatly exaggerated. The vague tales of a considerable population vanished before the accurate observation of the missionaries, who found in the wide wilderness of Illinois scarcely three or four villages. On the discovery of America, the number of the scattered tenants of the territory which now forms the states of Ohio and Michigan, of Indiana, and Illinois, and Kentucky, could hardly have exceeded eighteen thousand.

Marest Compare Hennepin, Tonti Joutel

CHAP. XXII.

In the early part of the eighteenth century, the Potawatomies had crowded the Miamis from their dwellings at Chicago: the intruders came from the islands near the entrance of Green Bay, and were a branch of the great nation of the Chippewas. That nation, or, as some write, the Ojibwas,—the Algonquin tribes of whose dialect, mythology, traditions, and customs, we have the fullest accounts,—held the country from the mouth of Green Bay to the head waters of Lake Superior, and were early visited by the French at Sault St. Mary and Chegoimegon. They adopted into their tribes many of the Ottáwas from Upper Canada, and were themselves often included by the early French writers under that name.

Schoolcraft, 1825, p. 360

Ottáwa is but the Algonquin word for "trader;" and Mascoutins are but "dwellers in the prairie." The latter hardly implies a band of Indians distinct from the Chippewas; but history recognizes, as a separate Algonquin tribe near Green Bay, the Menomonies, who were found there in 1669, who retained their ancient territory long after the period of French and of English supremacy, and who prove their high antiquity as a nation by the singular character of their dialect.

South-west of the Menomonies, the restless Sacs and Foxes, ever dreaded by the French, held the passes from Green Bay and Fox River to the Mississippi, and, with insatiate avidity, roamed, in pursuit of contest, over the whole country between the Wisconsin and the upper branches of the Illinois. The Shawnees are said to have an affinity with this nation: that the Kickapoos, who established themselves, by conquest, in the north of Illinois, are but a branch of it, is demonstrated by their speech.

Morse, App. 222.

So numerous and so widely extended were the tribes of the Algonquin family. They were scattered over a moiety, or perhaps more than a moiety, of the territory east of the Mississippi and south of the St. Lawrence, and constituted about one half of the original population of that territory.

II. North-west of the Sacs and Foxes, west of the Chippewas, bands of the SIOUX, or DAHCOTAS, had encamped on prairies east of the Mississippi, vagrants between the head waters of Lake Superior and the Falls of St. Anthony. They were a branch of the great family which, dwelling for the most part west of the Mississippi and the Red River, extended from the Saskatchawan to lands south of the Arkansas. French traders discovered their wigwams in 1659; Hennepin was among them, on his expedition to the north; Joseph Marest and another Jesuit visited them in 1687, and again in 1689. There seemed to exist a hereditary warfare between them and the Chippewas. Their relations to the colonists, whether of France or England, were, at this early period, accidental, and related chiefly to individuals. But one little community of the Dahcota family had penetrated the territory of the Algonquins; the Winnebagoes, dwelling between Green Bay and the lake that bears their name, preferred rather to be environed by Algonquins than to stay in the dangerous vicinity of their own kindred. Like other western and southern tribes, their population appears of late to have greatly increased.

Charlevoix, iii. 291

III. The nations which spoke dialects of the HURON-IROQUOIS, or, as it has also been called, of the WYANDOT, were, on the discovery of America, found powerful in numbers, and diffused over a wide territory. The peninsula enclosed between Lakes Huron.

CHAP. XXII. Erie, and Ontario, had been the dwelling-place of the five confederated tribes of the Hurons. After their defeat by the Five Nations, a part descended the St. Lawrence, and their progeny may still be seen near Quebec; a part were adopted, on equal terms, into the tribes of their conquerors; the Wyandots fled beyond Lake Superior, and hid themselves in the dreary wastes that divided the Chippewas from their western foes. In 1671, they retreated before the powerful Sioux, and made their home first at St. Mary's and at Michilimackinac, and afterwards near the post of Detroit. Thus the Wyandots within our borders were emigrants from Canada. Having a mysterious influence over the Algonquin tribes, and making treaties with the Five Nations, they spread along Lake Erie, and, leaving to the Miamis the country beyond the Miami of the Lakes, they gradually acquired a claim to the whole territory from that river to the western boundary of New York.

The immediate dominion of the Iroquois—where the Mohawks, Oneidas, Onondagas, Cayugas, and Senecas, were first visited by the trader, the missionary, or the war parties of the French—stretched, as we have seen, from the borders of Vermont to Western New York, from the lakes to the head waters of the Ohio, the Susquehannah, and the Delaware. The number of their warriors was declared by the French, in 1660, to have been two thousand two hundred; and, in 1677, an English agent, sent on purpose to ascertain their strength, confirmed the precision of the statement. Their geographical position made them umpires in the contest of the French for dominion in the west. Besides, their political importance was increased by their conquests. Not only did they claim some supremacy

Relation 1660. Chalmers, 607–609.

in Northern New England as far as the Kennebec, and to the south as far as New Haven, and were acknowledged as absolute lords over the conquered Lenape, — the peninsula of Upper Canada was their hunting-field by right of war; they had exterminated the Eries and the Andastes, both tribes of their own family, the one dwelling on the south-eastern banks of Lake Erie, the other on the head waters of the Ohio; they had triumphantly invaded the tribes of the west as far as Illinois; their warriors had reached the soil of Kentucky and Western Virginia; and England, to whose alliance they steadily inclined, availed itself of their treaties for the cession of territories, to encroach even on the empire of France in America.

Nor had the labors of the Jesuit missionaries been fruitless. The few families of the Iroquois who migrated to the north of Lake Ontario, and raised their huts round Fort Frontenac, remained in amity with the French; and two villages of Iroquois converts, the Cahnewagas of New England writers, were established near Montreal, a barrier against their heathen countrymen and against New York.

The Huron tribes of the north were environed by Algonquins. At the south, the Chowan, the Meherrin, the Nottoway, villages of the Wyandot family, have left their names to the rivers along which they dwelt; and the Tuscaroras, kindred with the Five Nations, were the most powerful tribe in North Carolina. In 1708, its fifteen towns still occupied the upper country on the Neuse and the Tar, and could count twelve hundred warriors, as brave as their Mohawk brothers.

IV. South of the Tuscaroras, the midlands of Carolina sheltered the CATAWBAS. Its villages included the Woccons and the nation spoke a language of its

CHAP. XXII. own: that language is now almost extinct, being known only to less than one hundred persons, who linger on the banks of a branch of the Santee. Imagination never assigned to the Catawbas, in their proudest days, more than twelve hundred and fifty warriors; the oldest enumeration was made in 1743, and gives but four hundred. It may therefore be inferred, that, on the first appearance of Europeans, their language was in the keeping of not more than three thousand souls. History knows them chiefly as the hereditary foes of the Iroquois tribes, before whose prowess and numbers they dwindled away.

Adair. Ramsay

V. The mountaineers of aboriginal America were the CHEROKEES, who occupied the upper valley of the Tennessee River, as far west as Muscle Shoals, and the highlands of Carolina, Georgia, and Alabama—the most picturesque and most salubrious region east of the Mississippi. Their homes were encircled by blue hills rising beyond hills, of which the lofty peaks would kindle with the early light, and the overshadowing ridges envelop the valleys like a mass of clouds There the rocky cliffs, rising in naked grandeur, defy the lightning, and mock the loudest peals of the thunder-storm; there the gentler slopes are covered with magnolias and flowering forest-trees, decorated with roving climbers, and ring with the perpetual note of the whip-poor-will; there the wholesome water gushes profusely from the earth in transparent springs; snow-white cascades glitter on the hill-sides; and the rivers, shallow, but pleasant to the eye, rush through the narrow vales, which the abundant strawberry crimsons, and coppices of rhododendron and flaming azalea adorn. At the fall of the leaf, the fruit of the hickory and the chestnut is thickly strown on the ground. The fertile soil teems with luxuriant herbage, on which the roebuck fattens; the vivifying breeze is laden with fragrance; and daybreak is ever welcomed by the shrill cries of the social nighthawk and the liquid carols of the mocking-bird. Through this lovely region were scattered the little villages of the Cherokees, nearly fifty in number, each consisting of but a few cabins, erected where the bend in the mountain stream offered at once a defence and a strip of alluvial soil for culture. Their towns were always by the side of some creek or river, and they loved their native land; above all, they loved its rivers—the Keowee, the Tugeloo, the Flint, and the beautiful branches of the Tennessee. Running waters, inviting to the bath, tempting the angler, alluring wild fowl, were necessary to their paradise. Their language, like that of the Iroquois, abounds in vowels, and is destitute of the labials. Its organization has a common character, but etymology has not yet been able to discover conclusive analogies between the roots of words. The "beloved" people of the Cherokees were a nation by themselves. Who can say for how many centuries, safe in their undiscovered fastnesses, they had decked their war-chiefs with the feathers of the eagle's tail, and listened to the counsels of their "old beloved men"? Who can tell how often the waves of barbarous migrations may have broken harmlessly against their cliffs, where nature was the strong ally of the defenders of their land?

Smith. Barton.

Adair, 31, 33

VI. South-east of the Cherokees dwelt the UCHEES. They claimed the country above and below Augusta, and, at the earliest period respecting which we can surmise, seem not to have extended beyond the Chata-hoo-chee; yet they boast to have been the oldest inhabitants of that region. They now constitute an

CHAP XXII. inconsiderable band in the Creek confederacy, and are known as a distinct family, not from political organization, but from their singularly harsh and guttural language. When first discovered, they were but a remnant,—bewildering the inquirer by favoring the conjecture, that, from the north and west, tribe may have pressed upon tribe; that successions of nations may have been exterminated by invading nations; that even languages, which are the least perishable monument of the savages, may have become extinct.

VII. The NATCHEZ, also, are now merged in the same confederacy; but they, with the Taensas, were known to history as a distinct nation, residing in scarcely more than four or five villages, of which the largest rose near the banks of the Mississippi. That they spoke but a dialect of the Mobilian, is an inference which the memoirs of Dumont would have warranted, and which more recent travellers have confirmed, without reservation,—while the diffuse Du Pratz represents them as using at once the Mobilian and a radically different speech of their own. The missionary station among them was assigned to Franciscans; and the Jesuits who have written of them are silent respecting the tongue, which they themselves had no occasion to employ. The opinion of the acute Vater was in favor of its original character; and, by the persevering curiosity of Gallatin, it is at last known that the Natchez were distinguished from the tribes around them less by their customs and the degree of their civilization than by their language, which, as far as comparisons have been instituted, has no etymological affinity with any other whatever. Here, again, the imagination too readily kindles to invent theories; and the tradition has been widely received, that the domin-

Dumont, i. 182. Chateaubriand and Bartram. Du Pratz, Hist. de la Louis. ii. 214, 218, 219, 222, 323. Charlevoix. Le Petit, in Lett. Ed. iv. Mithridates, iii 285.

ion of the Natchez once extended even to the Wabash, that they are emigrants from Mexico; that they are the kindred of the incas of Peru. The close observation of the state of the arts among them, tends to dispel these illusions; and history knows them only as a feeble and inconsiderable nation, the occupants of a narrow territory round the spot where the Christian church, and the dwellings of emigrants from Europe and from Africa, have displaced the rude abode of their Great Sun, and the artless cabin of the chosen guardians of the sacred fire, which they vainly hoped should never die.

VIII. With these exceptions of the Uchees and the Natchez, the whole country south-east, south, and west of the Cherokees, to the Atlantic and the Gulf of Mexico, to the Mississippi and the confluence of the Tennessee and Ohio, was in the possession of one great family of nations, of which the language was named by the French the MOBILIAN, and is described by Gallatin as the MUSKHOGEE–CHOCTÀ. It included three considerable confederacies, each of which still exists, and perhaps even with some increase of numbers.

The country bounded on the Ohio at the north, on the Mississippi at the west, on the east by a line drawn from the bend in the Cumberland River to the Muscle Shoals of the Tennessee, and extending at the south into the territory of the state of Mississippi, was the land of the cheerful, brave Chickasas, the faithful, the invincible allies of the English. Marquette found them already in possession of guns, obtained probably through Virginia; La Salle built Fort Prudhomme on one of their bluffs; but their chosen abodes were on the upland country, which gives birth to the Yazoo and the Tombecbee, the finest and most fruitful on the

Bossu i. 309

CHAP XXII. continent,—where the grass is verdant in midwinter; the olue-bird and the robin are heard in February; the springs of pure water gurgle up through the white sands, to flow through natural bowers of evergreen holly; and, if the earth be but carelessly gashed to receive the kernel of maize, the thick corn springs abundantly from the fertile soil. The region is as happy as any beneath the sun; and the love which it inspired made its occupants, though not numerous, yet the most intrepid warriors of the south.

Below the Chickasas, between the Mississippi and the Tombecbee, was the land of the Choctas, who were gathered, on the eastern frontier, into compact villages, but elsewhere were scattered through the interior of their territory. Dwelling in plains or among gentle hills, they excelled every North American tribe in their agriculture,—subsisting chiefly on corn, and placing little dependence on the chase. Their country was healthful, abounding in brooks. The number of their warriors perhaps exceeded four thousand. Their dialect of the Mobilian so nearly resembles that of the Chickasas, that they almost seemed but one nation. The Choctas were allies of the French, yet preserving their independence: their love for their country was intense, and, in defending it, they utterly contemned danger.

The ridge that divided the Tombecbee from the Alabama, was the line that separated the Choctas from the groups of tribes which were soon united in the confederacy of the Creeks or Muskhogees. Their territory, including all Florida, reached, on the north, to the Cherokees; on the north-east and east, to the country on the Savannah and to the Atlantic. Along the sea, their northern limit seems to have extended

Roberts' Florida, 13.

almost to Cape Fear; at least, the tribes with which the settlers at Charleston first waged war, are enumerated by one writer as branches of the Muskhogees. Their population, spread over a fourfold wider territory, did not exceed that of the Choctas in number. Their towns were situated on the banks of beautiful creeks, in which their country abounded; the waters of their bold rivers, from the Coosa to the Chatahoochee, descended rapidly, with a clear current, through healthful and fertile regions; they were careful in their agriculture, and, before going to war, assisted their women to plant. In Florida, they welcomed the Spanish missionaries; and, throughout their country, they derived so much benefit from the arts of civilization, that their numbers soon promised to increase; and, being placed between the English of Carolina, the French of Louisiana, the Spaniards of Florida,—bordering on the Choctas, the Chickasas, and the Cherokees,—their political importance made them esteemed as the most powerful Indian nation north of the Gulf of Mexico. They readily gave shelter to fugitives from other tribes; and their speech became so modified, that, with radical resemblances, it has the widest departure from its kindred dialects. The Yamassees, on the Savannah, seem certainly to have been one of their bands; and the Seminoles of Florida are but "wild men," lost from their confederacy, and abandoning agriculture for the chase.

CHAP XXII

Bernard Roman's Hist. of Florida 91

Such is a synopsis of the American nations east of the Mississippi. It is not easy to estimate their probable numbers at the period of their discovery. Many of them—the Narragansetts, the Illinois—boasted of the superior strength of their former condition; and, from wonder, from fear, from the ambition of exciting

CHAP. XXII.

surprise, early travellers often repeated the exaggerations of savage vanity. The Hurons of Upper Canada were thought to number many more than thirty thousand, perhaps even fifty thousand, souls; yet, according to the more exact enumeration of 1639, they could not have exceeded ten thousand. In the heart of a wilderness, a few cabins seemed like a city; and to the pilgrim, who had walked for weeks without meeting a human being, a territory would appear densely peopled where, in every few days, a wigwam could be encountered. Vermont, and North-western Massachusetts, and much of New Hampshire, were solitudes; Ohio, a part of Indiana, the largest part of Michigan, remained open to Indian emigration long after America began to be colonized by Europeans. From the portage between the Fox and the Wisconsin to the Des Moines, Marquette saw neither the countenance nor the footstep of man. In Illinois, so friendly to the habits of savage life, the Franciscan Zenobe Mambré, whose journal is preserved by Le Clercq, describes the "only large village," as containing seven or eight thousand souls; Father Rasle imagined he had seen in one place twelve hundred fires, kindled for more than two thousand families: other missionaries who made their abode there describe their appalling journeys through absolute solitudes; they represent their vocation as a chase after a savage, that was scarce ever to be found; and they could gather hardly five, or even three, villages in the whole region. Kentucky, after the expulsion of the Shawnees, remained the wide park of the Cherokees. The banished tribe easily fled up the valley of the Cumberland River, to find a vacant wilderness in the highlands of Carolina; and a part of them for years roved to and fro in wildernesses west of the

Gallatin, 70.

Le Clercq, Etablissement de la Foi dans la Nouvelle France, ii. 172.

Lett. Ed. iv 208.

Cherokees. On early maps, the low country from the Mobile to Florida is marked as vacant. The oldest reports from Georgia exult in the entire absence of Indians from the vicinity of Savannah, and will not admit that there were more than a few within four hundred miles. There are hearsay and vague accounts of Indian war parties composed of many hundreds: those who wrote from knowledge furnish the means of comparison and correction. The whole population of the Five Nations could not have varied much from ten thousand; and their warriors strolled as conquerors from Hudson's Bay to Carolina,—from the Kennebec to the Tennessee. Very great uncertainty must, indeed, attend any estimate of the original number of Indians east of the Mississippi and south of the St. Lawrence and the chain of lakes. The diminution of their population is far less than is usually supposed. They have been exiled, but not exterminated. The use of iron, of gunpowder, of horses, has given to the savage dominion over the beasts of the forest, and new power over nature. The Cherokee and Mobilian families of nations are more numerous now than ever. We shall approach, and perhaps exceed, a just estimate of their numbers two hundred years ago, if to the various tribes of the Algonquin race we allow about ninety thousand; of the Eastern Sioux, less than three thousand; of the Iroquois, including their southern kindred, about seventeen thousand; of the Catawbas, three thousand; of the Cherokees, twelve thousand; of the Mobilian confederacies and tribes,—that is, of the Chickasas, Choctas, and Muskhogees,—fifty thousand; of the Uchees, one thousand; of the Natchez, four thousand;—in all, it may be, not far from one hundred and eighty thousand souls.

CHAP. XXII.

Compare Volney

CHAP. XXII.

The study of the structure of the dialects of the red men sheds light on the inquiry into their condition. Language is their oldest monument, and the record and image of their experience. No savage horde has been caught with it in a state of chaos, or as if just emerging from the rudeness of undistinguishable sounds. No American language bears marks of being an arbitrary aggregation of separate parts; but each is possessed of an entire organization, having unity of character, and controlled by exact rules. Each appears, not as a slow formation by painful processes of invention, but as a perfect whole, springing directly from the powers of man. A savage physiognomy is imprinted on the dialect of the dweller in the wilderness; but each dialect is still not only free from confusion, but is almost absolutely free from irregularities, and is pervaded and governed by undeviating laws. As the bee builds his cells regularly, yet without the recognition of the rules of geometry, so the unreflecting savage, in the use of words, had rule, and method, and completeness. His speech, like every thing else, underwent change; but human pride errs in believing that the art of cultivated man was needed to resolve it into its elements, and give to it new forms, before it could fulfil its office. Each American language was competent, of itself, without improvement from scholars, to exemplify every rule of the logician, and give utterance to every passion. Each dialect that has been analyzed has been found to be rich in derivatives and compounds, in combinations and forms. As certain as every plant which draws juices from the earth has roots and sap vessels, bark and leaves, so certainly each language has its complete organization,—including the same parts of speech, though some of them

Relation 1633, 37

may lie concealed in mutual coalitions. Human consciousness and human speech exist every where, indissolubly united. A tribe has no more been found without an organized language, than without eyesight or memory.

The American savage has tongue, and palate, and lips, and throat; the power to utter flowing sounds, the power to hiss: hence the primitive sounds are essentially the same. The savage had, indeed, never attempted their analysis; but the analogies are so close, that they may almost all be expressed by the alphabet of European use. The tribes vary in their capacity or their custom of expressing sounds: the Oneidas always changed the letter *r;* the rest of the Iroquois tribes rejected the letter *l.* The Algonquins have no *f;* the whole Iroquois family never use the semivowel *m,* and want the labials entirely. The Cherokees, also, employing the semivowels, are in like manner destitute of the labials. Of the several dialects of the Iroquois, that of the Oneidas is the most soft, being the only one that admits the letter *l;* that of the Senecas is rudest and most energetic. The Algonquin dialects, especially those of the Abenakis, heap up consonants with prodigal harshness; the Iroquois abound in a concurrence of vowels; in the Cherokee, every syllable ends with a vowel, and the combinations with consonants are so few and so simple, that the "old beloved speech," like the Japanese, admits a syllabic alphabet, of which the signs need not exceed eighty-five.

Huron Grammar, in Quebec Lit. and Hist. Trans. ii. 94, 95.

Quickened by conversation with Europeans, Sequoah, an ingenious Cherokee, recently completed an analysis of the syllables of his language, and invented symbols to express them. But, before acquaintance with Europeans, no red man had discriminated the

CHAP. XXII. sounds which he articulated: in all America there was no alphabet, and to the eye knowledge was conveyed only by rude imitations. In a picture of an animal drawn on a sheet of birch bark, or on a smooth stone, or on a blazed tree, an Indian will recognize the symbol of his tribe; and the figures that are sketched around will give him a message from his friends. Pictorial hieroglyphics were found in all parts of America, —in Southern Louisiana, and in the land of the Wyandots, among Algonquins and Mohawks. The rudest painting, giving its story at a glance, constituted the only writing of the Indian.

Edwin James, in Am. Quar. Rev. iii. 396. Schoolcraft, 1836, 146, 147. Vater's Mithridates, iii. 324.

As his mode of writing was by imitation of visible objects, so his language itself was held in bonds by external nature. Abounding in words to designate every object of experience, it had none to express a spiritual conception; materialism reigned in it. The individuality of the barbarian and of his tribe, stamps itself upon his language. Nature creates or shapes expressions for his sensations and his desires, and his language was always vastly copious in words for objects within his knowledge, for ideas derived from the senses; but for "spiritual matters" it was poor; it had no name for continence or justice, for gratitude or holiness. That each American language has been successfully used by Christian missionaries, comes not from an original store of words expressing moral truth, but from the reciprocal pliability of ideas and their signs. It required, said Loskiel, the labor of years to make the Delaware dialect capable of expressing abstract truth; it was necessary to forge a new language out of existing terms by circumlocutions and combinations; and it was the glory of Eliot, that his benevolent simplicity intuitively caught the analogies by which moral truth could be

Relation 1633, 36, 37, 114.

Loskiel. Le Jeune. Lafitau.

Compare Lafitau, ii. 481.

conveyed to nations whose language had not yet emancipated itself from nature.

In another point of view, this materialism contributed greatly to the picturesque brilliancy of American discourse. Prosperity is as a bright sun or a cloudless sky; to establish peace, is to plant a forest-tree, or to bury the tomahawk; to offer presents as a consolation to mourners, is to cover the grave of the departed; and if the Indian from the prairies would speak of griefs and hardships, it is the thorns of the prickly pear that penetrate his moccasons. Especially the style of the Six Nations was adorned with noble metaphors, and glowed with allegory.

Edwin James. Sir Wm. Johnson, in Phil. Trans.

If we search for the distinguishing traits of our American languages, we shall find the synthetic character pervading them all, and establishing their rules. The American does not separate the component parts of the proposition which he utters; he never analyzes his expressions; his thoughts rush forth in a troop. The picture is presented at once and altogether. His speech is as a kindling cloud, not as radiant points of light. This absence of all reflective consciousness, and of all logical analysis of ideas, is the great peculiarity of American speech. Every complex idea is expressed in a group. Synthesis governs every form; it pervades all the dialects of the Iroquois and the Algonquin, and equally stamps the character of the language of the Cherokee.

Jarvis, in N. Y. Hist. Coll. Pickering, Notes to Eliot. Duponceau, Mem. 95.

This synthetic character is apparent in the attempt to express, in the simplest manner, the name of any thing. The Algonquin, the Iroquois, could not say *father;* they must use a more definite expression. Their nouns implying relation, says Brebeuf, always include the signification of one of the three persons of the possessive

CHAP. XXII. pronoun. They cannot say *father*, *son*, *master*, separately; the noun must be limited by including within itself the pronoun for the person to whom it relates. The missionaries could not, therefore, translate the doxology literally, but chanted among the Hurons, and doubtless at Onondaga, "Glory be to our Father, and to his Son, and to their Holy Ghost."

Brebeuf, 81.

Edwards.

Just so, the savage could not say *tree*, or *house*; the word must always be accompanied by prefixes defining its application. The only pronoun which can, with any plausibility, be called an article, is always blended with the noun.

Duponceau, on Zeisberger, 99. Eliot, Grammar, xv

In like manner, the languages are defective in terms that express generalizations. Our forests abound, for example, in various kinds of oak: the Algonquins have special terms for each kind of oak, but no generic term including them all. The same is even true of the verb. No activity is generalized; and hence come multitudes of words to express the same action, as modified by changes of its object. So, too, they have no noun expressing simply the idea of existence; the idea is always blended with locality. And, in this connection, it may be added, that not one of the families of languages of which we treat possessed the simple substantive verb. As the idea of being, when expressed by a noun, was always blended with that of place, so the verb *to be* was never used abstractly, but included within itself the idea of place and time. Thus arises a marvellous fertility of expression, and a wonderful precision; and yet this very copiousness is a defect, springing from the total want of reflection and analysis.

The same synthetic character appears in the formation of words. The noun receives into itself not only

CHAP XXII.

Sir Wm Johnson.

Eliot's Indian Bible, Mark i. 40.

the affixed forms designating relation, but those also which express a quality. The noun and the adjective are, with the pronoun, blended into one word. The power of combination, common to every original language, is possessed in an unlimited degree; and, as a new object is presented to an Indian, he will inquire its use, and promptly give it a name, including within itself, perhaps, an entire definition. The Indian never kneels; so, when Eliot translated *kneeling*, the word which he was compelled to form fills a line, and numbers eleven syllables. As, in early days, books were written in unbroken lines, without any division of the parts of a sentence, so the savage, in his speech, runs word into word, till at last a single one appears to include the whole proposition. By this process of aggregation, a simple root is often buried beneath its environments; rapidity of movement and grace are lost; and speech is encumbered with the expressive masses which it has heaped together. The words that enter into the compound are not melted into each other; nothing resembling a chemical affinity takes place; but the compound word is like patchwork; the masses that are joined together remain heterogeneous. The union resembles clumsy mechanism, where the contrivance lies bare, and forces itself upon the eye. The cultivated man, with select instruments, expresses every idea; the savage is forever coining words; and the original character of his language permits him to multiply them at will.

Still more is the character of synthesis observable in the pronoun. That part of speech hardly existed in a separated form—at least, in a separate form, was rarely in use. Its principal office, in the Algonquin dialects, is to define the relations of the noun and the

CHAP. XXII. verb. The pronoun knows no distinction of genders for male and female; one form is common to both; another form is for the neuter, as in Latin there is sometimes a common gender, in contradistinction to the neuter. Hence, as nouns are always used in connection with pronouns, there is in the form no distinction between masculine and feminine, but only between the form common to both genders, on the one hand, and the form applied to the neuter, on the other,—in a word, between the animate and the inanimate. The plural of animate nouns appears to be formed by an amalgamation with the pronoun of the third person, and the plural of inanimate words by an amalgamation with the corresponding neuter pronoun.

The use of the pronoun is, therefore, to modify nouns and verbs. The ideas which we imply by case, with the exception of the possessive, are not ideas having relation to pronouns: the Indian languages have, therefore, all the modifications of the noun that can come from the use of pronouns: but, with the exception of the genitive, as expressing possession, and marked, as in the Hebrew, by a pronominal affix, they have no series of cases. The relations of case are expressed by means of pronouns affixed to the verb.

Zeisberger's Gram 99

The use of the adjective is in a still greater degree synthetical. There is no such separate word, in an Algonquin dialect, as a simple adjective. As the noun is used only in its relation, so the adjective is used with reference to that which it qualifies. Its form, when it stands alone, is that of an impersonal verb.

But the peculiar economy of the American languages is best illustrated in their verbs. Though destitute of the substantive verb, of which feeble and uncertain traces only can be found in the Chippewa, and perhaps in the Muskhogee, and those only after the presence of Europeans,—yet the verb is the dominant part of speech, swallowing up, as it were, and including within itself, the pronoun, the substantive, and the adjective. Declension, cases, articles, are deficient; but every thing is conjugated. The adjective assumes a verbal termination, and is conjugated as a verb; the idea expressed by a noun is clothed in verbal forms, and at once does the office of a verb.

Here, also, the synthetic character predominates. Does an adjective assume a verbal form, it takes to itself also the person or thing which it qualifies; and the adjective, the pronoun representing the subject, and the verbal form, are included in one word. Thus far the American dialects have analogies with the Greek and Latin. But the American go farther. The accessory idea of case is represented in a form of the verb by means of a pronominal affix. An Algonquin cannot say *I love*, or *I hate;* he must also, and simultaneously, express the object of the love or hatred. As each noun is blended with a pronominal prefix; as each adjective amalgamates with the subject which it qualifies; so each active verb includes in one and the same word one pronoun representing its subject, and another representing its object also. Nor does the synthetic tendency stop here. An adjective may first be melted into the substantive, and the compound word may then assume verbal forms, and thus receive all the changes, and include within itself all the relations, which those forms can express.

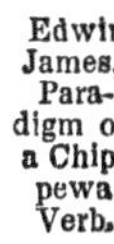
Edwin James, Paradigm of a Chippewa Verb.

There are in the American dialects no genuine declensions; it is otherwise with conjugations. The verbs have true grammatical forms, as fixed and as regular as those of Greek or Sanscrit. The relations of number and person, both with regard to the agent and the object, are included in the verb by means of significant pronominal syllables, which are prefixed, inserted, or annexed. The relations of time are expressed by the insertion, in part, of unmeaning, in part, it may be, of significant, syllables; and, as many supplementary syllables may not always be easily piled one upon another, changes of consonants, as well as, in a slight degree, changes of vowels, and elisions, take place; and sometimes, also, unmeaning syllables are inserted for the sake of euphony. Inflection, agglutination, and euphonic changes, all take place in the conjugation of the Chippewa verb. Of varieties of terminations and forms, the oldest languages, and those in the earliest stage of development, have the most.

But not only does the Algonquin verb admit the number of forms required for the diversity of time and mode; it also has numerous conjugations. An action may be often repeated, and a frequentative conjugation follows. The idea of causation, which the Indian does not conceive abstractly, and can express only synthetically, makes a demand, as in the Hebrew, for a new conjugation. Every verb may be used negatively, as well as positively; it may include in itself an animate object, or the object may be inanimate; and whether it expresses a simple action, or, again, is a frequentative, it may have a reflex signification, like the middle voice of a Greek verb; and every one of these accidents gives birth to an entire series of new forms. Then, since the Indian verb includes within itself the agent and the object, it may pass through as many transitions as the persons and numbers of the pronouns will admit of different combinations; and each of these combinations may be used positively or negatively, with a reflex or a causative signification. In this manner, changes are so multiplied, that the number of possible forms of a Chippewa verb is said to amount to five or six thousand: in other words, the number of possible variations is indefinite.

Such are the cumbersome processes by which synthetical languages express thought. For the want of analysis, the savage obtains no mastery over the forms of his language; nay, the forms themselves are used in a manner which to us would seem anomalous, and to the Indian can appear regular only because his mind receives the complex thought without analysis. To a verb having a nominative singular and an accusative plural, a plural termination is often affixed. The verb, says Eliot, is thus changed to an adnoun. Again: if with a verb which is qualified by an adverb, the idea of futurity is to be connected, the sign of futurity is attached promiscuously either to the verb or the adverb; the Indian is satisfied on finding the expression of futurity somewhere in the group.

Edwin James, in Am. Q. Rev iii. 405. Eliot's Massachusetts Grammar.

From these investigations two momentous conclusions follow. The grammatical forms which constitute the organization of a language, are not the work of civilization, but of nature. It is not writers, nor arbitrary conventions, that give laws to language: the forms of grammar, the power of combinations, the possibility of inversions, spring from within us, and are a consequence of our own organization. If language is a human invention, it was the invention of savage man; and this creation of barbarism would be a higher trophy to human power than any achievement of civilization. The study of these rudest dialects tends to prove, if it does not conclusively prove, that it was not man who made language, but He who made man gave

Duponceau, on Zeisberger, 249.

Alex. Humboldt, Voyage iii 305.

CHAP. XXII.

him utterance. Speech in copiousness, and with abundance and regularity of forms, belongs to the American savage, because it belongs to man. From the country of the Esquimaux to the Oronoco, and from the burning climes on the borders of that stream to the ice of the Straits of Magellan, the primitive American languages, entirely differing in their roots, have, with slight exceptions, one and the same physiognomy. Remarkable analogies of grammatical structure pervade the most refined, as well as the most gross. Idioms as unlike as Sclavonic and Celtic resemble each other in their internal mechanism. In the Esquimaux there is an immense number of forms, derived from the regimen of pronouns. The same is true of the Basque language in Spain, and of the Congo in Africa. Here is a marvellous coincidence in the structure of languages, at points so remote, among three races so different as the white man of the Pyrenees, the black man of Congo, and the copper-colored tribes of North America. Now, a characteristic so extensive is to be accounted for only on some general principle. It pervades languages of different races and different continents: it must, then, be the result of a law. As nature, when it rose from the chaos of its convulsions and its deluges, appeared with its mountains, its basins, and its valleys, all so fashioned that man could cultivate and adorn them, but not shape them anew at his will; so language, in its earliest period, has a fixed character, which culture, by weeding out superfluities, inventing happy connections, teaching the measure of ellipsis, and, through analysis, perfecting the mastery of the mind over its instruments, may polish, enliven, and improve, but cannot essentially change. Men have admired the magnificence displayed in the mountains,

Humboldt, Voyage, iii. 306. Mithridates, ii. Pt. ii. p. 385—409. Vater, Ueber America's Bevölkerung, 207. Vater's Mithridates, iii. Part iii. p. 441–444. W. Humboldt, on the Basque Lang. p. 58. Lafitau, ii. 474.

A. Humboldt, Voy. iii. 307; Researches, i. 19.

W. von Humboldt, Berl. Acad. xliv. 240

the rivers, the prolific vegetation, of the New World. In the dialect of the wildest tribe, the wilderness can show a nobler work, of a Power higher than that of man. CHAP. XXII.

Another and a more certain conclusion is this—that the ancestors of our tribes were rude like themselves. It has been asked if our Indians were not the wrecks of more civilized nations. Their language refutes the hypothesis; every one of its forms is a witness that their ancestors were, like themselves, not yet disenthralled from nature. The character of each Indian language is one continued, universal, all-pervading synthesis. They to whom these languages were the mother tongue, were still in that earliest stage of intellectual culture where reflection has not begun.

Meantime, from the first visit of Europeans, a change has been preparing in the American languages. The stage of progress, in the organic structure of a language, is that of intermixture. To the study of the American dialects the missionaries carried the habit of analysis, and enriched the speech of the barbarians with the experience of civilization. Hence new ideas are gaining utterance, and new forms are springing up. The half-breeds grow unwilling to indulge in diffuse combinations, but are ready to employ each word distinctly and by itself; and the wild man understands, if he does not approve, the innovation. Already the cultivated Chippewa is gaining the power of expressing a noun of relation, independent of its relations; and the substantive verb begins to glimmer in various tongues from Lake Superior to the homes of the Choctas.

"The sociableness of the nature of man appears in the wildest of them." To Indians returning to their

CHAP. XXII. family no one would offer hinderance, "thus confessing the sweetness of their homes." They love society, and the joining together of houses and towns. With long poles fixed in the ground, and bent towards each other at the top, covered with birch or chestnut bark, and hung on the inside with embroidered mats, having no door but a loose skin, no hearth but the ground, no chimney but an opening in the roof, the wigwam is quickly constructed and easily removed. Its size, whether it be round or oblong, is in proportion to the number of families that are to dwell together; and there, in one smoky cell, the whole clan—men, children, and women—are huddled together, careless of cleanliness, and making no privacy of actions of which some irrational animals seem ashamed.

Roger Williams.

Relation 1633, p. 92. T. Shepard's Clear Sunshine.

As the languages of the American tribes were limited by the material world, so, in private life, the senses held dominion. The passion of the savage was liberty; he demanded license to gratify his animal instincts. To act out himself, to follow the propensities of his nature, seemed his system of morals. The supremacy of conscience, the rights of reason, were not subjects of reflection to those who had no name for continence. The idea of chastity, as a social duty, was but feebly developed among them; and the observer of their customs would, at first, believe them to have been ignorant of restraint. If "the kindly flames of nature burned in wild humanity," their love never became a frenzy or a devotion; for indulgence destroyed its energy and its purity.

And yet no nation has ever been found without some practical confession of the duty of self-denial. "God hath planted in the hearts of the wildest of the sonnes of men a high and honorable esteem of the mar-

R. Williams, c. xxiii.

riage bed, insomuch that they universally submit unto it, and hold its violation abominable." Neither might marriages be contracted between kindred of near degree; the Iroquois might choose a wife of the same tribe with himself, but not of the same cabin; the Algonquin must look beyond those who used the same *totem*, or family symbol; the Cherokee would marry at once a mother and her daughter, but would never marry his own immediate kindred.

On forming an engagement, the bridegroom, or, if he were poor, his friends and neighbors, made a present to the bride's father, of whom no dowry was expected. The acceptance of the presents perfected the contract; the wife was purchased; and, for a season, at least, the husband, surrendering his gains as a hunter to her family, had a home in her father's lodge.

But, even in marriage, the Indian abhorred constraint; and, from Florida to the St. Lawrence, polygamy was permitted, though at the north it was not common. In a happy union, affection was fostered and preserved; and the wilderness could show wigwams where "couples had lived together thirty, forty years." Yet Love did not always light his happiest torch at the nuptials of the children of nature, and marriage among the forests had its sorrows and its crimes. The infidelities of the husband sometimes drove the helpless wife to suicide: the faithless wife had no protector; her husband insulted or disfigured her at will; and death for adultery was unrevenged. Divorce, also, was permitted, even for occasions beside adultery; it took place without formality, by a simple separation or desertion, and, where there was no offspring, was of easy occurrence. Children were the strongest bond; for, if the mother was discarded, it

Le Jeune.

was the unwritten law of the red man that she should herself retain those whom she had borne or nursed.

The sorrows of child-bearing were mitigated to the Indian mother, and her travail was comparatively easy and speedy. "In one quarter of an hour, a woman would be merry in the house, and delivered, and merry againe; and within two days, abroad; and after four or five dayes, at worke." Energy of will surmounted the pangs of child-birth. The woman who uttered complaints or groans was esteemed worthy to be but the mother of cowards. Yet death sometimes followed. The pregnant woman continued her usual toils, bore her wonted burdens, followed her family even in its winter rambles. How helpless the Indian infant, born, without shelter, amidst storms and ice! But fear nothing for him: God has placed near him a guardian angel, that can triumph over the severities of nature; the sentiment of maternity is by his side; and, so long as his mother breathes, he is safe. The squaw loves her child with instinctive passion; and, if she does not manifest it by lively caresses, her tenderness is real, wakeful, and constant. No savage mother ever trusted her babe to a hireling nurse; no savage mother ever put away her own child to suckle that of another. To the cradle, consisting of thin pieces of light wood, and gayly ornamented with quills of the porcupine, and beads, and rattles, the nursling is firmly attached, and carefully wrapped in furs; and the infant, thus swathed, its back to the mother's back, is borne as the topmost burden,—its dark eyes now cheerfully flashing light, now accompanying with tears the wailings which the plaintive melodies of the carrier cannot hush. Or, while the squaw toils in the field, she hangs her child, as spring does its blossoms, on the boughs of a tree, that it may be rocked by the breezes from the land of souls, and soothed to sleep by the lullaby of the birds. Does the mother die, the nursling—such is Indian compassion—shares her grave. Relation 1656, 1657, p. 179.

On quitting the cradle, the children are left nearly naked in the cabin, to grow hardy, and learn the use of their limbs. Juvenile sports are the same every where; children invent them for themselves; and the traveller, who finds every where in the wide world the same games, may rightly infer, that the Father of the great human family himself instructs the innocence of childhood in its amusements. Chateaubriand. There is no domestic government; the young do as they will. They are never earnestly reproved, injured, or beaten; a dash of cold water in the face is their heaviest punishment. If they assist in the labors of the household, it is as a pastime, not as a charge. Yet they show respect to the chiefs, and defer with docility to those of their cabin. The attachment of savages to their offspring is extreme; and they cannot bear separation from them. Joutel, 284. Hence every attempt at founding schools for their children was a failure: a missionary would gather a little flock about him, and of a sudden, writes Le Jeune, "my birds flew away." Relation 1634, p. 38. From their insufficient and irregular supplies of clothing and food, they learn to endure hunger and rigorous seasons; of themselves they become fleet of foot, and skilful in swimming; their courage is nursed by tales respecting their ancestors, till they burn with a love of glory to be acquired by valor and address. So soon as the child can grasp the bow and arrow, they are in his hand; and, as there was joy in the wigwam at his birth, and his first cutting of a tooth, so a festival is kept for his earliest success in the chase. The Indian young man is edu

CHAP. XXII. cated in the school of nature. The influences by which he is surrounded nurse within him the passion for war: as he grows up, he, in his turn, takes up the war-song, of which the echoes never die away on the boundless plains of the west: he travels the war-path in search of an encounter with an enemy, that he, too, at the great war-dance and feast of his band, may boast of his exploits; may enumerate his gallant deeds by the envied feathers of the war eagle that decorate his hair; and may keep the record of his wounds by shining marks of vermilion on his skin.

Cass.

The savages are proud of idleness. At home, they do little but cross their arms and sit listlessly; or engage in games of chance, hazarding all their possessions on the result; or meet in council; or sing, and eat, and play, and sleep. The greatest toils of the men were, to perfect the palisades of the forts; to manufacture a boat out of a tree by means of fire and a stone hatchet; to repair their cabins; to get ready instruments of war or the chase; and to adorn their persons. Woman is the laborer; woman bears the burdens of life. The food that is raised from the earth is the fruit of her industry. With no instrument but a wooden mattock, a shell, or a shoulder-blade of the buffalo, she plants the maize, the beans, and the running vines. She drives the blackbirds from the cornfield, breaks the weeds, and, in due season, gathers the harvest. She pounds the parched corn, dries the buffalo meat, and prepares for winter the store of wild fruits; she brings home the game which her husband has killed; she bears the wood, and draws the water, and spreads the repast. If the chief constructs the keel of the canoe, it is woman who stitches the bark with split ligaments of the pine root, and sears the seams with resinous

CHAP XXII.

gum. If the men prepare the poles for the wigwam, it is woman who builds it, and, in times of journeyings, bears it on her shoulders. The Indian's wife was his slave; and the number of his slaves was a criterion of his wealth. Lett.Ed iv. 202

The Indians of our republic had no calendar of their own; their languages have no word for *year*, and they reckon time by the return of snow or the springing of the flowers; their months are named from that which the earth produces in them; and their almanac is kept in the sky by the birds, whose flight announces the progress of the seasons. The brute creation gives them warning of the coming storm; the motion of the sun marks the hour of the day; and the distinctions of time are noted, not in numbers, but in words that breathe the grace and poetry of nature.

The aboriginal tribes of the United States depended for food on the chase, the fisheries, and agriculture. They kept no herds; they never were shepherds. The bison is difficult to tame, and its female yields little milk, of which the use was unknown to the red man: water was his only drink. The moose, the bear, the deer, and at the west the buffalo, besides smaller game and fowl, were pursued with arrows tipped with hart's-horn, or eagles' claws, or pointed stones. With nets and spears fish were taken, and, for want of salt, were cured by smoke. Wild fruits, and abundant berries, were a resource in their season; and troops of girls, with baskets of bark, would gather the fragrant fruit of the wild strawberry. But all the tribes south of the St. Lawrence, except remote ones on the north-east and the north-west, cultivated the earth. Unlike the people of the Old World, they were at once hunters and tillers of the ground. The con-

CHAP. XXII.

trast was due to the character of their grain. Wheat or rye would have been a useless gift to the Indian, who had neither plough nor sickle. The maize springs luxuriantly from a warm, new field, and in the rich soil, with little aid from culture, outstrips the weeds; bears, not thirty, not fifty, but a thousand fold; if once dry, is hurt neither by heat nor cold; may be preserved in a pit or a cave for years, ay, and for centuries; is gathered from the field by the hand, without knife or reaping-hook; and becomes nutritious food by a simple roasting before a fire. A little of its parched meal, with water from the brook, was often a dinner and supper; and the warrior, with a small supply of it in a basket at his back, or in a leathern girdle, and with his bow and arrows, is ready for travel at a moment's warning. The tobacco-plant was not forgotten; and the cultivation of the vine which we have learned of them to call the squash, with beans, completed their husbandry.

During the mild season, there may have been little suffering. But thrift was wanting; the stores collected by the industry of the women were squandered in festivities. The hospitality of the Indian has rarely been questioned. The stranger enters his cabin, by day or by night, without asking leave, and is entertained as freely as a thrush or a blackbird that regales himself on the luxuries of the fruitful grove. He will take his own rest abroad, that he may give up his own skin or mat of sedge to his guest. Nor is the traveller questioned as to the purpose of his visit; he chooses his own time freely to deliver his message. Festivals, too, were common, at some of which it was the rule to eat every thing that was offered; and the indulgence of appetite surpassed belief. But what could be more miserable than the tribes of the north and north-west,

R. Williams, 36. Relation 1633, p. 44. Bartram

in the depth of winter,—suffering from an annual famine; driven by the intense cold to sit indolently in the smoke round the fire in the cabin, and to fast for days together; and then, again, compelled, by faintness for want of sustenance, to reel into the woods, and gather moss or bark for a thin decoction, that might, at least, relieve the extremity of hunger?

Relation 1662, 1663, p 100.

Famine gives a terrible energy to the brutal part of our nature. A shipwreck will make cannibals of civilized men; a siege changes the refinements of urbanity into excesses at which humanity shudders; a retreating army abandons its wounded. The hunting tribes have the affections of men; but among them, also, extremity of want produces like results. The aged and infirm meet with little tenderness; the hunters, as they roam the wilderness, desert their old men; if provisions fail, the feeble drop down, and are lost, or life is shortened by a blow.

Relation 1633, p. 64. James, on Tanner, 293 Lewis and Clarke, ii. 138. Lafitau i 438

The fate of the desperately ill was equally sad. Diseases were believed to spring, in part, from natural causes, for which natural remedies were prescribed. Of these, the best was the vapor bath, prepared in a tent covered with skins, and warmed by means of hot stones; or decoctions of bark, or roots, or herbs, were used. Graver maladies were inexplicable, and their causes and cures formed a part of their religious superstitions; but those who lingered with them, especially the aged, were sometimes neglected, and sometimes put to death.

The clothing of the natives was, in summer, but a piece of skin, like an apron, round the waist; in winter, a bear-skin, or, more commonly, robes made of the skins of the fox and the beaver. Their feet were protected by soft moccasons; and to these were bound

CHAP XXII. the broad snow-shoes, on which, though cumbersome to the novice, the Indian hunter could leap like the roe. Of the women, head, arms, and legs, were uncovered; a mat or a skin, neatly prepared, tied over the shoulders, and fastened to the waist by a girdle, extended from the neck to the knees. They glittered with tufts of elk hair, brilliantly dyed in scarlet; and strings of the various kinds of shells were their pearls and diamonds. The summer garments, of moose and deer skins, were painted of many colors; and the fairest feathers of the turkey, fastened by threads made from wild hemp and nettle, were curiously wrought into mantles. The claws of the grisly bear formed a proud collar for a war-chief; a piece of an enemy's scalp, with a tuft of long hair, painted red, glittered on the stem of their war-pipes; the wing of a red-bird, or the beak and plumage of a raven, decorated their locks; the skin of a rattlesnake was worn round the arm of their chiefs; the skin of the polecat, bound round the leg, was their order of the garter—emblem of noble daring. A warrior's dress was often a history of his deeds. His skin was also tattooed with figures of animals, of leaves, of flowers, and painted with lively and shining colors.

R. Williams, 107

Some had the nose tipped with blue, the eyebrows, eyes, and cheeks, tinged with black, and the rest of the face red; others had black, red, and blue stripes drawn from the ears to the mouth; others had a broad, black band, like a ribbon, drawn from ear to ear across the eyes, with smaller bands on the cheeks. When they made visits, and when they assembled in council, they painted themselves gloriously, delighting especially in vermilion.

Relation 1632, p. 18. 1633, p. 27. Joutel, 220, 221.

There can be no society without government; but

CHAP. XXII.

among the Indian tribes on the soil of our republic, there was not only no written law,—there was no traditionary expression of law; government rested on opinion and usage, and the motives to the usage were never imbodied in language; they gained utterance only in the fact, and power only from opinion. No ancient legislator believed that human society could be maintained with so little artifice. Unconscious of political principles, they remained under the influence of instincts. Their forms of government grew out of their passions and their wants, and were therefore every where nearly the same. Without a code of laws, without a distinct recognition of succession in the magistracy by inheritance or election, government was conducted harmoniously by the influence of native genius, virtue, and experience.

Prohibitory laws were hardly sanctioned by savage opinion. The wild man hates restraint, and loves to do what is right in his own eyes. "The Illinois," writes Marest, "are absolute masters of themselves, subject to no law." The Delawares, it was said, "are, in general, wholly unacquainted with civil laws and proceedings, nor have any kind of notion of civil judicatures, of persons being arraigned and tried, condemned or acquitted." As there was no commerce, no coin, no promissory notes, no employment of others for hire, there were no contracts. Exchanges were but a reciprocity of presents, and mutual gifts were the only traffic. Arrests and prisons, lawyers and sheriffs, were unknown. Each man was his own protector, and, as there was no public justice, each man issued to himself his letter of reprisals, and became his own avenger. In case of death by violence, the departed shade could not rest till appeased by a retaliation.

Brainerd.

CHAP. XXII. His kindred would "go a thousand miles, for the purpose of revenge, over hills and mountains; through large cane swamps, full of grape vines and briers; over broad lakes, rapid rivers, and deep creeks; and all the way endangered by poisonous snakes, exposed to the Adair, 180, 181. extremities of heat and cold, to hunger and thirst." And blood being once shed, the reciprocity of attacks involved family in the mortal strife against family, tribe against tribe, often continuing from generation to generation. Yet mercy could make itself heard even among barbarians; and peace was restored by atoning presents, if they were enough to cover up the graves of the dead.

The acceptance of the gifts pacified the families of those who were at variance. In savage life, which admits no division of labor, and has but the same pursuit for all, the bonds of relationship are widely extended. Families remain undivided, having a common emblem, which designates all their members as effectually as with us the name. The limit of the family is the limit of the interdicted degrees of consanguinity for marriage. They hold the bonds of brotherhood so dear, that a brother commonly pays the debt of a deceased brother, and assumes his revenge and his perils. There are no beggars among them, no fatherless children unprovided for. The families that dwell together, hunt together, roam together, fight together, constitute a tribe. Danger from neighbors, favoring union, leads to alliances and confederacies, just as pride, which is a pervading element in Indian character, and shelters Schoolcraft, 1836, p. 92. itself in every lodge, leads to subdivisions. Of national affinity, as springing from a common language, the Algonquin, the Wyandot, the Dahcota, the Mobilian, each was ignorant. They did not themselves know their respective common lineage, and neither of them had a name embracing all its branches.

As the tribe was but a union of families, government was a consequence of family relations, and the head of the family was its chief. The succession depended on birth, and was inherited through the female line. Even among the Narragansetts, the colleague of Canonicus was his nephew. This rule of descent, which sprung from the general licentiousness, and was known throughout various families of tribes, was widely observed, but most of all among the Natchez. Elsewhere, the hereditary right was modified by opinion. Opinion could crowd a civil chief into retirement, and could dictate his successor. Nor was assassination unknown. The organization of the savage communities was like that which with us takes place at the call of a spontaneous public meeting, where opinion in advance designates the principal actors; or, as with us, at the death of the head of a large family, opinion within the family selects the best fitted of its surviving members to settle its affairs. Doubtless the succession appeared sometimes to depend on the will of the surviving matron; sometimes to have been consequent on birth; sometimes to have been the result of the free election of the wild democracy, and of silent opinion. There have even been chiefs who could not tell when, where, or how, they obtained power.

In like manner, the different accounts of the power of the chief are contradictory only in appearance. The limit of his authority would be found in his personal character. The humiliating subordination of one will to another was every where unknown. The Indian chief has no crown, or sceptre, or guards; no outward symbols of supremacy, or means of giving va-

CHAP XXII. lidity to his decrees. The bounds of his authority float with the current of opinion in the tribe; he is not so much obeyed as followed with the alacrity of free volition; and therefore the extent of his power depends on his personal character. There have been chiefs whose commanding genius could so overawe and sway the common mind, as to gain, for a season, an almost absolute rule,—while others had little authority, and if they used menaces, were abandoned.

Long, i. 223. Marest in Lett Ed. iv. 197

Each village governed itself as if independent, and each after the same analogies, without variety. If the observer had regard to the sachems, the government seemed monarchical; but as, of measures that concerned all, "they would not conclude aught unto which the people were averse," and every man of due age was admitted to council, it might also be described as a democracy. In council, the people were guided by the eloquent, were carried away by the brave; and this influence, which was recognized, and regular in its action, appeared to constitute an oligarchy. The governments of the aborigines scarcely differed from each other, except as accident gave a predominance to one or the other of these elements. It is of the Natchez that the most wonderful tales of despotism and aristocratic distinctions have been promulgated. Their chiefs, who, like those of the Hurons, were esteemed descendants of the sun, had greater power than could have been established in the colder regions of the north, where the severities of nature compel the savage to rely on himself and to be free; yet as the Natchez, in exterior, resembled the tribes by which they were surrounded, so their customs and institutions were but more marked developments of the same characteristics. Every where at the north, there was the same distribution into families, and the same order in each separate town. The affairs relating to the whole nation were transacted in general council, and with such equality, and such zeal for the common good, that, while any one might have dissented with impunity, the voice of the tribe would yet be unanimous in its decisions.

Their delight was in assembling together, and listening to messengers from abroad. Seated in a semicircle on the ground, in double or triple rows, with the knees almost meeting the face,—the painted and tattooed chiefs adorned with skins and plumes, with the beaks of the red-bird or the claws of the bear,—each listener perhaps with a pipe in his mouth, and preserving deep silence,—they would give solemn attention to the speaker, who, with great action and energy of language, delivered his message; and, if his eloquence pleased, they esteemed him as a god. Decorum was never broken; there were never two speakers struggling to anticipate each other; they did not express their spleen by blows; they restrained passionate invective; the debate was never disturbed by an uproar; questions of order were unknown.

The record of their treaties was kept by strings of wampum; these were their annals. When the envoys of nations met in solemn council, gift replied to gift, and belt to belt; by these the memory of the speaker was refreshed: or he would hold in his hand a bundle of little sticks, and for each of them deliver a message. To do this well required capacity and experience. Each tribe had, therefore, its heralds or envoys, selected with reference only to their personal merit, and because they could speak well; and often an orator, without the aid of rank as a chief, by the brilliancy of his eloquence, swayed the minds of a

CHAP. XXII. confederacy. That the words of friendship might be transmitted safely through the wilderness, the red men revered the peace-pipe. The person of him that travelled with it was sacred; he could disarm the young warrior as by a spell, and secure himself a fearless welcome in every cabin. Each village also had its calumet, which was adorned by the chief with eagles' feathers, and consecrated in the general assembly of the nation. The envoys from those desiring peace or an alliance, would come within a short distance of the town, and, uttering a cry, seat themselves on the ground. The great chief, bearing the peace-pipe of his tribe, with its mouth pointing to the skies, goes forth to meet them, accompanied by a long procession of his clansmen, chanting the hymn of peace. The strangers rise to receive them, singing also a song, to put away all wars, and to bury all revenge. As they meet, each party smokes the pipe of the other, and peace is ratified. The strangers are then conducted to the village; the herald goes out into the street that divides the wigwams, and makes repeated proclamation that the guests are friends; and the glory of the tribe is advanced by the profusion of bear's meat, and flesh of dogs, and hominy, which give magnificence to the banquets in honor of the embassy.

But, if councils were their recreation, war alone was the avenue to glory. All other employment seemed unworthy of human dignity; in warfare against the brute creation, but still more against man, they sought liberty, happiness, and renown; thus was gained an honorable appellation, while the mean and the obscure among them had not even a name. Hence to ask an Indian his name was an offence: a chief would push the question aside with scorn; for it implied that his deeds and the titles conferred by them, were unknown.

R. Williams, 29.

CHAP. XXII.

The code of war of the red men attests the freedom of their life. No war-chief was appointed on account of birth, but was, in every case, elected by opinion; and every war party was but a band of volunteers, enlisted for one special expedition, and for no more. Any one who, on chanting the war-song, could obtain volunteer followers, became a war-chief. This was true of the Algonquins, and true of the Natchez.

Solemn fasts and religious rites precede the departure of the warriors; the war-dance must be danced, and the war-song sung. They express in their melodies a contempt of death, a passion for glory; and the chief boasts that "the spirits on high shall repeat his name." A belt painted red, or a bundle of bloody sticks, sent to the enemy, is a declaration of defiance. As the war party leave the village, they address the women in a farewell hymn:—"Do not weep for me, loved woman, should I die; weep for yourself alone. I go to revenge our relations fallen and slain: our foes shall lie like them; I go to lay them low." And, with the pride which ever marks the barbarian, each one adds, "If any man thinks himself a great warrior, I think myself the same."

Schoolcraft, 1825, p. 428, 432.

James and Tanner, 381

The wars of the red men were terrible, not from their numbers; for, on any one expedition, they rarely exceeded forty men: it was the parties of six or seven which were the most to be dreaded. Skill consisted in surprising the enemy. They follow his trail, to kill him when he sleeps; or they lie in ambush near a village, and watch for an opportunity of suddenly surprising an individual, or, it may be, a woman and her children; and, with three strokes to each, the scalps of the victims being suddenly taken off, the brave flies back with his companions, to hang the trophies in his

Marest, in Lett. Ed. iv. 221.

CHAP. XXII. cabin, to go from village to village in exulting procession, to hear orators recount his deeds to the elders and the chief people, and, by the number of scalps taken with his own hand, to gain the high war titles of honor. Nay, war parties of but two or three were not uncommon. Clad in skins, with a supply of red paint, a bow and quiver full of arrows, they would roam through the wide forest as a bark would over the ocean; for days and weeks, they would hang on the skirts of their enemy, waiting the moment for striking a blow. From the heart of the Five Nations, two young warriors would thread the wilderness of the south; would go through the glades of Pennsylvania, the valleys of Western Virginia, and steal within the mountain fastnesses of the Cherokees. There they would hide themselves in the clefts of rocks, and change their places of concealment, till, provided with scalps enough to astonish their village, they would bound over the ledges, and hurry home. It was the danger of such inroads, that, in time of war, made every English family on the frontier insecure.

The Romans, in their triumphal processions, exhibited captives to the gaze of the Roman people; the Indian conqueror compels them to run the gantlet through the children and women of his tribe. To inflict blows that cannot be returned, is proof of full success, and the entire humiliation of the enemy; it is, moreover, an experiment of courage and patience. Those who show fortitude are applauded; the coward becomes an object of scorn.

Fugitives and suppliants were often incorporated into a victorious tribe, which had waged an unrelenting warfare against their nation. The Creek confederacy was recruited by emigrants from friends and foes;

the Iroquois welcomed the defeated Hurons. Sometimes a captive was saved, to be adopted in place of a warrior who had fallen. In that event the allegiance, and, as it were, the identity, of the captive, the current of his affections and his duties, became changed. The children and the wife whom he had left at home, are to be blotted from his memory: he is to be the departed chieftain, resuscitated and brought back from the dwelling-place of shadows, to cherish those whom he cherished; to hate those whom he hated; to rekindle his passions; to retaliate his wrongs; to hunt for his cabin; to fight for his clan. And the foreigner thus adopted is esteemed to stand in the same relations of consanguinity, and to be bound by the same restraints in regard to marriage.

More commonly, it was the captive's lot to endure torments and death, in the forms which Brebeuf has described. On the way to the cabins of his conquerors, the hands of an Iroquois prisoner were crushed between stones, his fingers torn off or mutilated, the joints of his arms scorched and gashed, while he himself preserved his tranquillity, and sang the songs of his nation. Arriving at the homes of his conquerors, all the cabins regaled him, and a young girl was bestowed on him, to be the wife of his captivity and the companion of his last loves. At one village after another, he was present at festivals which were given in his name, and at which he was obliged to sing. The old chief, who might have adopted him in place of a fallen nephew, chose rather to gratify revenge, and pronounced the doom of death. "That is well," was his reply. The sister of the fallen warrior, into whose place it had been proposed to receive him, still treated him with tenderness as a brother, offering him

CHAP. XXII. food, and serving him with interest and regard; her father caressed him as though he had become his kinsman, gave him a pipe, and wiped the thick drops of sweat from his face. His last entertainment, made at the charge of the bereaved chief, began at noon. To the crowd of his guests he declared,—"My brothers, I am going to die; make merry around me with good heart: I am a man; I fear neither death nor your torments:" and he sang aloud. The feast being ended, he was conducted to the cabin of blood. They place him on a mat, and bind his hands; he rises, and dances round the cabin, chanting his death-song. At eight in the evening, eleven fires had been kindled, and these are hedged in by files of spectators. The young men selected to be the actors are exhorted to do well, for their deeds would be grateful to Areskoui, the powerful war-god. A war-chief strips the prisoner, shows him naked to the people, and assigns their office to the tormentors. Then ensued a scene the most horrible: torments lasted till after sunrise, when the wretched victim, bruised, gashed, mutilated, half-roasted, and scalped, was carried out of the village, and hacked in pieces. A festival upon his flesh completed the sacrifice. Such were the customs that Europeans have displaced.

The solemn execution of the captive seems to have been, in part at least, an act of faith, and a religious sacrifice. The dweller in the wilderness is conscious of his dependence; he feels the existence of relations with the universe by which he is surrounded and an invisible world; he recognizes a nature higher than his own. His language, which gave him no separate word for causation, could give him no expression for a first cause; and, since he had no idea of existence except in connection with space and time, he could have no idea of an Infinite and Eternal Being. But, as the ideas of existence and causation were blended with words expressing action or quality, so the idea of divinity was blended with nature, and yet not wholly merged in the external world. So complete was this union, many travellers denied that they had any religion. "As to the knowledge of God," says Joutel of the south-west, "it did not seem to us that they had any definite notion about it. True, we found upon our route some who, as far as we could judge, believed that there was something exalted, which is above all, but they have neither temples, nor ceremonies, nor prayers, marking a divine worship. That they have no religion, can be said of all whom we saw." "The northern nations," writes Le Caron, "recognize no divinity from motives of religion; they have neither sacrifice, nor temple, nor priest, nor ceremony of worship." Le Jeune also affirms, "There is among them very little superstition; they think only of living and of revenge; they are not attached to the worship of any divinity." And yet they believed that some powerful genius had created the world; that unknown agencies had made the heavens above them and the earth on which they dwelt. The god of the savage was what the metaphysician endeavors to express by the word *substance*. The red man, unaccustomed to generalization, obtained no conception of an absolute substance, of a self-existent being, but saw a divinity in every power. Wherever there was being, motion, or action, there to him was a spirit; and, in a special manner, wherever there appeared singular excellence among beasts or birds, or in the creation, there to him was the presence of a divinity. When he feels his pulse throb, or his heart beat, he knows that it is a

Joutel, 224, 225.

Le Clercq, ii. 268, 269.

Relation 1632, 28.

St. Mary of the Incarnation, lettre lxxxvi. p. 652.
R. Williams, c. xxi.

Joseph Le Caron, in Le Clercq, i 186.

R. Williams

CHAP XXII.

spirit. A god resides in the flint, to give forth the kindling, cheering fire; in the mountain cliff; in the cool recesses of the grottoes which nature has adorned; in each "little grass" that springs miraculously from the earth. "The woods, the wilds, and the waters, respond to savage intelligence; the stars and the mountains live; the river, and the lake, and the waves, have a spirit." Every hidden agency, every mysterious influence, is personified. A god dwells in the sun, and in the moon, and in the firmament; the spirit of the morning reddens in the eastern sky; a deity is present in the ocean and in the fire; the crag that overhangs the river has its genius; there is a spirit to the waterfall; a household god makes its abode in the Indian's wigwam, and consecrates his home; spirits climb upon the forehead, to weigh down the eyelids in sleep. Not the heavenly bodies only, the sky is filled with spirits that minister to man. To the savage, divinity, broken, as it were, into an infinite number of fragments, fills all place and all being. The idea of unity in the creation may have existed contemporaneously; but it existed only in the germ, or as a vague belief derived from the harmony of the universe. Yet faith in the Great Spirit, when once presented, was promptly seized and appropriated, and so infused itself into the heart of remotest tribes, that it came to be often considered as a portion of their original faith. Their shadowy aspirations and creeds assumed, through the reports of missionaries, a more complete development; and a religious system was elicited from the pregnant but rude materials.

James's Tanner, 323

Schoolcraft, Algic Res. ii. 226

Von Reck's Kurze Nachricht, in Urlsperger's Ausführliche Nachricht, i. 192.

Loskiel

It is not fear which generates this faith in the existence of higher powers. The faith attaches to every thing, but most of all to that which is excellent; it is the undefined consciousness of the existence of inexplicable relations towards powers of which the savage cannot solve the origin or analyze the nature. His gods are not the offspring of terror; universal nature seems to him instinct with divinity. The Indian venerates what excites his amazement or interests his imagination. "The Illinois," writes the Jesuit Marest, "adore a sort of genius, which they call *manitou:* to them it is the master of life, the spirit that rules all things. A bird, a buffalo, a bear, a feather, a skin—that is their manitou." Lett. Ed. iv 203.

No tribe worshipped its prophets, or deified its heroes; no Indian adored his fellow-man, or paid homage to the dead. He turns from himself to the animal world, which he believes also to be animated by spirits. The bird, that mysteriously cleaves the air, into which he cannot soar; the fish, that hides itself in the depths of the clear, cool lakes, which he cannot fathom; the beasts of the forest, whose unerring instincts, more sure than his own intelligence, seem like revelations; —these enshrine the deity whom he adores. On the Ohio, Mermet questioned a medicine man, who venerated the buffalo as his manitou. He confessed that he did not worship the buffalo, but the invisible spirit which is the type of all buffaloes. "Is there such a manitou to the bear?"—"Yes."—"To man?"—"Nothing more certain; man is superior to all."—"Why do you not, then, invoke the manitou of man?" And the juggler knew not what to answer. It has been said by speculative philosophy, that no Indian ever chose the manitou of a man for his object of adoration, because he adored only the unknown, and man is the being most intimately known to him. It seems, also, that the very instinct which prompted the savage

Adair, 19, 22, 25. Benjamin Constant, De la Religion i. 159

Marest, iv. 205.

CHAP. XXII.

to adore, was an instinct which prompted him to recognize his closer connection with the world. To have worshipped the manitou of a man, would have been to put himself only in nearer relations with his own kind; the gulf between him and the universe would have remained as wide as ever. The instincts towards man led to marriage, society, and political institutions. The sentiment of devotion sought to pass beyond the region of humanity, and enter into intimate communion with nature and the beings to whom imagination intrusted its control,—with the sun and moon, the forests, the rivers, the lakes, the fishes, the birds,—all which has an existence independent of man, and manifests a power which he can neither create nor destroy.

Nor did the savage distrust his imaginations. Something within him affirmed with authority, that there was more in them than fancies which his mind had called into being. Infidelity never clouded his mind; the shadows of skepticism never darkened his faith.

The piety of the savage was not merely a sentiment of passive resignation—he sought to propitiate the unknown, to avert their wrath, to secure their favor. If, at first, no traces of religious feeling were discerned, closer observation showed that, every where among the red men, even among the roving tribes of the north, they had some kind of sacrifice and of prayer. If the harvest was abundant, if the chase was successful, they saw in their success the influence of a manitou; and they would ascribe even an ordinary accident to the wrath of the god. "O manitou!" exclaimed an Indian, at daybreak, with his family about him, lamenting the loss of a child, "thou art angry with me; turn thine anger from me, and spare the rest of my children." Canonicus, the great sachem of the Narragansetts, when bent with age, having

Le Caron. Relation 1633, p. 79.

R. Williams.

buried his son, "burned his own dwelling, and all his goods in it, in part as a humble expiation to the god who, as they believe, had taken his sonne from him." At their feasts, they were careful not to profane the bones of the elk, the beaver, and of other game, lest the spirits of these animals should pass by and behold the indignity; and then the living of the same species, instructed of the outrage, would ever after be careful to escape the toils and the arrows of the hunter. There were also occasions on which nothing of the flesh was carried forth out of the wigwam, though a part might be burned as food for the dead, and when, of the beasts which were consumed, it was the sacred rule that not a bone should be broken. On their expeditions, they keep no watch during the night, but pray earnestly to their fetiches; and the band of warriors sleep securely under the safeguard of the sentinels whom they have invoked. They throw tobacco into the fire, on the lake or the rapids, into the crevices in the rocks, on the war-path, to propitiate the genius of the place The evil that is in the world they also ascribe to spirits, that are the dreaded authors of their woes. The evil demon of war was to be propitiated only by acts of cruelty; yet they never sacrificed their own children or their own friends. The Iroquois, when Jogues was among them, sacrificed an Algonquin woman in honor of Areskoui, their war-god, exclaiming, "Areskoui, to thee we burn this victim; feast on her flesh, and grant us new victories;" and her flesh was eaten as a religious rite. Hennepin found a beaver robe hung on an oak, as an oblation to the spirit that dwells in the Falls of St Anthony. The guides of Joutel in the southwest, on killing a buffalo, offered several slices of the meat as a sacrifice to the unknown spirit of that wil

Le Caron, in Le Clercq, i. 218.

Jogues, in Creuxius, 86

Joutel, 321

CHAP. XXII. derness. As they passed the Ohio, its beautiful stream was propitiated by gifts of tobacco and dried meat; and worship was paid to the rock just above the Missouri.

Even now, in the remote west, evidence may be found of the same homage to the higher natures, which the savage divines, but cannot fathom. Nor did he seek to win their favor by gifts alone; he made a sacrifice of his pleasures; he chastened his passions. To calm the rising wind, when the morning sky was red, he would repress his activity, and give up the business of the day. To secure success in the chase, by appeasing the tutelary spirits of the animals to be pursued, severe fasts were kept; and happy was he to whom they appeared in his dreams, for it was a sure augury of abundant returns. The warrior, preparing for an expedition, often sought the favor of the god of battle by separating himself from woman, and mortifying the body by continued penance. The security of female captives was, in part, the consequence of the vows of chastity, by which the warrior was bound till after his return. The Indian, detesting restraint, was perpetually imposing upon himself extreme hardships, that by penance and suffering he might atone for his offences, and by acts of self-denial might win for himself the powerful favor of the invisible world.

Alloüez, 58.

Adair, 382.

Nor is the Indian satisfied with paying homage to the several powers whose aid he may invoke in war, in the chase, or on the river; he seeks a special genius to be his companion and tutelary angel through life. On approaching maturity, the young Chippewa, anxious to behold God, blackens his face with charcoal, and, building a lodge of cedar-boughs, it may be on the summit of a hill, there begins his fast in solitude

Alloüez, 108, 109. Schoolcraft's Algic Researches, i. 220.

The fast endures, perhaps, ten days, sometimes even without water, till, excited by the severest irritation of thirst, watchfulness, and famine, he beholds a vision of God, and knows it to be his guardian spirit. That spirit may assume fantastic forms, as a skin or a feather, as a smooth pebble or a shell; but the fetich, when obtained, and carried by the warrior in his pouch, is not the guardian angel himself, but rather the token of his favor, and the pledge of his presence in time of need. A similar probation was appointed for the warriors of Virginia, and traces of it are discerned beyond the Mississippi. That man should take up the cross, that sin should be atoned for, are ideas that dwell in human nature; they were so diffused among the savages, that Le Clercq believed some of the apostles must have reached the American continent.

The gifts to the deities were made by the chiefs, or by any Indian for himself. In this sense, each Indian was his own priest; the right of offering sacrifices was not reserved to a class; any one could do it for himself, whether the sacrifice consisted in oblations or acts of self-denial. But the Indian had a consciousness of man's superiority to the powers of nature, and sorcerers sprung up in every part of the wilderness. They were prophets whose prayers would be heard. "They are no other," said the Virginian Whitaker, "but such as our English witches;" and, as their agency was most active in healing disease, they are now usually called *medicine men.*

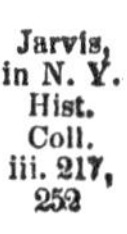
Jarvis, in N. Y. Hist. Coll. iii. 217, 252

Here, too, the liberty of the desert appears. As the war-chief was elected by opinion, and served voluntarily, so the medicine men were self-appointed. They professed an insight into the laws of nature, and power over those laws; but belief was free; there was no

CHAP. XXII. monopoly of science, no close priesthood. He who could inspire confidence might come forward as a medicine man. The savage puts his faith in auguries; he casts lots, and believes nature will be obedient to the decision, he puts his trust in the sagacity of the sorcerer, who comes forth from a heated, pent-up lodge, and, with all the convulsions of enthusiasm, utters a confused medley of sounds as oracles.

Adair, 85. Tanner, 343. Bartram. Relation 1638, 1639, p. 162. The medicine man boasts of his power over the elements; he can call water from above, and beneath, and around; he can foretell a drought, or bring rain, or guide the lightning; by his spells he can give attraction and good fortune to the arrow or the net; he conjures the fish, that dwell in the lakes or haunt the rivers, to suffer themselves to be caught; he can pronounce spells which will infallibly give success in the chase, which will compel the beaver to rise up from beneath the water, and overcome the shyness and cunning of the moose; he can, by his incantations, draw the heart of woman; he can give to the warrior vigilance like the rising sun, and power to walk over the earth and through the sky victoriously. If an evil spirit has introduced disease into the frame of a victim, the medicine man can put it to flight; and, should his Garest remedies chance to heal, he exclaims, "Who can resist my spirit? Is he not, indeed, the master of life?" Or disease, it was believed, might spring from a want of harmony with the outward world. If some innate desire has failed to be gratified, life can be saved only by the discovery and gratification of that secret longing of the soul; and the medicine man reveals the momentous secret. Were he to assert that the manitou Relation 1633, p. 81 orders the sick man to wallow naked in the snow, or to scorch himself with fire, he would do it. But let

CHAP. XXII.

not the wisdom of civilization wholly deride the savage: the same superstition long lingered in the cities and palaces of Europe; and, in the century after the Huron missions began, the English moralist Johnson was carried, in his infancy, to the British monarch, to be cured of scrofula by the great medicine of her touch.

Purchas, v. 951. Bernard Romans. Charlevoix, iii, 417, 418. Adair 210.

Little reverence was attached to time or place. It could not be perceived that the savages had any set holidays; only in times of triumph, at burials, at harvests, the nation assembled for solemn rites. Each Chocta town had a house in which the bones of the dead were deposited for a season previous to their final burial. The Natchez, like their kindred the Taënsas, kept a perpetual fire in a rude cabin, in which the bones of their great chiefs were said to be preserved. The honest Charlevoix, who entered it, writes, "I saw no ornaments, absolutely nothing, which could make me know that I was in a temple;" and, referring to the minute relations which others had fabricated of an altar, and a dome, of cones wrapped in skins, and the circle of the bodies of departed chiefs, he adds, "I saw nothing of all that: if things were so formerly, they must have changed greatly." And Adair confidently insinuates, that the Koran does not more widely differ from the Gospels, than the romances respecting the Natchez from the truth. The building was probably a charnel-house, not a place of worship. No tribes whatever, east of the Mississippi, or certainly none except those of the Natchez family, had a consecrated spot, or a temple, where there was believed to be a nearer communication between this world and that which is unseen.

Dreams are to the wild man the avenue to the in-

CHAP. XXII. visible world; he reveres them as divine revelations, and believes he shall die unless they are carried into effect. The capricious visions in a feverish sleep are obeyed by the village or the tribe; the whole nation would contribute its harvest, its costly furs, its belts of beads, the produce of its chase, rather than fail in their fulfilment; the dream must be obeyed, even if it re-
Relation 1638, 1639, p. 125. quired the surrender of women to a public embrace. The faith in the spiritual world, as revealed by dreams, was universal. On Lake Superior, the nephew of a Chippewa squaw having dreamed that he saw a
Relation 1655, 1656, p. 97. French dog, the woman travelled four hundred leagues, in midwinter, over ice and through snows, to obtain
1654, 1655, 96-99. it. Life itself was hazarded, rather than fail to listen to the message conveyed through sleep; and, if it could not be fulfilled, at least some semblance would be made. Happy was the hunter who, as he went forth to the chase, obtained a vision of the great spirit of the animal which he was to pursue; the sight was a warrant of success. But if the dream should be threatening, the savage would rise in the night, or prevent the dawn with prayer; or he would call around him his friends and neighbors, and himself keep waking and
R. Williams, 40. fasting, with invocations, for many days and nights.

The Indian invoked the friendship of spirits, and sought the mediation of medicine men; but he never would confess his fear of death. To him, also, intelligence was something more than a transitory accident; and he was unable to conceive of a cessation of life. His faith in immortality was like that of the child, who weeps over the dead body of its mother, and believes that she yet lives. At the bottom of a grave, the
Relation 1634, 20, 21. melting snows had left a little water; and the sight of it chilled and saddened his imagination. "You

have had no compassion for my poor brother"—such was the reproach of an Algonquin;—"the air is pleasant, and the sun so cheering, and yet you do not remove the snow from his grave to warm him a little;" and he knew no contentment till this was done.

Le Jeune, 1632, 50, 51.

The same motive prompted them to bury with the warrior his pipe and his manitou, his tomahawk, quiver, and bow ready bent for action, and his most splendid apparel; to place by his side his bowl, his maize, and his venison, for the long journey to the country of his ancestors. Festivals in honor of the dead were also frequent, when a part of the food was given to the flames, that so it might serve to nourish the departed. The traveller would find in the forests a dead body placed on a scaffold erected upon piles, carefully wrapped in bark for its shroud, and attired in warmest furs. If a mother lost her babe, she would cover it with bark, and envelop it anxiously in the softest beaver-skins; at the burial-place, she would put by its side its cradle, its beads, and its rattles; and, as a last service of maternal love, would draw milk from her bosom in a cup of bark, and burn it in the fire, that her infant might still find nourishment on its solitary journey to the land of shades. Yet the new-born babe would be buried, not, as usual, on a scaffold, but by the wayside, that so its spirit might secretly steal into the bosom of some passing matron, and be born again under happier auspices. On burying her daughter, the Chippewa mother adds, not snow-shoes, and beads, and moccasons, only, but (sad emblem of woman's lot in the wilderness!) the carrying-belt and the paddle. "I know my daughter will be restored to me," she once said, as she clipped a lock of hair as a memorial; "by this lock of hair I shall dis-

Relation 1633, p. 53.

Relation 1633, p. 50. 1634, p. 25.

Brebeuf.

Henry's Travels, 150.

CHAP. XXII.

cover her, for I shall take it with me,"—alluding to the day when she, too, with her carrying-belt and paddle, and the little relic of her child, should pass through the grave to the dwelling-place of her ancestors.

Brebeuf

It was believed, even, that living men had visited the remote region where the shadows have their home; and that once, like Orpheus of old, a brother, wandering in search of a cherished sister, but for untimely curiosity, would have drawn her from the society of the dead, and restored her to the cabin of her fathers. In the flashes of the northern lights, men believed they saw the dance of the dead. But the south-west is the great subject of traditions. There is the court of the Great God; there is the paradise where beans and maize grow spontaneously; there are the shades of the forefathers of the red men.

Tanner, 322.

R. Williams, 21.

Portuguese Relation c xxx.

Tales of the North-west, 282.

Lett. Ed. iv.

Du Pratz.

This form of faith in immortality had also its crimes. It is related that the chief within whose territory De Soto died, selected two young and well-proportioned Indians to be put to death, saying the usage of the country was, when any lord died, to kill Indians to wait on him and serve him by the way. Traces of an analogous superstition may be found among Algonquin tribes, and among the Sioux; the Winnebagoes are said to have observed the usage within the memory of persons now living; it is affirmed, also, of the Natchez, and doubtless with truth, though the details of the sacrifice are described with wild exaggeration. Even now, the Dahcotas will slay horses on the grave of a warrior: news has come from the Great Spirit, that the departed chief is still borne by them in the land of shades; and the spirits of the mighty dead have sometimes been seen, as they ride, in the night-time, through the sky.

CHAP. XXII

The savage believed that to every man there is an appointed time to die; to anticipate that period by suicide, was detested as the meanest cowardice. For the dead he abounds in his lamentations, mingling them with words of comfort to the living: to him death is the king of terrors. He never names the name of the departed; to do so is an offence justifying revenge. To speak generally of brothers to one who has lost her own, would be an injury, for it would make her weep because her brothers are no more; and the missionary could not speak of the Father of man to orphans, without kindling indignation. And yet they summon energy to speak of their own approaching death with tranquillity "Full happy am I," sings the warrior, "full happy am I to be slain within the limits of the land of the enemy!" While yet alive, the dying chief sometimes arrayed himself in the garments in which he was to be buried, and, giving a farewell festival, calmly chanted his last song, or made a last harangue, glorying in the remembrance of his deeds, and commending to his friends the care of those whom he loved; and when he had given up the ghost, he was placed by his wigwam in a sitting posture, as if to show that, though life was spent, the principle of being was not gone; and in that posture he was buried. Every where in America this posture was adopted at burials. From Canada to Patagonia, it was the usage of every nation—an evidence that some common sympathy pervaded the continent, and struck a chord which vibrated through the heart of a race. The narrow house, within which the warrior sat, was often hedged round with a light palisade; and, for six months, the women would repair to it thrice a day to weep. He that should despoil the dead was accursed.

Schoolcraft, 1825, p. 432

Creuxius, 91 92

CHAP XXII.

The faith, as well as the sympathies, of the savage descended also to inferior beings. Of each kind of animal they say there exists one, the source and origin of all, of a vast size, the type and original of the whole class. From the immense invisible beaver come all the beavers, by whatever run of water they are found; the same is true of the elk and buffalo, of the eagle and the robin, of the meanest quadruped of the forest, of the smallest insect that buzzes in the air. There lives for each class of animals this invisible, vast type, or elder brother. Thus the savage established his right to be classed by philosophers in the rank of realists; and his chief effort at generalization was a reverent exercise of the religious sentiment. Where these elder brothers dwell they do not exactly know; yet it may be that the giant manitous, which are brothers to beasts, are hid beneath the waters, and that those of the birds make their homes in the blue sky. But the Indian believes also, of each individual animal, that it possesses the mysterious, the indestructible principle of life: there is not a breathing thing but has its shade, which never can perish. Regarding himself, in comparison with other animals, but as the first among coördinate existences, he respects the brute creation, and assigns to it, as to himself, a perpetuity of being. "The ancients of these lands" believed that the warrior, when released from life, renews the passions and activity of this world; is seated once more among his friends; shares again the joyous feast; walks through shadowy forests, that are alive with the spirits of birds; and there, in his paradise,

Compare Jos. Le Caron, in Le Clercq, i 273

"By midnight moons, o'er moistening dews,
In vestments for the chase arrayed,
The hunter still the deer pursues—
The hunter and the deer a shade."

Philip Freneau

To the Indian the prospect of his own paradise was dear. "We raise not our thoughts," they would say to the missionaries, "to your heaven; we desire only the paradise of our ancestors." To the doctrine of a future life they listened readily. The idea of retribution, as far as it has found its way among them, was derived from Europeans. The future life was to the Indian, like the present, a free gift; some, it was indeed believed, from feebleness or age, did not reach the paradise of shades; but no red man was so proud as to believe that its portals were opened to him by his own good deeds.

Relation 1655, 1656, p. 95

Their notion of immortality was, as we have seen, a faith in the continuance of life; they did not expect a general resurrection; nor could they be induced, in any way, to believe that the body will be raised up. Yet no nations paid greater regard to the remains of their ancestors. Every where among the Choctas and the Wyandots, Cherokees and Algonquins, they were carefully wrapped in choicest furs, and preserved with affectionate veneration. Once every few years, the Hurons collected from their scattered cemeteries the bones of their dead, and, in the midst of great solemnities, cleansed them from every remainder of flesh, and deposited them in one common grave: these are their holy relics. Other nations possess, in letters and the arts, enduring monuments of their ancestors; the savage red men, who can point to no obelisk or column, whose rude implements of agriculture could not even raise a furrow on the surface of the earth, excel all races in veneration for the dead. The grave is their only monument,—the bones of their fathers the only pledges of their history.

A deeper interest belongs to the question of the

CHAP. XXII. natural relation of the aborigines of America to those before whom they have fled. "We are men," said the Illinois to Marquette. After illustrating the weaknesses of the Wyandots, Brebeuf adds, "They are men." The natives of America were men and women of like endowments with their more cultivated conquerors; they have the same affections, and the same powers; are chilled with an ague, and burn with a fever. We may call them savage, just as we call fruits wild; natural right governs them. They revere unseen powers; they respect the nuptial ties; they are careful of their dead: their religion, their marriages, and their burials, show them possessed of the habits of humanity, and bound by a federative compact to the race. They had the moral faculty which can recognize the distinction between right and wrong; nor did their judgments of relations bend to their habits and passions more decidedly than those of the nations whose laws justified, whose statesmen applauded, whose sovereigns personally shared, the invasion of a continent to steal its sons. If they readily yielded to the impetuosity of selfishness, they never made their own personality the centre of the universe. They were faithless treaty-breakers; but, at least, they did not exalt falsehood into the dignity of a political science, or scoff at the supremacy of justice as the delusive hope of fools; and, if they made every thing yield to self-preservation, they never avowed their interest to be the first law of international policy. They had never risen to the conceptions of a spiritual religion, but as between the French and the natives, the latter —such is the assertion of St. Mary of the Incarnation— had even a greater tendency to devotion. Under the instructions of the Jesuits, they learned to swing censers, and to chant aves. Gathering round Eliot, in Massachusetts, the tawny choir sang the psalms of David, in Indian, "to one of the ordinary English tunes, melodiously;" and in the school of Brainerd, thirty Lennape boys could answer to all the questions in the Westminster Assembly's Catechism. There were instances of the submission of warriors to the penance imposed by the Roman church; and the sanctity of a Mohawk maiden,—the American Geneveva,—who preserved her vows of chastity, is celebrated in the early histories of New France. They recognized the connection between the principles of Christian morals; there were examples among them of men who, under the guidance of missionaries, became anxious for their salvation, having faith enough for despair, if not for conversion; and even in the doctrine of the divine unity, they seemed to find not so much a novelty as the revival of a slumbering reminiscence. They were not good arithmeticians; their tales of the number of their years, or of the warriors in their clans, are little to be relied on; and yet every where they counted like Leibnitz and La Place, and, from the influence of some law that pervades humanity, they began to repeat at ten. They could not dance like those trained to attitudes of grace; they could not sketch light ornaments like Raphael; yet, under every sky, they delighted in a rhythmic repetition of forms and sounds,—would move in cadence to wild melodies,—and, with great elegance and imitative power, they would tattoo their skins with harmonious arabesques. We call them cruel; yet they never invented the thumb-screw, or the boot, or the rack, or broke on the wheel, or exiled bands of their nations for opinion's sake; and never protected the monopoly of a medicine man by the gal-

Wilson.

Jonathan Edwards, iii 539.

Brainerd. Charlevoix

Charlevoix, i. 189

Shepard

CHAP. XXII. lows, or the block, or by fire. There is not a quality belonging to the white man, which did not also belong to the American savage; there is not among the aborigines a rule of language, a custom, or an institution, which, when considered in its principle, has not a counterpart among their conquerors. The unity of the human race is established by the exact correspondence between their respective powers; the Indian has not one more, has not one less, than the white man; the map of the faculties is for both identical.

When, from the general characteristics of humanity, we come to the comparison of powers, the existence of degrees immediately appears. The red man has aptitude at imitation rather than invention; he learns easily; his natural logic is correct and discriminating, and he seizes on the nicest distinctions in comparing objects. But he is deficient in the power of imagination to combine and bring unity into his floating fancies, and in the faculty of abstraction to lift himself out of the dominion of his immediate experience. He is nearly destitute of abstract moral truth,—of general principles; and, as a consequence, equalling the white man in the sagacity of the senses, and in judgments resting on them, he is inferior in reason and the moral qualities. Nor is this inferiority simply attached to the individual; it is connected with organization, and is the characteristic of the race.

This is the inference from history. Benevolence has, every where in our land, exerted itself to ameliorate the condition of the Indian,—above all, to educate the young. Jesuit, Franciscan, and Puritan, the Church of England, the Moravian, the benevolent founders of schools, academies, and colleges, all have endeavored to change the habits of the rising generation among the Indians; and the results, in every instance, varying in the degree of influence exerted by the missionary, have varied in little else. Woman, too, with her gentleness, and the winning enthusiasm of her self-sacrificing benevolence, has attempted their instruction, and has attempted it in vain. St. Mary of the Incarnation succeeded as little as Jonathan Edwards or Brainerd. The Jesuit Stephen de Carheil, revered for his genius, as well as for his zeal, was for more than sixty years, in the seventeenth and eighteenth centuries, a missionary among the Huron-Iroquois tribes; he spoke their dialects with as much facility and elegance as though they had been his mother-tongue; yet the fruits of his diligence were inconsiderable. Neither John Eliot nor Roger Williams was able to change essentially the habits and character of the New England tribes. The Quakers came among the Delawares in the spirit of peace and brotherly love, and with sincerest wishes to benefit the Indian; but the Quakers succeeded no better than the Puritans—not nearly as well as the Jesuits. Brainerd awakened in the Delawares a perception of the unity of Christian morals; and yet his account of them is gloomy and desponding: "They are unspeakably indolent and slothful; they discover little gratitude; they seem to have no sentiments of generosity, benevolence, or goodness." The Moravian Loskiel could not change their character; and, like other tribes, its fragments at last migrated to the west. The condition of the little Indian communities, that are enclosed within the European settlements in Canada, in Massachusetts, in Carolina, is hardly cheering to the philanthropist. In New Hampshire, and elsewhere, schools for Indian children were established; but, as they became fledged, they

CHAP. XXII. all escaped, refusing to be caged. Harvard College enrolls the name of an Algonquin youth among her pupils; but the college parchment could not close the gulf between the Indian character and the Anglo-American. The copper-colored men are characterized by a moral inflexibility, a rigidity of attachment to their hereditary customs and manners. The birds and the brooks, as they chime forth their unwearied canticles, chime them ever to the same ancient melodies, and the Indian child, as it grows up, displays a propensity to the habits of its ancestors.

This determinateness of moral character is marked, also, in the organization of the American savage. He has little flexibility of features or transparency of skin; and therefore, if he depicts his passions, it is by strong contortions, or the kindling of the eye, that seems ready to burst from its socket. He cannot blush; the movement of his blood does not visibly represent the movement of his affections: for him the domain of animated beauty is circumscribed; he cannot paint to the eye the emotions of moral sensibility.

This effect is heightened by a uniformity of intellectual culture and activity. Youth and manhood to all have but one character; and where villages were scattered only at widest distances in the wilderness,—where marriage, interdicted, indeed, between members of the same family badge, was yet usually limited to people of the same tribe,—ties of blood united the nation, and the purity of the race increased the uniformity of organization. Each individual was marked, not so much by personal peculiarities, as by the physiognomy of his tribe.

Thus Nature in the wilderness is true to her type, and deformity is almost unknown. How rare is it to find the red man squint-eyed, or with a diseased spine, halt or blind, or with any deficiency or excess in the organs! It is not merely that, in the savage state of equality, deformity would never perpetuate itself, by winning through the aid of fortune what it cannot win from love; it is not merely that, among barbarians, the feeble and the misshaped perish from neglect or fatigue; the most refined nation is most liable to produce varieties, and to degenerate; when the habits of uncivilized simplicity have been fixed for thousands of years, the hereditary organization is safe against monstrous deviations.

CHAP. XXII.

This inflexibility of organization will not even yield to climate: there is the same general resemblance of feature among all the aboriginal inhabitants, from the Terra del Fuego to the St. Lawrence; all have some shade of the same dull vermillion, or cinnamon, or reddish brown, or copper color, carefully to be distinguished from the olive,—the same dark and glossy hair, coarse, and never curling. They have beards, but generally of feeble growth; their eye is elongated, having an orbit inclining to a quadrangular shape; the cheek-bones are prominent; the nose is broad; the jaws project the lips are large and thick, giving to the mouth an expression of indolent insensibility; the forehead, as compared with Europeans, is narrow. The facial angle of the European is assumed to be eighty-seven; that of the American, by induction from many admeasurements, is declared to be seventy-five. The mean internal capacity of the skull of the former is eighty-seven cubic inches; of the barbarous tribes of the latter, it is found to be, at least, eighty-two.

Morton's Crania Americana, 260, 261

And yet the inflexibility of organization is not so absolute as to forbid hope. The color of the tribes

CHAP. XXII. differs in its hue; and some are of so fair a complexion, that the blood can be seen as it mantles to the cheek: the stature and form vary, so that not only are some nations tall and slender, but in the same nation there are contrasts.

Improvement, too, has pervaded every clan in North America. The Indian of to-day excels his ancestors in skill, in power over nature, and in knowledge; the gun, the knife, and the horse, of themselves made a revolution in his condition and the current of his ideas: that the wife of the white man is cherished as his equal, has already been dimly noised about in the huts of the Comanches; the idea of the Great Spirit, who is the master of life, has reached the remote prairies. How slowly did the condition of the common people of Europe make advances! For how many centuries did the knowledge of letters remain unknown to the peasant of Germany or France! How languidly did civilization pervade the valleys of the Pyrenees! How far is intellectual culture from having reached the peasantry of Hungary! Within the century and a half during which the Cherokees have been acquainted with Europeans, they have learned the use of the plough and the axe, of herds and flocks, of the printing-press and water-mills; they have gained a mastery over the fields, and have taught the streams to run for their benefit. And finally, in proof of progress, that nation, like the Choctas, the Creeks, the Chippewas, the Winnebagoes, and other tribes, has increased, not in intelligence only, but in numbers.

"Whence was America peopled?" was the anxious inquiry that followed its discovery. "Whence came its trees and its grasses?" was asked, by way of excuse for indifference. But we keep the record of the intro duction of many trees and grasses; and, though this continent was peopled before it became known to history, it is yet reasonable to search after traces of connection between the nations of America and those of the Old World. CHAP. XXII.

To aid this inquiry, the country east of the Mississippi has no monuments. The numerous mounds which have been discovered in the alluvial valleys of the west, have by some been regarded as the works of an earlier and more cultivated race of men, whose cities have been laid waste, whose language and institutions have been destroyed or driven away; but the study of the structure of the earth strips this imposing theory of its marvels. Where imagination fashions relics of artificial walls, geology sees but crumbs of decaying sandstone, clinging like the remains of mortar to blocks of greenstone that rested on it; it discovers in parallel intrenchments a trough, that subsiding waters have ploughed through the centre of a ridge; it explains the tessellated pavement to be but a layer of pebbles aptly joined by water; and, on examining the mounds, and finding them composed of different strata of earth, arranged horizontally to their very edge, it ascribes their creation to the Power that shaped the globe into vales and hillocks. When the waters had gently deposited their alluvial burden on the bosom of the earth, it is not strange that, of the fantastic forms shaped by the eddies, some should resemble the ruins of a fortress; that the channel of a torrent should seem even like walls that connected a town with its harbor; that natural cones should be esteemed monuments of inexplicable toil. But the elements, as they crumble the mountain, and scatter the decomposed rocks, do not measure their action as men measure the labor of

Hitchcock

CHAP. XXII.

their hands. The hunters of old, as more recently the monks of La Trappe, may have selected a mound as the site of their dwellings, the aid to their rude fortifications, their watchtower for gaining a vision of God, or, more frequently than all, as their burial-places. Most of the northern tribes, perhaps all, preserved the bones of their fathers; and the festival of the dead was the greatest ceremony of western faith. When Nature has taken to herself her share in the construction of the symmetrical hillocks, nothing will remain to warrant the inference of a high civilization, that has left its abodes or died away,—of an earlier acquaintance with the arts of the Old World. That there have been successive irruptions of rude tribes, may be inferred from the insulated fragments of nations, which are clearly distinguished by their language. The mounds in the valley of the Mississippi have also been used—the smaller ones, perhaps, have been constructed—as burial-places of a race, of which the peculiar organization, as seen in the broader forehead, the larger facial angle, the less angular figure of the orbits of the eye, the more narrow nose, the less evident projection of the jaws, the smaller dimensions of the palatine fossa, the flattened occiput, bears a surprisingly exact resemblance to that of the race of nobles who sleep in the ancient tombs of Peru. Retaining the general characteristics of the red race, they differ obviously from the present tribes of Miamis and Wyandots. These mouldering bones, from hillocks which are crowned by trees that have defied the storms of many centuries, raise bewildering visions of migrations, of which no tangible traditions exist; but the graves of earth from which they are dug, and the feeble fortifications that are sometimes found in their vicinity,

J. C. Warren, in Delafield's Antiquities, 30. Morton, Crania Americ. 228–230. Warren, on the Sensorial and Nervous System, 137, 138.

afford no special evidence of early connection with other continents. "Among the more ancient works," says a careful observer, who is not disposed to undervalue the significancy of these silent monuments, near which he dwells, and which he has carefully explored, "there is not a single edifice, nor any ruins which prove the existence, in former ages, of a building composed of imperishable materials. No fragment of a column, nor a brick, nor a single hewn stone large enough to have been incorporated into a wall, has been discovered. The only relics which remain to inflame curiosity, are composed of earth." Some of the tribes had vessels made of clay; near Natchez, an image was found, of a substance not harder than clay dried in the sun. These few memorials of other days may indicate revolutions among the barbarous hordes of the Americans themselves; they cannot solve for the inquirer the problem of their origin.

Drake's Picture of Cincinnati, p. 201. Compare Atwater, in Trans. of Am Antiq. Soc.

Nor is it safe to place implicit reliance on tradition. The ideas of uncultivated nations are vaguely connected; and pressing want compels the mind to be indifferent to the past, not less than careless of the future. Time obliterates facts, or introduces confusion of memory, or buries one tradition beneath another. Yet the tradition of the Delawares may be repeated in this connection,—that tribes of the Algonquin and Wyandot families expelled from the basin of the Ohio its ancient tenants, and that the fugitives descended the Mississippi to renew their villages under a warmer sun. Vague indeed as must be the shadows that glimmer across the silent darkness of intervening centuries, physiologists have yet convinced themselves that they can trace, in the bones which time has not wholly crumbled, evidence of the extent of the Toltecan fam-

Heckewelder

CHAP. XXII.

ily from the heart of North America to the Andes The inference has no natural improbability. We know the wide range of the Indian brave; the kindred of the Athapasca race spread from the Kinaïzian Gulf to Hudson's Bay; the Algonquin was spoken from the Missinipi to Cape Fear; the Dahcotas extend from the Saskatchawan beyond the basin of the Arkansas. It would not be strange if, in the thousands of years from which no echo is to reach us, men of one American family had bowed to the sun in the southern valley of the Mississippi and within the tropics. The Chitimechas of Louisiana, improperly confounded with the Natchez, were on the same low stage of civilization with the Chechemecas, who are described as having entered Mexico from the north. But comparative anatomy, as it has questioned the graves, and compared its deductions with the traditions and present customs of the tribes, has not even led to safe inferences respecting the relations of the red nations among themselves; far less has it succeeded in tracing their wanderings from continent to continent.

Du Pratz. Gallatin. Clavigero, Storia di Mexico

Neither do the few resemblances that have been discovered between the roots of words in American languages, on the one hand, and those of Asia or Europe, on the other, afford historical evidence of any connection. The human voice articulates hardly twenty distinct, primitive sounds or letters: would it not be strange, then, were there no accidental resemblances? Of all European languages, the Greek is the most flexible; and it is that which most easily furnishes roots analogous to those of America. Not one clear coincidence has been traced beyond accident. Hard by Pamlico Sound dwelt, and apparently had dwelt for centuries, branches of the Algonquin, the

Huron-Iroquois, and the Catawba families. But though these nations were in the same state of civilization, were mingled by wars and captures, by embassies and alliances; though they had a common character in the organization of their language, as well as in their customs, government, and pursuits; yet each was found employing a language of its own. If resemblances cannot be traced between two families that have dwelt side by side apparently for centuries, who will hope to recover the traces of the mother tongue in Siberia or China? The results of comparison have thus far rebuked, rather than satisfied, curiosity.

It is still more evident, that similarity of customs furnishes no basis for satisfactory conclusions. The same kinds of knowledge may have been repeatedly reached; the same customs are naturally formed under similar circumstances. The manifest repetition of artificial peculiarities would prove a connection among nations; but all the customs consequent on the regular wants and infirmities of the human system, would be likely of themselves to be repeated; and, as for inventions and arts, they only offer new sources for measuring the capacity of human invention in its barbarous or semi-civilized state.

It is chiefly on supposed analogies of customs and of language, that the lost tribes of Israel, "who took counsel to go forth into a farther country, where never mankind dwelt," have been discovered, now in the bark cabins of North America, now in the secluded valleys of the Tennessee, and again, as the authors of culture, on the plains of the Cordilleras. We cannot tell the origin of the Goths and Celts; proud as we are of our lineage, we cannot trace our own descent; and we strive to identify, in the most western part of Asia,

II. Esdras, c. xiii. v. 40-45

Boudinot, &c

Adair.

Aglio's Antiquities of Mexico, vol. vi.

CHAP. XXII. the very hills and valleys among which the ancestors of our red men had their dwellings! Humanity has a common character. The ingenious scholar may find analogies in language, customs, institutions, and religion, between the aborigines of America and any nation whatever of the Old World: the pious curiosity of Christendom, and not a peculiar coincidence, has created a special disposition to discover a connection between them and the Hebrews. Inquirers into Jewish history, observing faint resemblances between their own religious faith and that of the American, have sought to trace the origin of common ideas to tradition from the same nation and the same sacred books,—when they should not have rested in their pursuit of a common source, till they had reached the Fountain of all knowledge and the Author of all being.

The Egyptians used hieroglyphics; so did the Mexicans, and the Pawnees, and the Five Nations. Among the Algonquins now, a man is represented by a rude figure of a body, surmounted by the head of the animal which gives a badge to his family; on the Egyptian pictures, men are found designated in the same way. But did North America, therefore, send its envoys to the court of Sesostris?

The Carthaginians, of all ancient nations, cultivated the art of navigation with highest success. If they rivalled Vasco de Gama, why may they not have anticipated Columbus? And men have seen on rocks in America Phœnician inscriptions and proofs of Phœnician presence; but these disappear before an honest skepticism. Besides, the Carthaginians were historians also; and a Latin poet has preserved for us the express testimony of Himilco, "that the abyss beyond the Columns of Hercules was to them interminable,

Festi Avieni Ora Maritima, v. 380–384.

that no mariner of theirs had ever guided a keel into that boundless deep."

On a rock by the side of a small New England stream, where, even by the aid of the tides, small vessels can hardly pass, a rude inscription has been made in a natural block of gray granite. By unwarranted interpolations and bold distortions, in defiance of countless improbabilities, the plastic power of fancy transformed the rude etching into a Runic monument; a still more recent theory insists on the analogy of its forms with the inscriptions of Fezzan and the Atlas. Calm observers, in the vicinity of the sculptured rock, see nothing in the design beyond the capacity of the red men of New England; and to one intimately acquainted with the skill and manners of the barbarians, the character of the drawing suggests its Algonquin origin. Scandinavians may have reached the shores of Labrador; the soil of the United States has not one vestige of their presence.

Jomard, in Vail, Notice sur les Indians, 36, 37. J. Davis, in Trans. Am. Ac. Schoolcraft.

An ingenious writer on the maritime history of the Chinese, finds traces of their voyages to America in the fifth century, and thus opens an avenue for Asiatic science to pass into the kingdom of Anahuac; but the theory refutes itself. If Chinese traders or emigrants came so recently to America, there would be customs and language to give evidence of it. Nothing is so indelible as speech: sounds that, in ages of unknown antiquity, were spoken among the nations of Hindostan, still live in their significancy in the language which we daily utter. The winged word cleaves its way through time, as well as through space. If Chinese came to civilize, and came so recently, the shreds of Asiatic civilization would be still clinging visibly to all their works.

De Guignes Acad. des Inscrip. t. xxviii.

CHAP. XXII.

Nor does the condition of astronomical science in aboriginal America prove a connection with Asia. The red men could not but observe the pole-star; and even their children could give the names and trace the motions of the more brilliant groups of stars, of which the return marked the seasons; but they did not divide the heavens, nor even a belt in the heavens, into constellations. It is a curious coincidence, that among the Algonquins of the Atlantic and of the Mississippi, alike among the Narragansetts and the Illinois, the north star was called the *bear*. This accidental agreement with the widely-spread usage of the Old World, is far more observable than the imaginary resemblance between the signs of the Mexicans for their days and the signs on the zodiac for the month in Thibet. The American nation had no zodiac, and could not, therefore, for the names of its days, have borrowed from Central Asia the symbols that marked the path of the sun through the year. Nor had the Mexicans either weeks or lunar months; but, after the manner of barbarous nations, they divided the days in the year into eighteen scores, leaving the few remaining days to be set apart by themselves. This division may have sprung directly from their system of enumeration; it need not have been imported. It is a greater marvel, that the indigenous inhabitants of Mexico had a nearly exact knowledge of the length of the year, and, at the end of one hundred and four years, made their intercalation more accurately than the Greeks, the Romans, or the Egyptians. The length of their tropical year was almost identical with the result obtained by the astronomers of the caliph Almamon; but let no one derive this coincidence from intercourse, unless he is prepared to believe that, in the ninth century of our

R Williams, 80. Le Clercq, Relation de la Gaspesie, 152, 153. Charlevoix, iii. 400.

A von Humboldt.

La Place, Exposition du Système du Monde, l. v. c. iii

era, there was commerce between Mexico and Bagdad. The agreement favors clearly the belief that Mexico did not learn of Asia; for, at so late a period, intercourse between the continents would have left its indisputable traces. No inference is warranted, except that, in the clear atmosphere of the table lands of Central America, the observers may have watched successfully the progress of the seasons; that the sun ran his career as faithfully over the heights of the Cordilleras as over the plains of Mesopotamia.

CHAP. XXII

When to this is added, that, alone of mankind, the American nations universally were ignorant of the pastoral state; that they kept neither sheep nor kine; that they knew not the use of the milk of animals for food; that they had neither wax nor oil; that they had no iron;—it becomes nearly certain that the imperfect civilization of America is its own.

Yet the original character of American culture does not insulate the American race. It would not be safe to reject the possibility of an early communication between South America and the Polynesian world. Nor can we know what changes time may have wrought on the surface of the globe, what islands may have been submerged, what continents divided. But, without resorting to the conjectures or the fancies which geologists may suggest, every where around us there are signs of migrations, of which the boundaries cannot be set; and the movement seems to have been towards the east and south.

Lang's View of the Polynesian Nation

The number of primitive languages increases near the Gulf of Mexico; and, as if one nation had crowded upon another, in the cane-brakes of the state of Louisiana there are more independent languages than are found from the Arkansas to the pole. In like man

CHAP. XXII.

ner, they abounded on the plateau of Mexico, the natural highway of wanderers. On the western shore of America, also, there are more languages than on the east; on the Atlantic coast, as if to indicate that it had never been a thoroughfare, one extended from Cape Fear to the Esquimaux; on the west, between the latitude of forty degrees and the Esquimaux, there were at least four or five. The Californians derived their ancestors from the north; the Aztecks preserve a narrative of their northern origin, which their choice of residence in a mountain region confirmed.

Ribas, l. i. c. vi and l. iii c. iii.

At the north, the continents of Asia and America nearly meet. In the latitude of sixty-five degrees fifty minutes, a line across Behring's Straits, from Cape Prince of Wales to Cape Tschowkotskoy, would measure a fraction less than forty-four geographical miles; and three small islands divide the distance.

Beechey's Voyage to Behring's Straits.

But within the latitude of fifty-five degrees, the Aleutian Isles stretch from the great promontory of Alaska so far to the west, that the last of the archipelago is but three hundred and sixty geographical miles from the east of Kamschatka; and that distance is so divided by the Mednoi Island and the group of Behring, that, were boats to pass from islet to islet from Kamschatka to Alaska, the longest navigation in the open sea would not exceed two hundred geographical miles, and at no moment need the mariner be more than forty leagues distant from land: and a chain of thickly-set isles extends from the south of Kamschatka to Corea. Now, the Micmac on the north-east of our continent would, in his frail boat, venture thirty or forty leagues out at sea: a Micmac savage, then, steering from isle to isle, might in his birch-bark canoe have made the voyage from North-West America to China.

A. Humboldt's N. E. ii. 501, &c.

Water, ever a favorite highway, is especially the highway of uncivilized man: to those who have no axes, the thick jungle is impervious; emigration by water suits the genius of savage life; canoes are older than wagons, and ships than chariots; a gulf, a strait, the sea intervening between islands, divide less than the matted forest. Even civilized man emigrates by sea and by rivers, and has ascended two thousand miles above the mouth of the Missouri, while interior tracts in New York and Ohio are still a wilderness. To the uncivilized man, no path is free but the sea, the lake, and the river.

The American and the Mongolian races of men, on the two sides of the Pacific, have a near resemblance. Both are alike strongly and definitely marked by the more capacious palatine fossa, of which the dimensions are so much larger, that a careful observer could, out of a heap of skulls, readily separate the Mongolian and American from the Caucasian, but could not distinguish them from each other. Both have the orbit of the eye quadrangular, rather than oval; both, especially the American, have comparatively a narrowness of the forehead; the facial angle in both, but especially in the American, is comparatively small; in both, the bones of the nose are flatter and broader than in the Caucasian,—and in so equal a degree, and with apertures so similar, that, on indiscriminate selections of specimens from the two, an observer could not, from this feature, discriminate which of them belonged to the old continent; both, but especially the Americans, are characterized by a prominence of the jaws. The elongated occiput is common to the American and the Asiatic; and there is to each very nearly the same obliquity of the face. Between the Mongolian of South-

CHAP. XXII. ern Asia and of Northern Asia there is a greater difference than between the Mongolian Tâtar and the North American. The Iroquois is more unlike the Peruvian than he is unlike the wanderer on the steppes of Siberia. Physiology has not succeeded in defining the qualities which belong to every well-formed Mongolian, and which never belong to an indigenous American; still less can geographical science draw a boundary line between the races. The Athapascas cannot be distinguished from Algonquin Knisteneaux, on the one side, or from Mongolian Esquimaux, on the other. The dwellers on the Aleutian Isles melt into resemblances with the inhabitants of each continent; and, at points of remotest distance, the difference is still so inconsiderable, that the daring Ledyard, whose ardent curiosity filled him with the passion to circumnavigate the globe and cross its continents, as he stood in Siberia, with men of the Mongolian race before him, and compared them with the Indians who had been his old play-fellows and school-mates at Dartmouth, writes deliberately, that, "universally and circumstantially, they resemble the aborigines of America." On the Connecticut and the Oby, he saw but one race.

Sparks's Ledyard, 201. Compare 246, 255.

Mithridates, iii. 343.

He that describes the Tungusians of Asia seems also to describe the North American. That the Tschukchi of North-Eastern Asia and the Esquimaux of America are of the same origin, is proved by the affinity of their languages,—thus establishing a connection between the continents previous to the discovery of America by Europeans. The indigenous population of America offers no new obstacle to faith in the unity of the human race.

CHAPTER XXIII.

THE COLONIES OF FRANCE AND ENGLAND ENCROACH MORE AND MORE ON THE RED MEN.

CHAP XXIII.

THE Tuscaroras changed their dwelling-place before the treaty of Utrecht was completed. Their chiefs had become indignant at the encroachments of the proprietaries of Carolina, who had assigned their lands to unhappy German fugitives from the banks of the Neckar and the Rhine. De Graffenried, who had undertaken the establishment of the exiles, accompanied by Lawson, the surveyor-general for the northern province, in September of 1711, ascended the Neuse River in a boat, to discover how far it was navigable, and through what kind of country it flowed. Seized by a party of sixty well-armed Indians, both were compelled to travel all night long, till they reached a village of the Tuscaroras, and were delivered up to its chief. Before a numerous council of the principal men from various towns of the tribe, complaint was made of the conduct of the English in Carolina, and especially of the severity of Lawson. He who, with his compass and chain, had marked their territory into lots for settlers, was reproved as "the man who sold their land." After a discussion of two days, the death of the prisoners was decreed. The large fire was kindled; the ring was drawn round the victims, and strown with flowers. On the morning appointed for the execution, a council

Graffenried, in Williamson

1711. Sept.

CHAP. XXIII. 1711. assembled anew. Round the white men sat the chiefs in two rows; behind them were three hundred of the people, engaged in festive dances. Yet mercy was mingled with severity; and, if no reprieve was granted to Lawson, yet Graffenried, as the great chieftain of the Palatines, on pledging his people to neutrality, and promising to occupy no land without the consent of the tribe, was suffered, after a captivity of five weeks, to return through the woods on foot. He returned to desolated settlements. On the twenty-second of September, small bands of the Tuscaroras and Corees, acting in concert, approached the scattered cabins along the Roanoke and Pamlico Sound. As night came on, a whoop from a warrior called his fierce associates from the woods, to commence the indiscriminate carnage. The wretched Palatines, now tenants of the wilderness, encountered a foe more savage than Louvois and the hated Louis XIV. At Bath, the Huguenot refugees, and the planters in their neighborhood, were struck down by aid of the glare from the burning of their own cabins; and, with a lighted pine knot in one hand and the tomahawk in the other, the hunters after men pursued their game through the forests. In the three following days, they scoured the country on the Albemarle Sound, and did not desist from slaughter till they were disabled by fatigue.

Sept. 22. Martin. Williamson. Spotswood, MSS.

Not all the Tuscaroras had joined in the conspiracy; Spotswood sought immediately to renew with them an alliance; but, as the burgesses of Virginia engaged with him in a contest of power, no effectual aid came from the Old Dominion. But the assembly of South Carolina promptly voted relief; and, defying the hardships of a long march through the wilderness, Barnwell, with Cherokees, Creeks, Catawbas, and Yamas-

Spotswood, MSS.

Statutes at large ii 366.

sees, as allies, led a small detachment of militia to the banks of Neuse River. There, in the upper part of Craven county, the Indians were intrenched in a rude fort. With the aid of a few soldiers of North Carolina, the fort was besieged; but the province was rent by intestine divisions. Even imminent danger had not roused its inhabitants to harmonious action; they retained their hatred for the rule of the proprietaries; and, surrounded by difficulties, Barnwell could only negotiate with the Indians a treaty of peace.

CHAP. XXIII.

1712.

The troops of South Carolina, on their return, themselves violated the treaty, enslaving inhabitants of villages which should have been safe under its guaranties; and the massacres on Neuse River were renewed. The province was impoverished, the people dissatisfied with their government; in autumn, the yellow fever raged under its most malignant form; and the country south of Pamlico Sound seemed destined to become once more a wilderness. But Spotswood succeeded in dividing the Tuscaroras. Large reënforcements of Indians from South Carolina arrived, with a few white men, under James Moore; the enemy were pursued to their fort (within the limits of the present Greene county) on the Neuse; and, on its surrender, eight hundred became captives. The legislature of North Carolina, assembling in May, under a new governor, issued its first bills of credit, to the amount of eight thousand pounds; "the very refractory" among the people grew zealous to supply the forces with provisions; the enemy was chased across the lakes and swamps of Hyde county; the woods were patrolled by red allies, who hunted for prisoners to be sold as slaves, or took scalps for a reward. At last, the hostile part of the Tuscaroras abandoned their old hunting-

Spotswood

Sept.

Nov Dec.

1713. Mar.

June.

CHAP. XXIII. grounds, and, migrating to the vicinity of the Oneida Lake, were welcomed by their kindred of the Iroquois as the sixth nation of their confederacy. Their hum-
1715 bled allies were established as a single settlement in the precincts of Hyde. Thus the power of the natives of North Carolina was broken, and its interior forests became safe places of resort to the emigrant

1714 Aug Meantime, the house of Hanover had ascended the English throne—an event doubly grateful to the colonies. The contest of parties is the struggle, not between persons, but between ideas; and the abiding sympathy of nations is never won but by an appeal to the controlling principles of the age. George I. had imprisoned his wife; had, from jealousy, caused a young man to be assassinated; had had frequent and angry quarrels with his son; and now, being fifty-three years old, attended by two women of the Hanoverian aristocracy, who were proud of being known as his mistresses, he crossed the sea to become the sovereign of a country of which he understood neither the institutions, the manners, nor the language. Intrusting the administration to the whigs, he avowed his purpose of limiting his favor to them, as though he were himself a member of their party; and, in return, by a complaisant ministry, places in the highest ranks of the English aristocracy were secured to his mistresses, whose number he, in his sixty-seventh year, just before his death, was designing to enlarge. And yet, throughout English America, even the clergy heralded the elevation of George I. as an omen of happiness; and from the pulpit in Boston it was announced of its people that, in the whole land, "not a dog can wag his tongue to charge them with disloyalty." To the children of the Puritans, the accession of the house

Benjamin Colman's Fast Sermon, 1716, p. 31.

of Hanover was the triumph of Protestantism, and the guaranty of Protestant liberties. CHAP XXIII.

The advancement of the new dynasty was, moreover, a pledge of a pacific policy; and this pledge was redeemed. Louis XIV. drew near his end: he had outlived his children and every grandchild, except the new king of Spain,—his own glory,—the gratitude of those whom he had advanced. "My child," said he, as he gave a farewell blessing to his great-grandson, the boy of five years old, who was to be his successor, "you will be a great king; do not imitate me in my passion for war; seek peace with your neighbors, and strive to be, what I have failed to be, a solace to your people." "Sad task," madame de Maintenon had written, "to amuse a man who is past being amused;" and, quitting his bedside, she left him, after a reign of seventy-two years, to die alone. He had sought to extend his power beyond his life by establishing a council of regency; but the will was cancelled by the parliament, and his nephew, the brave, generous, but abandoned Philip of Orleans, became absolute regent. In the event of the early death of Louis XV., who should inherit the throne of France? By the treaty of Utrecht, Philip of Anjou, accepting the crown of Spain, renounced the right of succession to that of France. If the treaty were maintained, Philip of Orleans was heir-apparent; if legitimacy could sustain the necessary succession of the nearest prince, the renunciation of the king of Spain was invalid, and the integrity of his right unimpaired. Thus the personal interest of the absolute regent in France was opposed to the rigid doctrine of legitimacy, and sought an alliance with England; while the king of Spain, under the guidance of Alberoni, was moved not less by hereditary attachment to

1715 Aug.

Sept. 1.

CHAP. XXIII. legitimacy than by personal ambition to disregard the provisions of the treaty, and favor alike the pretensions of the Stuarts to the British throne and of himself to the succession in France. The French minister Torcy had avowed his faith that God has established the order of succession, which man cannot change; and the power of the gifted son of Colbert yielded to that of the wily, degenerate, avaricious Du Bois. By the influence of Protestant England, the recklessly immoral Du Bois, thrice infamous, as the corrupter of his pupil, as the licentious priest of a spiritual religion, and as a statesman in the pay of a foreign country, became cardinal, the successor of Fenelon in an archbishopric, and prime minister of France. Under such auspices was a happy peace secured to the colonies of rival nations

1727. Neither the death of George I. nor the coming of age of Louis XV. changed the dispositions of the governments. The character of Walpole was a pledge of moderation. Ignorant of theories, not familiar with the history or politics of foreign nations, he was profoundly versed in the maxims of worldly wisdom. Never boasting of his philosophy, he possessed that tranquillity which could lose office without excess of complaint, and meet death without fear. Destitute of fortune or alliances, he rose gradually to power, and exercised it temperately. Hope shed its light always on his path; he never distrusted his policy or himself. It was his weakness that he could endure no rival, and sought as friends men who were his inferiors; that his pleasures degenerated into coarse licentiousness; and that he was not indifferent to the vanity of magnificence. In the employment of means, he "plunged to the elbows in corruption," and had the daring to do wrong without compunction; and yet his policy rested mainly for its support on great views, which were in harmony with his age, fostering the commerce and diminishing the debt of England. Never palliating his conduct, and caring only for majorities,—trading for numbers, and not for talents or for appearances,—he followed honesty more than he professed to do it; and, if he never resisted his party from motives of moral right; if he had the weakness, at last, to yield the cardinal point of his policy, rather than leave the cabinet; he, at least, never parted from his friends to serve himself. The house of commons was his avenue to power; and his thoughts were chiefly engrossed by intrigues for majorities. Of the American colonies he knew little; but they profited by the character of a statesman who ever shunned measures that might lead to an insurrection,—who rejected every system of revenue that required the sabre and the bayonet to enforce it.

In his honorable policy, Walpole was favored by the natural moderation of Fleury, who, at the age of seventy-three, was called by Louis XV. to direct the affairs of France. The wise cardinal had a discriminating mind, and an equitable candor, which shunned intrigue and forbade distrust. The preservation of peace was his rule of administration; and he was the cnosen mediator between conflicting sovereigns. His clear perceptions anticipated impending revolutions; but he hushed the storm till his judgment sunk under the infirmities of fourscore. Happy period for the colonies! Let England judge as she will of the minister to whom she owes septennial parliaments, America blesses the memory of Walpole and of Fleury as of statesmen who preferred commerce to conquest, and desired no higher glory than that of guardians of

CHAP XXIII.

peace. For a quarter of a century, if less forbearance was shown towards Spain, the controversies of Great Britain and France respecting colonial boundaries, though they might lead to collisions, could not occasion a rupture.

The prospect of continued peace occasioned a rapid extension of the Indian traffic of South Carolina. Favored by the mild climate, its traders had their storehouses among the Chickasas and near the Natchez, and by intimidation, rather than by good will, gained admission even into villages of the Choctas. Still more intimate were their commercial relations with the branches of the Muskhogees in the immediate vicinity of the province, especially with the Yamassees, who, from impatience at the attempts at their conversion to Christianity, had deserted their old abodes in Florida, and planted themselves from Port Royal Island along the north-east bank of the Savannah River. The tribes of Carolina had been regarded as "a tame and peaceable people;" they were very largely in debt for the advances which had been made them; and "the traders began to be hard upon them, because they would be paid." The influence of Bienville, of Louisiana, prevailed with the Choctas, and the English were driven from their villages. The whole Indian world from Mobile River to Cape Fear was in commotion. The Yamassees renewed friendly relations with the Spaniards at St. Augustine; they won the alliance of the Catawbas and the Cherokees; and their messenger with "the bloody stick" threaded his way through flowering groves to the new towns of the Appalachian emigrants on the Savannah, to the ancient villages of the Uchees, and bounded across the rivers along which the various tribes of the Muskho-

Marston, in Hawks' MSS. i. 1.

Hawks' MSS. i. 29, 30.

Hassell, Marston, Le Jeu, in Hawks' MSS. i. 407, &c. Carroll's Coll. ii. 570, &c. 353, 548. Martin's Louisiana, i. 185.

gees had their dwellings; and they delayed their CHAP. XXIII.
rising till the deliberations of the grand council of the
Creeks should be finished, and the emblem of war Ramsay, i. 159.
be returned.

In passion-week of 1715, the traders at Pocotaligo observed the madness of revenge kindling among the Yamassees. On Thursday night, unaware of immediate danger, Nairne, the English agent, sent with proposals of peace, slept in the round house, with the civil chiefs and the war-captains. On the morning of Good 1715
Friday, the indiscriminate massacre of the English be- April 15.
gan. One boy escaped into the forest, and, after wandering for nine days, reached a garrison. Seaman Burroughs, a strong man and swift runner, broke through the ranks of the Indian band; and, though hotly pursued, and twice wounded, by running ten miles, and swimming one, he reached Port Royal, and alarmed the town. Its inhabitants, some in canoes, and some on board a ship, which chanced to be in the harbor, fled to Charleston. The numerous bands of the enemy, hiding by day in the swamps, and by night attacking the scattered settlements, drove the planters towards the capital. The Yamassees and their confederates advanced even as far as Stono, where they halted, that their prisoners—planters, with their wives and little ones—might be tormented and sacrificed at leisure. On the north, a troop of horse, insnared by a false guide in an ambush among large trees, thickly strown by a late hurricane, lost its commander, and retreated. The insurgent Indians carried their ravages even to the parish of Goose Creek; Charleston itself was in peril; the colony seemed near its ruin.

But the impulse of savage passion could not resist the deliberate courage of civilized man. The spirit of

CHAP. XXIII. 1715. the colony was aroused. On the north, the insulated band of invaders received a check, and vanished into the forests; on the south, Charles Craven, the governor of the province, himself promptly led the forces of Colleton district to the desperate conflict with the confederated warriors on the banks of the Salke-hachie. The April. battle was bloody and often renewed. The air resounded with savage yells; arrows, as well as bullets, were discharged, with fatal aim, from behind trees and coppices. At last, the savages gave way, and were pursued beyond the present limits of Carolina. The Yamassees retired into Florida, and at St. Augustine were welcomed with peals from the bells and a salute of guns, as though allies and friends had returned from victory. The Uchees left their old settlements below Broad River, and the Appalachians their new cabins near the Savannah, and retired towards Flint River. When Craven returned to Charleston, he was greeted with the applause which his alacrity, courage, and conduct, had merited. The colony had lost about four hundred of its inhabitants.

The war with the Yamassees was followed by a domestic revolution in Carolina. Its soil had been defended by its own people, and they resolved, under the sovereignty of the English monarch, to govern themselves. Scalping parties of Yamassees, from their places of refuge in Florida, continued to hover on the frontiers of a territory which the Spaniards still claimed as their own. The proprietaries took no efficient measures for protecting their colony. Instead of inviting settlers, they monopolized the lands which they had not contributed to defend. The measures adopted for the payment of the colonial debts were negatived, in part because they imposed a duty of ten pounds on the introduction of every negro from abroad. The polls for the election of representatives had hitherto been held for the whole province at Charleston alone; the provincial legislature permitted the votes to be given in each parish. But because the reform increased popular power, this also was negatived. Some of the members of the proprietary council had, by long residence, become attached to the soil and the liberties of their new country; and they were supplanted, or their influence destroyed, by an abrupt increase of the number of their associates. In consequence, at the next election of assembly, though it was chosen at Charleston, the agents of the proprietaries could not succeed in procuring the return of any one whom they desired. The members elect, at private meetings, "resolved to have no more to do with the proprietors;" and the people of the province entered "into an association to stand by their rights and privileges." It was remembered that the lords of trade had formerly declared the charter forfeit; that the house of peers had favored its prosecution; and, as the known hostility of Spain threatened an invasion, the assembly resolved "to have no regard to the officers of the proprietaries or to their administration," and begged Robert Johnson, the governor, "to hold the reins of government for the king." When Johnson, remaining true to his employers, firmly rejected their offer, they, with Arthur Middleton for their president, voted themselves "a convention delegated by the people;" and, resolved "on having a governor of their own choosing," they elected the brave James Moore, a favorite with the people, "whom all the country had allowed to be the fittest person" for undertaking its defence. The militia of Charleston was to be reviewed on the twenty-

CHAP. XXIII. 1719.

1719 Nov. 28.

Hawks' MSS. i. 414.

CHAP. XXIII. first of December; and that day was selected for proclaiming the new chief magistrate. To Parris, the

1719 commanding officer, Johnson issued particular orders to delay the muster, nor suffer a drum to be beat in the town. But the people of Carolina had, by the power of public opinion, renounced the government of the proprietaries; and, on the appointed day, with colors flying at the forts and on all the ships in the harbor, the militia, which was but the people in arms, drew up in the public square. It would be tedious to relate minutely by what menaces, what entreaties, what arguments, Johnson struggled to resist the insurrection. In the king's name, he commanded Parris to disperse his men; and Parris answered, "I obey the convention." "The revolutioners had their governor, council, and convention, and all of their own free election." Peacefully, and without bloodshed, palatines, landgraves, and caciques, were dismissed from Carolina, where they had become so little connected with the vital interests of the state, that history with difficulty preserves them from oblivion.

1720 The agent from Carolina obtained in England a ready hearing from the lords of the regency. The proprietors were esteemed to have forfeited their charter; measures were taken for its abrogation; and, in the mean time, Francis Nicholson—an adept in colonial governments, trained by experience in New York, in Virginia, in Maryland; brave, and not penurious, but narrow and irascible; of loose morality, yet a fervent supporter of the church—received a royal commission as provisional governor of the province. The bold act of the people of Carolina, which in England was respected as an evidence of loyalty, was remembered in America as an example for posterity. The introduction of the direct regal supremacy was a pledge of more than security to the southern frontier: no lines were either run or proposed; and the neglect was an omen that the limits of the stronger nation would be advanced by encroachments or conquest. CHAP. XXIII.

The first act of Nicholson confirmed peace with 1721
the natives. On the borders of the territory of the peaceful Cherokees, he was met, in congress, by the chiefs of thirty-seven different villages. They smoked with him the pipe of peace, and marked the boundaries between "the beloved nation" and the colonists; and they returned to their happy homes in the mountain vales pleased with their generous brother and new ally. A treaty of commerce and peace was also concluded with the Creeks, whose hunting-grounds it was solemnly agreed should extend to the Savannah. Yet the ambition of England was not bounded by that river; and on the forks of the Alatamaha, in defiance of remonstrances from Spain and from Florida, a fort was kept by a small English garrison.

The controversy was not adjusted when, in September, 1729, under the sanction of an act of parliament, 1729
and for the sum of twenty-two thousand five hundred pounds, seven eighths of the proprietaries sold to the crown their territory, the jurisdiction over it, and their arrears of quitrents. Lord Carteret alone, joining in the surrender of the government, reserved an eighth share in the soil. This is the period when a royal governor was first known in North Carolina. Its secluded hamlets had not imitated the popular revolution of the southern province.

So soon as the royal government was ful.y confirmed, it attempted, by treaties of union, to convert the Indians on the borders of Carolina into allies or

CHAP. XXIII. subjects; and, early in 1730, Sir Alexander Cumming, a special envoy, guided by Indian traders to Keowee summoned a general assembly of the chiefs of the Cherokees to meet at Nequassee, in the valley of the Tennessee. They came together in the month of April, and were told that King George was their sovereign. When they offered a chaplet, four scalps of their enemies, and five eagles' tails, as the records of the treaty, and the pledge of their fidelity, it was proposed to them to send deputies to England; and English writers interpreted their assent as an act of homage to the British monarch. In England, a treaty of alliance, offensive and defensive, was drawn up by the English, and signed by the name and seal of one party, by the emblems and marks of the other. No white men, except the English, might build cabins or plant corn upon the wide lands of the Cherokees. Thus a nation rose up as a barrier against the French. The seven envoys from the mountains of Tennessee, already bewildered by astonishment at the vastness of London, and the splendor and discipline of the English army, were presented at court; and when the English king claimed their land and all the country about them as his property, surprise and inadvertence extorted from one of their war-chieftains the irrevocable answer,
1730. Sept. "*To-eu-hah*,"—it is "a most certain truth;" and the delivery of eagles' feathers confirmed his words. The covenant promised that love should flow forever like the rivers, that peace should endure like the mountains; and it was faithfully kept, at least for one generation.

Of the maritime powers of Europe, it was Spain which chiefly took umbrage at the progress of the English settlements and the English alliances at the south. The questions at issue with France were attended with greater difficulty. The treaty of Utrecht surrendered to England Acadia and Nova Scotia, "with its ancient boundaries." Disputes were to arise respecting them; but even the eastern frontier of the province of Massachusetts was not vindicated without a contest. To the country between the Kennebec and the St. Croix a new claimant appeared in the Abenakis themselves. In 1716, the general court extended its jurisdiction to the utmost bounds of the province; the enterprise of the fishermen and the traders of New England, whom, at first, the convenience of commerce made welcome, not only revived the villages that had been desolated during the war, but, on the eastern bank of the Kennebec, laid the foundation of new settlements, and protected them by forts.

The red men became alarmed. Away went their chiefs across the forests to Quebec, to ask if France had indeed surrendered the country, of which they themselves were the rightful lords; and as Vaudreuil answered, that the treaty of which the English spoke made no mention of their country, their chief resisted the claim of the government of Massachusetts. "I have my land," said he, "where the Great Spirit has placed me; and while there remains one child of my tribe, I shall fight to preserve it." France could not maintain its influence by an open alliance, but its missionaries guided their converts. At Norridgewock, on the banks of the Kennebec, the venerable Sebastian Rasles, for more than a quarter of a century the companion and instructor of savages, had gathered a flourishing village round a church which, rising in the desert, made some pretensions to magnificence. Severely ascetic,—using no wine, and little food ex-

1717
1720

CHAP. XXIII. cept pounded maize,—a rigorous observer of the days of Lent,—he built his own cabin, tilled his own garden, drew for himself wood and water, prepared his own hominy, and, distributing all that he received, gave an example of religious poverty. And yet he was laborious in garnishing his forest sanctuary, believing the faith of the savage must be quickened by Lett, Ed. iv. 143. striking appeals to the senses. Himself a painter, he adorned the humble walls of his church with pictures. There he gave instruction almost daily. Following his pupils to their wigwams, he tempered the spirit of devotion with familiar conversation and innocent gayety, winning the mastery over their souls by his powers of persuasion. He had trained a little band of forty young savages, arrayed in cassock and surplice, to assist in the service and chant the hymns of the church; and their public processions attracted a great concourse of red men. Two chapels were built near the village,—one dedicated to the Virgin, and adorned with her statue in relief,—another to the guardian angel; and before them the hunter muttered his prayers, on his way to the river or the woods. When the tribe descended to the sea-side, in the season of wild fowl, they were followed by Rasles; and on some islet a little chapel of bark was quickly consecrated.

1717 The government of Massachusetts attempted, in turn, to establish a mission; and its minister made a mocking of purgatory and the invocation of saints, of the cross and the rosary. "My Christians," retorted Rasles, "believe the truths of the Catholic faith, but are not skilful disputants;" and he himself prepared a defence of the Roman church. Thus Calvin and Loyola met in the woods of Maine. But the Protestant minister, unable to compete with the Jesuit for the affections of the Indians, returned to Boston, while "the friar remained, the incendiary of mischief." CHAP. XXIII.

Several chiefs had, by stratagem, been seized by the New England government, and were detained as hostages. For their liberty a stipulated ransom had been paid; and still they were not free. The Abenakis then demanded that their territory should be evacuated, and the imprisoned warriors delivered up, or reprisals would follow. Instead of negotiating, the English seized the young baron de St. Castin, who, being a half-breed, at once held a French commission and was an Indian war-chief; and, after vainly soliciting the savages to surrender Rasles, in midwinter Westbrooke led a strong force to Norridgewock to take him by surprise. The warriors were absent in the chase, yet the Jesuit had sufficient warning to escape, with the old men and the infirm, into the forest; and the invaders gained nothing but his papers. These were important; for the correspondence with Vaudreuil proved a latent hope of establishing the power of France on the Atlantic. There was found, moreover, a vocabulary of the Abenaki language, which the missionary had compiled, and which has been preserved to this day. 1721 Mass Hist Coll. xviii. Lett. Ed. iv. July. 1722 Jan

These insults induced the Indians to hope for no peace but by inspiring terror. On returning from the chase, after planting their grounds, they resolved to destroy the English settlements on the Kennebec. They sent deputies to carry the hatchet and chant the war-song among the Hurons of Quebec, and in every village of the Abenakis. The war-chiefs met at Norridgewock, and the work of destruction began by the burning of Brunswick. 1722

The clear judgment of Rasles perceived the issue. The forts of the English could not be taken by the

CHAP. XXIII. 1722. feeble means of the natives: "unless the French should join with the Indians," he reported the land as lost. Many of his red people retired to Canada: he bid them go; but to their earnest solicitations that he would share their flight, the aged man, foreseeing the impending ruin of Norridgewock, replied, "I count not my life dear unto myself, so I may finish with joy the ministry which I have received."

July. The government of Massachusetts, by resolution, declared the eastern Indians to be traitors and robbers; and, while troops were raised for the war, it also stimulated the activity of private parties by offering for each Indian scalp at first a bounty of fifteen pounds, and afterwards of a hundred.

1723. March 4–9. The expedition to Penobscot was under public auspices. After five days' march through the woods, Westbrooke, with his company, came upon the Indian settlement, that was probably above Bangor, at Old Town. He found a fort, seventy yards long, and fifty in breadth, well protected by stockades, fourteen feet high, enclosing twenty-three houses regularly built. On the south side, near at hand, was the chapel, sixty feet long, and thirty wide, well and handsomely furnished within and without; and south of this stood the "friar's dwelling-house." The invaders arrived there on the ninth of March, at six in the evening. That night they set fire to the village, and by sunrise next morning every building was in ashes.

Williamson, ii. 60 and 121. See his letter of Mar. 23, 1722–3.

Twice it was attempted in vain to seize Rasles. 1724. At last, on the twenty-third of August, 1724, a party from New England reached Norridgewock unperceived, and escaped discovery till they discharged their guns at the cabins.

De la Chasse. There were then about fifty warriors in the place.

CHAP XXIII.

They seized their arms, and marched forth tumultuously, not to fight, but to protect the flight of their wives, and children, and old men. Rasles, roused to the danger by their clamors, went forward to save his flock by drawing down upon himself the attention of the assailants; and his hope was not vain. Meantime, the savages fled to the river, which they passed by wading and swimming, while the English pillaged the cabins and the church, and then, heedless of sacrilege, set them on fire.

After the retreat of the invaders, the savages returned to nurse their wounded and bury their dead. They found Rasles mangled by many blows, scalped, his skull broken in several places, his mouth and eyes filled with dirt; and they buried him beneath the spot where he used to stand before the altar.

De la Chasse

Thus died Sebastian Rasles, the last of the Catholic missionaries in New England; thus perished the Jesuit missions and their fruits,—the villages of the semi-civilized Abenakis and their priests. Rasles was in his sixty-seventh year, and had been thirty-seven years in the service of the church in America. He was naturally robust, but had wasted by fatigues, age, and fastings. He knew several dialects of the Algonquin, and had been as a missionary among various tribes from the ocean to the Mississippi. In 1721, Father de la Chasse had advised his return to Canada. "God has intrusted to me this flock"—such was his answer; "I shall follow its fortunes, happy to be immolated for its benefit." In New England, he was regarded as the leader of the insurgent Indians; the brethren of his order mourned for him as a martyr, and gloried in his happy immortality as a saint. The French ministry, intent on giving an example of forbearance, restrained

Vergennes 43

CHAP. XXIII. its indignation, and trusted that the joint commissioners for regulating boundaries would restore tranquillity.

The overthrow of the missions completed the ruin of French influence. The English themselves had grown skilful in the Indian warfare; and no war parties of the red men ever displayed more address or heroism than the brave John Lovewell and his companions. His volunteer associates twice returned laden

1725. April. with scalps. On a third expedition, falling into an ambush of a larger party of Saco Indians, he lost his life in Fryeburg, near a sheet of water which has taken his name; and the little stream that feeds it is still known to the peaceful husbandman as the Battle Brook.

Nov. At last, the eastern Indians, despairing of success, instigated, but not supported, by the French, unable to contend openly with their opponents, and excelled even in their own methods of warfare, concluded a

1726. Aug. 6. peace, which was solemnly ratified by the Indian chiefs as far as the St. John, and was long and faithfully maintained. Influence by commerce took the place of influence by religion, and English trading-houses supplanted French missions. The eastern boundary of New England was established.

Beyond New England no armed collisions took place. The coast between Kennebec and Nova Scotia had ever been regarded by the French as a part of their possessions. If the treaty of Utrecht had been silent as to this claim, the stipulations of that treaty respecting the country of the Iroquois seemed to preclude the idea of French jurisdiction; and yet the whole basin of the St. Lawrence was still considered as included within the limits of New France. The wilderness that divided the settlements of the contending claimants could but postpone hostilities. By the treaty of Utrecht, the subjects and friends of both nations might resort to each other for the reciprocal benefit of their trade; and an active commerce subsisted between Albany and Montreal by means of the Christian Iroquois. In the administration of Burnet, that commerce was prohibited; and, amidst the bitter hostility of the merchants whose trade was interrupted, New York established a commercial post at Oswego. This was the first in the series of measures which carried the bounds of the English colonies towards Michigan, and, in public opinion, annexed the north-west to our country. In 1727, this trading-post was converted into a fortress, in defiance of the discontent of the Iroquois and the constant protest of France. It was the avenue through which the west was reached by English traders, and the Miamis, and even the Hurons from Detroit, found their way to Albany.

CHAP. XXIII.

1722

The limit of jurisdiction, as between England and France, was not easy of adjustment. Canada, by its original charter, comprised the whole basin of the St. Lawrence; and that part of Vermont and New York which is watered by streams flowing to the St. Lawrence, had ever been regarded by France as Canadian territory. The boat of Champlain had entered the lake that makes his name a familiar word, in the same summer in which Hudson ascended the North River. Holland had never dispossessed the French; and the conquest and surrender of New Netherlands could transfer no more than the possessions of Holland There was, therefore, no act of France relinquishing its claim till the treaty of Utrecht. The ambiguous language of that treaty did, indeed, refer to "the Five Nations subject to England;" but French diplomacy would not

CHAP. XXIII. interpret an allusion to savage hordes as an express surrender of Canadian territory. The right of France, then, to that part of New York and Vermont which belongs to the basin of the St. Lawrence, sprung from discovery, occupation, the uniform language of its grants and state papers.

As the claims of discovery and earliest occupation were clearly with the French, the English revived and exaggerated the rights of the Five Nations. In the strife with France, during the government of De la Barre, some of their chiefs had fastened the arms of the duke of York to their castles; and this act was taken as a confession of irrevocable allegiance to England. The treaty of Ryswick made the condition at the commencement of hostilities the basis of occupation at the time of peace. Now, at the opening of the war, Fort Frontenac had been razed, and the country around it, and Montreal itself, were actually in possession of the Mohawks; so that all Upper Canada was declared to have become, by the treaty of Ryswick, a part of the domain of the Five Nations, and therefore subject to England.

Again: at the opening of the war of the Spanish succession,
1701 the chiefs of the Mohawks and Oneidas had appeared in Albany; and the English commissioners, who could produce no treaty, had seen cause to make a minute in their books of entry, that the Mohawks and the Oneidas had placed their hunting-grounds under the protection of the English. Immediately their hunting-grounds were interpreted to extend to Lake Nipissing; and, on old English maps, the vast region is included within the dominions of England, by virtue of an act of cession from the Iroquois.

But as a treaty, of which no record existed, could

hardly be cited by English lawyers as a surrender of lands, it was the object of Governor Burnet to obtain a confirmation of this grant. Accordingly, in the treaty concluded at Albany, in September, 1726, the cession of the Iroquois country west of Lake Erie, and north of Erie and Ontario, was confirmed; and, in addition, a strip of sixty miles in width, extending from Oswego to Cuyahoga River at Cleveland, was "submitted and granted," by sachems of the three western tribes, to "their sovereign lord, King George," "to be protected and defended by his said majesty, for the use of the said three nations." The chiefs could give no new validity to the alleged treaty of 1701; they had no authority to make a cession of land; nor were they conscious of attempting it. If France had renounced its rights to Western New York, it had done so only by the treaty of Utrecht. Each new ground for an English claim, was a confession that the terms of that treaty were far from being explicit.

CHAP. XXIII. 1726 Sept. 14.

But France did not merely remonstrate against the attempt to curtail its limits and appropriate its provinces. Entering Lake Champlain, it established, in 1731, the fortress of the Crown. The garrison of the French was at first stationed on the eastern shore of the lake, but soon removed to the Point, where its batteries defended the approach to Canada by water, and gave security to Montreal.

The fort at Niagara had already been renewed. Among the public officers of the French, who gained influence over the red men by adapting themselves, with happy facility, to life in the wilderness, was the Indian agent Joncaire. For twenty years he had been successfully employed in negotiating with the Senecas. He was become, by adoption, one of their own citizens

1721

CHAP. XXIII. and sons, and to the culture of a Frenchman added the fluent eloquence of an Iroquois warrior. "I have no happiness," said he in council, "like that of living with my brothers;" and he asked leave to build himself a dwelling. "He is one of our own children," it was said, in reply; "he may build where he will." And he planted himself in the midst of a group of cabins, at Lewiston, higher than where La Salle had driven a rude palisade, and where Denonville had designed to lay the foundations of a settlement. In May of 1721 a party arrived at the spot to take measures for a permanent establishment; among them were the son of the governor of New France, De Longeuil, from Montreal, and the admirable Charlevoix, best of early writers on American history. It was then resolved to construct a fortress. The party were not insensible to the advantages of the country; they observed the rich soil of Western New York, its magnificent forests, its agreeable and fertile slopes, its mild climate. "A good fortress in this spot, with a reasonable settlement, will enable us"—thus they reasoned—"to dictate law to the Iroquois, and to exclude the English from the fur-trade." And, in 1726, four years after Burnet had built the English trading-house at Oswego, the flag of France floated from Fort Niagara.

Charlevoix, iii. 226.

1721.

The fortress at Niagara gave a control over the commerce of the remote interior: if furs descended by the Ottawa, they went directly to Montreal; and if by way of the lakes, they passed over the portage at the falls. The boundless region in which they were gathered knew no jurisdiction but that of the French, whose trading-canoes were safe in all the waters, whose bark chapels rose on every shore, whose missions extended beyond Lake Superior. The implacable Foxes were chastised, and driven from their old abode on the borders of Green Bay. Except the English fortress at Oswego, the entire country watered by the St. Lawrence and its tributaries was possessed by France.

The same geographical view was applied by the French to their province of Louisiana. On the side of Spain, at the west and south, it was held to extend to the River del Norte; and on the map published by the French Academy, the line passing from that river to the ridge that divides it from the Red River followed that ridge to the Rocky Mountains, and then descended to seek its termination in the Gulf of California. On the Gulf of Mexico, it is certain that France claimed to the Del Norte. At the north-west, where its collision would have been with the possessions of the company of Hudson's Bay, no treaty, no commission, appears to have fixed its limits. Greenhow's Memoir 216.

On the east, the line as between Spain and France was the half way between the Spanish garrison at Pensacola and the fort which, in 1711, the French had established on the site of the present city of Mobile: with regard to England, Louisiana was held to embrace the whole valley of the Mississippi. Not a fountain bubbled on the west of the Alleghanies but was claimed as being within the French empire. Louisiana stretched to the head-springs of the Alleghany and the Monongahela, of the Kenawha and the Tennessee. "Half a mile from the head of the southern branch of the Savannah River is Herbert's Spring, which flows to the Mississippi: strangers, who drank of it, would say they had tasted of French waters." Adair 231.

The energy of the centralized government of New France enabled it to act with promptness; and, before the English government could direct its thoughts to the consequences, the French had secured their influence on the head-springs of the Ohio.

CHAP. XXIII. In 1698, a branch of the Shawnees, offended with the French, established themselves at Conestogo; in 1700, William Penn received them as a part of the people of Pennsylvania; and they scattered themselves along the upper branches of the Delaware and the Susquehannah. About the year 1724, the Delaware Indians, for the conveniency of game, migrated to the branches of the Ohio; and, in 1728, the Shawnees gradually followed them. They were soon met by Canadian traders; and Joncaire, the adopted citizen of the Seneca nation, found his way to them from Lake Erie. The wily emissary invited their chiefs to visit the governor at Montreal, and, in 1730, they descended with him to the settlement at that place. In the next year, more of them followed; and the warriors of the tribe put themselves wholly under the protection of Louis XV., having, at their whim, hoisted a white flag in their town. It was even rumored that, in 1731, the French were building strong houses for them. The government of Canada annually sent them presents and messages of friendship, and deliberately pursued the design of estranging them from the English.

James Logan, MSS.

The dangerous extent of the French claims had for a long time attracted the attention of the colonies. To resist it was one of the earliest efforts of Spotswood, who hoped to extend the line of the Virginia settlements far enough to the west to interrupt the chain of communication between Canada and the Gulf of Mexico. He caused, also, the passes in the mountains to be examined; desired to promote settlements beyond them; and sought to concentrate within his province bands of friendly Indians. Finding other measures unavailing, he planned the incorporation of a Virginia

1710, 1711.

Spotswood's MS. Letters.

Logan's Memorial

Indian company, which, from the emoluments of a monopoly of the traffic, should sustain forts in the western country. Disappointed by the determined opposition of the people to a privileged company, he was still earnest to resist the encroachments of the French. But from Williamsburg to Kaskaskia the distance was too wide; and though, by a journey across the mountains, the right of Virginia might be sustained, yet no active resistance would become possible till the posts of the two nations should be nearer. A wilderness of a thousand miles was a good guaranty against reciprocal invasions.

CHAP. XXIII.

Compare Hening's Statutes iv. 56.

In the more northern province of Pennsylvania, the subject never slumbered. In 1719, it was earnestly pressed upon the attention of the lords of trade by the governor of that colony, who counselled the establishment by Virginia of a fort on Lake Erie. But after the migration of the Delawares and Shawnees, James Logan, the mild and estimable secretary of Pennsylvania, could not rest from remonstrances, demanding the attention of the proprietary to the ambitious designs of France, which extended "to the heads of all the tributaries of the Ohio." "This," he rightly added, "interferes with the five degrees of longitude of this province;" and the attention of the council was solicited to the impending danger.

Keith's MS. Memorial.

1728. Oct.

Logan's MS Correspondence. Gordon's Pennsylvania 213, &c.

1732

Nor was this all. In the autumn of 1731, immediately after the establishment of Crown Point, Logan prepared a memorial on the state of the British plantations; and through Perry, a member of the British parliament, it was communicated to Sir Robert Walpole. But "the grand minister and those about him were too solicitously concerned for their own standing to lay any thing to heart that was at so great a distance."

CHAP. XXIII. Thus did England permit the French to establish their influence along the banks of the Alleghany to the Ohio. They had already quietly possessed themselves of the three other great avenues from the St. Lawrence to the Mississippi; for the safe possession of the route by way of the Fox and Wisconsin, they had no opponents but in the Sacs and Foxes; that by way of Chicago had been safely pursued since the days of Marquette; and a report on Indian affairs, written by Logan, in 1718, proves that they very early made use of the Miami of the Lakes, where, after crossing the carrying-place of about three leagues, they passed the summit level, and floated down a shallow branch into the Wabash and the Ohio. Upon this line of communication the French established a post; and of the population of Vincennes, a large part trace their lineage to early emigrants from Canada. Yet, as of Kaskaskia, so of Vincennes, it has not been possible to fix the date of its foundation with precision. The hero, whose name it bears, came to his end in 1736. This route may have been adopted at a very early period, after La Salle's return from Illinois; it was certainly in use early in the last century. Tradition preserves the memory of a release, in 1742, of lands, which, being ceded for the use of settlers, could not have been granted till after the military post had grown into a little village of Canadian French. It would seem that, in 1716, the route was established, and, in conformity to instructions from France, was secured by a military post. The year 1735, assumed by Volney as the probable date of its origin, is not too early. Thus began the commonwealth of Indiana. Travellers, as they passed from Quebec to Mobile or New Orleans, pitched their tents on the banks of the Wabash; till, at last,

Keith's MS. Memorial.

in 1742, a few families of resident herdsmen gained permission of the natives to pasture their beeves on the fertile fields above Blanche River. CHAP. XXIII.

That Louisiana extended to the head-spring of the Alleghany, and included the Laurel Ridge, the Great Meadows, and every brook that flowed to the Ohio, was, on the eve of the treaty of Utrecht, expressly asserted in the royal grant of the commerce of the province. Weary of fruitless efforts, Louis XIV. had assigned the exclusive trade of the unbounded territory to Anthony Crozat, a French merchant, who had "prospered in opulence to the astonishment of all the world." La Motte Cadillac, now the royal governor of Louisiana, became his partner; and the merchant proprietary and the founder of Detroit sought fortune by discovering mines and encroaching on the colonial monopolies of Spain. 1712 Sept. Joutel's editor, 380.

The latter attempt met with no success whatever. Hardly had the officers of the new administration landed at Dauphine Island, when a vessel was sent to Vera Cruz; but it was not allowed to dispose of its cargo. The deep colonial bigotry of Spain was strengthened by the political jealousy which soon disturbed the relations between the governments at Madrid and Paris,—while the French occupation of Louisiana was itself esteemed an encroachment on Spanish territory. Every Spanish harbor in the Gulf of Mexico was closed against the vessels of Crozat. 1713 May. Ensayo Cronologico, para la Hist. de la Florida, 327, &c.

It was next attempted to institute commercial relations by land. Had they been favored, they could not then have succeeded. But when St. Denys, after renewing intercourse with the Natchitoches, again ascended the Red River, and found his way from one Spanish post to another, till he reached a fortress in

CHAP. XXIII. Mexico, his enterprise was followed by his imprisonment; and even liberty of commerce across the wilderness was sternly refused.

1714 From the mines of Louisiana it was still hoped to obtain "great quantities of gold and silver;" and for many years the hope agitated France with vague but confident expectations. Two pieces of silver ore, left at Kaskaskia by a traveller from Mexico, were exhibited to Cadillac as the produce of a mine in Illinois; and, elated by the seeming assurance of success, he hurried up the river, to be, in his turn, disappointed,—finding in Missouri abundance of the purest ore of lead, but neither silver nor gold.

For the advancement of the colony Crozat accomplished nothing. The only prosperity which it possessed grew out of the enterprise of humble individuals, who had succeeded in instituting a little barter between themselves and the natives, and a petty trade with neighboring European settlements. These small sources of prosperity were cut off by the profitless but fatal monopoly of the Parisian merchant. The Indians were too numerous to be resisted by his factors. The English gradually appropriated the trade with the natives; and every Frenchman in Louisiana, except his agents, fomented opposition to his privileges. Crozat resigned his charter. On receiving it, Louisiana possessed twenty-eight French families: in 1717, when he abandoned it, the troops sent by the king, joined to the colonists, did not swell the inhabitants of the colony to more than seven hundred, including persons of every age, sex, and color. These few were extended

.714 1717 from the neighborhood of the Creeks to Natchitoches. On the head waters of the Alabama, at the junction of

1714. the Coosa and the Tallapoosa, with the aid of a band

CHAP. XXIII.

of Choctas, Fort Toulouse, a small military post, was built and garrisoned. After a short period of hostilities, which sprung, in part, from the influence of English traders among the Chickasas, the too powerful Bienville chanted the calumet with the great chief of the Natchez; and Fort Rosalie, built chiefly by the natives, protected the French commercial establishment in their village. Such was the origin of the city of Natchez. In the Mississippi valley, it takes rank, in point of age, of every settlement south of Illinois.

Meek's South-West, 14.

1716.

The monopoly of Crozat was terminated by its surrender. The mines, and commerce, and boundless extent, of Louisiana were now invoked to relieve the burden and renew the credit of the metropolis. The human mind is full of trust; men in masses always have faith in the approach of better times; humanity abounds in hope. The valley of the Mississippi inflamed the imagination of France: anticipating the future, the French nation beheld the certain opulence of coming ages as within their immediate grasp; and John Law, who possessed the entire confidence of the regent, obtained the whole control of the commerce of Louisiana and Canada.

The debt which Louis XIV. bequeathed to his successor, after arbitrary reductions, exceeded two thousand millions of livres; and, to meet the annual interest of eighty millions, the surplus revenues of the state did not yield more than nine millions. Hence the national securities were of uncertain value; and the national burdens exceeded the national resources. In this period of depression, John Law proposed to the regent a credit system, which should liberate the state from its enormous burden, not by loans, on which interest must be paid,—not by taxes, that would be burden-

CHAP. XXIII. some to the people,—but by a system which should bring all the money of France on deposit. It was the faith of Law, that the currency of a country is but the representative of its moving wealth; that this representative need not possess, in itself, an intrinsic value, but may be made, not of stamped metals only, but of shells or paper; that, where gold and silver are the only circulating medium, the wealth of a nation may at once be indefinitely increased by an arbitrary infusion of paper; that credit consists in the excess of circulation over immediate resources; and that the advantage of credit is in the direct ratio of that excess. Applying these maxims to all France, he gradually planned the whimsically gigantic project of collecting all the gold and silver of the kingdom into one bank At first, from his private bank, having a nominal capital of six million livres, of which a part was payable in
1716 government notes, bills were emitted with moderation; and, while the despotic government had been arbitrarily changing the value of its coin, his notes, being payable in coin at an unvarying standard of weight and fineness, bore a small premium. When Crozat resigned the commerce of Louisiana, it was transferred to the Western company, better known as the company of Mississippi, instituted under the auspices of Law. The stock of the corporation was fixed at two hundred thousand shares, of five hundred livres each, to be paid in any certificates of public debt. Thus nearly one hundred millions of the most depreciated of the public stocks were suddenly absorbed. The government thus changed the character of its obligations from an indebtedness to individuals to an indebtedness to a favored company of its own creation. Through the bank of Law, the interest on the debt was discharged

CHAP. XXIII.

punctually; and in consequence, the evidences of debt, which were received in payment for stock, rose rapidly from a depreciation of two thirds to par value. Although the union of the bank with the hazards of a commercial company was an omen of the fate of "the system," public credit seemed restored as if by a miracle. The ill success of La Salle, of Iberville, and Crozat, the fruitlessness of the long search for the mines of St. Barbe, were notorious; yet tales were revived of the wealth of Louisiana; its ingots of gold had been seen in Paris. The vision of a fertile empire, with its plantations, manors, cities, and busy wharves, a monopoly of commerce throughout all French North America, the certain products of the richest silver mines and mountains of gold, were blended in the French mind into one boundless promise of untold treasures. The regent, who saw opening before him unlimited resources,—the nobility, the churchmen, who competed for favors from the privileged institution,—the stockjobbers, including dukes and peers, marshals and bishops, women of rank, statesmen and courtiers,—eager to profit by the sudden and indefinite rise of stocks, conspired to reverence Law as the greatest man of his age.

It was in September, 1717, that the Western company obtained its grant. On the twenty-fifth day of the following August, after a long but happy voyage, the Victory, the Duchess of Noailles, and the Mary, bearing eight hundred emigrants for Louisiana, chanted their Te Deum as they cast anchor near Dauphine Island. 1718. Already had Bienville, in the midsummer of 1718, as he descended the Mississippi, selected on its banks a site for the capital of the new empire; and from the prince who denied God, and "trembled at a

B. de la Harpe, MS. Hist. Du Pratz, i. 24 and 58, with ii. 260.

CHAP. XXIII. star," the dissolute but generous regent of France, the promised city received the name of New Orleans. Instead of ascending the river in the ships, the emigrants disembarked on the crystalline sands of Dauphine Island, to make their way as they could to the lands that had been ceded to them. Some perished for want of enterprise, some from the climate; others prospered by their indomitable energy. The Canadian Du Tissenet, purchasing a compass, and taking an escort of fourteen Canadians, went fearlessly from Dauphine Island, by way of the Mobile River, to Quebec, and returned to the banks of the Mississippi with his family. The most successful colonists of Louisiana were the hardy emigrants from Canada, who brought with them little beyond a staff and the coarse clothes that covered them.

Du Pratz, i. 40.

1718. Of the recent emigrants from France, eighty convicts were sent amongst the coppices that overspread New Orleans, to prepare room for a few tents and cottages. At the end of more than three years, the place was still a wilderness spot, where two hundred persons, sent to construct a city, had but encamped among unsubdued canebrakes. And yet the enlightened traveller held America happy, as the land in which the patriot could sigh over no decay, could point in sorrow to no ruins of a more prosperous age; and, with cheerful eye looking into futurity, he predicted the opulence and vastness of the city which was destined to become the emporium of the noblest valley in the world. Still the emigrants of the company, though, in the winter of 1718, one of their ships had sailed up the river, blindly continued to disembark on the miserable coast; and, even in 1721, Bienville himself a second time established the head quarters of Louisiana at Biloxi.

La Harpe, MS. Hist.

Charlevoix, iii. 430 and 440.

Meantime, Alberoni, the active minister of Spain, CHAP. XXIII.
having, contrary to the interests of France and of
Spain, involved the two countries in a war, De Serigny 1719.
arrived in February of 1719, with orders to take possession of Pensacola. This is the bay called, in the
days of De Soto, Anchusi, afterwards Saint Mary, and 1558. 1693.
Saint Mary of Galve. In 1696, Don Andrés de Arriola had built upon its margin a fort, a church, and a few houses, in a place without commerce or agriculture, or productive labor of any kind. By the capture of the fort, which, after five hours' resistance, surrendered, the French hoped to extend their power along
the Gulf of Mexico from the Rio del Norte to the Atlantic. 1719. May 14.
But within forty days the Spaniards recovered
the town, and attempted, in their turn, to conquer the June 29.
French posts on Dauphine Island and on the Mobile. In September, the French recovered Pensacola, which, by the treaty of 1721, reverted to Spain. The tidings
of peace were welcomed at Biloxi with heartfelt joy. 1722.

During the period of hostility, La Harpe, in a letter 1720
to the nearest Spanish governor, had claimed "Texas Jan. 8.
to the Del Norte as a part of Louisiana." La Harpe, MSS.
France was too feeble to stretch its colonies far to the west; but its rights were esteemed so clear, that, in time of peace,
the attempt to occupy the country was renewed. This 1722
second attempt of Bernard de la Harpe to plant a colony near the Bay of Matagorda had no other results than to incense the natives against the French, and to stimulate the Spaniards to the occupation of the country by a fort. Yet the French ever regarded the mouth of the Del Norte as the western limit of Louisiana on
the Gulf of Mexico; and English geography recognized See Popple's Map.
the claim.

But a change had taken place in the fortunes of the

CHAP. XXIII. Mississippi company. By its connection with the bank of Law, its first attempts at colonization were conducted with careless prodigality. The richest prairies, the most inviting fields, in the southern valley of the Mississippi, were conceded to companies or to individuals who sought principalities in the New World. Thus it was hoped that at least six thousand white colonists would be established in Louisiana. To Law himself there was conceded on the Arkansas one of those vast prairies, of which the wide-spreading waves of verdure are bounded only by the azure of the sky. There he designed to plant a city and villages; his investments rapidly amounted to a million and a half of livres; through the company, which he directed, possessing a monopoly of the slave-trade for the French colonies, he had purchased three hundred negroes, mechanics from France, and a throng of German emigrants, were engaged in his service or as his tenants, his commissioners lavished gifts on the tribes with whom they smoked the calumet. But when, in 1727, a Jesuit priest arrived there, he found only thirty needy Frenchmen, who had been abandoned by their employer, and had no consolation but in the blandness of the climate and the unrivalled fertility of the soil. The decline of Louisiana was a consequence of financial changes in France.

Du Poisson, in Lett. Ed. iv. 235.

1719.

1719 Jan. 1. In January of 1719, the bank of Law became, by a negotiation with the regent, the Bank of France; and a government which had almost absolute power of legislation conspired to give the widest extension to what was called credit. "Law might have regulated at his pleasure the interest of money, the value of stocks, the price of labor and of produce." The contest between paper and specie began to rage,—the

Marmontel.

CHAP. XXIII.

F. C. Schlosser, i. 267.

one buoyed up by despotic power, the other appealing to common sense. Within four years, a succession of decrees changed the relative value of the livre not less than fifty times, that, from disgust at fluctuation, paper at a fixed rate might be preferred. All taxes were to be collected in paper; at last, paper was made the legal tender in all payments. To win the little gold and silver that was hoarded by the humbler classes, small bills, as low even as of ten livres, were put in circulation. The purchase of the bank by the government met less opposition, when a second scheme was devised for absorbing its issues. Two kinds of paper —bills payable on demand and certificates of stock— were put abroad together; and the stupendous project was formed of paying off the public debt in bank bills, to absorb which new shares in the Mississippi company, under its title of Company of the Indies, were constantly created and offered for sale. The extravagance of hope was nourished by the successive surrender to that corporation of additional monopolies,—the trade in Africans, the trade on the Indian seas, the sale of tobacco, the profits of the royal mint, the profits of farming the whole revenue of France,—till a promise of a dividend of forty per cent., from a company which had the custody of all the revenues and the benefit of all the commerce of France, obtained belief, and the shares which might be issued after a payment of a first instalment of five hundred livres, rose in price a thousand per cent. Avarice became a frenzy; its fury seized every member of the royal family, men of letters, prelates, women. Early in the morning, the exchange opened with beat of drum and sound of bell, and closed at night on avidity that could not slumber. To doubt the wealth of Louisiana provoked anger,

CHAP. XXIII. New Orleans was famous at Paris as a beautiful city almost before the canebrakes began to be cut down. The hypocrisy of manners, which, in the old age of Louis XIV., made religion become a fashion, revolted to libertinism; and licentious pleasure was become the parent of an equally licentious cupidity. Thus the regent, purchasing directly of the company a share for five hundred livres, was able to sell it at a great advance, perhaps for five thousand. The public creditor paid virtually ten livres of public debt for one livre of the stock, and, instead of holding government securities, became a stockholder in an untried company. In this manner, in the course of sixteen months, more than two thousand millions of bills were emitted; and the regent's mother could write that "all the king's debts were paid." The extravagances of stockjobbing were increased by the latent distrust alike of the shares and of the bills; men purchased stock because they feared the end of the paper system, and because with the bills they could purchase nothing else. The fraud grew to be apparent; the parliament protested that private persons were by the system defrauded of three fifths of their income. To stifle doubt, Law, who had
1720. Jan. 5. made himself a Catholic, was appointed comptroller-
Feb. 27 general; and the new minister of finance perfected the triumph of paper by a decree that no person or corporation should have on hand more than five hundred livres in specie; the rest must be exchanged for paper; and all payments, except for sums under one hundred livres, must be paid in paper. Terror and the dread of informers brought, within three weeks, forty-four
March 11. millions into the bank. In March, a decree of council fixed the value of the stock at nine thousand livres for five hundred, and forbade certain corporations to in-

vest money in any thing else; all circulation of gold and silver, except for change, was prohibited; all payments must be made in paper, except for sums under ten livres. He who should have attempted to convert a bill into specie, would have exposed his specie to forfeiture and himself to fines. Confidence disappeared, and in May bankruptcy was avowed by a decree which reduced the value of bank notes by a moiety. When men are greatly in the wrong, and especially when they have embarked their fortunes in their error, they wilfully resist light. So it had been with the French people: they remained faithful to their delusion, till France was impoverished, public and private credit subverted, the income of capitalists annihilated, and labor left without employment,—while, in the midst of the universal wretchedness of the middling class, a few wary speculators gloried in the unjust acquisition and enjoyment of immense wealth.

CHAP. XXIII. 1720 May 21.

Such was the issue of Law's celebrated system, which left to the world a lesson the world was slow to learn—that the enlargement of the circulation quickens industry so long only as the enlargement continues, for prices then rise, and every kind of labor is remunerated; that when this increase springs from artificial causes, it must meet with a check, and be followed by a reaction; that when the reaction begins, the high remunerating prices decline, labor fails to find an equivalent, and each evil opposite to the previous advantages ensues; that therefore every artificial expansion of the currency, every expansion resting on credit alone, is a source of confusion and ultimate loss to the community, and brings benefits to none but to those who are skilful in foreseeing and profiting by the fluctuations. The chancellor d'Aguesseau, who was driven from office be-

CHAP. XXIII. cause he could show no favor to the system, was, after a short period of retirement, restored to greater honors than before, and lives in the memory of the world as a tolerant and incorruptible statesman,—while those who yielded to the reckless vanity and promises of Law, have been rescued from infamy only by oblivion.

The downfall of Law abruptly curtailed expenditures for Louisiana. But a colony was already planted, destined to survive all dangers, even though in France Louisiana was involved in disgrace. Instead of the splendid visions of opulence, the disenchanted public would now see only unwholesome marshes, which were the tombs of emigrants; its name was a name of disgust and terror. The garrison of Fort Toulouse
1722. revolted; and of the soldiers six-and-twenty departed
A. B. Meek's South-West, 15. for the English settlements of Carolina. Overtaken by Villemont, with a body of Choctas, the unhappy wretches were in part massacred, in part conducted to Mobile and executed. Even the wilderness could not moderate the barbarisms of military discipline.

The Alabama River had been a favorite line of communication with the north. From the easier connection of Mobile with the sea, it remained a principal post; but, in August of 1723, the quarters of Bienville were transferred to New Orleans. Thus the central point of French power, after hovering round Ship Island and Dauphine Island, the Bays of Biloxi and Mobile, was at last established on the banks of the Mississippi; and the emigrants to Arkansas gathered into settlements along the river nearer to New Orleans.

The villages of the Natchez, planted in the midst of the most fertile climes of the south-west, rose near the banks of the Mississippi. Each was distinguished by a receptacle for the dead. In the sacred building, of an oval shape, having a circumference of one hundred feet,—a simple hut, without a window, and with a low and narrow opening on the side for the only door,—were garnered up the choicest fetiches of the tribe, of which some were moulded from clay and baked in the sun. There, too, were gathered the bones of the dead; there an undying fire was kept burning by appointed guardians, as if to warm, and light, and cheer, the departed. On the palisades around this edifice, which has been called a temple, the ghastly trophies of victories were arranged. Once, when, during a storm, such as in those regions sometimes blends the elements, rocks the forest, and bows the hearts of the bravest, the sacred edifice caught fire from the lightning, seven or eight mothers won the applause of the terror-stricken tribes by casting their babes into the flames to appease the unknown power of evil.

CHAP. XXIII.

Lett. Ed. iv. 265.

Lett. Ed iv. 267.

The grand chief of the tribe was revered as of the family of the sun, and he could trace his descent with certainty from the nobles; for the inheritance of power was transmitted exclusively by the female line. Hard by the temple, on an artificial mound of earth, stood the hut of the Great Sun: around it were grouped the cabins of the tribe. There, for untold years, the savage had freely whispered his tale of love; had won his bride by a purchase from the father; had placed his trust in his manitous; had turned, at daybreak, towards the east, to hail and worship the beams of morning; had listened to the revelations of dreams; had invoked the aid of the medicine men to dance the medicine dance; had achieved titles of honor by prowess in war; had tortured and burned his prisoners. There were the fields where, in spring, the whole tribe had gone forth to cultivate the maize and vines; there the

CHAP. XXIII. scenes of the glad festivals at the gathering of the harvest; there the natural amphitheatres, where councils were convened, and embassies received, and the calumet of reconciliation passed in solemn ceremony from lip to lip. There the dead had been arrayed in their proudest apparel; the little baskets of food for the first month after death set apart for their nurture; the requiem chanted by the women in mournful strains over their bones; and there, when a great chief died, persons of the same age were strangled, that they might constitute his escort into the realm of shades.

Nowhere was the power of the grand chieftain so nearly despotic. The race of nobles was so distinct, that usage had moulded language into forms of reverence. In other respects, there was among the Natchez no greater culture than among the Choctas; and their manners hardly differed from those of northern tribes, except as they were modified by climate.

The French, who were cantoned among the Natchez, coveted their soil; the commander, Chopart, swayed by a brutal avarice, demanded as a plantation the very
Adair, 353. site of their principal village. They listened to the counsels of the Chickasas; they prevailed in part with the Choctas; and a general massacre of the intruders was concerted. The arrival of boats from New Orleans with merchandise hastened the rising of the
1729. Natchez. On the morning of the twenty-eighth of
Nov. 28. November, 1729, the work of blood began, and before noon nearly every Frenchman in the colony was murdered.

The Great Sun, taking his seat under the storehouse of the company, smoked the calumet in complacency, while the head of Chopart was laid at his feet. One after another, the heads of the principal officers at the post were ranged in order around it, while their bodies were left abroad to be a prey to dogs and buzzards. At that time, the Jesuit Du Poisson was the appointed missionary among the Arkansas. Two years before, he had made his way up the Mississippi from New Orleans. On each of the nearest plantations which he saw in his progress, bands of sixty negroes had already succeeded in cultivating maize, tobacco, indigo, and rice. His companions, as thev advanced, now dragged the boat along shore, now stemmed the torrent by rowing. At night, they made a resting-place by spreading canvass over boughs of trees heaped together on the miry bank; or, making their boat fast to some *raft* that, covering many roods, had floated down the stream till it became entangled in the roots of trees overthrown but not wholly loosened from the soil, they would upon the raft itself kindle their evening fire and prepare their meal,—and prepare it exultingly, if the huntsman of the party had chanced to kill a deer or a bear; or, toiling through the mud, and forests, and canes, they would make their way to the cabin of some petty chief, and intrude on the hospitality of the red dwellers in the morasses; or would seek, as at Point Coupee, the humble mansion of some French settler, who, amidst the giant forests, had raised a cabin on piles, as a security against the overflowing of the river,—where, by the side of the immense activity of vegetative power, an overseer and a few negroes exhibited the puny efforts of man at mastering nature, in contrast with the majesty of the stream, whose waters flooded, whose alluvial deposits fertilized, the wide expanse of lowlands. Thus the pilgrim had ascended the Mississippi, now drinking the turbid but wholesome waters with a reed; now tasting

CHAP. XXIII. the wild and as yet unripe grapes, which grew by the banks of the river; now hiding from the clouds of mosquitoes beneath a stifling awning; now accompanied in the boat by one army of insects, and, as he passed near a coppice of willows or a canebrake, overwhelmed by another; till he reached the prairies that had been selected for the plantations of Law, and smoked the calumet with the southernmost tribes of the Dahcotas. Desiring to plan a settlement near the margin of
Nov 26. the Mississippi, he had touched at Natchez, in search of counsel, had preached on the first Sunday in advent, had visited the sick, and was returning with the host from the cabin of a dying man, when he, too, was struck to the ground, and beheaded. The Arkansas, hearing of his end, vowed that they would avenge him with a vengeance that should never be appeased. Du Codère, the commander of the post among the Yazoos, who had drawn his sword to defend the missionary, was himself killed by a musket ball, and scalped be-
Dumont, ii. 145. cause his hair was long and beautiful. The planter De Koli, a Swiss by birth, one of the most worthy men, zealous for the colony, had come, with his son, to take possession of a tract of land on St. Catharine's Creek; and both were shot. The Capuchin missionary among the Natchez chanced to be absent when the massacre began; returning, he was shot near his cabin, and a negro slave by his side. Two white men, both mechanics, and two only, were saved. The number of victims was reckoned at two hundred. Women were spared for menial services; children, also, were detained as captives. When the work of death was finished, pillage and carousals began.

The news spread dismay in New Orleans. Messengers were sent with the tidings to the Illinois, by way

of the Red River, and to the Choctas and Cherokees. CHAP. XXIII.
Each house was supplied with arms; the city fortified by a ditch. Danger appeared on every side. The negroes, of whom the number was about two thousand, half as large as the number of the French, showed symptoms of revolt. But the brave, enterprising Le Sueur, repairing to the Choctas, ever ready to engage in excursions, won them to his aid, and was followed across the country by seven hundred of their warriors. On the river the forces of the French were assembled, and placed under the command of Loubois.

Le Sueur was the first to arrive in the vicinity of 1730
the Natchez. Not expecting an attack, they were celebrating festivities, which were gladdened by the spoils of the French. Mad with triumph, and exulting in their success, on the evening of the twenty-eighth of January, they gave themselves up to sleep, after the careless manner of the wilderness. On the following morning, at daybreak, the Choctas broke upon their villages, liberated their captives, and, losing but two of their own men, brought off sixty scalps, with eighteen prisoners.

On the eighth of February, Loubois arrived, and 1730 Feb. 8
completed the victory. Of the Natchez, some fled to neighboring tribes for shelter; the remainder of the nation crossed the Mississippi to the vicinity of Natchitoches. They were pursued, and, partly by stratagem, 1731
partly by force, their place of refuge was taken. Some fled still farther to the west. Of the scattered remnants, some remained with the Chickasas; others found a shelter among the Muskhogees. The Great 1732
Sun and more than four hundred prisoners were shipped to Hispaniola, and sold as slaves.

Thus perished the nation of the Natchez. Their

CHAP. XXIII. peculiar language,—which has been still preserved by the descendants of the fugitives, and is, perhaps, now on the point of expiring,—their worship, their division into nobles and plebeians, their bloody funereal rites, —invite conjecture, and yet so nearly resemble in character the distinctions of other tribes, that they do but irritate, without satisfying, curiosity.

The cost of defending Louisiana exceeding the returns from its commerce and from grants of land, the company of the Indies, seeking wealth by conquests or
1732 traffic on the coast of Guinea and Hindostan, solicited leave to surrender the Mississippi wilderness; and, on the tenth of April, 1732, the jurisdiction and control over its commerce reverted to the crown of France. The company had held possession of Louisiana for fourteen years, which were its only years of comparative prosperity. The early extravagant hopes had not subsided till emigrants had reached its soil; and the emigrants, being once established, took care of themselves. In 1735, the Canadian Bienville reappeared to assume the command for the king.

It was the first object of the crown to establish its supremacy throughout the borders of Louisiana. The Chickasas were the dreaded enemies of France; it was they who had hurried the Natchez to bloodshed and destruction; it was they whose cedar barks, shooting boldly into the Mississippi, interrupted the connection between Kaskaskia and New Orleans. Thus they maintained their savage independence, and weakened by dividing the French empire. No settlements on the eastern bank of the Mississippi were safe; and from Natchez, or even from the vicinity of New Orleans, to Kaskaskia, none existed. The English traders from Carolina were, moreover, welcomed to their villages. Nay, more: resolute in their hatred, they had even endeavored to debauch the affections of the Illinois, and to extirpate French dominion from the west. But the tawny envoys from the north descended to New Orleans, and presented the pipe of friendship. "This," said Chicago to Perrier, as he concluded an offensive and defensive alliance; "this is the pipe of peace or war. You have but to speak, and our braves will strike the nations that are your foes."

To secure the eastern valley of the Mississippi, it was necessary to reduce the Chickasas; and nearly two years were devoted to preparations for the enterprise. At last, in 1736, the whole force of the colony at the south, with D'Artaguette and troops from his command in Illinois, and probably from the Wabash, was directed to meet, on the tenth of May, in the land of the Chickasas. The government of France had itself given directions for the invasion, and its eye was turned anxiously to watch the issue of the strife. 1736

From New Orleans the little fleet of thirty boats and as many pirogues departed for Fort Condé at Mobile, which it did not leave till the fourth of April. In sixteen days, it ascended the river to Tombecbee, a fort which an advance party had constructed on the west bank of the river, two hundred and fifty miles above the bay. Of the men employed in its construction, some had attempted to escape, and enjoy the liberty of the wilderness: in the wilds of Alabama, a court martial sentenced them to death, and they were shot. 1736. Mar.

The Choctas, lured by gifts of merchandise, and high rewards for every scalp, gathered at Fort Tombecbee to aid Bienville. Of these red auxiliaries the number was about twelve hundred; and the whole party slowly sounded its way up the windings of the Tombecbee May 4-25

CHAP. XXIII. 1736. A. B. Meek's South-West, 17

to the point where Cotton Gin Port now stands, and which was but about twenty-one miles south-east of the great village of the Chickasas. There the artillery was deposited in a temporary fortification; and the solitudes of the quiet forests and blooming prairies between the head-sources of the Tombecbee and the Tallahatchie were disturbed by the march of the army towards the long house of their enemy. After the manner of Indian warfare, they encamped, on the evening of the twenty-fifth of May, at the distance of a league from the village. In the morning, before day, they advanced to surprise the Chickasas. In vain. The brave warriors, whom they had come to destroy, were on the watch; their intrenchments were strong; English flags waved over their fort; English traders had assisted them in preparing defence. Twice, during the day, an attempt was made to storm their log citadel; and twice the French were repelled, with a loss of thirty killed, of whom four were officers. The next day saw skirmishes between parties of Choctas and Chickasas. On the twenty-ninth, the final retreat began; on the thirty-first of May, Bienville dismissed the Choctas, having satisfied them with presents, and, throwing his cannon into the Tombecbee, his party ingloriously floated down the river. In the last days of June, he landed on the banks of the Bayou St. John.

May 25.

Lett. Ed, iv 291.

But where was D'Artaguette, the brave commander in the Illinois, the pride of the flower of Canada? And where was the gallant Vincennes, whose name, in honor of the founder of a state, is borne by the oldest settlement of Indiana?

Du Petit, in Lett. Ed. iv. 291.

The young D'Artaguette had already gained glory in the war against the Natchez, braving death under every form. Advanced to the command in the Illinois,

CHAP. XXIII.

1736.

he obeyed the summons of Bienville; and, with an army of about fifty French soldiers and more than a thousand red men, accompanied by Father Senat, and by the Canadian De Vincennes, the careful hero stole cautiously and unobserved into the country of the Chickasas, and, on the evening before the appointed May 9. day, encamped near the rendezvous among the sources of the Yalabusha. But the expected army from below did not arrive. For ten days he retained his impatient allies in the vicinity of their enemy; at last, as they menaced desertion, he consented to an attack. May 20. His measures were wisely arranged. One fort was carried, and the Chickasas driven from the cabins which it protected; at the second, the intrepid youth was equally successful; on attacking the third fort, he received one wound, and then another, and, in the moment of victory, was disabled. The red men from Illinois, dismayed at the check, fled precipitately. Voisin, a lad of but sixteen years old, conducted the retreat, having the enemy at his heels for five-and-twenty leagues, marching forty-five leagues without food, while his men carried with them such of the wounded as could bear the fatigue. The unhappy D'Artaguette lay weltering in his blood, and by his side fell others of his bravest troops. The Jesuit Senat might have fled: he remained to receive the last sigh of the wounded, regardless of danger, mindful only of duty. Vincennes, too, the Canadian, refused to fly, and shared the captivity of his gallant leader. After the Indian custom, their wounds were stanched; tney were received into the cabins of the Chickasas, and feasted bountifully. At last, when Bienville had retreated, the Chickasas brought the captives into a field; and, while one was spared to relate the deed,

Du mont, ii. Du Pratz, iii. 418 &c. Charlevoix, ii. 501, 502 Martin, i. 304

CHAP. XXIII. the adventurous D'Artaguette; the faithful Senat, true to his mission; Vincennes, whose name will be perpet-
1736. uated as long as the Wabash shall flow by the dwellings of civilized man;—these, with the rest of the captives, were bound to the stake; and neither valor nor piety could save them from death by slow torments and fire.—Such is the early history of Mississippi.

Ill success did but increase the disposition to con-
1737 tinue the war. To advance the colony, a royal edict permitted a ten years' freedom of commerce between the West India Islands and Louisiana; while a new expedition against the Chickasas, receiving aid not from Illinois only, but even from Montreal and Que-
1739. bec, and from France, made its rendezvous in Arkansas, on the St. Francis River. In the last of June, the whole army, composed of twelve hundred whites, and twice that number of red and black men, took up its quarters in Fort Assumption, on the bluff of Memphis. But autumn wasted itself in languor and weariness of spirit; the recruits from France, the Canadians, sunk under the climate. When, in March, 1740, a small detachment proceeded towards the Chickasa country, they were met by messengers, who supplicated for peace; and Bienville gladly accepted the calumet. The fort at Memphis was razed; the troops from Illinois and from Canada drew back; the fort on the St. Francis was dismantled; and Bienville returned, to conceal his shame under false pretences. Peace, it was said, was established between France and the Chickasas; but the settlements between Lower Louisiana and the Illinois were interrupted. From Kaskaskia to Baton Rouge was a wilderness; the Chickasas remained the undoubted lords of their country; and, in the great expanse of territory claimed by

DEATH OF VINCENNES.

Designed and etched for Bancroft's History of the U. States.

France, the jurisdiction of her monarch was but a name. The French were kept out of the country of the Chickasas by that nation itself; red men protected the English settlements on the west.

Such was Louisiana more than a half century after the first attempt at colonization by La Salle. Its population may have been five thousand whites and half that number of blacks. Louis XIV. had fostered it with pride and liberal expenditures; an opulent merchant, famed for his successful enterprise, assumed its direction; the company of the Mississippi, aided by boundless but transient credit, had made it the foundation of their hopes; and, again, Fleury and Louis XV. had sought to advance its fortunes. Priests and friars, dispersed through nations, from Biloxi to the Dahcotas, propitiated the favor of the savages. But still the valley of the Mississippi was nearly a wilderness. All its patrons—though among them it counted kings and ministers of state—had not accomplished for it, in half a century, a tithe of the prosperity which, within the same period, sprung naturally from the benevolence of William Penn to the peaceful settlers on the Delaware.

The progress of the Anglo-American colonies was advanced, not by anticipating strife with the natives, but by the progress of industry. In 1738, there were built in Boston forty-one topsail vessels, burden in all six thousand three hundred and twenty-four tons. In its vicinity the increase of population justified the frequent division of townships; and the husbandmen of the West Farms in Cambridge, as if anticipating for their posterity a place in the world's annals, claimed also to be organized separately, as the village of Lexington. Peace on the eastern frontier revived the youthful

1712

CHAP XXIII. maritime enterprise of Maine, and its settlements began to obtain a fixed prosperity. The French, just before occupying Crown Point, pitched their tents on the opposite eastern shore, in the township of Addison. But already, in 1724, the government of Massachusetts had established Fort Dummer, on the site of Brattleborough; and thus, one hundred and fifteen years after the inroad of Champlain, a settlement of civilized man was made in Vermont. That Fort Dummer was within the limits of Massachusetts, was not questioned by the French; for the fort at Saybrook, according to the French rule, gave to England the whole basin of the river. Of Connecticut the swarming population spread over all its soil, and occupied even its hills; for its whole extent was protected against the desolating inroads of savages. The selfish policy of its governors and its royalist party delayed the increase of New York. Pennsylvania, as the land of promise, was still the refuge of the oppressed. We shall "soon have a German
1726, 1729 colony," wrote Logan, "so many thousands of Palatines are already in the country." "We are also very much surprised at the vast crowds of people pouring in upon us from the north of Ireland. Both these sorts sit frequently down on any spot of vacant land. They say the proprietary invited people to come and settle his country. Both pretend they would pay, but not one in twenty has any thing to pay with." Nor did the south-west range of mountains, from the James to the Potomac, fail to become occupied by emigrants, and enlivened by county courts; and, in 1732, the valley of Virginia received white inhabitants. West of the Alleghany there were no European settlements, except as traders, especially from Carolina, had ventured among the Indians, and, becoming wild like the

men with whom they trafficked, had established their houses among the Cherokees, the Muskhogees, and the Chickasas. There existed no settlement, even of Carolina, on streams that flow westward. The abodes of civilized man reached scarcely a hundred miles from the Atlantic; the more remote ones were made by herdsmen, who pastured beeves upon canes and natural grasses; and the cattle, hardly kept from running wild, were now and then rallied at central "Cowpens." Thus, unheeded of the savage, herdsmen were the pioneers of colonization in the wilderness of Carolina. Philanthropy opened the way beyond the Savannah. The growth of the colonies excited astonishment in England; and a British poet pointed with admiration across the Atlantic:—

> "Lo! swarming southward on rejoicing suns,
> Gay colonies extend,—the calm retreat
> Of undeserved distress, the better home
> Of those whom bigots chase from foreign lands.
> Not built on rapine, servitude, and woe,
> But bound by social freedom, firm they rise."

While the Palatinate poured forth its sons from their devastated fields; while the Scotch, who had made a sojourn in Ireland, abandoned the culture of lands where they were but tenants, and, crowding to America, established themselves as freeholders in almost every part of the United States, from New Hampshire to Carolina,—the progress of colonization was mainly due to the rapid increase of the descendants of former settlers. At the peace of Utrecht, the inhabitants in all the colonies could not have been far from four hundred thousand. Before peace was again broken, they had grown to be not far from eight hundred thousand. Happy America! to which Providence gave the tran-

CHAP. XXIII. quillity necessary for her growth, as well as the trials which were to discipline her for action.

The effects of the American system of social freedom were best exhibited in the colonies which approached the most nearly to independence. More than a century ago, "the charter governments were celebrated for their excellent laws and mild administration; for the security of liberty and property; for the encouragement of virtue, and suppression of vice; for promoting letters by erecting free schools and colleges." Among the most distinguished sons of Ireland of that day was George Berkeley, who, like Penn and Locke, garnered up his hopes for humanity in America. Versed in ancient learning, exact science, and modern literature; disciplined by polished society, by travel, and reflection; he united innocence, humility, and extensive knowledge, with the sagacity and confidence of intuitive reason. Adverse factions agreed in ascribing to him "every virtue under heaven." Beloved and cherished by those who were the pride of English letters and society, favored with unsolicited dignities and revenues, his mind asked, for its happiness, not fortune or preferment, but a real progress in knowledge; so that he dedicated his age, as well as his early years—the later growth, as well as the first fruits—at the altar of truth. The material tendencies of the age in which he lived were hateful to his purity of sentiment; and, having a mind kindred with Plato and the Alexandrine philosophers, with Barclay and Malebranche, he held that the external world was wholly subordinate to intelligence; that of spirits alone true existence can be predicated. He did not distrust the senses, being rather a close and exact observer of their powers, and finely discriminating be-

Dummer's Defence 21.

tween impressions made on them and the inferences of reason. Far from being skeptical, he sought to give to faith the highest certainty, by deriving all knowledge from absolutely perfect intelligence—from God. If he could but "expel matter out of nature;" if, in a materialist age, he could establish the supremacy of spirit as the sole creative power and active being, —then would the slavish or corrupt theories of Epicurus and of Hobbes be cut up by the roots and totally extirpated. Thus he sought "gently to unbind the ligaments which chain the soul to the earth, and to assist her flight upwards towards the sovereign good." For the application of such views, Europe of the eighteenth century offered no theatre. He longed to divest himself of European dignities; and, regarding "the well-being of all men of all nations" as the design in which the actions of each individual should concur, he repaired to the new hemisphere to found a university. The Island of Bermuda, so famed in Europe for its delicious climate, at first selected as its site, was abandoned for a spot within our America, of which he was for more than two years a resident. But opinion in England did not favor his design. "From the labor and luxury of the plantations," it was said, "great advantages may ensue to the mother country; yet the advancement of literature, and the improvement in arts and sciences in our American colonies, can never be of any service to the British state." Such seems to have been the opinion of Sir Robert Walpole. The funds that had been regarded as pledged to the university,—in which Indians were to be trained in wisdom, missionaries educated for works of good, science and truth cherished, pursued, and disseminated,—were diverted to pay the dowry of the

Gulian C. Verplanck. Sir Jas. Mackintosh. Dugald Stewart. Berkeley's Works.

Keith's Virginia, 187.

CHAP XXIII. princess royal. Disappointed, yet not irritated, Berkeley returned to Europe, to endow a library in Rhode Island; to cherish the interests of Harvard; to gain a right to be gratefully remembered at New Haven; to encourage the foundation of a college at New York. Advanced to a bishopric, the heart of the liberal and catholic prelate was in America. He loved the simplicity and gentle virtues which its villages illustrated; and, as he looked into futurity, the ardor of his benevolence dictated his prophecy—

"In happy climes, the seat of innocence,
 Where nature guides, and virtue rules;
Where men shall not impose for truth and sense
 The pedantry of courts and schools;—

"There shall be sung another golden age,—
 The rise of empire and of arts,—
The good and great inspiring epic rage—
 The wisest heads and noblest hearts.

"Not such as Europe breeds in her decay;
 Such as she bred when fresh and young,
When heavenly flame did animate her clay,
 By future poets shall be sung.

"Westward the course of empire takes its way.
 The four first acts already past,
A fifth shall close the drama with the day.
 Time's noblest offspring is the last."

To free schools and colleges the periodical press had been added, and newspapers began their office in America as the ministers to curiosity and the guides and organs of opinion. On the twenty-fourth day of April, in 1704, the Boston News-Letter, the first ever published on the western continent, saw the light in the metropolis of New England. In 1719, it obtained a rival at Boston, and was imitated at Philadelphia.

In 1740, the number of newspapers in the English colonies on the continent had increased to eleven, of which one appeared in South Carolina, one in Virginia, three in Pennsylvania,—one of them being in German,—one in New York, and the remaining five in Boston. The sheet at first used was but of the foolscap size; and but one, or even but a half of one, was issued weekly. The papers sought support rather by modestly telling the news of the day, than by engaging in conflicts; they had no political theories to enforce, no revolutions in faith to hasten. In Boston, indeed, where the pulpit had marshaled Quakers and witches to the gallows, one newspaper, the New England
Courant, the fourth American periodical, was estab- 1721 Aug. 21.
lished, as an organ of independent opinion, by James Franklin. Its temporary success was advanced by Benjamin, his brother and apprentice, a boy of fifteen, who wrote pieces for its humble columns, worked in composing the types, as well as in printing off the sheets, and himself, as carrier, distributed the papers to the customers. The little sheet satirized hypocrisy, and spoke of religious knaves as of all knaves the worst. This was described as tending "to abuse the ministers of religion in a manner which was intolerable." "I can well remember," writes Increase Mather, then more than fourscore years of age, "when the civil government would have taken an effectual course to
suppress such a cursed libel." In July, 1722, a 1722
resolve passed the council, appointing a censor for the press of James Franklin; but the house refused its concurrence. The ministers persevered; and, in January, 1723, a committee of inquiry was raised by the legislature. Benjamin Franklin, being examined, escaped with an admonition; James, the publisher,

CHAP. XXIII. refusing to discover the author of the offence, was kept in jail for a month; his paper was censured as reflecting injuriously on the reverend ministers of the gospel; and, by vote of the house and council, he was forbidden to print it, "except it be first supervised."

1723 Vexed at the arbitrary proceedings of the assembly; willing to escape from a town where good people pointed with horror at his freedom; indignant, also, at the tyranny of a brother, who, as a passionate master, often beat his apprentice,—Benjamin Franklin, then
Oct. but seventeen years old, sailed clandestinely for New York; and, finding there no employment, crossed to Amboy; went on foot to the Delaware; for want of a wind, rowed in a boat from Burlington to Philadelphia; and, bearing marks of his labor at the oar, weary, hungry, having for his whole stock of cash a single dollar, the runaway apprentice—greatest of the sons of New England of that generation, the humble pupil of the free schools of Boston, rich in the boundless hope of youth and the unconscious power of genius, which modesty adorned—stepped on shore to seek food, occupation, shelter, and fortune.

On the deep foundations of sobriety, frugality, and industry, the young journeyman built his fortunes and fame; and he soon came to have a printing-office of his own. Toiling early and late, with his own hands he set types and worked at the press; with his own hands would trundle to the office in a wheelbarrow the reams of paper which he was to use. His ingenuity was such, he could form letters, make types and wood cuts, and engrave vignettes in copper. The assembly of Pennsylvania respected his merit, and chose him its printer. He planned a newspaper; and, when he became its proprietor and editor, he fearlessly defend-

CHAP XXIII.

ed absolute freedom of thought and speech, and the inalienable power of the people. Desirous of advancing education, he proposed improvements in the schools of Philadelphia; he invented the system of subscription libraries, and laid the foundation of one that was long the most considerable library in America; he suggested the establishment of an academy, which has ripened into a university; he saw the benefit of concert in the pursuit of science, and gathered a philosophical society for its advancement. The intelligent and highly cultivated Logan bore testimony to his merits before they had burst upon the world:—"Our most ingenious printer has the clearest understanding, with extreme modesty. He is certainly an extraordinary man,"—"of a singularly good judgment, but of equal modesty,"—"excellent, yet humble." "Do not imagine," he adds, "that I overdo in my character of Benjamin Franklin, for I am rather short in it." When the scientific world began to investigate the wonders of electricity, Franklin excelled all observers in the marvellous simplicity and lucid exposition of his experiments, and in the admirable sagacity with which he elicited from them the laws which they illustrated. It was he who first suggested the explanation of thunder-gusts and the northern lights on electrical principles, and, in the summer of 1752, going 1749
out into the fields, with no instrument but a kite, no companion but his son, established his theory by obtaining a line of connection with a thunder-cloud. Nor did he cease till he had made the lightning a household pastime, taught his family to catch the subtile fluid in its inconceivably rapid leaps between the earth and the sky, and compelled it to give warning of its passage by the harmless ringing of bells.

CHAP. XXIII.

With placid tranquillity, Benjamin Franklin looked quietly and deeply into the secrets of nature. His clear understanding was never perverted by passion, or corrupted by the pride of theory. The son of a rigid Calvinist, the grandson of a tolerant Quaker, he had from boyhood been familiar not only with theological subtilties, but with a catholic respect for freedom of mind. Skeptical of tradition as the basis of faith, he respected reason, rather than authority; and, after a momentary lapse into fatalism, escaping from the mazes of fixed decrees and free will, he gained, with increasing years, an increasing trust in the overruling providence of God. Adhering to none "of all the religions" in the colonies, he yet devoutly, though without form, adhered to religion. But though famous as a disputant, and having a natural aptitude for metaphysics, he obeyed the tendency of his age, and sought by observation to win an insight into the mysteries of being. Loving truth, without prejudice and without bias, he discerned intuitively the identity of the laws of nature with those of which humanity is conscious; so that his mind was like a mirror, in which the universe, as it reflected itself, revealed her laws. He was free from mysticism, even to a fault. His morality, repudiating ascetic severities, and the system which enjoins them, was indulgent to appetites of which he abhorred the sway; but his affections were of a calm intensity; in all his career, the love of man gained the mastery over personal interest. He had not the imagination which inspires the bard or kindles the orator; but an exquisite propriety, parsimonious of ornament, gave ease of expression and graceful simplicity even to his most careless writings. In life, also, his tastes were delicate. Indifferent to the pleasures of the table, he relished the delights of music and harmony, of which he enlarged the instruments. His blandness of temper, his modesty, the benignity of his manners, made him the favorite of intelligent society; and, with healthy cheerfulness, he derived pleasure from books, from philosophy, from conversation,—now calmly administering consolation to the sorrower, now indulging in the expression of light-hearted gayety. In his intercourse, the universality of his perceptions bore, perhaps, the character of humor; but, while he clearly discerned the contrast between the grandeur of the universe and the feebleness of man, a serene benevolence saved him from contempt of his race, or disgust at its toils. To superficial observers, he might have seemed as an alien from speculative truth, limiting himself to the world of the senses; and yet, in study, and among men, his mind always sought, with unaffected simplicity, to discover and apply the general principles by which nature and affairs are controlled,—now deducing from the theory of caloric improvements in fireplaces and lanterns, and now advancing human freedom by firm inductions from the inalienable rights of man. Never professing enthusiasm, never making a parade of sentiment, his practical wisdom was sometimes mistaken for the offspring of selfish prudence; yet his hope was steadfast, like that hope which rests on the Rock of Ages, and his conduct was as unerring as though the light that led him was a light from heaven. He never anticipated action by theories of self-sacrificing virtue; and yet, in the moments of intense activity, he, from the highest abodes of ideal truth, brought down and applied to the affairs of life the sublimest principles of goodness, as noiselessly and unostentatiously as became the man who, with a kite and

CHAP. XXIII. hempen string, drew the lightning from the skies. He separated himself so little from his age, that he has been called the representative of materialism; and yet, when he thought on religion, his mind passed beyond reliance on sects to faith in God; when he wrote on politics, he founded the freedom of his country on principles that know no change; when he turned an observing eye on nature, he passed always from the effect to the cause, from individual appearances to universal laws; when he reflected on history, his philosophic mind found gladness and repose in the clear anticipation of the progress of humanity.

Thus did America, by its increase in population, and by the genius of its sons, ripen for independence. But still there was no union: neither danger from abroad, nor English invasions of liberty, had as yet roused the colonies to a common resistance. Not even the proposal to abrogate charters could excite a united opposition. Public sentiment in America so little respected the proprietary governments, that, in 1720, the three New England charter governments were left to contend for their privileges alone. It was asserted, on the side of those who desired to merge colonial liberties in the royal prerogative, that the charter governments had neglected the defence of the country; had exercised power arbitrarily; had disregarded the acts of trade; had made laws repugnant to English legislation; and, most dangerous of all, by fostering the numbers and wealth of their inhabitants, were creating formidable antagonists to English industry, and nursing a disposition to rebellion.

To this it was answered, by the agent for Massachusetts, that the three New England colonies held their charters by compact, having obtained them as a consideration for the labor of those who redeemed the wilderness and annexed it to the English dominions; that, if the planters had foreseen that their privileges would be such transitory things, they never would have engaged in their costly and hazardous enterprise; that, but for them, France would have multiplied its settlements till she had reigned sole mistress of North America; that, far from neglecting their defence, the glorious deeds of their soldiers, if they must not shine in British annals, would consecrate their memory in their own country, and there, at least, transmit their fame to the latest posterity; that the charters themselves contained the strongest barriers against arbitrary rule, in the annual election of magistrates; that the violations of the acts of navigation, which occurred also in every seaport in England, were the frauds of individuals, not the fault of the community; that, in the existing state of things, all the officers of the revenue were appointed by the crown, and all breaches of the acts of trade cognizable only in the court of admiralty; that colonial laws, repugnant to those of England, far from effecting a forfeiture of the charters, were of themselves, by act of parliament, illegal, null, and void; that the colonies, even "if it were possible they could contrive so wild and rash an undertaking as to rebel," would not be able to execute their purpose, "unless they could first strengthen themselves by a confederacy of all the parts;" that the crown had no interest to resume the charters, since it could derive no benefit but from the trade of the colonies, and the nursery of trade is a free government, where the laws are sacred; that justice absolutely forbade a bill of attainder against the liberties of states; that it would be a severity without a precedent, if a people, unsummoned and unheard,

CHAP. XXIII.

7 and 8 Will. c. xxii § 9

CHAP. XXIII. should in one day be deprived of all the valuable privileges which they and their fathers had enjoyed for near a hundred years. Such were the arguments urged by Jeremiah Dummer, a native of New England, who, "in the scarcity of friends to those governments," gained a tongue to defend the liberties of his country. Nor was it then known that, though the charters should be burned, freedom itself would rise again from their ashes in forms more beautiful than before. But at that time the bill for abrogating them was dropped; and when, in 1726, the charter of Massachusetts was explained, it was done, not by parliament, but by the act of the king, and the change was held to require the assent of the colony. Nor was liberty only curtailed; after a long strife, the territory of Massachusetts was unjustly abridged in favor of the royal government of New Hampshire.

These controversies produced no effect beyond New England. The post-office had no political influence. The wars with the savages on the eastern and southern frontier were insulated. The relations with the Iroquois had a greater tendency to effect concert; they interested New England on the east; and, at a con-
1722. gress in Albany, Virginia, as well as Pennsylvania, was represented by its governor.

The necessity of joint action, for purposes of defence, had led even Spotswood, of Virginia, to suggest
1711. to the board of trade that "the regulation of that assistance should not be left to the precarious humor of an assembly;" and he invited the government in
Spotswood, MSS. England "to consider some more proper method for rendering it effectual." But no attempt was made from England to tax America. It is true that, in 1728, the profligate Sir William Keith—once the governor

CHAP XXIII.

of Pennsylvania, and afterwards, for selfish purposes, a fiery patriot, boisterous for liberty and property, meaning a new issue of paper money—submitted to the king the inquiry, "whether the duties of stamps upon parchment and paper in England may not, with good reason, be extended by act of parliament to all the American plantations." The suggestion, which, probably, was not original with Keith, met with no favor from the commissioners of trade. The influence of Sir Robert Walpole, disinclined by character to every measure of violence, and seeking to conciliate the colonies by his measured forbearance, was a guaranty against its adoption. "I will leave the taxing of the British colonies"—such are the words attributed to him towards the close of his ministry, and such, certainly, were his sentiments—"for some of my successors, who may have more courage than I have, and be less a friend to commerce than I am. It has been a maxim with me," he added, "during my administration, to encourage the trade of the American colonies to the utmost latitude: nay, it has been necessary to pass over some irregularities in their trade with Europe; for, by encouraging them to an extensive, growing foreign commerce, if they gain five hundred thousand pounds, I am convinced that, in two years afterwards, full two hundred and fifty thousand pounds of this gain will be in his majesty's exchequer, by the labor and produce of this kingdom, as immense quantities of every kind of our manufactures go thither; and, as they increase in the foreign American trade, more of our produce will be wanted. This is taxing them more agreeably to their own constitution and laws."

Burke's Virginia, iii. 159.

Annual Register for 1765.

Tribute was therefore levied on America by means of its consumption. That the British creditor might

CHAP. XXIII. be secure, lands in the plantations were, by act of parliament, made liable for debts. Every branch of consumption was, as far as practicable, secured to English manufacturers; every form of competition in industry, in the heart of the plantations, was discouraged or forbidden. In the land of furs, it was found that hats were well made: the London company of hatters remonstrated; and their craft was protected by an act forbidding hats to be transported from one plantation to another. The proprietors of English iron works were jealous of American industry; and, in 1719, the house of commons declared, "that the erecting of manufactories in the colonies tended to lessen their dependence on Great Britain." Under pretence of encouraging the importation of American naval stores, they voted a clause that "none in the plantations should manufacture iron wares of any kind whatsoever;" and the house of peers added a prohibition of every "forge going by water for making bar or rod iron." The opposition of the northern colonies defeated the bill. Of the purpose, which was never abandoned, the mildly conservative Logan plainly saw the tendency. "Some talk of an act of parliament," he observed, in 1728, "to prohibit our making bar iron, even for our own use. Scarce any thing could more effectually alienate the minds of the people in these parts, and shake their dependence upon Britain."

5 Geo. II. c. 7.

5 Geo. II c. 22.

1719.

Ross, 78.

Anderson, iii. 88, 89.

1728

After the peace of Utrecht, the English continental colonies grew accustomed to a humble commerce with the islands of the French and Dutch, purchasing of them sugar, rum, and molasses, in return for provisions, horses, and lumber. The British sugar colonies, always eager for themselves to engage in contraband trade with the Spanish provinces, demanded of parliament a prohibition of all intercourse between the northern colonies and any tropical islands but the British. CHAP. XXIII.

In the formation of the colonial system, each European nation valued most the colonies of which the products least interfered with its own. Jealous of the industry of New England, England saw with exultation the increase of its tropical plantations. It was willing, therefore, to check the north, and to favor the south. Hence permission was given to the planters 2 Geo. II. c. xxviii. and xxxiv.
of Carolina, and afterwards of Georgia, to ship their rice directly to any port in Europe south of Cape Finisterre. Hence special restrictions on colonial maritime enterprise; so that when, in imitation of the French policy, the act of navigation was modified, and liberty 12 Geo. II. c. xxx.
granted for carrying sugar from the British sugar plantations directly to foreign markets, ships built and ships owned in the American plantations were excluded from the privilege. Ashley's Memoirs c. ii
Hence, also, the tropical products, especially the products of the cane, formed the central point of colonial policy. To monopolize sugar and slaves—to engross the culture of the first, and the exclusive traffic in the second—became the cardinal hope of English commercial ambition.

The interests of the northern plantations were therefore esteemed subordinate to those of the sugar colonies; and, after two years' discussion, an act of par- 1733
liament, recognizing the prosperity of "the sugar colonies in America as of the greatest consequence to 6 Geo. II. c. xiii
the trade of England," imposed a duty of ninepence on every gallon of rum, sixpence on every gallon of molasses, and five shillings on every hundred weight of sugar, imported from foreign colonies into any of the British plantations.

Here was an act of the British parliament, to be

CHAP. XXIII. executed by officers of royal appointment, levying a tax on consumption in America. In England, it was afterwards appealed to as a precedent; in America, the sixpence duty on molasses had all the effect of a prohibition, and led only to clandestine importations. Even in case of forfeitures, nobody appeared to demand the third part given to the king for the colony. The act of parliament produced no revenue, and appeared to be no more than a regulation of commerce, a new development of the colonial system. The enactment had its motive in the desire to confirm the monopoly of the British sugar plantations, and, so long as it brought no income to the crown, it was complained of as a grievance, but not resisted as a tax. Thus the colonial system subjected the trade of the northern colonies to that of the West Indies, with the design of promoting the interest of England. But here a new difficulty arose. The commercial dependence on the metropolis kept the colonies in debt to England, and the indebtment increased as the mercantile system was rigidly enforced.

Hutch. Hist. iii. 108 Polit. Reg. i. 17. Hutch iii 89

It is the nature of a new country to desire credit, — to submit even to extortion and expedients, rather than renounce its use. Where nature invited to the easy and rapid development of its resources, hope saw the opportunity of golden advantages, if credit could be obtained; and, in the want of it, an eager cupidity was ever fruitful in devices that might be employed in its stead. The condition of a young country, soliciting labor, but not yet enriched by the results of labor; the impediments to progress consequent on colonial dependence; the influence of men of business on legislation,—combined to bring about extraordinary results, which nothing but the simplicity of colonial life, and purity of colonial morals, could have rendered tolerable. The constant state of debt to the mother country created a demand for remittances; so that specie disappeared. America was left without a currency: she was incapable of the voluntary self-denial requisite to recover a specie currency from commerce with England; could adopt no counteracting policy; and was debarred from such traffic as would have furnished a supply from other nations. The consequence was, a policy which the history of the world had never yet witnessed. The progress of European civilization had endowed commerce with legislative power. Its counsels prevailed in England, where it dictated the national policy, prescribed alliances, and menaced wars. In America, the political influence of commerce sprung, not from progress, but from sympathy with the movement of Europe; and it was, less gloriously, content with introducing new maxims of legislation and new systems of finance. That it is the duty of government to provide a currency for commerce, was the maxim that came into vogue in every colony but one; and, as the impossibility of maintaining a metallic currency, in a state of colonial dependence, was assumed as undeniable, the maxim, reduced to practice, led to the perilous use of paper money. The provinces were invited to manufacture bills of credit, and to institute loan offices. The credit of the colonies was invoked in behalf of borrowers. The first emissions of provincial paper had their origin in the immediate necessities of government. In times of peace, provinces which had an empty treasury issued bills of credit, redeemable at a remote day, and put in circulation, by means of loans to citizens, at a low rate of interest, on the mortgage of lands The bills, in

CHAP. XXIII. themselves almost worthless, from the remoteness of the day of payment, were made a lawful tender. The borrower, who received them, paid annual interest on his debt to the state; and this interest constituted a public revenue, obtained, it was boasted, without taxation. The system spread rapidly. In 1712, South Carolina issued, in this manner, "a bank" of forty-eight thousand pounds. Massachusetts, which for twenty years had used bills of credit for public purposes, in 1714, authorized an emission of fifty thousand pounds in bills, to be put into the hands of five trustees, and let out at five per cent. on safe mortgages of real estate, to be paid back in five annual instalments. The debts were not thus paid back; but an increased clamor was raised for greater emissions. In 1716, an additional issue of one hundred thousand pounds was made, and committed to the care of county trustees. The scarcity of money was even more and more complained of: "all the silver money was sent into Great Britain to make returns for what was owing there." Yet the system was imitated in every colony but Virginia. Franklin, who afterwards perceived its evil tendencies, assisted, in 1723, in introducing it into Pennsylvania, where silver had circulated; and the complaint was soon heard, that, "as their money was paper, they had very little gold and silver, and, when any came in, it was accounted as merchandise." Rhode Island, on one occasion, combined the old system of payments, made in the staple products of industry, with the new system of credit, and, in 1721, "issued a bank of forty thousand pounds," on which the interest was payable in hemp or flax.

Felt's Mass. Currency, 68.

1728

Logan, MSS.

E. R. Potter's Brief Account of R. I. Paper Money, 5, 6.

In Massachusetts, a struggle ensued for a new application of the credit system, by the establishment of a land bank. The design was long resisted as "a fraudulent undertaking," and was acknowledged as tending to give to the company "power and influence in all public concerns, more than belonged to them, more than they could make a good use of, and therefore unwarrantable;" yet, but for the interference of parliament, it would at last have been chartered, and "the authority of government"—such is the language of a royalist historian of the last century—"would have been entirely in the land bank company."

The first effects of the unreal enlargement of the currency appeared beneficial; and men rejoiced in the seeming impulse given to trade. It was presently found that specie was repelled from the country by the system; that the paper furnished but a depreciated currency, fluctuating in value with every new emission; that, from the interest of debtors, there was between the colonies some rivalship in issues; that the increase of paper, far from remedying the scarcity of money, excited a thirst for new issues; that, as the party of debtors, if it prevailed in the legislature but once in ten years, could flood the country with bills of credit, men had an interest to remain in debt; that the income of widows and orphans, and all who had salaries or annuities, was ruinously affected by the fluctuations; that administrators were tempted to delay settlements of estates, as each year diminished the value of the inheritances which were to be paid; and, finally, that commerce was corrupted in its sources by the uncertainty attending the expressions of value in every contract.

This uncertainty rapidly pervaded the country. In 1738, the New England currency was worth but one hundred for five hundred; that of New York, New

CHAP. XXIII. Jersey, Pennsylvania, and Maryland, one hundred for one hundred and sixty or seventy, or two hundred; of South Carolina, one for eight; while of North Carolina—of all the states the least commercial in its character—the paper was in London esteemed worth but one for fourteen, in the colony but one for ten. And yet the policy itself was not repudiated. The statesmen of England never proposed or desired to raise the domestic currency of the colonies to an equality with that of the great commercial world; and the system which Franklin had advocated found an apologist in Pownall, and was defended by Edmund Burke, except that Burke, instead of a currency of depreciated paper, proposed an emission of base coin.

Williamson, ii. 42.

The disputes about the currency led to collisions between the provinces and England. The proclamation of Queen Anne was nugatory. It pretended to give to coin one value in England, another in the colonies; but as the coin, being an actual product of labor, could not change, it was, in fact, but giving to the words pounds, shillings, and pence, a different signification in America from that which they bore in Europe. A queen's proclamation could not affect the value of gold or silver. As little could a royal proclamation fix the value of the colonial paper, which was contingent on the results of the past legislation, on the character of the future policy, of ten or twelve disconnected colonial governments.

Thus the great topic of variance between England and her continental colonies of America, lay in the mercantile system and its consequences. Controversies were also occurring in every part of the country

Anderson, iii 39, 129, 153.

Did the lumberers in Maine, on any land first purchased since the grant of the new charter of Massachusetts, cut some stately pine tree into logs for the saw-mill, the officer of the British crown came to measure its diameter, and to arraign them for a trespass in destroying a mast reserved for the English navy. The colonial legislatures hated the restriction, and parliament repeatedly interfered to extend and confirm the royal monopoly in the American forests.

The ministers of Massachusetts, by the hand of Cot- 1725
ton Mather, desire a synod, "to recover and establish the faith and order of the gospel." The council assents; the house hesitates, and, by a reference to the next session, gives opportunity for instructions from the people. The bishop of London anticipates their decision; and a reprimand from England forbids "the authoritative" meeting, as a bad precedent for dissenters. An English prelate was once more the opponent of the religion of New England.

The people of Massachusetts resolutely withheld a regular salary from the governor of royal appointment, but, by its legislature, voted, each year, such a grant
as his good offices might seem to merit. Burnet is 1728
instructed to insist on an established salary. The legislature refuse to modify the constitution by relinquishing any part of their power over the annual appropriations; and, by forbidding their adjournment, the governor seeks to weary them into an assent. The rustic patriots, firmly asserting every source of popular influence over the executive, scorned "to betray the great trust reposed in them by their principals." Burnet hinted that the parliament of England might be invoked as arbiter of the strife, and the charter of Massachusetts be dissolved by its act. The representatives at once appealed to their constituents, transmitting a statement of the controversy to the several towns

CHAP. XXIII. in the colony. Boston, in town meeting, unanimously
applauded the refusal to fix a salary; and, to escape
1728. the influence of that town, the general court was ad-
Oct. 24. journed to Salem. The board of trade reproved the
conduct of the house; the agents of Massachusetts ad-
1729. vised concession, lest parliament should interfere; but
the representatives answered, "It is better that the liberties of the people should be taken from them, than given up by themselves." Burnet, dying, bequeathed
1730. the contest to Belcher, his successor. "The assembly of Massachusetts," it was said in his instructions, "for some years last past, have attempted, by unwarrantable practices, to weaken, if not cast off, the obedience they owe to the crown, and the dependence which all colonies ought to have on their mother country;" and an appeal to parliament was formally menaced. The general court still persevered in its stubbornness; and, at last, as Belcher obtained leave of the crown to accept the annual grants, the controversy subsided, leaving victory to the strong will of Massachusetts.

1733. In 1733, the province of Massachusetts Bay presented a memorial to the house of commons, praying to be heard by counsel on the subject of grievances, and the grief complained of was a royal instruction. This petition to parliament against the king was voted to be frivolous and groundless,—a high insult, "tending to shake off the dependency of said colony." The opinion of censure by the representatives of Massachusetts was, at the same time, voted to be "an audacious proceeding."

Dalrymple's Rights of Great Britain, 35

1728. The farmers of Connecticut loved to divide their domains among their children. In regard to intestate estates, their law was annulled in England, and the English law, favoring the eldest born, was declared to be in force among them. Republican equality seemed endangered; but, in the short conflict between the European system and the American system, the new legislation triumphed; and the king receded from the vain project of enforcing English rules of descent on the husbandmen of New England. CHAP. XXIII.

At New York, the people and the governor are in collision. Cosby, imitating Andros in Massachusetts, insists on new surveys of lands and new grants, in lieu of the old. To the objection of acting against law he answers, "Do you think I mind that? I have a great interest in England." The house of assembly, chosen under royalist influences, and continued from year to year, offered no resistance. The right of the electors was impaired, for the period of the assembly was unlimited. The courts of law were not so pliable; and Cosby, displacing the chief justice, himself appointed judges, without soliciting the consent of the council, or waiting for the approbation of the sovereign.

Complaint could be heard only through the press. A newspaper was established to defend the popular cause; and, in about a year after its establishment, its 1734.
printer, John Peter Zenger, was imprisoned, on the Nov 17.
charge of publishing false and seditious libels. The grand jury would find no bill against him, and the attorney-general filed an information. The counsel of Zenger took exceptions to the commissions of the judges, because they ran during pleasure, and because they had been granted without the consent of council. The court answered the objection by excluding those who offered it from the bar. At the trial, the publishing was confessed; but the aged Andrew Hamilton, a lawyer of Philadelphia, pleading for Zenger, justified the publication by asserting its truth. "You cannot

CHAP. XXIII. be admitted," interrupted the chief justice, "to give the truth of a libel in evidence."—"Then," said Hamilton to the jury, "we appeal to you for witnesses of the facts. The jury have a right to determine both the law and the fact, and they ought to do so." "The

Dunlap, i 310. question before you," he added, "is not the cause of a poor printer, nor of New York alone; it is the best cause—the cause of liberty. Every man who prefers freedom to a life of slavery, will bless and honor you as men who, by an impartial verdict, lay a noble foundation for securing to ourselves, our posterity, and our neighbors, that to which nature and the honor of our country have given us a right—the liberty of opposing arbitrary power by speaking and writing truth." The jury gave their verdict, "Not guilty;" the people of the colonies exulted in the victory of freedom; Hamilton received of the common council of New York the franchises of the city for "his learned and generous defence of the rights of mankind." A patriot of the rev-

Gouverneur Morris olution esteemed this trial to have been the morning star of the American revolution. But it was not one light alone that ushered in the dawn of our independence: the stars of a whole constellation sang together for joy.

In Pennsylvania, there existed the fewest checks on the power of the people. "Popular zeal raged as high

Logan to John Penn. there as in any country;" and Logan wrote despondingly to the proprietary,—"Faction prevails among the people; liberty and privileges are ever the cry." The world was inexperienced in the harmlessness of the ferment of the public mind, where that mind deliberates, decides, and governs. To the timid eye of that

1729. day, there seemed "a real danger of insurrection." The assemblies were troublesome; the spirit of insubordination grew by indulgence; "squatters" increased so rapidly, that their number threatened to become their security. And Maryland was as restless as Pennsylvania; Lord Baltimore, though "a very reasonable gentleman, was most insolently treated by some of his assemblies." The result was inexplicable on the old theories of government. "One perplexity had succeeded another, as waves follow waves in the sea, while the settlement of Penn had still prospered and thriven at all times since its beginning." And yet Logan could not shake off distrust of the issue of the experiment. "This government under you," he warns the proprietary, "is not possibly tenable, without a miracle." With "a long enjoyment of a free air and almost unrestrained liberty, we must not have the least appearance even of a militia, nor any other officers than sheriffs chosen by the multitude themselves, and a few constables, part of themselves, to enforce the powers of government; to which add a most licentious use of thinking, in relation to those powers, most industriously inculcated and fomented."

CHAP. XXIII.

1728

1729

Through the press, no one had been so active as Benjamin Franklin. His newspaper defended absolute freedom of speech and of the press; for he held that Falsehood alone dreads attack, and cries out for auxiliaries, while Truth scorns the aid of the secular arm, and triumphs by her innate strength. He rejected with disdain the "policy of arbitrary government," which can esteem truth itself to be a libel. Nor did he fail to defend "popular governments, as resting on the wisest reasons." In "the multitude, which hates and fears ambition," he saw the true counterpoise to unjust designs; and he defended the mass, as unable "to judge amiss on any essential

Franklin, ii. 292, 310.

CHAP. XXIII. points." "The judgment of a whole people,"—such was the sentiment of Franklin,—"if unbiased by faction, undeluded by the tricks of designing men, is infallible." That the voice of the people is the voice of God, he declared to be universally true; and therefore "the people cannot, in any sense, divest themselves of the supreme authority." Thus he asserted the common rights of mankind, by illustrating "eternal truths, that cannot be shaken even with the foundations of the world." Such was public opinion in Pennsylvania more than a century ago.

Virginia was still more in contrast with England. The eighteenth century was the age of commercial ambition; and Virginia relinquished its commerce to foreign factors. It was the age when nations rushed into debt, when stockjobbers and bankers competed with landholders for political power; and Virginia paid its taxes in tobacco, and alone of all the colonies, alone of all civilized states, resisting the universal tendency of the age, had no debts, no banks, no bills of credit, no paper money. The committee of its burgesses did not fear "to speak irreverently of the king's government;" even royalists acknowledged that the people esteemed "a friendship for the governor incompatible with the interest of the country;" but the people, though fond of independence, had no sullen griefs, no brooding discontent.

Thus were the colonies forming a character of their own. Throughout the continent, national freedom and independence were gaining vigor and maturity. They were not the offspring of deliberate forethought; they were not planted or watered by the hand of man; they grew like the lilies, which neither toil nor spin.

CHAPTER XXIV.

ENGLISH ENCROACHMENTS ON THE COLONIAL MONOPOLIES OF SPAIN PREPARE AMERICAN INDEPENDENCE.

CHAP XXIV.

The moral world is swayed by general laws. They extend not over inanimate nature only, but over man and nations,—over the policy of rulers and the opinion of masses. Event succeeds event according to their influence: amidst the jars of passions and interests, amidst wars and alliances, commerce and conflicts, they form the guiding principle of civilization, which marshals incongruous incidents into their just places, and arranges checkered groups in clear and harmonious order. Yet let not human arrogance assume to know intuitively, without observation, the tendency of the ages. Research must be unwearied, and must be conducted with indifference; as the student of natural history, in examining even the humblest flower, seeks instruments that may unfold its wonderful structure, without color and without distortion. For the historic inquirer to swerve from exact observation, would be as absurd as for the astronomer to break his telescopes, and compute the path of a planet by conjecture Of success, too, there is a sure criterion; for, as every false statement contains a contradiction, truth alone possesses harmony. Truth also, and truth alone, is permanent. The selfish passions of a party are as evanescent as the material interests involved in the transient

CHAP. XXIV. conflict: they may deserve to be described; they never can inspire; and the narrative which takes from them its bias will hurry to oblivion as rapidly as the hearts in which they were kindled moulder to ashes. But facts faithfully ascertained, and placed in proper contiguity, become of themselves the firm links of a brightly burnished chain, connecting events with their causes, and marking the line along which the electric power of truth is conveyed from generation to generation.

Events that are past are beyond change, and where they merit to be known, can, in their general aspect, be known accurately. The constitution of the human mind varies only in details; its elements are the same always; and the multitude, possessing but a combination of the powers and passions of which each one is conscious, is subject to the same laws which control individuals. Humanity, also, constantly enriched and cultivated by the truths it develops and the inventions it amasses, has a life of its own, and yet possesses no element that is not common to each of its members. By comparison of document with document; by an analysis of facts, and the reference of each of them to the laws of the human mind which it illustrates; by separating the idea which inspires combined action from the forms it assumes; by comparing events with the great movement of humanity,—historic truth may establish itself as a science; and the principles that govern human affairs, extending like a path of light from century to century, become the highest demonstration of the superintending providence of God.

The inference that there is progress in human affairs, is also warranted. The trust of our race has ever been in the coming of better times. Universal history does

CHAP. XXIV. 1739

but seek to relate "the sum of all God's works of providence." In America, the first conception of its office, in the mind of Jonathan Edwards, though still cramped and perverted by theological forms not derived from observation, was nobler than the theory of Vico: more grand and general than the method of Bossuet, it embraced in its outline the whole "work of redemption,"—the history of the influence of all moral truth in the gradual regeneration of humanity. The meek New England divine, in his quiet association with the innocence and simplicity of rural life, knew that, in every succession of revolutions, the cause of civilization and moral reform is advanced. "The new creation"—such are his words—"is more excellent than the old. So it ever is, that when one thing is removed by God to make way for another, the new excels the old."—"The wheels of Providence," he adds, "are not turned about by blind chance, but they are full of eyes round about, and they are guided by the spirit of God. Where the spirit goes, they go." Nothing appears more self-determined than the volitions of each individual; and nothing is more certain than that the providence of God will overrule them for good. The finite will of man, free in its individuality, is, in the aggregate, subordinate to general laws. This is the reason why evil is self-destructive; why truth, when it is once generated, is sure to live forever; why freedom and justice, though resisted and restrained, renew the contest from age to age, confident that messengers from heaven fight on their side, and that the stars in their courses war against their foes. There would seem to be no harmony, and no consistent tendency to one great end, in the confused events of the reigns of George II. of England and Louis XV. of France, where legisla-

Works of Edwards, ii. 377 and 382

CHAP. XXIV. tion was now surrendered to the mercantile passion for gain, was now swayed by the ambition and avarice of the mistresses of kings,—where the venal corruption of public men, the open profligacy of courts, the greedy cupidity of trade, conspired in exercising dominion over the civilized community. The political world was without form and void; yet the spirit of God was moving over the chaos of human passions and human caprices, bringing forth the firm foundations on which better hopes were to rest, and setting in the firmament the bright lights that were to serve as guides to the nations.

England, France, and Spain, occupied all the continent, nearly all the islands, of North America; each established over its colonies an oppressive metropolitan monopoly. Had they been united, no colony could have rebelled successfully; but Great Britain, in the pride of opulence, vigorously enforced her own acts of navigation, and disregarded those of Spain. Strictly maintaining the exclusive commerce with her own colonies, she coveted intercourse with the Spanish islands and main; and, intent on her object, she was about to give to the world, for the first time in its history, the spectacle of a war for trade. One colonial power encroached on another, and, in its passion for gain, not content with oppressing its own plantations, strove to appropriate to itself the wealth and commerce of the colonies of its rival. Thus the metropolitan monopolists were divided against themselves. Their divisions were to their colonies reciprocally a promise of an ally in case of rebellion. The war, engendered by the grasping avidity of England, against the colonial monopoly of Spain, hastened the approach of commercial freedom, and contained for the colonies an augury of independence.

CHAP XXIV

A part of the creditors of England had been incorporated into a company, with the exclusive trade to the South Seas. But as Spain, having acquired the American coast in those seas, possessed a monopoly of its commerce, the grant was nugatory and worthless, unless the monopoly of Spain could be successfully invaded; and, for this end, the benefit of the assiento treaty was assigned to the South Sea company.

In 1719, the capital of the company was increased by new subscriptions of national debts; and, in the next year, it was proposed to incorporate into its stock all the national debt of England. The system resembled that of Law; but the latter was connected with a bank of issue, and became a war against specie. In England, there was no attempt, directly or indirectly, to exile specie, no increase of the circulating medium, but only an increase of stocks. The parties implicated suffered from fraud and folly; the stockjobbers—they who had parted with their certificates of the national debt for stock in the company—they who, hurried away by a blind avidity, had engaged in other "bubbles"—were ruined; but the country was not impoverished.

Enough of the South Sea company survived the overthrow of hopes which had no foundation but in fraud or delusion, to execute the contract for negroes, and to covet an illicit commerce with Spanish America. Cupidity grew the more earnest from having been baffled; and, at last, "ambition, avarice, distress, disappointment, and all the complicated vices that tend to render the mind of man uneasy, filled all places and all hearts in the English nation." Dreams of the conquest of Florida, with the possession of the Bahama Channel,—of the conquest of Mexico and Peru, with

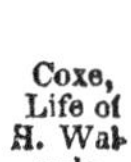
Coxe, Life of H. Walpole

CHAP. XXIV. their real and their imagined wealth,—rose up to dazzle the minds of the restless. While the opportunity of conquest and rapine was anxiously waited for, Jamaica became the centre of an extensive smuggling trade; and slave ships, deriving their passport from the assiento treaty, were the ready instruments of contraband cupidity.

The great activity of the English slave trade does not acquire its chief interest for American history by the transient conflict to which it led. While the South Sea company satisfied but imperfectly its passion for wealth, by a monopoly of the supply of negroes for the Spanish islands and main, the African company and independent traders were still more busy in sending negroes to the colonies of England. To this eagerness, encouraged by English legislation, fostered by royal favor, and enforced for a century by every successive ministry of England, it is due, that one sixth part of the population of the United States—a moiety of those who dwell in the five states nearest the Gulf of Mexico—are descendants of Africans.

The colored men who were imported into our colonies, sometimes by way of the West Indies, and sometimes, especially for the south, directly from the Old World, were sought all along the African coast, for thirty degrees together, from Cape Blanco to Loango St. Pauls; from the Great Desert of Sahara to the kingdom of Angola, or perhaps even to the borders of the land of the Caffres. It is not possible to relate precisely in what bay they were respectively laden, from what sunny cottages they were kidnapped, from what more direful captivity they were rescued. The traders in men have not been careful to record the lineage of their victims. They were chiefly gathered from gangs

B. Edwards, ii. 58.

that were marched from the far interior; so that the freight of a single ship might be composed of persons of different languages, and of nations altogether strange to each other. Nor was there uniformity of complexion: of those brought to our country, some were from tribes of which the skin was of a tawny yellow.

The purchases in Africa were made, in part, of convicts punished with slavery, or mulcted in a fine, which was discharged by their sale; of debtors sold, though but rarely into foreign bondage; of children sold by their parents; of kidnapped villagers; of captives taken in war. Hence the sea-coast and the confines of hostile nations were laid waste. But the chief source of supply was from swarms of those born in a state of slavery; for the despotisms, the superstitions, and the usages of Africa had multiplied bondage. In the upper country, on the Senegal and the Gambia, three fourths of the inhabitants were not free; and the slave's master was the absolute lord of the slave's children. The trade in slaves, whether for the caravans of the Moors or for the European ships, was chiefly supplied from the natural increase. In the healthy and fertile uplands of Western Africa, under the tropical sun, the reproductive power of the prolific race, combined with the imperfect development of its moral faculties, gave to human life, in the eye of man himself, an inferior value. Humanity did not respect itself in any of its forms,—in the individual, in the family, or in the nation. Our systems of morals will not explain the phenomenon: its cause is not to be sought in the suppression of moral feeling, but rather in the condition of a branch of the human family not yet conscious of its powers, not yet fully possessed of its moral and ra-

Ritter, Vergleich. Geog. i. 383.

CHAP. XXIV. tional life. In the state of humanity itself, in Senegambia, in Upper and Lower Guinea, the problem of the slave trade finds its solution. The habits of life of the native tribes of America rendered its establishment with them impossible. The quick maturity of Ritter, i. 384 385. life, the facility of obtaining sustenance, the nature of the negro, as influenced by a hot sun, a healthful and fertile clime, an undeveloped intelligence, and the fruitfulness of the race, explain why, from century to century, the slave ships could find a freight, and yet the population of the interior be constantly replenished.

England valued Africa as returning for her manufactures abundant laborers for her colonies, and valued it for nothing else. Africans of more than thirty years of age were rejected by the traders as too old, and few were received under fourteen. Of the whole number, not more than one third part was composed of women, and a woman past two-and-twenty was hardly deemed worth transportation. The English slave ships were laden with the youth of Africa.

Slavery, and even a change of masters, were familiar to the African; but to be conducted to the shores of the Western Ocean, to be doomed to pass its boundless deep, and enter on new toils, in an untried clime, and amidst an unknown race, was appalling to the black man. The horrors of the passage, also, corresponded with the infamy of the trade. Small vessels, of little more than two hundred tons burden, were prepared for the traffic; for these could most easily penetrate the bays and rivers of the coast, and, quickly obtaining a lading, could soonest hurry away from the deadly air of Western Africa. In such a bark five hundred negroes and more have been stowed, exciting wonder that men could have lived, within the tropics, cribbed in so few inches of room The inequality of force between the crew and the cargo led to the use of manacles; the hands of the stronger men were made fast together, and the right leg of one was chained to the left of another. The avarice of the trader was a partial guaranty of the security of life, as far as it depended on him; but death hovered always over the slave ship. The negroes, as they came from the higher level to the sea-side,—poorly fed on the sad pilgrimage, sleeping at night on the damp earth without covering, and often reaching the coast at unfavorable seasons,—imbibed the seeds of disease, which confinement on board ship quickened into feverish activity. There have been examples where one half of them—it has been said, even, where two thirds of them—perished on the passage. The total loss of life on the voyage is computed to have been, on the average, fifteen, certainly full twelve and a half, in the hundred: the harbors of the West Indies proved fatal to four and a half more out of every hundred. No scene of wretchedness could surpass a crowded slave ship during a storm at sea, unless it were that same ship dismasted, or suffering from a protracted voyage and want of food, its miserable inmates tossed helplessly to and fro under the rays of a vertical sun, vainly gasping for a drop of water.

Of a direct voyage from Guinea to the coast of the United States no journal is known to exist, though slave ships from Africa entered nearly every considerable harbor south of Newport.

In the northern provinces of English America, the few negroes were lost in the larger number of whites; and only in the lowlands of South Carolina and Virginia did they constitute a great majority of the in

CHAP. XXIV. habitants. But they came with the limited faculties of uncivilized man: when they met on our soil, they were as strange to one another as to their masters. Coming from places in Africa a thousand miles asunder, the negro emigrants to America brought with them no common language, no abiding usages, no worship, no nationality. They were compelled to adopt a new dialect for intercourse with each other; and broken English became their tongue not less among themselves than with their masters. Hence there was no unity among them, and no immediate political danger from their joint action. Once an excitement against them raged in New York, through fear of a pretended plot; but the frenzy grew out of a delusion. Sometimes the extreme harshness of taskmasters may have provoked resistance; or sometimes an African, accustomed from birth to freedom, and reduced to slavery by the chances of war, carried with him across the Atlantic the indomitable spirit of a warrior; but the instances of insurrection were insulated, and without result. Destitute of common traditions, customs, and laws, the black population existed in fragments, having no bonds of union but color and misfortune. Thus the negro slave in America was dependent on his master for civilization; he could be initiated into skill in the arts only through him; through him only could he gain a country; and, as a consequence, in the next generation, if dissatisfied with his condition, he had yet learned to love the land of his master; it was his country also.

It is not easy to conjecture how many negroes were imported into the English continental colonies. The usual estimates far exceed the truth. Climate came in aid of opinion to oppose the introduction of them. As their limited number diminished the danger from their presence, they, from the first, appear to have increased, though, owing to the inequality of the sexes, not rapidly in the first generation. Previous to the year 1740, there may have been introduced into our country nearly one hundred and thirty thousand; before 1776, a few more than three hundred thousand. In 1727, "the vast importation of negroes" was a subject of complaint in South Carolina. The German traveller Von Reck, in 1734, reported the number of negroes in that province at thirty thousand, and for the annual importation gave the greatly exaggerated estimate of nearly three thousand.

Urlsperger, Ausführliche Nachricht, &c. i 79

In the Northern and the Middle States, the negro was employed for menial offices and in the culture of wheat and maize. Almost all the tobacco exported from Maryland and Virginia, all the indigo and rice of Carolina, were the fruit of his toils. Instead of remaining in a wild and unproductive servitude, his labor contributed to the wealth of nations,—his destiny, from its influence on commerce, excited interest throughout the civilized world.

With new powers of production, the negro learned new wants, which were at least partially supplied. At the north, he dwelt under the roof of his master; his physical well-being was provided for, and opinion protected him against cruelty. At the south, his home was a rude cabin of his own, constructed of logs or slabs,—to him, but for the abundance of fuel, a feeble protection against winter. The early writers tell us little of his history, except the crops which he raised.

The physical constitution of the negro decided his home in the New World: he loved the sun; even the climate of Virginia was too chill for him. His labor, therefore, increased in value as he proceeded south;

CHAP. XXIV. and hence the relation of master and slave came to be essentially a southern institution: to the southern colonies, mainly, Providence intrusted the guardianship and the education of the colored race.

The concurrent testimony of tradition represents the negroes, at their arrival, to have been gross and stupid, having memory and physical strength, but undisciplined in the exercise of reason and imagination. Their organization seemed analogous to their barbarism. But, at the end of a generation, all observers affirmed the marked progress of the negro American. In the midst of the horrors of slavery and the slave trade, the masters had, in part at least, performed the office of advancing and civilizing the negro.

The thought of general emancipation early presented itself. Massachusetts, where the first planters assumed to themselves "a right to treat the Indians on the foot of Canaanites or Amalekites," always opposed the introduction of slaves from abroad; and, in 1701, the town of Boston instructed its representatives "to put a period to negroes' being slaves." In 1712, to a general petition for the emancipation of negro slaves by law, the legislature of Pennsylvania answered that "it was neither just nor convenient to set them at liberty;" and yet George Keith, the early abolitionist, was followed by the eccentric Benjamin Lay,—by Ralph Sandiford, who held slavery to be inconsistent alike with the rights of man and the principles of Christianity,—and, at a later day, by the amiable enthusiast Anthony Benezet.

Berkeley, iii. 247

But did not Christianity enfranchise its converts? The Christian world of that day almost universally revered in Christ the impersonation of the divine wisdom. Could an intelligent being, who, through the

CHAP. XXIV.

Mediator, had participated in the Spirit of God, and, by his own inward experience, had become conscious of a Supreme Existence, and of relations between that Existence and humanity, be rightfully held in bondage? From New England to Carolina, the "notion" prevailed, that "being baptized is inconsistent with a state of slavery;" and this early apprehension proved a main obstacle to the culture and "conversion of these poor people." The sentiment was so deep and so general, that South Carolina in 1712, Maryland in 1715, Virginia repeatedly from 1667 to 1748, gave a negative to it by special enactments. The lawyers, also, declared the fear groundless; and "the opinion of his majesty's attorney and solicitor-general, Yorke and Talbot, signed with their own hands, was accordingly printed in Rhode Island, and dispersed through the plantations." "I heartily wish," adds Berkeley, "it may produce the intended effect;" and, at the same time, he rebuked "the irrational contempt of the blacks," which regarded them "as creatures of another species, having no right to be instructed." In like manner, Gibson, the bishop of London, declared that "Christianity and the embracing of the gospel does not make the least alteration in civil property;" while he besought the masters to regard the negroes "not barely as slaves, but as men-slaves and women-slaves, having the same frame and faculties with themselves." Thus was strife with the lawyers and the planters avoided by friends to the negro, who were anxious for his improvement, and yet willing to leave his emancipation to be decided by the result.

Berkeley's Works, iii. 247. Bacon's Laws of Maryland. Laws of S. Carolina, 1712. Dalcho. 94, &c.

Hen. ii. 260; iii. 448, &c.

1727 May 19

But for the difference of color, this question would at once have been decided in the affirmative. There is not, in all the colonial legislation of America, one

CHAP. XXIV. single law which recognizes the rightfulness of slavery in the abstract. Every province favored freedom as such. The real question at issue was, from the first, not one of slavery and freedom generally, but of the relations to each other of the Ethiopian and American races. The Englishman in America tolerated and enforced not the slavery of man, but the slavery of the man who was

> "guilty of a skin
> Not colored like his own."

In the skin lay unexpiated, and, as it was held, inexpiable, guilt. The negro, whom the benevolence of his master enfranchised, was not absorbed into the mass of the free population: his color adhered to him, and still constituted him a separate element in society. Hence arose laws restricting the right of emancipation. The indelible mark of his species remained unfaded and unchanged; and, in the state of opinion, for him to rise by single merit was impracticable; the path to social equality was not open to him; he could not raise himself from humiliation without elevating his race.

T J Randolph, 17.

Our country might well have shrunk from assuming the guardianship of the negro. Hence the question of tolerating the slave trade and the question of abolishing slavery rested on different grounds. The one related to a refusal of a trust; the other, to the manner of its exercise. The English continental colonies, in the aggregate, were always opposed to the African slave trade. Maryland, Virginia, even Carolina,—alarmed at the excessive production and the consequent low price of their staples, at the heavy debts incurred by the purchase of slaves on credit, and at the dangerous increase of the colored population,—each showed an anxious preference for the introduction of white men; and laws designed to restrict importations of slaves, are scattered copiously along the records of colonial legislation. The first continental congress which took to itself powers of legislation, gave a legal expression to the well-formed opinion of the country, by resolving "that no slaves be imported into any of the thirteen united colonies."

CHAP XXIV.

1776. April 6.

Journals of Congress, i 307

Before America legislated for herself, the interdict of the slave trade was impossible. England was inexorable in maintaining the system, which gained new and stronger supporters by its excess. The English slave trade began to attain its great activity after the assiento treaty. From 1680 to 1700, the English took from Africa about three hundred thousand negroes, or about fifteen thousand a year. The number, during the continuance of the assiento, may have averaged not far from thirty thousand. Raynal considers the number of negroes exported by all European nations from Africa before 1776, to have been nine millions; and the considerate German historian of the slave trade, Albert Hüne, deems his statement too small. A careful analysis of the colored population in America at different periods, and the inferences to be deduced from the few authentic records of the numbers imported, corrected by a comparison with the commercial products of slave labor, as appearing in the annals of English commerce, seem to prove, beyond a doubt, that even the estimate of Raynal is larger than the reality. We shall not err very much, if, for the century previous to the prohibition of the slave trade by the American congress, in 1776, we assume the number imported by the English into the Spanish, French, and English West Indies, as well as the English continental colonies, to have been, collectively, nearly three millions; to which are to be added more than a

B. Edwards, ii.

CHAP. XXIV. quarter of a million purchased in Africa, and thrown into the Atlantic on the passage. The gross returns to English merchants, for the whole traffic in that number of slaves, may have been not far from four hundred millions of dollars. Yet, as at least one half of the negroes exported from Africa to America were carried in English ships, it should be observed that this estimate is by far the lowest ever made by any inquirer into the statistics of human wickedness. After every deduction, the trade retains its gigantic character of crime.

In an age when the interests of trade guided legislation, this branch of commerce possessed paramount attractions. Not a statesman exposed its enormities; and, if Richard Baxter echoed the opinions of Puritan Massachusetts; if Southern drew tears by the tragic tale of Oronooko; if Steele awakened a throb of indignation by the story of Inkle and Yarico; if Savage and Shenstone pointed their feeble couplets with the wrongs of "Afric's sable children;" if the Irish metaphysician Hutcheson, struggling for a higher system of morals, justly stigmatized the traffic; yet no public opinion lifted its voice against it. English ships, fitted out in English cities, under the special favor of the royal family, of the ministry, and of parliament, stole from Africa, in the years from 1700 to 1750, probably a million and a half of souls, of whom one eighth were buried in the Atlantic, victims of the passage; and yet in England no general indignation rebuked the enormity; for the public opinion of the age was obedient to materialism. Wars had been for the balance of power, as though the safeguards of nations lay in force alone. Protestantism itself had, in the political point of view, been the triumph of materialism over the spiritual authority of the church. The same influence exhibited itself in philosophy and letters. Shaftesbury, who professed to be its antagonist, degrading conscience to the sphere of sensibility, enlarged, rather than subverted, the philosophy of the senses. The poetical essayist on man, in exquisite diction, exalted self-love into an identity with social, and celebrated its praise as the source of the most capacious philanthropy. Bolingbroke, in his attacks on religion, was but a caviler at historical difficulties. Of the large school of English deists, some were only disposed to make war upon human authority; while others, led astray by materialism, in their theories of necessity, so lost sight of the creative power of mind, as to make of the universe but one vast series of results consequent on laws of nature. Even Hume did not reject a system, which, as he demonstrated, led to nothing absolute but skepticism. The philosophy of that day furnished to the African no protection against oppression; and the interpretation of English common law was equally regardless of human freedom. The colonial negro, who sailed to the metropolis, found no benefit from touching the soil of England, but returned a slave. Such was the approved law of Virginia in the first half of the last century; such was the opinion of Yorke and Talbot, the law officers of the crown, as expressed in 1729, and, after a lapse of twenty years, repeated and confirmed by one of the same authorities, as chancellor of England.

Hening, iii. 448 v. 548.

Clarkson, ii.

The influence of the manufacturers was still worse. They clamored for the protection of a trade which opened to them an African market. Thus the party of the slave trade dictated laws to England. A resolve of the commons, in the days of William and Mary, proposed to lay open the trade in negroes "for the better supply of the plantations:" and the statute-book of

CHAP. XXIV. England soon declared the opinion of its king and its parliament, that "the trade is highly beneficial and advantageous to the kingdom and the colonies." In 1708, a committee of the house of commons report that "the trade is important, and ought to be free;" in 1711, a committee once more report that "the plantations ought to be supplied with negroes at reasonable rates," and recommend an increase of the trade. In June, 1712, Queen Anne, in her speech to parliament, boasts of her success in securing to Englishmen a new market for slaves in Spanish America. In 1729, George II. recommended a provision, at the national expense, for the African forts; and the recommendation was followed. At last, in 1749, to give the highest activity to the trade, every obstruction to private enterprise was removed, and the ports of Africa were laid open to English competition; for "the slave trade"—such are the words of the statute—"the slave trade is very advantageous to Great Britain."—"The British senate," wrote one of its members, in February, 1750, "have this fortnight been pondering methods to make more effectual that horrid traffic of selling negroes. It has appeared to us that six-and-forty thousand of these wretches are sold every year to our plantations alone."

1695. 8 and 10 Wil. III. c. xxvi.

23 Geo. II. c. xxxi.

Horace Walpole to Sir H. Mann, ii. 438. 1750 Feb. 25.

But, while the partial monopoly of the African company was broken down, and the commerce in men was opened to the competition of Englishmen, the monopoly of British subjects was rigidly enforced against foreigners. That Englishmen alone might monopolize all wealth to be derived from the trade, Holt and Pollexfen, and eight other judges, in pursuance of an order in council, had given their opinion "that negroes are merchandise," and that therefore the act of navigation was to be extended to the English trade in them, to the exclusion of aliens.

The same policy was manifested in the relations CHAP XXIV.
between the English crown and the colonies. Land
from the public domain was given to emigrants, in one
West India colony, at least, on condition that the resident owner would "keep four negroes for every hundred acres." The eighteenth century was, as it were,
ushered in by the royal instruction of Queen Anne to the 1702
governor of New York and New Jersey, "to give due
encouragement to merchants, and in particular to the
royal African company of England." That a similar
instruction was given generally, is evident from the
apology of Spotswood for the small importations of
slaves into Virginia. In that commonwealth, the
planters beheld with dismay the increase of negroes.
A tax checks their importation; and, in 1726, 1726.
Hugh Drysdale, the deputy-governor, announces to May 12.
the house that "the interfering interest of the African company has obtained the repeal of that law."
Long afterwards, a statesman of Virginia, in full view
of the course of colonial legislation and English counteracting authority, unbiased by hostility to England,
bore true testimony that "the British government constantly checked the attempts of Virginia to put a stop Madison
to this infernal traffic." On whatever ground Virginia Papers, iii. 1390
opposed the trade, the censure was just.

The white man, emigrating, became a dangerous
freeman: it was quite sure that the negroes of that
century would never profess republicanism; their presence in the colonies increased dependence. This reasoning was avowed by "a British merchant," in 1745, 1745
in a political tract entitled "The African Slave Trade
the great Pillar and Support of the British Plantation
Trade in America." "Were it possible for white men
to answer the end of negroes in planting," it is there
contended, "our colonies would interfere with the

CHAP. XXIV.

manufactures of these kingdoms. In such case, indeed, we might have just reason to dread the prosperity of our colonies; but while we can supply them abundantly with negroes, we need be under no such apprehensions." "Negro labor will keep our British colonies in a due subserviency to the interest of their mother country; for, while our plantations depend only on planting by negroes, our colonies can never prove injurious to British manufactures, never become independent of their kingdom." This policy of England knew no relenting. "My friends and I," wrote Oglethorpe, "settled the colony of Georgia, and by charter were established trustees. We determined not to suffer slavery there; but the slave merchants and their adherents not only occasioned us much trouble, but at last got the government to sanction them." South Carolina, in 1760, from prudential motives, attempted restrictions, and gained only a rebuke from the English ministry. Great Britain, steadily rejecting every colonial limitation of the slave trade, instructed the governors, on pain of removal, not to give even a temporary assent to such laws; and, but a year before the prohibition of the slave trade by the American congress, in 1776, the earl of Dartmouth illustrated the tendency of the colonies and the policy of England, by addressing to a colonial agent these memorable words:—"We cannot allow the colonies to check, or discourage in any degree, a traffic so beneficial to the nation."

The African Slave Trade, &c. p. 14 and 13.

The assiento treaty, originally extorted from Spain by force of arms, remained a source of jealousy between that kingdom and England. Other collisions were preparing on the American frontier, where Spain resolutely claimed to extend her jurisdiction north of the Savannah River, as far, at least, as St. Helena Sound. The foundation of St. Augustine had preceded that of Charleston by a century; national pride still clung to the traditions of the wide extent of Florida; the settlement of the Scottish emigrants at Port Royal had been successfully dispersed; Indians and negroes were received as ready allies against English encroachments; and it was feebleness alone which had tolerated the advancement of the plantations of South Carolina towards the Savannah. Meantime, England resolved to pass that stream, and carry her flag still nearer the walls of St. Augustine.

Mountgomery's Discourse concerning a New Colony, &c. 1717.

The resolution was not hastily adopted. In 1717, a proposal was brought forward, by one whose father had been interested in the unfortunate enterprise of Lord Cardross, to plant a new colony south of Carolina, in the region that was heralded as the most delightful country of the universe. The land was to be tilled by British and Irish laborers, exclusively, without "the dangerous help of blackamoors." Three years afterwards, in the excited season of English stockjobbing and English anticipations, the suggestion was revived. When Carolina became, by purchase, a royal province, Johnson, its governor, was directed to mark out townships as far south as the Alatamaha; and, in 1731, a site was chosen for a colony of Swiss in the ancient land of the Yamassees, but on the left bank of the Savannah. The country between the two rivers was still a wilderness, over which England held only a nominal jurisdiction, when the spirit of benevolence formed a partnership with the selfish passion for extended territory, and, heedless of the objection that "the colonies would grow too great" for England, "and throw off their dependency," resolved to plant the sunny clime with the children of misfortune,—with those who in England had neither land nor shelter,

1728.

Purry's Description of Carolina, 1731.

Reasons for establishing the Colony of Georgia, in Georgia Hist. Coll. i. 213

CHAP. XXIV.

and those on the continent to whom, as Protestants bigotry denied freedom of worship and a home.

Reasons for establishing Georgia, &c

Samuel Smith's Sermon before the Trustees of Georgia, 23.

In the days when protection of property was avowed to be the end of government, the gallows was set up as the penalty for a petty theft; and each year, in Great Britain, at least four thousand unhappy men were immured in prison for the misfortune of poverty. A small debt exposed to a perpetuity of imprisonment; one indiscreet contract doomed the miserable dupe to life-long confinement. The subject won the attention of James Oglethorpe, a member of the British parliament; a man of an heroic mind and a merciful disposition; in the full activity of middle life; rich in varied experience; who had been disciplined alike in the schools of learning and action; a pupil of the university of Oxford; an hereditary loyalist; receiving his first commission in the English army during the ascendency of Bolingbroke; a volunteer in the family of Prince Eugene; present at the siege of Belgrade, and in the brilliant campaign against the Turks on the Danube. To him, in the annals of legislative philanthropy, the honor is due of having first resolved to redress the griefs that had so long been immured from the public gaze,—to lighten the lot of debtors. Touched with the sorrows which the walls of a prison could not hide from his merciful eye, he searched into the gloomy horrors of jails,

T. M. Harris, Memorials of Oglethorpe.

> "Where sickness pines, where thirst and hunger burn,
> And poor misfortune feels the lash of vice."

In 1728, he invoked the interference of the English parliament; and, as a commissioner for inquiring into the state of the jails in the kingdom, his benevolent zeal persevered, till, "from extreme misery, he restored to light and freedom multitudes, who, by long confinement for debt, were strangers and helpless in the country of their birth." He did more. For them, and for persecuted Protestants, he planned an asylum and a new destiny in America, where former poverty would be no reproach, and where the simplicity of piety could indulge the spirit of devotion, without fear of persecution from men who hated the rebuke of its example.

It was not difficult for Oglethorpe to find associates in his disinterested purpose. To further this end, a charter from George II., dated the ninth day of June, 1732, erected the country between the Savannah and the Alatamaha, and from the head-springs of those rivers due west to the Pacific, into the province of Georgia, and placed it, for twenty-one years, under the guardianship of a corporation, "in trust for the poor." The common seal of the corporation, having on one side a group of silk-worms at their toils, with the motto, *Non sibi, sed aliis*,—Not for themselves, but for others,—expressed the disinterested purpose of the patrons, who, by their own request, were restrained from receiving any grant of lands, or any emolument whatever. On the other side of the seal, the device represented two figures reposing on urns, emblematic of the boundary rivers, having between them the genius of "Georgia Augusta," with a cap of liberty on her head, a spear in one hand, the horn of plenty in the other. But the cap of liberty was, for a time at least, a false emblem; for all executive and legislative power, and the institution of courts, were, for twenty-one years, given exclusively to the trustees, or their common council, who were appointed during good behavior. The trustees, men of benevolence and of leisure, ignorant of the value or the nature of popular power, held these grants

1732 June 9.

Establishment of the Colony of Georgia

Charter of Georgia.

CHAP. XXIV.

Estab-lish-ment, &c. 5.

to contain but "proper powers for establishing and governing the colony." The land, open to Jews, was closed against "Papists." At the head of the council stood Shaftesbury, fourth earl of that name; but its most celebrated member was Oglethorpe. So illustrious were the auspices of the design, that hope at once painted brilliant visions of an Eden that was to spring up to reward the ardor of such disinterested benevolence. The kindly sun of the new colony was to look

Georgia, a poem.

down on the abundance of purple vintages, and the silkworm yield its thread to enrich the British merchant, and employ the British looms. The benevolence of England was aroused; the charities of an opulent and an enlightened nation were to be concentrated on the new plantation; individual zeal was kindled in its favor; the Society for propagating the Gospel in Foreign Parts sought to promote its interests; and parliament showed its good will by at once contributing ten thousand pounds.

But, while others gave to the design their leisure, their prayers, or their wealth, Oglethorpe, heedless of danger, devoted himself to its fulfilment. In Novem-
1732. Nov. 17–28. ber, 1732, embarking with about one hundred and
1733. twenty emigrants, he began the voyage to America, and
Jan. 13. in fifty-seven days arrived off the bar of Charleston.
Jan. 13–24. Accepting a hasty welcome, he sailed directly for Port
Jan. 20–31. Royal. While the colony was landing at Beaufort, its patron ascended the boundary river of Georgia, and chose for the site of his chief town the high bluff on which Savannah now stands. At the distance of a half mile dwelt the Yamacraws, a branch of the Muskhogees, who, with Tomo-chichi, their chieftain, sought security by an alliance with the English. "Here is a little present," said the red man, as he

CHAP. XXIV.

1733

offered a buffalo skin, painted on the inside with the head and feathers of an eagle. "The feathers of the eagle are soft, and signify love; the buffalo skin is warm, and is the emblem of protection. Therefore love and protect our little families." On the first day of February, or, according to the new style of computation, on the twelfth, the colonists, on board of a small sloop and periaguas, arrived at the place intended for the town, and before evening encamped on shore near the edge of the river. Four beautiful pines protected the tent of Oglethorpe, who, for near a twelvemonth, sought no other shelter. In the midst of the pleasant region, the streets of Savannah were laid out with greatest regularity; in each quarter a public square was reserved; the houses were planned and constructed on one model—each a frame of sawed timber, twenty-four feet by sixteen, floored with rough deals, the sides with feather-edged boards unplaned, and the roof shingled. Such a house Oglethorpe afterwards hired as his residence, when in Savannah. Erelong a walk, cut through the native woods, led to the large garden on the river side, destined as a nursery of European fruit and of the wonderful products of America. Thus began the commonwealth of Georgia. The humane reformer of prison discipline was already the father of a state, "the place of refuge for the distressed people of Britain and the persecuted Protestants of Europe."

New Voyage to Georgia.

Von Reck, in Urlsperger, i. 184

The fame of the hero penetrated the wilderness; and, in May, the chief men of the eight towns of the Lower Muskhogees, accepting his invitation, came down to make an alliance. Long King, the tall and aged civil chief of the Oconas, spoke for them all:—"The Great Spirit, who dwells every where around,

May 29.

CHAP. XXIV. and gives breath to all men, sends the English to instruct us." Claiming the country south of the Savan-
1733 nah, he bade the strangers welcome to the lands which his nation did not use; and, in token of sincerity, he laid eight bundles of buckskins at Oglethorpe's feet. "Tomo-chichi," he added, "though banished from his nation, has yet been a great warrior; and for his wisdom and courage, the exiles chose him their king." Tomo-chichi entered timorously, and, bowing very low, gave thanks that he was still permitted "to look for good land among the tombs of his ancestors." The chief of Coweta stood up and said, "We are come twenty-five days' journey to see you. I was never willing to go down to Charleston, lest I should die on the way; but when I heard you were come, and that you are good men, I came down, that I might hear good things." He then gave leave to the exiles to summon the kindred that loved them out of each of the Creek towns, that they might dwell together. "Recall," he added, "the Yamassees, that they may be buried in peace among their ancestors, and may see their graves before they die." On the first of June, a treaty of peace was signed, by which the English claimed sovereignty over the land of the Creeks as far south as the St. Johns; and the chieftains departed laden with presents.

A Cherokee appeared among the English. "Fear nothing," said Oglethorpe, "but speak freely;" and the mountaineer answered, "I always speak freely. Why should I fear? I am now among friends; I never feared even among my enemies." And friendly relations were cherished with the Cherokees. In the
1734 July. following year, Red Shoes, a Chocta chief, proposed commerce. "We came a great way," said he, "and

1733. we are a great nation. The French are building forts about us, against our liking. We have long traded with them, but they are poor in goods; we desire that a trade may be opened between us and you." And when commerce with them was begun, the English coveted the harbors on the Gulf of Mexico.

Description of Georgia, 1741

The good faith of Oglethorpe, in the offers of peace, his noble mien and sweetness of temper, conciliated the confidence of the red men; and he, in his turn, was pleased with their simplicity, and sought for means to clear the glimmering ray of their minds, to guide their bewildered reason, and teach them to know the God whom they ignorantly adored.

While the neighboring province of South Carolina displayed "a universal zeal for assisting its new ally and bulwark," the persecuted Protestants known to us as Moravians heard the message of hope, and, on the invitation of the Society in England for propagating the Gospel, prepared to emigrate to the Savannah. A free passage; provisions in Georgia for a whole season; land for themselves and their children, free for ten years, then to be held for a small quitrent; the privileges of native Englishmen; freedom of worship;—these were the promises made, accepted, and honorably fulfilled. On the last day of October, 1733, "the evangelical community,"—well supplied with Bibles and hymn-books, catechisms and books of devotion,—conveying in one wagon their few chattels, in two other covered ones their feebler companions, and especially their little ones,—after a discourse, and prayer, and benedictions,—cheerfully, and in the name of God, began their pilgrimage. History need not stop to tell what charities cheered them on their journey, what towns were closed against them by Roman Catholic

Von Reck, Nachricht von dem Etablissement derer Salzburgischen Emigranten zu Ebenezer

Oct. 31.

CHAP XXIV. 1733 magistrates, or how they entered Frankfort on the Maine, two by two, in solemn procession, singing spiritual songs. As they floated down the Maine, and between the castled crags, the vineyards, and the white-walled towns that adorn the banks of the Rhine, (Umständlicher Vorbericht, 16) their conversation, amidst hymns and prayers, was of justification, and of sanctification, and of standing fast (Nov. 27.) in the Lord. At Rotterdam, they were joined by two preachers, Bolzius and Gronau, both disciplined in (Nov. 27.) charity at the Orphan House in Halle. A passage of (Dec. 3.) six days carried them from Rotterdam to Dover, where several of the trustees visited them and provided considerately for their wants. In January, 1734, they set (Reise Diarium.) sail for their new homes. The majesty of the ocean quickened their sense of God's omnipotence and wisdom; and, as they lost sight of land, they broke out into a hymn to his glory. The setting sun, after a calm, so kindled the sea and the sky, that words could not express their rapture; and they cried out, "How lovely the creation! How infinitely lovely the Creator!" When the wind was adverse, they prayed; and, as it changed, one opened his mind to the other on the power of prayer, even the prayer "of a man subject to like passions as we are." As the voyage excited weariness, a devout listener confessed himself to be an unconverted man; and they reminded him of the promise to him that is poor and of a contrite spirit, and trembleth at the word. As they sailed pleasantly, with a favoring breeze, at the hour of evening prayer, they made a covenant with each other, like Jacob of old, and resolved, by the grace of Christ, to cast all the strange gods which were in their hearts into the depths of the sea. A storm grew so high, that not a sail could (Feb. 18.) be set; and they raised their voices in prayer and song amidst the tempest; for to love the Lord Jesus as a brother gave consolation. At Charleston Oglethorpe bade them welcome; and, in five days more, the wayfaring men, whose home was beyond the skies, pitched their tents near Savannah.

CHAP. XXIV.

1734. March 18. 12–23.

It remained to select for them a residence. To cheer their principal men, as they toiled through the forest and across brooks, Oglethorpe, having provided horses, himself joined the little party. By the aid of blazed trees and Indian guides, he made his way through morasses; a fallen tree served as a bridge over a stream, which the horses swam, for want of a ford; at night, he encamped with them abroad round a fire, and shared every fatigue, till the spot for their village was chosen, and, like the little stream which formed its border, was named Ebenezer. There they built their dwellings, and there they resolved to raise a column of stone, in token of gratitude to God, whose providence had brought them safely to the ends of the earth.

Von Reck, Diarium, in Urlsperger, i. 86

March 17–28.

Oglethorpe's letter to Sir John Philips.

Vorbericht, 32

In the same year, the town of Augusta was laid out, soon to become the favorite resort of Indian traders. The good success of Oglethorpe made the colony increase rapidly by volunteer emigrants. "His under taking will succeed," said Johnson, the governor of South Carolina; "for he nobly devotes all his powers to serve the poor, and rescue them from their wretchedness." "He bears a great love to the servants and children of God," wrote the pastor of Ebenezer. "He has taken care of us to the utmost of his ability." "God has so blessed his presence and his regulations in the land, that others would not in many years have accomplished what he has brought about in one."

1734.

Oldmixon, i. 537.

Kurze Nachricht von Georgia, in Urlsperger, i. 177.

Reise Diarium, 91.

At length, in April, 1734, after a residence in America of about fifteen months, Oglethorpe sailed for Eng-

Tailfer &c.

CHAP. XXIV.

land, taking with him Tomo-chichi and others of the Creeks, to do homage at court, and to invigorate the confidence of England in the destiny of the new colony, which was shown to possess the friendship of the surrounding Indian nations.

His absence left Georgia to its own development. For its franchises, it had only the system of juries, and, though it could not prosper but by self-reliance, legislation by its own representatives was not begun.

The laws, too, which the trustees had instituted, were irksome. To prevent the monopoly of lands, to insure an estate even to the sons of the unthrifty, to strengthen a frontier colony, the trustees, deceived by reasonings from the system of feudal law, and by their own prejudices as members of the landed aristocracy of England, had granted lands only in tail male. Here was a grievance that soon occasioned a just discontent.

Another regulation, which prohibited the introduction of ardent spirits, could not be enforced: it led only to clandestine traffic.

Run-dle's Sermon to recommend the Charity for Georgia, &c. p. 15. 1733-1734. Feb. 16

A third rule forbade the introduction of slaves. "No settlement was ever before established on so humane a plan." Such was the praise of Georgia uttered in London in 1734. "Slavery, the misfortune, if not the dishonor, of other plantations, is absolutely proscribed. Let avarice defend it as it will, there is an honest reluctance in humanity against buying and selling, and regarding those of our own species as our wealth and possessions." "The name of slavery is here unheard and every inhabitant is free from unchosen masters and oppression." And the testimony of Oglethorpe, who yet had once been willing to employ negroes, and once, at least, ordered the sale of a slave, explains the motive of the prohibition. "Slavery," he relates, "is

Ibid. p. 18.

Stephens's Journal.

Memoirs of Sharpe, i. 234.

against the gospel, as well as the fundamental law of England. We refused, as trustees, to make a law permitting such a horrid crime." "The purchase of negroes is forbidden," wrote Von Reck, "on account of the vicinity of the Spaniards;" and this was doubtless "the governmental view." The colony was also "an asylum to receive the distressed. It was necessary, therefore, not to permit slaves in such a country; for slaves starve the poor laborer." But, after a little more than two years, several "of the better sort of people in Savannah" addressed a petition to the trustees "for the use of negroes."

CHAP. XXIV.

Voyage in Georgia Hist Coll. 96.

Tailfer, 23

During his stay in England, Oglethorpe won universal favor for his colony, the youngest child of the colonial enterprise of England. Parliament continued its benefactions; the king expressed interest in a province which bore his name. While the jealousy of the maritime powers on the continent was excited, new emigrants continued to be sent from England. The voice of mercy reached the Highlands of Scotland; and a company of Gaelic mountaineers, as brave as the bravest warriors of the Creek nation, some of them kindred to the loyalists who fell victims to their fidelity to the Stuarts, embarked for America, and established New Inverness, in Darien,

1734
1735

"Where wild Altama murmured to their woe."

Within a few weeks, a new company of three hundred emigrants, conducted by Oglethorpe himself, whose care of them during the voyage proved him as considerate as he was brave, ascended a rising ground, not far from Tybee Island, "where they all knelt and returned thanks to God for having safely arrived in Georgia." Among that group was a reënforcement of Moravians;—men who had a faith above fear; "whose

1736
Feb. 6

Wesley

CHAP. XXIV. wives and children even were not afraid to die;" whose simplicity and solemnity, in their conferences

1736 and prayers, seemed to revive the primitive "assemblies, where form and state were not, but Paul, the tent-maker, or Peter, the fisherman, presided with the demonstration of the Spirit." There, too, were John and Charles Wesley,—the latter selected as the secretary to Oglethorpe, the former eager to become an apostle to the Indians,—fervent enthusiasts, who, by their own confession, were not yet disciplined to a peaceful possession of their souls. "That they were simple of heart, but yet that their ideas were disturbed," was the judgment of Zinzendorf. "Our end in leaving our native country," said they, "is not to gain riches and honor, but singly this—to live wholly to the glory of God." They desired to make Georgia a religious colony, having no theory but devotion, no ambition but to quicken the sentiment of piety. The reformation of Luther and Calvin had included a political revolution; its advocates went abroad on the whirlwind, eager to overthrow the institutions which time had consecrated and selfishness perverted. The age in which religious and political excitements were united, had passed away; with the period of commercial influence fanaticism had no sympathy. Mystic piety, more intense by its aversion to the theories of the eighteenth century, appeared as the rainbow; and Wesley was as the sower, who comes after the clouds have been lifted up, and the floods have subsided, and scatters his seed in the serene hour of peace. The new devotees, content to remain under the guardianship of the established government, sought to enjoy the exquisite delights of religious sensibility, not to overthrow dynasties, or to break the bonds of colonial dependence. By John Wesley, therefore, who resided in America less than two years, no share in moulding the political institutions of Georgia was desired or exerted. As he strolled through natural avenues of palmettoes and evergreen hollies, and woods sombre with hanging moss, his heart gushed forth in addresses to God.

> "Is there a thing beneath the sun,
> That strives with Thee my heart to share?
> Ah! tear it thence, and reign alone,—
> The Lord of every motion there."

The austerity of his maxims involved him in controversies with the mixed settlers of Georgia: and his residence in America preceded his influence on the religious culture of its people. His brother was still less suited to shape events: fainting under fatigue, he sighed for sympathy; the privations and hardships of the wilderness, among rough associates, plunged his gentle nature into the depths of melancholy and homesickness; and, at this time, his journal, of which extracts have unwisely been made public, is not a record of events around him, but rather a chronicle of what passed within himself—the groundless jealousies of a pure mind, rendered suspicious by pining disease. When afterwards George Whitefield came, his intrepid nature did not lose its cheerfulness in the encounter with the wilderness; his eager benevolence, led by the example of the Moravians and the fame of the Orphan House at Halle, founded and sustained an orphan house at Savannah by contributions which his eloquence extorted. He became more nearly identified with America, visited all the provinces from Florida to the northern frontier, and made his grave in New England; but he, also, swayed no legislatures, and is chiefly remembered for his fervor and his power of melting the multitude.

CHAP XXIV 1736 Feb. 6–17. 9–20. At once, Oglethorpe visited the Moravians at Ebenezer, to praise their good husbandry, and to select the site of their new settlement—of which the lines were no sooner drawn, and the streets laid out by an engineer, than huts covered with bark rose up as a shelter, and the labors of the field were renewed. In a few Von Reck's Nachricht, 36. years, the produce of raw silk by the Germans amounted to ten thousand pounds a year; and indigo also became a staple. In earnest memorials, they long deprecated the employment of negro slaves, pleading the ability of the white man to toil even under the suns of Georgia. Their religious affections bound them together in the unity of brotherhood; their controversies were decided among themselves; every event of life had its moral; and the fervor of their worship never disturbed their healthy tranquillity of judgment. They were cheerful, and at peace.

Feb. 16. From the Moravian towns Oglethorpe hastened to the southward, passing in a scout boat through the narrow inland channels, which delighted the eye by their clear, sea-green color and stillness, and were sheltered by woods of pines, and evergreen oaks, and cedars, that grew close to the water's side. On the Feb. 18. second day, aided by the zeal of his own men, and by Indians skilful in using the oar, he arrived at St. Simon's Island. A fire, kindling the long grass on an old Indian field, cleared a space for the streets of Frederica; Moore's Voyage to Georgia. and, amidst the carols of the great numbers of the red and the mocking bird, and the noisy mirth of the rice bird, a fort was constructed on the centre of the bluff, with four bastions, commanding the river, and protecting the palmetto cabins, which, appearing like a camp, with bowers instead of tents, and smooth leaves, of a pleasing color, for canvass, each twenty feet by fourteen, were set up on forks and poles in regular rows—a tight and convenient shelter for the emigrants. CHAP XXIV.

It was but ten miles from Frederica to the Scottish settlement at Darien. To give heart to them by his presence, Oglethorpe, in the Highland costume, sailed up the Alatamâha; and all the Highlanders, as they perceived his approach, assembled, with their plaids, broadswords, targets, and fire-arms, to bid him welcome. The brave men were pleased that a town was to be settled, and ships to come up, so near them, and also that they now had a communication by land with Savannah. The "boggy places" proved to be not quite impassable; "two rivers," that had no ford, could be crossed by swimming; and trees had been blazed all the way for a "horse-road."

It remained to vindicate the boundaries of Georgia. The messenger who, in February, had been despatched to St. Augustine, had not returned. Oglethorpe resolved himself to sustain the pretensions of Great Britain to the territory as far south as the St. John's, and the Highlanders volunteered their service. With their aid, he explored the channels south of Frederica; and on the island to which Tomo-chichi gave the name of Cumberland, he marked out a fort to be called St. Andrew's. But Oglethorpe still pressed forward to the south. Passing Amelia Island, and claiming the St. John's River as the southern boundary of the territory possessed by the Indian subjects of England at the time of the treaty at Utrecht, on the southern extremity of the island at the entrance of that stream, where myrtles and palmettoes abounded, and wild grape vines, climbing to the summit of trees, formed as beautiful walks as art could have designed, he planted the Fort St. George, as the defence of the British frontier.

1736 April. Von Reck's Reise Diarium in Urlsperger, i. 846.

April 18.

Von Reck, in Urlsperger i. 848

CHAP XXIV. 1736. Indignant at the near approach of the English, the Spaniards of Florida threatened opposition. The messengers of Oglethorpe were detained as prisoners, and he resolved to claim their liberty. The rumors of his May. intended expedition had reached the wilderness; and the Uchees, all brilliantly painted, came down to form an alliance, and to grasp the hatchet. Long speeches and the exchange of presents were followed by the May 23. war-dance. Tomo-chichi appeared, also, with his warriors, ever ready to hunt the buffalo along the frontiers of Florida, or to engage in warfare with the few planters on the peninsula; and an embarkation was made for the purpose of regulating the southern boundary of the British colonies.

Oglethorpe knew his danger: the Spaniards had been tampering with his allies, and were willing to cut off the settlements in Georgia at a blow; the promised succors, which he awaited from England, had not arrived. But, in his enthusiasm, regardless of incessant toil, regardless of himself,—unlike Baltimore and Penn, securing domains not to his family, but to emigrants,—unlike so many royal governors at the north, amassing no lands, and not even appropriating to himself permanently a cottage, or a single lot of fifty acres, —he resolved to assert the claims of England, and preserve his colony as the bulwark of English North America. Southey's Wesley, i 113. "To me," said he to Charles Wesley, "death is nothing." "If separate spirits," he added, "regard our little concerns, they do it as men regard the follies of their childhood." The people at Frederica declared to him their readiness to die in defence of the place, grieving only at his exposure to danger without them.

But, for that season, active hostilities were avoided by negotiation. The Spaniard did, indeed, claim peremptorily the whole country as far as St. Helena's

CHAP. XXIV

Sound; but the English envoys at St. Augustine were set free; and, if the English post on St. George was abandoned, St. Andrew's, commanding the approach to the St. Mary's, was maintained. Hence the St. Mary's ultimately became the boundary of the colony of Oglethorpe.

Impartial Inquiry, in Georgia Hist. Coll. i. 182

The friendship of the red men insured the safety of the English settlements. The Chickasas, animated by their victory over the Illinois and D'Artaguette, came down to narrate how unexpectedly they had been attacked, how victoriously they had resisted, with what exultations they had consumed their prisoners by fire. Ever attached to the English, they now sent their deputation of thirty warriors, with their civil sachem and war chief, to make an alliance with Oglethorpe, whose fame had reached the Mississippi. They brought for him an Indian chaplet, made from the spoils of their enemies, glittering with feathers of many hues, and enriched with the horns of buffaloes. Thus the Creeks, the Cherokees, the Chickasas, were his unwavering friends, and even the Choctas had covenanted with him to receive English traders. To hasten preparations for the impending contest with Spain, Oglethorpe embarked for England. He could report to the trustees, "that the colony was doing well; that Indians from seven hundred miles' distance had confederated with him, and acknowledged the authority of his sovereign."

1736 July.

Von Reck's Diarium in Urlsperger, i. 850. John Wesley, Journal.

Nov. 23.

1737 Jan. 19.

Receiving a commission as brigadier-general, with a military command extending over South Carolina, Oglethorpe himself, in Great Britain, raised and disciplined a regiment; and, after an absence of more than a year and a half, he returned to Frederica. There, by the industry of his soldiers, the walls of the fortress

Aug

1738. Sept.

CHAP. XXIV. 1738. were completed. Their ivy-mantled ruins are still standing; and the village, now almost a deserted one, in the season of its greatest prosperity, is said to have contained a thousand men.

Oct. 20. At Savannah, he was welcomed by salutes and bonfires. But he refused any alteration in the titles of land. The request for the allowance of slaves he rejected sternly, declaring that, if negroes should be introduced into Georgia, "he would have no further concern with the colony;" and he used his nearly arbitrary power as the civil and military head of the state, the founder and delegated legislator of Georgia, to interdict negro slavery. The trustees applauded this decision, and, notwithstanding "repeated applications," "persisted in denying the use of negroes,"—even though many of the planters, believing success impossible with "white servants," prepared to desert the colony.

Tailfer, 36.

Tailfer, 79.

The openness and fidelity of Oglethorpe preserved the affection of the natives. Muskhogees and Chickasas came round him once more, to renew their covenants of friendship. The former had, from the first, regarded him as their father; and, as he had made some progress in their language, they appealed to him directly in every emergency.

Urlsperger, i. 191.

1739. Aug. Nor was this all. In the summer of 1739, the civil and war chiefs of the Muskhogees held a general council in Cowetas, and adjourned it to Cusitas, on the Chattahouchee; and Oglethorpe, making his way through solitary paths, fearless of the suns of summer, the night dews, or the treachery of some hireling Indian, came also into the large square of their council-place, to distribute presents to his red friends; to renew and explain their covenants; to address them

Stephens's Journal of Proceedings in Georgia, ii. 67-142 Von Reck, 30-33. Spalding, 263.

in words of affection; and to smoke with their nations the pipe of peace. It was then agreed, that the ancient love of the tribes to the British king should remain unimpaired; that the lands from the St. John's to the Savannah, between the sea and the mountains, belonged, of ancient right, to the Muskhogees. Their cession to the English of the land on the Savannah, as far as the Ogeechee, and along the coast to the St. John's, as far into the interior as the tide flows, was, with a few reservations, confirmed; and the entrance to the rest of their domains was barred forever against the Spaniards. The right of preëmption was reserved for the trustees of Georgia alone; nor might they enlarge their possessions, except with the consent of the ancient proprietaries of the soil.

Oct.

The news of this treaty could not have reached England before the negotiations with Spain were abruptly terminated. Walpole desired peace; he pleaded for it in the name of national honor, of justice, and of the true interests of commerce. But the active English mind had become debauched by the hopes of sudden gains, and soured by disappointment, and was now resolved on illicit commerce, or on plunder and conquest. A war was desired, not because England insisted on cutting logwood in the Bay of Honduras, where Spain claimed a jurisdiction, and had founded no settlements; nor because the South Sea company differed with the king of Spain as to the balances of their accounts; nor yet because the boundary between Carolina and Florida was still in dispute;—these differences could all have been adjusted;—but because English "merchants were not permitted to smuggle with impunity." A considerable part of the population of Jamaica was sustained by the profits of the contraband trade with Spanish ports; the annual

Lord Mahon's History of England, iii. 5

CHAP. XXIV.

ship to Porto Bello, which the assiento permitted, was followed at a distance by smaller vessels; and fresh bales of goods were nightly introduced in the place of those that had been discharged during the day. Not only did the slave ships assist in violating the revenue laws of Spain; British smuggling vessels, also, pretending distress, would claim the right by treaty to enter the Spanish harbors on the Gulf of Mexico. In consequence, the colonial commerce of Spain was almost annihilated. In former days, the tonnage of the fleet of Cadiz had amounted to fifteen thousand tons; it was now reduced to two thousand tons, and had no office but to carry the royal revenues from America.

The monarch of Spain, the victim of bigoted scruples, busy in celebrating auto-da-fes and burning heretics, and regarding as an affair of state the question who should be revered as the true patron saint of his kingdom, was at last roused to angry impatience. His complaints, when addressed to England, were turned aside; and when the Spanish officers showed vigor in maintaining the commercial system of their sovereign, the English merchants resented their interference as the ebullitions of pride, and the wanton aggressions of tyranny. One Jenkins, who to the pursuits of smuggling had joined maraudings which might well have been treated as acts of piracy, was summoned to the bar of the house of commons to give evidence. The tale, which he was disciplined to tell, of the loss of his ears by Spanish cruelty, of dishonor offered to the British flag and the British crown, was received without distrust. "What were your feelings, when in the hands of such barbarians?" was asked by a member, as his mutilated ears were exhibited. "I commended my soul to my God," answered the impudent fabler, "and my cause to my country."—"We

Gentleman's Magazine, Feb. 1739, p. 121. Lord Mahon. Tindal T. Southey's W. Indies, ii. 265

have no need of allies to enable us to command justice; the story of Jenkins will raise volunteers:" such was the cry of Pulteney, resolved to find fault at any rate, and to embarrass and overthrow the administration of Walpole. The clamor of orators was seconded by the greatest poets of that age: Pope, in his dying notes, sneered at the timidity which was willing to shun giving offence,

> "And own the Spaniard did a waggish thing,
> Who cropped our ears, and sent them to the king;"

and the early genius of Johnson, in more energetic strains, indignant at the supporters of Walpole, as men who explained away the rights of their country, and openly pleaded for pirates, vindicated the right of England to the territory which Oglethorpe had colonized:—

> "Has Heaven reserved, in pity to the poor,
> No pathless waste, or undiscovered shore?
> No secret island in the boundless main?
> No peaceful desert yet unclaimed by Spain?"

At last, a convention was signed. The mutual claims for damages sustained in commerce were balanced and liquidated; and, while the king of Spain demanded of the South Sea company sixty-eight thousand pounds, as due to him for his share of their profits, he agreed to pay, as an indemnity to British merchants for losses sustained by unwarranted seizures, the sum of ninety-five thousand pounds. On these questions no dispute remained but the trivial one, whether the British government should guaranty to Spain the acknowledged debt of the South Sea company. The question with regard to the boundaries of Florida was equally well settled; the actual possessions of each nation were to remain without change till commissioners could mark the boundary. In other words, England 1739 Jan.

CHAP. XXIV. was to hold undisturbed jurisdiction over the country as far as the mouth of the St. Mary's.

It is to the honor of Walpole, that he dared to resist the clamor of the mercantile interest, and, opposing the imbecile duke of Newcastle, boldly advocated the acceptance of the convention. "It requires no great abilities in a minister," he exclaimed, "to pursue such measures as may make a war unavoidable. But how many ministers have known the art of avoiding war by making a safe and honorable peace?"—"The convention," said William Pitt, afterwards Lord Chatham, —giving an augury, in his first speech on American affairs, that his political career might be marked by energy, but not by an elevated political faith,—"The convention is insecure, unsatisfactory, and dishonorable: I think, from my soul, it is nothing but a stipulation for national ignominy. The complaints of your despairing merchants, the voice of England, has condemned it. Be the guilt of it upon the head of the advisers; God forbid that this committee should share the guilt by approving it." What judgment posterity would form of Pulteney, was foreshadowed in the poetry of Akenside; but there was no need of awaiting the judgment of posterity, or listening to the indignation of contemporary patriotism; Pulteney and his associates stand self-condemned. The original documents demonstrate "the extreme injustice" of their opposition. "It was my fortune," said Edmund Burke, "to converse with those who principally excited that clamor. None of them, no, not one, did in the least defend the measure, or attempt to justify their conduct."

1739 Oct. 23. In an ill hour for herself, in a happy one for America, England declared war against Spain. If the rightfulness of the European colonial system be conceded, the declaration was a wanton invasion of it for immediate selfish purposes; but, in endeavoring to open the ports of Spanish America to the mercantile enterprise of her own people, England was also, though unconsciously, making war on monopoly, and advancing the cause of commercial freedom. The struggle was now, not for European conquests, or the balance of power, or religion, but for the opportunity of commerce with the colonies of Spain. That a great nation, like Spain, should be compelled by force of arms to admit a contraband trade with any part of its dominions, was an absurdity. England, therefore, could gain her purpose only by destroying the colonial system of Spain; and she began a career, which could not end till American colonies of her own, as well as of Spain, should obtain independence. CHAP. XXIV.

To acquire possession of the richest portions of Spanish America, Anson was sent, with a small squadron, into the Pacific; but disasters at sea compelled him to renounce the hope of conquest, and seek only booty. As he passed Cape Horn, the winds, of which the fury made an ordinary gale appear as a gentle breeze, scattered his ships; one after another of them was wrecked or disabled; and at last, with a single vessel, after circumnavigating the globe, he returned to England, laden with spoils, rich in adventures, having won a merited celebrity by his sufferings, his good judgment, and his cheerful perseverance,—while the brilliant sketches of the Ladrones, by the historian of his voyage, made his name familiar to the lovers of romance throughout Europe. 1740 to 1744

In November, 1739, Edward Vernon, with six men-of-war, appeared off Porto Bello. The attack on the 1739

CHAP. XXIV. feeble and ill-supplied garrison began on the twenty-first; and, on the next day, Vernon, losing but seven men, was in possession of the town and the castles. A booty of ten thousand dollars, and the pleasure of demolishing the fortifications of the place, were the sole fruits of the enterprise; and, having acquired no rightful claim to glory, Vernon returned to Jamaica. Party spirit, in free governments, sometimes vitiates the contemporary verdict of opinion. Vernon belonged to the opposition; and the enemies of Walpole exalted his praises, till his heroism was made a proverb, his birthday signalized by lights and bonfires, and his head selected as the favorite ornament for signposts.

1740. Meantime, he took and demolished Fort Chagre, on this side of the Isthmus of Darien; but without result; for the gales near Cape Horn had prevented the coöperation of Anson at Panama.

The victory, in its effects, was sad for the northern colonies. England prepared to send to the West Indies by far the largest fleet and army that had ever appeared in the Gulf of Mexico, and summoned the colonies north of Carolina to contribute four battalions to the armament. No colony refused its quota; even Pennsylvania voted a contribution of money, and thus enabled its governor to enlist troops for the occasion. "It will not be amiss," wrote Sir Charles Wager to Admiral Vernon, "for both French and Spaniards to be a month or two in the West Indies before us, that they may be half dead, and half roasted, before our fleet arrives." So the expedition from England did not begin its voyage till October, and, after stopping for water at Dominica, where Lord Cathcart, the commander of the land forces, fell a victim to the climate,

1741. Jan. 9. reached Jamaica in the early part of the following year.

CHAP. XXIV.

How has history been made the memorial of the passionate misdeeds of men of mediocrity! The death of Lord Cathcart left the command of the land forces with the inexperienced, irresolute Wentworth; the naval force was under the impetuous Vernon, who was impatient of contradiction, and ill disposed to endure even an associate. The enterprise, instead of having one good leader, had two bad ones. Smollett.

Wasting at Jamaica the time from the ninth of January, 1741, till near the end of the month, at last, with a fleet of twenty-nine ships of the line, beside about eighty smaller vessels, with fifteen thousand sailors, with twelve thousand land forces, equipped with all sorts of warlike instruments, and every kind of convenience, Vernon weighed anchor, without any definite purpose. Havana lay within three days' sail; its conquest would have made England supreme in the Gulf of Mexico. But Vernon insisted on searching for the fleet of the French and Spaniards; and the French had already left the fatal climate. 1741

The council of war, yielding to the vehement direction of Admiral Vernon, resolved to attack Carthagena, the strongest place in Spanish America. The fleet appeared before the town on the fourth of March, and lost five days in inactivity. Fifteen days were required to gain possession of the fortress that rose near the entrance to the harbor; the Spaniards themselves abandoned Castillo Grande. It remained to storm Fort San Lazaro, which commanded the town. The attack, devised without judgment, was made by twelve hundred men with intrepidity; but the assailants were repulsed, with the loss of half their number,—while the admiral gave no timely aid to the land forces; and discord aggravated defeat. Erelong, rains set in; the

CHAP. XXIV. days were wet, the nights brilliant with vivid lightning. The fever of the low country in the tropics began its rapid work; men perished in crowds; the dead were cast into the sea, sometimes without winding-sheet or sinkers; the hospital ships were crowded with miserable sufferers. In two days, the effective force on land dwindled from six thousand six hundred to three thousand two hundred. Men grew as jealous as they were wretched, and inquired if there were not Papists in the army. The English could only demolish the fortifications and retire. "Even the Spaniards," wrote Vernon, "will give us a certificate that we have effectually destroyed all their castles."

In July, an attack on Santiago, in Cuba, was meditated, and abandoned almost as soon as attempted.

Such were the fruits of an expedition which was to have prepared the way for conquering Mexico and Peru. Of the recruits from the colonies, nine out of ten fell victims to the climate and the service. When the fleet returned to Jamaica, late in November, 1741, the entire loss of lives is estimated to have been about twenty thousand, of whom few fell by the enemy. Vernon attributed the failure to his own want of a sole command. It is certain that nothing had been accomplished.

In March, 1742, Vernon and Wentworth planned an expedition against Panama; but, on reaching Porto Bello, the design was voted impracticable, and they returned. Meantime, the commerce of England with Spain itself was destroyed; the assiento was interrupted; even the contraband was impaired; while English ships became the plunder of privateers. England had made no acquisitions, and had inflicted on the Spanish West Indies far less evil than she herself had suffered.

CHAP. XXIV.

1739 Sept.

The disasters in the West Indies prevented the conquest of Florida. Having, in September, 1739, received instructions from England of the approaching war with Spain, Oglethorpe hastened, before the close of the year, to extend the boundaries of Georgia once more to the St. John's, and immediately, in December, urged upon the province of South Carolina the reduction of the Spaniards at St. Augustine. "As soon as the sea is free," he adds, "they will send a large body of troops from Cuba." His own intrepidity would brook no delay, and, in the first week of 1740, he entered Florida. "Dear Mr. Oglethorpe," wrote the Moravian ministers, "is now exposed to much danger; for the Spaniards wish nothing more than to destroy his health and life. He does not spare himself, but, in the common soldier's dress, he engages in the most perilous actions. Since the new year, he has captured two small fortified places of the Spaniards, which were the outposts of St. Augustine, and now waits only for more Indians and more soldiers to attack that important fortress itself."

Oglethorpe, in Harris, ii 339

1740. Feb. 14.

Bolzius and Gronau, in Urlsperger, i. 2555.

In March, Oglethorpe hurried to Charleston, to encourage the zeal of South Carolina; but the forces, which that province voted in April, were not ready till May; and when the expedition, composed of six hundred regular troops, four hundred militia from Carolina, beside Indian auxiliaries, who were soon reduced to two hundred, advanced to the walls of St. Augustine, the garrison, commanded by Monteano, a man of courage and energy, had already received supplies. A vigorous sally was successful against a detached party, chiefly of Highlanders, at Fort Moosa. Yet, for nearly five weeks, Oglethorpe endeavored, in defiance of his own weakness and the strength of the

June 2.

Urlsperger, ii. 545.

CHAP. XXIV.

Harris, ii. 339, 340. Stephens's Journal, ii. 461. Urlsperger, ii. 576. Harris, ii. 340.

place, to devise measures for victory, till "the Carolina troops, enfeebled by the heat, dispirited by sickness, and fatigued by fruitless efforts, marched away in large bodies." The small naval force also resolved, in council, "to take off all their men, and sail away," and thus "put an end to the enterprise." Oglethorpe returned without molestation to Frederica. His conduct throughout the summer was a commentary on his character. The few prisoners whom he made were kindly treated; the cruelties of the savages were reproved and restrained; not a field, or a garden, or a house, near St. Augustine, was injured, unless by the Indians,—for burning them he thought the worst use to which they could be devoted. "He endured more fatigues than any of his soldiers; and, in spite of ill health consequent on exposure to perpetual damps, he was always at the head in every important action."

Urlsperger, ii. 576.

1742. The English still asserted their superiority on the southern frontier. St. Augustine had not fallen; the Spaniards had not been driven from Florida; but Oglethorpe maintained the extended limits of Georgia; his Indian alliances gave him the superiority in the wilderness as far as the land of the Choctas.

Oglethorpe's Letters. McCall, i. 196.

At last, to make good its pretensions, the Spanish government resolved on invading Georgia. It collected its forces from Cuba, and a large fleet, with an armament of which the force has been greatly exaggerated, sailed towards the mouth of the St. Mary's. Fort William, which Oglethorpe had constructed at the southern extremity of Cumberland Island, defended the entrance successfully, till, fighting his way through Spanish vessels, which endeavored to intercept him, the general himself reënforced it. Then, promptly returning to St. Simon's, having no aid from Carolina,

CHAP. XXIV.

1742 June 24.

with less than a thousand men, by his vigilant activity, trusting in Providence, he prepared for defence. "We are resolved not to suffer defeat"—such was his cheering message to Savannah;—"we will rather die, like Leonidas and his Spartans, if we can but protect Carolina and the rest of the Americans from desolation." And, going on board one of the little vessels that chanced to be at hand, he called on the seamen to stand by their liberties and country. "For myself," he added, "I am prepared for all dangers. I know the enemy are far more numerous than we; but I rely on the valor of our men, and, with the aid of God, I do not doubt we shall be victorious."

Nachricht vom Einfall der Spanier in Georgien, in Urlsperger ii. 1254. Smith's letter, in Spalding, 276.

July 5

On the fifth of July, seven days after it first came to anchor off Simon's Bar, the Spanish fleet of thirty-six vessels, with the tide of flood and a brisk gale, entered St. Simon's Harbor, and succeeded in passing the English batteries on the southern point of the island. The general signalled his ships to run up to Frederica, and, spiking the guns of the lower fort, withdrew to the town; while the Spaniards landed at Gascoin's Bluff, and took possession of the camps which the English had abandoned. But, in constructing the road to Frederica, Oglethorpe had left a morass on the one side, and a dense oak wood on the other. A party of Spaniards advance; they are within a mile of the town; they are met by Oglethorpe himself, with the Highland company, are overcome, pursued, and most of the party killed or taken prisoners. A second party of the Spaniards march to the assault; they come to a place where the narrow avenue, bending with the edge of the morass, forms a crescent: as they reach the fatal spot, Highland caps rise up in the wood, and, under the command of Mackay and Sutherland, an

Jones. Oglethorpe

July 7

CHAP. XXIV. 1742. attack is begun. The opposing grenadiers at first stood firm, and discharged volley after volley at an enemy whom the thicket concealed. But, as Oglethorpe hastened to the scene, he found the victory already complete, except as a Highland shout or the yell of an Indian announced the discovery of some straggling Spaniard. The enemy had retreated, with a loss of about two hundred men, leaving to the ground, which was now strown with the dead, the name of "the Bloody Marsh."

Despairing of success, and weakened by divisions,—deceived, too, by an ingenious stratagem,—the Spaniards, on the night of the fourteenth, reëmbarked, (July 14.) leaving a quantity of ammunition and guns behind them. On the eighteenth, on their way to the south, they renewed their attack on Fort William, which was bravely defended by Stuart and his little garrison of fifty men. The English boats watched the movements of the retreating squadron till it was south of the St. John's; and, on the twenty-fourth day of July, Oglethorpe could publish an order for a general thanksgiving for the end of the invasion.

Thus was Georgia colonized and defended; its frontiers were safe against inroads; and, though Florida still lingered under the jurisdiction of Spain, its limits were narrowed. To meet the complaints of the disaffected, Oglethorpe, after a year of tranquillity, sailed for England, never again to behold the colony (1743 July) with which the disinterested toils of ten years had identified his fame. For the welfare of Georgia, he had renounced ease and the enjoyment of fortune, to (New Voyage, 5.) scorn danger, and fare "much harder than any of the people that were settled there." Yet his virtues were the result of sentiment, not of reflection, and were colored by the prejudices of his nation, the hatred of Papists, the aversion to Spain. But the gentleness of his nature appeared in all his actions: he was merciful to the prisoner; a father to the emigrant; the unwavering friend of Wesley; the constant benefactor of the Moravians; honestly zealous for the conversion of the Indians; invoking for the negro the panoply of the gospel. His heart throbbed warmly for all around him; he loved to relieve the indigent, to soothe the mourner; and his name became known as another expression for "vast benevolence of soul."

Urlsperger, ii. 1264. Tailfer.

Urlsperger, i. 84.

Of an honorable lineage; from boyhood devoted to the profession of arms; by hereditary attachment, and by personal character, a friend to legitimacy; he was, for a commercial age, the representative of that chivalry which knew neither fear nor reproach, and felt a stain on honor like a wound. There are men filled with the sentiment of humanity, yet having a predilection for hierarchical forms,—revering the institutions of aristocracy, with a genuine faith in them,—willing to protect the humble, rather than to surrender power and establish equality. Such was Oglethorpe. Loyal and brave; choleric, yet merciful; versed in elegant letters; affable even to talkativeness; slightly boastful, and tinged with vanity,—he was ever ready to shed blood, rather than brook an insult, and yet more ready to expose life for those who looked to him for defence. A monarchist in the state, friendly to the church, he seemed, even in youth, like one who had survived his times,—like the relic of a former century and a more chivalrous age,—illustrating to the modern world of business what a crowd of virtues and charities could cluster round the heart of a Cavalier.

The life of Oglethorpe was prolonged to near five-

CHAP. XXIV. score; and, even in the last year of it, he was extolled as "the finest figure" ever seen, the impersonation of venerable age; his faculties were as bright as ever, and his eye was undimmed; ever "heroic, romantic, and full of the old gallantry," he was like the sound of the lyre, as it still vibrates, after the spirit of the age that sweeps its strings has passed away. But, as he belonged to the past, he could not found enduring institutions. He could not mould the future, and his legislation did not outlive his power. The system of tail male went gradually into oblivion; the importation of rum was no longer forbidden; slaves from Carolina were hired by the planter, first for a short period, then for life or a hundred years. Slavers from Africa sailed directly to Savannah, and the laws against them were not rigidly enforced. Whitefield, who believed that God's providence would certainly make slavery terminate for the advantage of the Africans, pleaded before the trustees in its favor, as essential to the prosperity of Georgia; even the poorest people earnestly desired the change. The Moravians still expressed regret, moved partly by a hatred of oppression, and partly by antipathy to the race of colored men. At last, they too began to think that negro slaves might be employed in a Christian spirit; and it was agreed that, if the negroes are treated in a Christian manner, their change of country would prove to them a benefit. A message from Germany served to hush their scruples. "If you take slaves in faith, and with the intent of conducting them to Christ, the action will not be a sin, but may prove a benediction."

Hannah More. Boswell.

Urlsperger, iii. 479.

Urlsperger, iii. 482. Compare Americanisches Ackerwerke, Gottes, 4.

1751.

After the departure of Oglethorpe, the southern colonies enjoyed repose; for the war for colonial commerce had become merged in a vast European

James Oglethorpe

struggle, involving the principles and the designs which had agitated the civilized world for centuries. In France, Fleury, like Walpole, desiring to adhere to the policy of peace, was, like Walpole, overruled by the selfishness of his rivals. He looked anxiously upon the commotions in Europe, and saw no way of escape. It appeared to him as if the end of the world was at hand; and it was so with regard to the world of feudalism and Catholic legitimacy. He expressed his aversion to all wars; and when the king of Spain—whom natural melancholy, irritated by ill health and losses, prompted to abdicate the throne—obtained of Louis XV., under his own hand, a promise of fifty ships of the line, the prime minister explained his purposes:—"I do not propose to begin a war with England, or to seize or to annoy one British ship, or to take one foot of land possessed by England in any part of the world. Yet I must prevent England from accomplishing its great purpose of appropriating to itself the entire commerce of the West Indies." "France, though it has no treaty with Spain, cannot consent that the Spanish colonies should fall into English hands." "It is our object," said the statesmen of France, "not to make war on England, but to induce it to consent to a peace."

CHAP. XXIV.

1740 Aug. 11.

Von Raumer's Friedrich II. u. seine zeit. 26

Raumer, 28.

Raumer, 30, 31

Such was the wise disposition of the aged Fleury, when, by the death of Charles VI., the extinction of the male line of the house of Hapsburg raised a question on the Austrian succession. The pragmatic sanction, to which France was a party, secured the whole Austrian dominions to Maria Theresa, the eldest daughter of Charles VI.; while, from an erudite genealogy or previous marriages, the sovereigns of Spain, of Saxony, and of Bavaria, each derived a claim to the

CHAP. XXIV undivided heritage. The interest of the French king, his political system, his faith as pledged by a solemn treaty, the advice of his minister, demanded of him the recognition of the rights of Maria Theresa in their integrity; and yet, swayed by the intrigues of the Belle Isles and the hereditary hatred of Austria, without one decent pretext, he constituted himself the centre of an alliance against her. Each of his associates in the war claimed the entire Austrian succession; and France, which aimed at its dismemberment, could engage in the strife only as the common supporter of their several unfounded pretensions to the whole. But individuals, who are bound to each other from selfishness only, are ever ready to prove false; humanity is the same in masses. Louis XV. united his allies by no honest principles, by no definite policy, and was deserted by them, as the selfishness of each could in another manner be better gratified. Thus the condition of European political relations was that of tangled intrigues. No statesman of that day, except Frederick, seemed in any degree to perceive the tendency of events As England, by its arrogant encroachments on Spain, unconsciously enlarged the commercial freedom, or began the independence, of colonies; so France, by its unjustifiable war on Austria, floated from its moorings, and foreboded the wreck of Catholic legitimacy.

In the great European contest, England, true to its policy of connecting itself with the second continental
1744 power, gave subsidies to Austria. The fleets of Eng-
Feb. land and France meet in the Mediterranean; the fleet
March 15. of England is victorious. France declares war against England also; and the little conflicts in America are lost in the universal conflagration of Europe.

Never did history present such a scene of confusion.

While the selfishness which had produced the general war, was itself without faith, it made use of all the resources that were offered by ancient creeds or ancient animosities, by Protestantism and the Roman church, legitimacy and the mercantile system, the ancient rivalry of France and Austria, the reciprocal jealousies of France and England. The enthusiasm of other centuries in religious strifes was extinct; and the new passion for popular power was but just beginning to swell. Europe rocked like the ocean on the lulling of a long storm, when the opposite wind has just sprung up, throwing the heaving billows into tumultuous conflict.

The absence of purity in public life extinguished attachment to the administration, and left an opportunity to the Pretender to invade Great Britain, to conquer Scotland, to advance within four days' march of London. This invasion had no partisans in America, where the house of Hanover was respected as the representative of Protestantism. In England, where monarchy was established, the vices of the reigning family had produced disgust and indifference; but the friends of revolution did not look beyond a choice of dynasty. America was destined to choose, not between kings, but between forms of government.

On the continent France gained fruitless victories. Her flag waved over Prague only to be struck down by Austria. Saxony, Bavaria, her allies on the borders of Austria, one after another, abandoned her. The fields 1745
of blood at Fontenoy, at Raucoux, at Laffeldt, were 1746
barren of results; for the collision of armies was but 1747
an unmeaning collision of brute force, guided by selfishness. Statesmen scoffed at Virtue, and she avenged herself by bringing their counsels to nought. In vain

CHAP. XXIV. did they marshal all Europe in hostile array; they had no torch of truth to pass from nation to nation; and therefore, though they could besiege cities, and burn the granges of the peasant, yet, except as their purposes were overruled, their lavish prodigality of treasure, and honor, and life, was fruitless to humanity.

One result, however, of which the character did not at first appear, was, during the conflict, achieved in the north. Protestantism was represented on the continent by no great power. Frederick II., a pupil of the philosophy of Leibnitz and Wolf, took advantage of the confusion, and, with the happy audacity of youth, and a discreet ambition, which knew where to set bounds to its own impetuosity, wrested Silesia from Austria. Indifferent to alliances with powers which, having no fixed aims, could have no fixed friendships, he entered into the contest, and withdrew from it, alone. Twice assuming arms, and twice con-
1742. 1745. cluding a separate peace, he retired, with a guaranty from England of the acquisitions which, aided by the power of opinion, constituted his monarchy the central point of political interest on the continent of Europe.

Nor was the war limited to Europe and European colonies: in the East Indies, the commercial companies of France and England struggled for supremacy. The empire of the Great Mogul lay in ruins, inviting a restorer. But who should undertake its reconstruction? An active instinct urged the commercial world of England to seek a nearer connection with Hindostan; again the project of discovering a north-western pas-
1742- 1747. sage to India was renewed; and, to encourage the spirit of adventurous curiosity, the English parliament promised liberal rewards for success. Meantime, the French company of the Indies, aided by the king, had

confirmed its power at Pondicherry; and, as the Sorbonne had published to a credulous nation, that dividends on the stock of the commercial company would be usurious, and therefore a crime against religion, the corporation was unfortunate, though private merchants were gaining wealth in the Carnatic and on the Ganges. The brave mariner from St. Malo, the enterprising La Bourdonnais, from his government in the Isle of France, had devised schemes of conquest. But the future was not foreseen; and, limited by instructions from the French ministers to make no acquisitions of territory whatever, though, with the aid of the governor of Pondicherry, he might have gained for France the entire ascendency in Hindostan, he pledged his word of honor to restore Madras to the English, in the very hour of victory, when he proudly planted the flag of France on its fortress, and made himself master of the city which, next to Goa and Batavia, was the most opulent of the European establishments in India.

CHAP. XXIV.

Mills, British India, iii. Raynal Voltaire.

1746 Sept.

Russia, also, was invoked to take part in the contest; and, in her first political associations with our country, she was on the side of our fathers, the ally of Austria, the stipendiary of England. Thus did Russia, hastening by her interference the approach of peace, indirectly act upon the fortunes of America. But, at an earlier period of the war, she had, in the opposite direction, drawn near our present borders. After the empire of the czars had been extended over Kamtschatka, Peter the Great had planned a voyage of discovery along the shores of Asia; and, in 1728, Behring demonstrated the insulation of that continent on the east. In 1741, the same intrepid navigator, sailing with two vessels from Ochotzk, discovered the narrow straits which divide the continents; caught glimpses of the

1741 June 4.

CHAP. XXIV. mountains of North-West America; traced the line of the Aleutian archipelago; and, tossed by storms, in 1741. the midst of snows and ice, fell a victim to fatigue Dec. 8. on a desert island of the group which bears his name. The gallant Danish mariner did not know that he had seen America; and, though Russia, by right of discovery, thus gained the north-west of our continent, no conception dawned on the lewd revellers who surrounded the empress Elizabeth, of the political institutions which already felt the weight of her influence in diplomacy, and were one day to extend their power to the borders of the empire bequeathed to her successors.

While the states of Europe, by means of their wide relations, were fast forming the nations of the whole world into one political system, the few incidents of war in our America could obtain no interest. In themselves they were destitute of grandeur, and, though productive of individual distress, had no abiding influence whatever; it was felt that the true theatre of the war was not there. A proposition was brought forward by Coxe to form a union of all the colonies, for the purposes of defence; but danger was not so universal or so imminent as to furnish a sufficient motive for a confederacy. The peace of the central provinces was unbroken; the government of Virginia feared dissenters more than Spaniards. Morris, in one of its interior counties, in the south-west range, chanced to have a copy of Luther on Galatians, and Bunyan's works, and read from them, every Lord's day, to his neighbors. At last, a meeting-house was built for him to read in.
1743 His fame spread, and he was taken up for examina-
Hawks, Virginia 102, 103. tion; but when asked of what sect he was, he could not tell. In the glens of the Old Dominion, he had not heard of sects; he knew not that men could disa-

gree. The strifes of the world, in opinion and in arms, had not disturbed the scattered planters of Virginia.

1744. The ownership of the west was still in dispute; and at Lancaster, in Pennsylvania, the governor of that state, with commissioners from Maryland and from Virginia, met the deputies of the Iroquois, who, since the union with the Tuscaroras, became known as the Six Nations. "We conquered," said they, "the country of the Indians beyond the mountains: if the Virginians ever gain a good right to it, it must be by us." And, for about four hundred pounds, the deputies of the Six Nations made "a deed recognizing the king's right to all the lands that are or shall be, by his majesty's appointment, in the colony of Virginia." The lands in Maryland were, in like manner, confirmed to Lord Baltimore, but with definite limits; the deed to Virginia extended the claim of that colony indefinitely in the west and north-west.

Colden, ii. 87-152.

July 2.

The events of the war of England with France were then detailed, and the conditions of the former treaties of alliance were called to mind. "The covenant chain between us and Pennsylvania," replied Canassatego, "is an ancient one, and has never contracted rust. We shall have all your country under our eye. Before we came here, we told Onondio, there was room enough at sea to fight, where he might do what he pleased; but he should not come upon our land to do any damage to our brethren." After a pause, it was added—"The Six Nations have a great authority over the praying Indians, who stand in the very gates of the French: to show our further care, we have engaged these very Indians and other allies of the French; they have agreed with us they will not join against you." Then the chain of union was made as bright as the sun.

CHAP. XXIV. The Virginians proposed to educate the children of the Iroquois at their public school. "Brother Assaragoa,"
1744. they replied, "we must let you know we love our children too well to send them so great a way; and the Indians are not inclined to give their children learning. Your invitation is good, but our customs differ from yours." And then, acknowledging the rich gifts from the three provinces, they continued, as if aware of their doom—"We have provided a small present for you; but, alas! we are poor, and shall ever remain so, as long as there are so many Indian traders among us. Theirs and the white people's cattle eat up all the grass, and make deer scarce." And they presented three bundles of skins. At the close of the conference, the Indians gave, in their order, five *yo-hahs;* and the
July 4. English agents, after a health to the king of England and the Six Nations, put an end to the assembly by three loud huzzas. Thus did Great Britain at once acquire and confirm its claims to the basin of the Ohio, and, at the same time, protect its northern frontier.

Yet the sense of danger led the Pennsylvanians, for the first time, to a military organization, effected, by a voluntary system, under the influence of Franklin. "He was the sole author of two lotteries, that raised above six thousand pounds, to pay for the charge of (Logan's MSS.)
1747. batteries on the river;" and he "found a way to put the country on raising above one hundred and twenty companies of militia, of which Philadelphia raised ten, of about a hundred men each." "The women were so zealous, that they furnished ten pairs of silk colors, wrought with various mottoes." Of the Quakers, many admitted the propriety of self-defence. "I principally esteem Benjamin Franklin," wrote Logan, "for saving the country by his contriving the militia. He

was the prime actor in all this;" and when elected to the command of a regiment, he declined the distinction, and, as a humble volunteer, "himself carried a musket among the common soldiers." CHAP. XXIV.

While the central provinces enjoyed tranquillity, a body of French from Cape Breton, before the news of the declaration of war with France had been received in New England, surprised the little English garrison at Canseau; destroyed the fishery, the fort, and the other buildings there, and removed eighty men, as prisoners of war, to Louisburg. The fortifications of Annapolis, the only remaining defence of Nova Scotia, were in a state of ruin. An attack made upon it by Indians in the service of the French, accompanied by Le Loutre, their missionary, was with difficulty repelled. The inhabitants of the province, sixteen thousand in number, were of French origin; and a revolt of the people, with the aid of Indian allies, might have once more placed France in possession of its ancient colony While William Shirley, the governor of Massachusetts, foresaw the danger, and solicited aid from England, the officers and men taken at Canseau, after passing the summer in captivity at Louisburg, were sent to Boston on parole. They brought accurate accounts of the condition of that fortress; and Shirley resolved on an enterprise for its reduction. The fishermen, especially of Marblehead, interrupted in their pursuits by the war, disdained an idle summer, and entered readily into the design. The legislature of Massachusetts, after some hesitation, resolved on the expedition by a majority of one vote. Solicited to render assistance, New York sent a small supply of artillery, and Pennsylvania of provisions; New England alone furnished men; of whom Connecticut raised five hun-

1744. May.

Memoirs of Last War.

1745 Jan.

CHAP. XXIV. dred and sixteen; New Hampshire—to whose troops Whitefield gave, as Charles Wesley had done to Oglethorpe, the motto, "Nothing is to be despaired of, with Christ for the leader"—contributed a detachment of three hundred and four; while the forces levied for the occasion by Massachusetts exceeded three thousand volunteers. Three hundred men sailed from Rhode Island, but too late for active service. Of Commodore Warren at Antigua, an express-boat requested the coöperation with such ships as could be spared from the Leeward Islands; but, on a consultation with the captains of his squadron, it was unanimously resolved by them, in the absence of directions from England, not to engage in the scheme.

1745. April. Thus, then, relying on themselves, the volunteers of New Hampshire and Massachusetts, with a merchant, William Pepperell of Maine, for their chief commander, met at Canseau. The inventive genius of New England had been aroused; one proposed a model of a flying bridge, to scale the walls even before a breach should be made; another was ready with a caution against mines; a third, who was a minister, presented to the merchant general, ignorant of war, a plan for encamping the army, opening trenches, and placing batteries. Shirley, wisest of all, gave instructions for the fleet of a hundred vessels to arrive together at a precise hour; heedless of the surf, to land in the dark on the rocky shore; to march forthwith, through thicket and bog, to the city, and beyond it; and to take the fortress and royal battery by surprise before daybreak. Such was the confiding spirit at home. The expedition itself was composed of fishermen, who, in time of war, could no longer use the hook and line

Seth Pomroy's MS. Journal of Louisburg Expedition. R. Wolcott's MS. Journal, &c. Letters, in Mass. Hist. Coll. i. Memoirs of Last War. MS. Letters. Belknap, i 273.

on the Grand Bank, but, with prudent forethought, took CHAP XXIV
with them their codlines; of mechanics, skilled from
childhood in the use of the gun; of lumberers, inured 1745
to fatigue and encampments in the woods; of husbandmen from the interior, who had grown up with arms in their hands, accustomed to danger, keenest marksmen, disciplined in the pursuit of larger and smaller game; all volunteers; all commanded by officers from among themselves; many of them church-members; almost all having wives and children. On
the first Sabbath, how did "the very great company April 7.
of people" come together on shore, to hear the sermon on enlisting as volunteers in the service of the Great Captain of our salvation! As the ice of Cape Breton was drifting in such heaps that a vessel could not enter its harbors, the New England fleet was detained many days at Canseau,—when, under a clear sky and a
bright sun, the squadron of Commodore Warren hap- April 23.
pily arrived. Hardly had his council at Antigua declined the enterprise, when instructions from England bade him render every aid to Massachusetts; and, learning at sea the embarkation of the troops, he sailed
directly to Canseau. The next day arrived nine ves- 24.
sels from Connecticut, with the forces from that colony, in high spirits and good health.

On the last day of April, an hour after sunrise, the armament, in a hundred vessels of New England, entering the Bay of Chapeaurouge, or Gabarus, as the English called it, came in sight of Louisburg. Its walls, raised on a neck of land on the south side of the harbor, forty feet thick at the base, and from twenty to thirty feet high, all swept from the bastions, surrounded by a ditch eighty feet wide, were furnished with one hundred and one cannon, seventy-six swivels,

CHAP. XXIV. 1745. and six mortars; its garrison was composed of more than sixteen hundred men; the harbor was defended by an island battery of thirty twenty-two pounders, and by the royal battery on the shore, having thirty large cannon, a moat and bastions, all so perfect that R. Wolcott. it was thought two hundred men could have defended it against five thousand. On the other hand, the New England forces had but eighteen cannon and three mortars; but no sooner did they come in sight of the city, than, letting down the whale-boats, "they flew to shore, like eagles to the quarry." The French, that came down to prevent the landing, were put to flight, May 1. and driven into the woods. On the next day, a detachment of four hundred men, led by William Vaughan, a volunteer from New Hampshire, marched by the city, which it greeted with three cheers, and took post near the north-east harbor. The French who held the royal battery, struck with panic, spiked its guns, and abandoned it in the night. In the morning, boats from the city came to recover it; but Vaughan and thirteen men, standing on the beach, kept them from landing till a reënforcement arrived. To a major in one of the regiments of Massachusetts, Seth Pomroy, from Northampton, a gunsmith, was assigned the oversight of above twenty smiths in drilling the cannon, which were little injured; and the fire from the city and the island battery was soon returned. "Louisburg," wrote Pomroy to his family, "is an exceedingly strong place, and seems impregnable. It looks as if our campaign would last long; but I am willing to stay till God's time comes to deliver the city into our hands." "Suffer no anxious thought to rest in your mind about me," replied his wife, from the bosom of New England. "The whole town is much engaged with concern for the expedition, how Providence will order the affair, for which religious meetings every week are maintained. I leave you in the hand of God."

The troops made a jest of technical military terms; they laughed at proposals for zigzags and epaulements. The light of nature, however, taught them to erect fascine batteries at the west and south-west of the city. Of these the most effective was commanded by Tidcomb, whose readiness to engage in hazardous enterprises was justly applauded. As it was necessary, for the purposes of attack, to drag the cannon over boggy morasses, impassable for wheels, Meserve, a New Hampshire colonel, who was a carpenter, constructed sledges; and on these the men, with straps over their shoulders, sinking to their knees in mud, drew them safely over. Thus the siege proceeded in a random manner. The men knew little of strict discipline; they had no fixed encampment; destitute of tents to keep off the fogs and dews, their lodgings were turf and brush houses; their bed was the earth—dangerous resting-place for those of the people "unacquainted with lying in the woods." Yet the weather was fair; and the atmosphere, usually thick with palpable fogs, was, during the whole siege, singularly dry. All day long, the men, if not on duty, were busy with amusements,—firing at marks, fishing, fowling, wrestling, racing, or running after balls shot from the enemy's guns. The feebleness of the garrison, which had only six hundred regular soldiers, with about a thousand Breton militia, prevented sallies; the hunting parties, as vigilant for the trail of an enemy as for game, rendered a surprise by land impossible; while the fleet of Admiral Warren guarded the approaches by sea.

Hutchinson, i. 375

Belknap.

Douglass.

Pomroy MS. Journal

Belknap 278.

Four or five attempts to take the island battery,

CHAP. XXIV. which commanded the entrance to the harbor, had failed. The failure is talked of among the troops; a
1745 party of volunteers, after the fashion of Indian expeditions, under a chief of their own election, enlist for a vigorous attack by night; "but now Providence
May 26. seemed remarkably to frown upon the affair." The assailants are discovered; a murderous fire strikes their boats before they land; only a part of them reach the island; a severe contest for near an hour ensues; those who can reach the boats escape, with the loss of sixty killed, and one hundred and sixteen taken prisoners.

To annoy the island battery, the Americans, under the direction of Gridley of Boston, with persevering toil, erect a battery near the north cape of the harbor, on the Light-House Cliff; while, within two hundred yards of the city, trenches had been thrown up near an advanced post, which, with guns from the royal battery, played upon the north-west gate of Louisburg.

Still no breach had been effected, while the labors of the garrison were making the fortifications stronger than ever. The expedition must be abandoned, or the walls of the city scaled. The naval officers, who had been joined by several ships-of-war, ordered from England on the service, agree to sail into the harbor, and bombard the city, while the land forces are to attempt to enter the fortress by storm. But, strong as were the works, the garrison was discontented, and Duchambon, their commander, ignorant of his duties. The Vigilant, a French ship of sixty-four guns, laden with military stores for his supply, was decoyed by Douglas, of the Mermaid, into the English fleet, and, after an engagement of some hours, was taken,
1745. June 15. in sight of the besieged town. The desponding gov-
16. ernor sent out a flag of truce; terms of capitula-

tion were accepted; on the seventeenth of June, the city, the fort, the batteries, were surrendered; and a New England minister soon preached in the French 1745. chapel. As the troops, entering the fortress, beheld the strength of the place, their hearts, for the first time, sunk within them. "God has gone out of the way of his common providence," said they, "in a re- Wolcott. Pomroy. markable and almost miraculous manner, to incline the hearts of the French to give up, and deliver this strong city into our hands." When the news of success reached Boston, the bells of the town were rung mer- July 3. rily, and all the people were in transports of joy. Thus did the strongest fortress of North America capitulate to an army of undisciplined New England mechanics, and farmers, and fishermen. It was the greatest success achieved by England during the war.

The capture of Louisburg seemed to threaten a 1746 transfer of the scene of earnest hostilities to America. France planned its recovery, and the desolation of the English colonies; but, in 1746, the large fleet from France, under the command of the duke d'Anville, wasted by storms and shipwrecks, and pestilential disease; enfeebled by the sudden death of its commander, and the delirium and suicide of his successor,—did not even attack Annapolis. In the next year, the French 1747 fleet, with troops destined for Canada and Nova Scotia, was encountered by Anson and Warren; and all its intrepidity could not save it from striking its colors. The American colonies suffered only on the frontier. Fort Massachusetts, in Williamstown, the post nearest to Crown Point, having but twenty-two men for its garrison, capitulated to a large body of French and In- 1746 Aug. 20. dians. In the wars of Queen Anne, Deerfield and Haverhill were the scenes of massacre. It marks the

CHAP. XXIV. 1746. progress of settlements, that danger was now repelled from Concord, on the Merrimac, and from the township
1747, April. now called Charlestown, on the Connecticut.

Repairing to Louisburg, Shirley, with Warren, had concerted a project for reducing all Canada; and the
1746 duke of Newcastle replied to their proposals by directing preparations for the conquest. The colonies north of Virginia voted to raise more than eight thousand men; but no fleet arrived from England; and the French were not even driven from their posts in Nova
1747. Scotia. The summer of the next year passed in that inactivity which attends the expectation of peace; and in September, the provincial army, by direction of the duke of Newcastle, was disbanded. Men believed that England, from motives of policy, had not desired success. "There is reason enough for doubting whether the king, if he had the power, would wish to drive the French from their possessions in Canada." Such was public opinion at New York, in 1748, as pre-
1748. Nov. served for us by the Swedish traveller, Peter Kalm.
Kalm, ii. Pinkerton, ii. 461. "The English colonies in this part of the world," he continues, "have increased so much in wealth and population, that they will vie with European England But to maintain the commerce and the power of the metropolis, they are forbid to establish new manufactures, which might compete with the English; they may dig for gold and silver only on condition of shipping them immediately to England; they have, with the exception of a few fixed places, no liberty to trade to any parts not belonging to the English dominions, and foreigners are not allowed the least commerce with these American colonies. And there are many similar restrictions. These oppressions have made the inhabitants of the English colonies less tender

towards their mother land. This coldness is increased by the many foreigners who are settled among them; for Dutch, Germans, and French, are here blended with English, and have no special love for Old England. Besides, some people are always discontented, and love change; and exceeding freedom and prosperity nurse an untamable spirit. I have been told, not only by native Americans, but by English emigrants, publicly, that, within thirty or fifty years, the English colonies in North America may constitute a separate state, entirely independent of England. But, as this whole country is towards the sea unguarded, and on the frontier is kept uneasy by the French, these dangerous neighbors are the reason why the love of these colonies for their metropolis does not utterly decline. The English government has therefore reason to regard the French in North America as the chief power that urges their colonies to submission."

The Swede heard but the truth, though that truth lay concealed from British statesmen. Even during the war, the jealous spirit of resistance to tyranny was kindled into a fury at Boston. Sir Charles Knowles, the British naval commander, whom Smollett is thought to have described justly as "an officer without resolution, and a man without veracity," having been deserted by some of his crew, while lying off Nantasket, early one morning, sent his boats up to Boston, and impressed seamen from vessels, mechanics and laborers from the wharves. "Such a surprise could not be borne here," wrote Hutchinson, who was present, and he assigns, as the reason of impatience, that "the people had not been used to it." "Men would not be contented with fair promises from the governor;" "the seizure and restraint of the commanders and other offi-

Scott's Life of Smollett.

1747 Nov. 17

Hutchinson, ii. 387

CHAP. XXIV. cers who were in town, was insisted upon, as the only effectual method to procure the release of the inhabitants aboard the ships." And the mob executed what the governor declined. At last, after three days of rage and resentment, through the mediation of the house of representatives, order was restored. The officers were liberated from their irregular imprisonment; and, in return, most, if not all, of the impressed citizens of Boston were dismissed from the English fleet.

The alliance of Austria with Russia hastened negotiations for the pacification of Europe; and a congress convened at Aix la Chapelle to restore tranquillity to the civilized world. As between England and Spain, and between France and England, after eight years of reciprocal annoyance, after an immense accumulation of national debt, the condition of peace was a return to the state before the war. Nothing was gained. Humanity had suffered, without a purpose, and without a result. In the colonial world, Madras was restored for Cape Breton; the boundaries between the British and the French provinces in America were left unsettled, neither party acknowledging the right of the other to the basin of the Penobscot or of the Ohio; the frontier of Florida was not traced. Neither did Spain relinquish the right of searching English vessels suspected of smuggling; and, though it was agreed that the assiento treaty should continue for four years more, the right was soon abandoned, under a new convention, for an inconsiderable pecuniary indemnity. The principle of the freedom of the seas was asserted only by Frederick II. Holland, remaining neutral as long as possible, claimed, under the treaty of 1674, freedom of Heeren, 350 goods for her free ships; but England, disregarding the treaty, captured and condemned her vessels. On occasion of the war between Sweden and Russia, the principle was again urged by the Dutch, and likewise rejected by the Swedes. Even Prussian ships were seized; but the monarch of Prussia indemnified the sufferers by reprisals on English property. Of higher questions, in which the interests of civilization were involved, not one was adjusted. To the balance of power, sustained by standing armies of a million of men, the statesmen of that day intrusted the preservation of tranquillity, and, ignorant of the might of principles to mould the relations of states, saw in Austria the certain ally of England, in France the natural ally of Prussia.

Thus, after long years of strife, of repose, and of strife renewed, England and France solemnly agreed to be at peace. The treaties of Aix la Chapelle had been negotiated, by the ablest statesmen of Europe, in the splendid forms of monarchical diplomacy. They believed themselves the arbiters of mankind, the pacificators of the world,—reconstructing the colonial system on a basis which should endure for ages,—confirming the peace of Europe by the nice adjustment of material forces. At the very time of the congress of Aix la Chapelle, the woods of Virginia sheltered the youthful George Washington, the son of a widow. Born by the side of the Potomac, beneath the roof of a Westmoreland farmer, almost from infancy his lot had been the lot of an orphan. No academy had welcomed him to its shades, no college crowned him with its honors: to read, to write, to cipher—these had been his degrees in knowledge. And now, at sixteen years of age, in quest of an honest maintenance, encountering intolerable toil; cheered onward by being

CHAP. XXIV.

1748.

Washington's Diary, in Sparks's Washington, ii. 416–420.

able to write to a schoolboy friend, "Dear Richard, a doubloon is my constant gain every day, and sometimes six pistoles;" "himself his own cook, having no spit but a forked stick, no plate but a large chip;" roaming over spurs of the Alleghanies, and along the banks of the Shenandoah; alive to nature, and sometimes "spending the best of the day in admiring the trees and richness of the land;" among skin-clad savages, with their scalps and rattles, or uncouth emigrants, "that would never speak English;" rarely sleeping in a bed; holding a bearskin a splendid couch; glad of a resting-place for the night upon a little hay, straw, or fodder, and often camping in the forests, where the place nearest the fire was a happy luxury;—this stripling surveyor in the woods, with no companion but his unlettered associates, and no implements of science but his compass and chain, contrasted strangely with the imperial magnificence of the congress of Aix la Chapelle. And yet God had selected, not Kaunitz, nor Newcastle, not a monarch of the house of Hapsburg, nor of Hanover, but the Virginia stripling, to give an impulse to human affairs, and, as far as events can depend on an individual, had placed the rights and the destinies of countless millions in the keeping of the widow's son.

WASHINGTON THE SURVEYOR.

INDEX

TO THE

HISTORY OF COLONIZATION.

D.

M.

N.

O.

P.

Q.

R.

S.

Y.

Z.

END OF

HISTORY OF COLONIZATION.

www.ingramcontent.com/pod-product-compliance
Lightning Source LLC
LaVergne TN
LVHW021320110826
845150LV00003B/628